Thine the *the* AMEN

Essays on Lutheran Church Music in Honor of Carl Schalk

Edited by
Carlos R. Messerli

Foreword by
Martin E. Marty

LUTHERAN UNIVERSITY PRESS
MINNEAPOLIS, MINNESOTA

Thine the Amen
Essays on Lutheran Church Music
in Honor of Carl Schalk

Carlos R. Messerli, editor

Library of Congress Cataloging-in Publication Data
Thine the amen : essays on Lutheran church music in honor of Carl Schalk / edited by Carlos R. Messerli; foreword by Martin E. Marty
    p. cm.
    Includes bibliographical references.
    "The works of Carl Schalk": p.
    Contents: Music of the Lutheran heritage—The Lutheran heritage and worship in the twenty-first century—The life and work of Carl Schalk.
        ISBN-13: 978-1-932688-11-5 (pbk. : alk. paper)
        ISBN-10: 1-932688-11-0 (pbk. : alk. paper)
        1. Church music—Lutheran Church. 2. Public worship—Lutheran Church. I. Schalk, Carl. II. Messerli, Carlos R.

ML3168.T55 .2005
781.71'41—dc22

2005044925

Lutheran University Press, PO Box 390759, Minneapolis, MN 55439
Manufactured in the United States of America

Table of Contents

Part Two

The Lutheran Musical Heritage and Worship in the Twenty-first Century

Part Three

The Life and Works of Carl Schalk

CARLOS R. MESSERLI

Preface

The custom of honoring a person of distinction by means of a *Festschrift* (festival writing) on the occasion of a birthday or other noteworthy event has a long and distinguished history. Although hundreds of the genre have been published in many fields of learning, the custom has come into common use among musicians only since the early part of the twentieth century as the field of historical musicology developed.

Thine the Amen is presented as a *Festschrift* celebrating the ministry of Carl Flentge Schalk. It addresses the area of Lutheran church music because that is the field to which Carl has dedicated most of his life. The authors who have contributed to this publication form a group of distinguished colleagues and friends who are musicologists, teachers, or church musicians. All have a deep interest in Lutheran worship and its practice. The articles within these covers are written as a tribute to Carl to bring to life Lutheran music of the past, and to suggest that church music practice of the present can be informed with insights gleaned from the past.

Paul Bouman is Director of Music Emeritus, Grace Lutheran Church, River Forest, Illinois, where he served as parochial school teacher, choir director, and organist. He is an Honorary Lifetime Member of the Association of Lutheran Church Musicians, published composer, and a recognized authority on children's and youth choirs. Here he identifies, on the basis of his long experience, thirty classic choral pieces for Lutheran worship. The article, in the form of a letter to a young church musician, also presents a few guidelines for effective choral leadership for worship.

William H. Braun is Professor of Music, Wisconsin Lutheran College, Milwaukee, Wisconsin, where he also has served as Chair of the Humanities Division and of the Music Department. A prolific author of journal articles and reviews, and a lecturer and composer, he is the compiling editor of *Not Unto Us: A Celebration of the Ministry of Kurt J. Eggert* (Northwestern Publishing House, 2001). His present article surveys recent musical settings of the Passion of Christ in order to encourage the revival of a liturgical practice of great devotional value. He suggests that these settings be sung to interpret effectively the Good Friday Gospel on the day traditionally reserved for its performance in worship.

Robert Buckley Farlee places this book in the current context in his introduction. Senior editor for worship and music at Augsburg Fortress Publishers, he currently serves as the president of the Association of Lutheran Church Musicians.

Joseph Herl brings the training of a musicologist and a background of experience as parish leader of church music and teacher in the Concordia system of the Lutheran Church–Missouri Synod to the study of the chorale. He is Assistant Professor of Music at Concordia University, Seward, Nebraska. He is the author of the thought provoking publication *Worship Wars in Early Lutheranism: Choir, Congregation, and Three Centuries of Conflict* (Oxford, 2004), and here calls on worship leaders to conduct the liturgy mindful of seven principles that reflect its importance, vitality, and relevance to Lutheran worship today.

Natalie Jenne, Professor Emerita of Music at Concordia University, River Forest, Illinois, is also a well-recognized keyboardist and author. Her article suggests that performers of Bach's music become informed about the composer's familiarity with the formal dances of his day. While her *Dance and the Music of J. S. Bach* (Indiana, 1991, 2001) explores the topic in broad terms, her present article challenges the church musician to discover the importance of dance rhythms in the performance of Bach's cantatas.

Robin A. Leaver is Professor of Sacred Music at Westminster Choir College of Rider University, Visiting Professor at the Juilliard School, New York City, and immediate past-president of the American Bach Society. He has lectured and written extensively on the subject of Lutheran music in books and articles, one of which is the chief study on the subject in *The New Grove Dictionary of Music and Musicians* (2nd ed., 2001). Recently, he completed a substantial book on Luther's liturgical music. His *J. S. Bach and Scripture* (Concordia, 1985) examines Bach's own markings in his personal Bible. In his present article he explores the difficult task of rendering in English the often earthy, yet profound biblical truths contained in Luther's German chorales.

Martin E. Marty began his career as a Lutheran pastor who, incidentally, had a deep love for and understanding of worship and church music. He is presently the Fairfax M. Cone Distinguished Service Professor Emeritus at the University of Chicago, where he taught chiefly in the Divinity School. An author of great output and influence, he has written more than fifty books and five thousand articles. Past president and director of several associations and institutions, he has served St. Olaf College, Northfield, Minesota, as Regent, Board Chair, and Interim President. He has also been awarded more than seventy honorary doctorates.

Carlos R. Messerli, Founding Director Emeritus of Lutheran Music Program, had earlier been a Lutheran elementary and high school teacher and Professor of Music at Concordia College (now University), Seward, Nebraska. A long-time church musician, he founded and directed Lincoln (Nebraska) Lutheran Choir. He held several positions on the board of Lutheran Society for Worship, Music, and the Arts and is past-president and Honorary Lifetime Member of the Association of Lutheran Church Musicians. He also was a member of the Inter-Lutheran Commission on Worship and is co-author of *Manual on the Liturgy, Lutheran Book of Worship* (Augsburg, 1979).

Barbara J. Resch is Associate Professor and Director of Music Education at Indiana University–Purdue University, Fort Wayne, Indiana, and Director of Children's Choirs, St. Paul's Lutheran Church and School. She is editor of *The Indiana Musicator,* journal of the Indiana Music Educators Association and contributing editor, *Spotlight on Music* basal music series (McGraw–Hill, 2005). Her experience at various levels in education and in church music leads her to the conclusion that the church often limits the achievement of youth in music through its own misconceptions of what is possible. Her article successfully brings the Lutheran chorale into the lives of twenty-first century children.

Evangeline Rimbach is Professor Emerita of Concordia University, River Forest, Illinois. She was a contributing editor of *Church Music* journal and now serves as editor of *Grace Notes,* the newsletter of the Association of Lutheran Church Musicians. She is the author of a mini-revival of the works of the neglected eighteenth-century composer, Johann Kuhnau, Bach's immediate predecessor in Leipzig. Her transcriptions have helped to inspire performances of Kuhnau's music in worship and concert, as well as on recordings. Here, she provides an introduction to Kuhnau's sacred vocal music.

Frank C. Senn, Pastor of Immanuel Lutheran Church in Evanston, Illinois, is also a Senior of the Society of the Holy Trinity and past President of both the North American Academy of Liturgy and the Liturgical Conference. A prolific writer, he is the author of eight books, including the massive *Christian Liturgy: Catholic and Evangelical* (Fortress, 1997). His article in the present book offers advice to pastors and church musicians that is theologically sound, liturgically informed, and practical.

Mary Benson Stahlke, a musicologist and director of church music at St. John Lutheran Church in Chicago, has found among the works of Johann Krieger, an older colleague of Bach, an unusual treatment in one composition of an important concept rooted in Scripture and in the Augsburg Confession: Law and Gospel. Johann Krieger, who was highly regarded by both Bach and Handel, coordinated two differing approaches to composition in one work in order to highlight twin aspects of Lutheran doctrine.

Steven Wente serves Concordia University, River Forest, Illinois, as Professor of Music and Organist to the Chapel of Our Lord. He also is chair of the music department and coordinator of the graduate music programs at Concordia. A veteran church musician, he presently is minister of music at United Lutheran Church, Oak Park, Illinois. He writes of the life and accomplishments of Carl Schalk, not only from the particular vantage points of former pupil and later colleague, but also as participant in national Lutheran church music activity.

Paul Westermeyer is Professor of Church Music at Luther Seminary, St. Paul, Minnesota, Cantor for the Seminary, and Director of the Master of Sacred Music program with St. Olaf College. He has been national Chaplain of the American Guild of Organists, President of the Hymn Society, and Director of Ecclesiastical Concerns for the Association of Lutheran Church Musicians. He is the author of several books, including *The Church Musician* (Fortress, 1988, 1997) and *Te Deum: The Church and Music* (Fortress, 1998). His present article uses historical precedent to challenge the church to expand musical limitations in its worship.

Christoph Wolff is Adams University Professor at Harvard University. He has also served there as Chair of the Department of Music, Acting Director of the University Library, and Dean of the Graduate School of Arts and Sciences. He is the current director of the Bach Archive in Leipzig, Germany. The son of a Lutheran pastor, he is generally recognized as the foremost Bach scholar of the day. His *Johann Sebastian Bach, the Learned Musician* (Norton, 2000) approached the great Lutheran master in a new and refreshing light that can serve as an inspiration to any church musician. Dr. Wolff's article reveals in some detail the informed care for spiritual and musical matters that Bach brought to the creation of three cantatas.

Daniel Zager is Librarian and Chief Administrator, Sibley Music Library, Associate Professor of Musicology, and Affiliate Faculty Member of the Organ Department, Eastman School of Music, Rochester, New York. For five years he was editor of *Notes: Quarterly Journal of the Music Library Association* and for three years editor of *CrossAccent: Journal of the Association of Lutheran Church Musicians.* His article brings special insight to a study of Lutheran music in its early years as the canon of Reformation chorales was being formed. He notes the importance Lutherans of that time attached to the retention of Latin chant even as the "new" chorales were being written.

Thine the Amen, Thine the Praise

Thine the a-men, thine the praise al-le-lu-ias an-gels raise

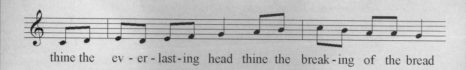

thine the ev-er-last-ing head thine the break-ing of the bread

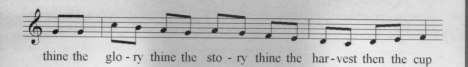

thine the glo-ry thine the sto-ry thine the har-vest then the cup

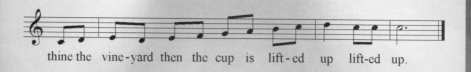

thine the vine-yard then the cup is lift-ed up lift-ed up.

Text: Herbert Brokering, b. 1926
Tune: Carl Schalk, b. 1929

THINE

MARTIN E. MARTY

Foreword

The late musicologist Howard Brown and I shared space in a parking lot and on walkways to our classrooms at The University of Chicago. Though he was a man of catholic tastes, he could not comprehend my love for hymnody. In a cavalier dismissal of the genre, he said, "Hymns all sound the same to me. Once you've heard one, you've heard them all." Recovering from my astonishment over such an un-bright comment, I set out to demonstrate something of the variety in the world of chorales and hymns. I'd hum a line or three now and then as we walked. The way I hum, however, leaves musical lines so undifferentiated that they may indeed all have sounded alike.

Now I wish I could hand just this one book to Professor Brown, and back it with some CDs, beckon him to live performances or, better, to worship, where the highly diverse forms of church music here referenced, described, and interpreted, receive at least brief mention and often considerable elaboration.

One could begin with Carl Schalk's own compositions, often hymn-based as they are. His outpouring, described by Paul Bouman as "simple, yet memorable and lyrical vocal lines" includes some complex, yet memorable and lyrical vocal lines. By the way, for musical amateurs like me, it is easier to remember the simple ones. I'd change the sentence to "memorable because of the simple lyrical vocal lines." I've heard and sometimes sung many scores of Schalk's scores, and find in them both a distinctive voice—you can't miss the manner and mien and bearing of this composer in his work—and a tremendous range of emotional, textual, and theological accents and nuances.

As I read the manuscript, it occurred to me that what the readers hold in their hands is not so much a book as a reference library.

I hope that after it has had its run as a best-selling book it will be scanned so that with "word-search" on the internet the lists will be easily available to choir directors, pastors, and music-lovers in general. The reference pages herein are not so much to be read as to be used; one's eyes glaze over when lists run pages-long, and yet the book is to do more than dazzle. It also instructs.

Time magazine once made reference to a Christian missionary school where illiterate children gained the tools of access to learning. I remember almost verbatim a summary by one child. "When I first came to this place, I did not know *anything*. Now already I know several things." I did not know how much I did *not* know about elements in church music past and present, and found many essays to have a quiet pedagogical tone, so I learned "several things."

Naturally that was the case in the helpful close-ups of giants in the tradition: Franz Eler, Johann Kuhnau, and Johann Krieger in essays by Daniel Zager, Evangeline Rimbach, and Mary Benson Stahlke. A quick run with Robin A. Leaver through the work of translators of Luther's hymns from Coverdale through Winkworth—that ubiquitous name at the bottom of so many hymnal pages in books with which we grew up—and then others into our own time, introduced problems of translating the blunt, angular, bold, rugged works of Luther himself. I've profited much from Christoph Wolff's writings on the technical side of Bach. How good it was here to see him dealing with the marriage of Bible and hymnal in this lineage. .

We are also likely to toe-tap more rhythmically during performances of Bach as we learn from Natalie Jenne the list—get this, for variety!—of dance styles in Bach's music: "bourées, gavottes, minuets, passepieds, sarabandes, loures, forlanas, . . . gigues/gigas," which she later elaborates as forms called "giga, jig, jigg, gique."

Nothing about Carl Schalk's work is archaic, antique, nostalgic, or sentimental, as several writers make clear even when they do not use those four terms. Because he has a long memory, it is clear to our writers that Schalk does not live "back there," but engages the world of contemporary choirs and worshippers (or choirs as being among and leading the worshippers).

What is more enduring *and* current than back-stage or sacristy-loft "wars" between some pastors and some musicians? Frank Senn, however, serves us not by dwelling on the psychology of the collaborators—many pastors and musicians *do* get along well—but by drawing us back all the way to the books of Chronicles, with stops along the way through history. Like so many other essayists, Senn includes practical advice.

Similarly, Paul Westermeyer is not alone in finding it impossible to make at least passing reference to the debasement of church music among what we might call market-oriented and mega-mall churches. Like others, he also shows why certain kinds of music old and new better serve the people's song and service (*leitourgia*).

I've recently directed a three-year project on "The Child in Religion, Law and Society," and anything about children piques my interest, so I was ready for Barbara Resch's tutoring and recommendations. Bizarrely, many scholarly works on church music forget that children have always been integral to the development of church music. And to read William H. Braun's catalog and comments on recent musical Passions, most of them written by people born more recently than I was, was a bracing and inviting introduction, a signal that creativity in church music is abundant today.

Like so many others, Joseph Herl presents lists, this time of seven habits. By visiting the sixteenth through the eighteenth centuries, he offers guidance for the twenty-first, counsel that should be helpful to those who would acquire a *habitus*, a set of conventions, an ease with the worship traditions, in our own time.

Steven Wente is given the chance to speak at length for all of us and to all of us of the life and work of Carl Schalk, whom this collection honors. Carl's is a household and church-hold name to so many of us. He is a cherished gift of God who uses the gifts of God to produce gifts for the people of God. So I'd close with the hope that he will be giving more for years to come, in a tradition to which this book bears testimony. The familiar greeting of hope, then, is *ad multos annos.* As quickly as he reads that, Schalk is like to set the phrase to music. If I had a search-engine run through all the works and all his pages, I would no doubt find that he already has done so! And it would end with *Amen.*

ROBERT BUCKLEY FARLEE

Introduction

A volume such as this can be appreciated in many ways. One, of course, is as a tribute to one of the finest church musicians of our time, Dr. Carl Schalk. And on behalf of the Association of Lutheran Church Musicians (ALCM), I am pleased to offer our congratulations and deep gratitude to him for the many gifts he has shared with the Lutheran and wider Christian church. Dr. Schalk is one of our own, a recipient of the Honorary Lifetime Membership in ALCM as well as a frequent presenter at our conferences and a contributor to several association projects. In addition, he has been a teacher of many of our members, and of course, his hymn tunes and choral arrangements have enriched the worship lives of our congregations. This honor is well-deserved.

But there is more to recommend this book. It is a collection of essays by some of the finest scholars in our field at this time. As such it is well worth reading for its own sake. Its contents demonstrate that the scholarship that has been a hallmark of Lutheran liturgical and musical studies over the centuries remains a vital force. Among the sampling addressed by the contributors one can find both attention to the heritage that continues to nourish us today, and a more explicit exploration of the ways in which today's church grapples with issues that are at the same time new and old. We owe editor (and ALCM past president) Carlos Messerli a debt of gratitude for gathering such a distinguished passel of writers.

Besides being a tribute to Carl Schalk, besides being a contribution to the scholarly conversation, this book can be seen as a time capsule—a snapshot, if you will, of what matters to church musicians (Lutheran and other) at the beginning of the twenty-first century. As such, it is certainly not all-encompassing; ours is, after all, a broad and diverse community. But by reading both on and between the lines, one can learn much about who we are and what matters to us, what spurs us onward.

Lutheran church musicians (for that is the tradition from which both this book and its honoree spring) have deep roots in the northern European lands, especially Germany. Recent decades have seen efforts to expand that identity (with mixed results), but few of us in the musical arena would wish to turn our backs on that heritage. The Lutheran chorale alone is, as Schalk has never tired of reminding us, an inexhaustible storehouse of riches. That treasury, as well as other historic contributions of the church catholic, continues to be explored, interpreted, and added to by today's cantors, following in the footsteps of luminous predecessors like Walter, Krieger, Kuhnau, and of course, Sebastian Bach.

It needs to be emphasized that American Lutherans' frequent looking across the sea and back through the centuries for repertoire is not a case of mere repristination, of living in the past. Works such as cantatas by the Baroque masters were born from a conviction that biblical truths of law and gospel could, and indeed must, be communicated also using musical means. Martin Luther established that principle, and it has guided us ever since. Modern sensibilities may not often or in many places allow for as deep an immersion as the weekly cantata performance of the eighteenth century, yet the use of chorales, cantata movements, and works influenced by cantatas continues to keep the tradition alive. Here and there, similar remnants of other parts of the tradition also survive, such as the use of Passions and Sequences. Where this takes place, hearers still find their faith deepened and enhanced. And occasionally, one can even hear a new work composed bearing these lineages.

No one would claim, however, that such northern European usage is as widespread as in past generations, let alone growing. Where does that leave the American Lutheran musical and worship tradition, since it has been identified so closely with its Germanic roots? Is it destined, over coming years, to be gradually but completely subsumed into the larger and blander cultural scene, becoming merely a historical footnote? Much will depend on how the generation instructed and inspired by Carl Schalk responds to the challenges they face. If they try to create cultural islands untouched by contemporary concerns and forces, those islands will continue to shrink, washed away by inexorable tides. If and where that happens, we confess with confidence that God's word will still thrive, for it doesn't depend on our stylistic purity or even our success.

But the Lutheran tradition, at its best, is adaptive, devoted finally not to any one style or form but rather to proclaiming in word, deed, and through the arts the cross of Christ as the sole source of life. Yes, specific means such as the chorale, the cantata, the liturgy have served that goal, and we hope will continue to do so, given creative adaptation by gifted cantors and pastors. And we can be certain that since the living gospel is the foundation of our art and craft, tomorrow's church music will also appear in new and unforeseen garb. If we have learned from teachers and exemplars like Carl Schalk, church music will continue, in ever new ways, to witness to the truth that the final word, the Amen—the "let it be so"—belongs to God.

Part One

Music of the
Lutheran Heritage

ROBIN A. LEAVER

Figs and Thistles:
Luther's Hymns in English[1]

Luther's hymns are distinctively German. Although there is a commonality of iambic stress-patterns in both German and English, grammar and sentence structure are significantly different in the two languages, to say nothing of the ubiquity of weak endings in German poetry, and the early appearance of the verb in English sentences, compared with the opposite necessity in German. Thus the task of translating German poetry into acceptable English verse is not an easy one, especially when the German is Luther's rugged rhymes and rhythms expressed in a sixteenth-century language that was then in a very fluid state. Nevertheless, even while Luther was still alive, there were those who felt compelled to attempt to render into Anglo-Saxon these Teutonic-Saxon songs of faith and theology. In later generations many translators followed the earlier pioneers, some with greater success than others in getting Luther to sing in English.

What follows here is an overview of some of the primary translators, from Luther's day to our own, who have built on each other's work in order to give English-language worshipers the opportunity to sing the substance of Luther's hymns and to sing them to their associated melodies, which in many cases were also the creation of the Wittenberg reformer. As one reviews the work of these translators one cannot but be impressed by their achievements, and their struggles to find the right word, phrase, and rhythm should fill us with humility, respect, and gratitude—even if the result is sometimes less than perfect!

Sixteenth-Century Translators

Miles Coverdale was the first to translate Luther's hymns into English in a consistent, singable form.[2] In the 1530s, having broken with the papacy in Rome, King Henry VIII in England was feeling vulnerable, and he feared an attack from European Catholic princes. It was at this time that he began to think of the possibility of joining the Schmalkaldic League of Lutheran princes who had pledged to defend each other's territories should they be attacked. In order to join, Henry would have to become a Lutheran. Some of his subjects were well ahead of him and were already well-read in Lutheran literature, and some, like William Tyndale, Robert Barnes, and Miles Coverdale, had been in Germany and had experienced the Lutheran Reformation first-hand. So, for a short period Lutheran theology and practice were openly discussed and considered in England. Like Luther, Miles Coverdale had produced a complete vernacular Bible, published in 1535, the year after Luther's complete Bible had been issued in German. Like Luther, Coverdale produced a vernacular hymnal. But, unlike Luther, Coverdale was not the creator of such hymns but rather the translator. Coverdale's hymnal, *Goostly psalmes and spirituall songes* (c.1535), contained forty-one hymns, virtually all of them translations from the German, or, in the case of one or two, written in a Germanic style. Of the twenty-nine hymns Luther had published by 1535, Coverdale translated eighteen (listed here in the sequence they appear in Coverdale's hymnal):[3]

Luther	*Coverdale*
Komm, Heiliger Geist, Herre Gott (1524)	Come holy Spirite moste blessed lorde
Nun bitten wir den Heiligen Geist (1524)	Thou holy Spirite we pray to the
Gott der Vater wohn uns bei (1524)	God the Father dwel us by
Dies sind die heilgen zehn Gebot (1524)	These are the holy commaundementes ten
Mensch wilt du leben seliglich (1524)	Man wylt thou lyve ryght vertuously
Wir glauben all an einen Gott (1524)	We beleve all upon one God
Nun freut euch lieben Christen gmein (1523)	Be glad now all ye christen men

Mitten wir im Leben sind (1524)	In the myddest of our lyvynge
Gelobet seist du, Jesu Christ (1524)	Now blessed be thou Christ Jesu
Christ lag in Todesbanden (1524)	Christ dyed and suffred great payne
Mit Fried und Freud ich fahr dahin (1524)	With peace and with joyfull gladnesse
Ach Gott vom Himmel sieh darein (1524)	Helpe now O Lorde and loke on us
Ein feste Burg ist unser Gott (1529)	Oure God is a defence and towre
Wär Gott nicht mit uns dieser Zeit (1524)	Except the lorde had bene with us
Wohl dem, der in Gottes Furcht steht (1524)	Blessed are all that feare the lorde
Aus tiefer Not schrei ich zu dir (1524)	Out of the depe crye I to the
Es wollt uns Gott gnädig sein (1523)	God be mercyfull unto us
Es spricht der Unweisen Mund wohl (1524)	The foolysh wicked men can saye

These Coverdale translations, which have often been characterized as unpoetical and mundane doggerel, nevertheless have a
rugged angularity that closely approximates Luther's German style.
However, these translations are usually somewhat free, especially
those based on specific texts. The translator accepted the general
metrical pattern of the melody and the leading ideas of the original
text but then followed the scriptural passage on which the original
is based, in his own independent way, rather than slavishly following the German text.[4] A notable example is Coverdale's version of
Ein feste Burg, which has five stanzas to Luther's four:

1. Our God is a defence and tower,
   a good armour and good weapon.
   He hath been ever our help and succour
   in all the troubles that we have been in.
   Therefore will we never dread
   for any wondrous deed,
   by water or by land
   in hills or the sea sand;
   Our God hath them all in his hand.

2. Though we be alway greatly vexed
   with many a great temptation,
   yet thanked be God we are refreshed;
   his sweet Word comforteth our mansion.
   It is God's holy place,
   he dwelleth here by grace;
   among us is he
   both night and day truly;
   he helpeth us all and that swiftly.

3. The wicked heathen besiege us straitly,
   and many great Kingdoms take their part;
   they are gathered against us truly
   and are sore moved in their heart.
   But God's Word as clear as day
   maketh them shrink away.
   The Lord God of power
   standeth by us every hour;
   the God of Jacob is our strong tower.

4. Come hither now, behold and see
   the noble acts and deeds of the Lord,
   what great things he doth for us daily,
   and comforteth us with his sweet Word.
   For when our enemies would fight
   then brake he their might,
   their bow and their spear
   (so that we need not fear),
   and burnt their chariots in the fire.

5. "Therefore," saith God, "take heed to me;
   Let me alone and I shall help you;
   Know me for your God, I say, only,
   among all heathen that reign now."
   Wherefore then should we dread,
   seeing we have no need.
   For the Lord God of power
   standeth by us every hour;
   the God of Jacob is our strong tower.[5]

Although rarely recognized, a section of a Coverdale translation of a Luther hymn was embedded within one of the services of the Book of Common Prayer of 1549 and repeated in subsequent editions. This is the English version of the *Media vita in morte sumus*, which is found in "The Ordre for the Buriall of the dead."[6] In the Prayer Book order it appears to be a simple prose translation from the text of the Sarum Latin rite, *Inhumatio defuncti*, but when the sources are compared it becomes clear that Cranmer (or whoever drew up the burial service) made substantial use of Coverdale's translation of Luther's German version of the Latin antiphon, *Mitten wir im Leben sind*: In the myddest of our lyvynge. See page 26 for the comparison.

The Prayer Book version occasionally omits a word from Coverdale's translation and in other places makes small additions, but the general dependence on Coverdale is unmistakable. Several lines are not present in the Latin text and are clearly taken from Coverdale's text, which in turn is a translation of Luther's *du ewiger Gott* in stanza three of his German version (given in italics below):

Luther	*Coverdale*
. . . . .	. . . . .
Heiliger Herre Gott	O lorde god most holy
Heiliger Starker Gott	O lorde god most myghtie
Heiliger Barmhertziger Heiland	O holy and mercyfull Savioure
du ewiger Gott	*Thou most worthy god eternall*
las vns nicht entfallen	Suffre us not at oure last houre
von des rechten glauben trost.	Thorow despare from the to fall.
Kyrieleison.	Kirieleyson.

In one line the Prayer Book version prefers "iudge eternall" to Coverdale's "god eternall," and "for any paynes of death" replaces Coverdale's "Thorow despare." But since the Prayer Book version was prose rather than rhymed verse, there were few constraints to slavishly follow the English versification of Luther's German. Here is an indication of the durability and influence of Coverdale's *Goostly psalmes*, in that it became an essential source for the reformed English liturgy. But what is extremely important is that one of Luther's hymns made this fundamental contribution to the Book of Common Prayer, the classic anthology of worship that in many ways defined Anglicanism for centuries.

What Coverdale began was taken up by others in succeeding decades, and many were grateful to build on his translations. John Wedderburn from Dundee fled from his native Scotland to Wittenberg in 1539 where he associated with Luther and his colleagues.

Sarum	BCP 1549	Coverdale
. . .	. . .	. . .
Sancte deus.	yet O Lorde God moste holy,	O lorde god most holy
Sancte fortis.	O Lorde moste mightie,	O lorde god most myghtie
Sancte & misericors saluator:	O holy and most mercifull sauiour,	O holy and mercyfull Savioure
amare morti ne tradas nos.	delyver vs not into the bytter	
	paynes of eternall deathe	
. . .	. . .	. . .
Sancte fortis	But spare vs Lorde moste holy,	O lorde god most holy
sancte et misericors saluator	O God moste mightye,	O lorde god most myghtie
	O holye and mercifull sauioure,	O holy and mercyfull Savioure
amare morti ne tradas nos.	thou most woorthie *iudge* eternall,	Thou most worthy god eternall
	suffre vs not at our last houre	Suffre us not at oure last houre
	for any paynes of death,	Thorow despare
	to fall from thee.	from the to fall.

Sometime between 1540 and 1550 he translated some of the hymns of the Wittenberg hymn writers, such as his version of *Vom Himmel hoch* in vigorous Scottish dialect (and metrical deficiencies). Here are the first three stanzas:

1. I come from hevin to tell
   The best nowellis that ever befell,
   To zow thir tythingis trew I bring,
   And I will of them say and sing.

2. This day, to zow, is borne ane childe
   Of Marie meik, and Virgin milde.
   That blissit bairne bening and kynde,
   Sall zow reioyis, baith hart and mynde.

3. It is the Lord, Christ, God and Man,
   He will do for zow quhat he can:
   Him self zour Saviour will be,
   Fra sin and hell, to mak zow free.[7]

Some of Wedderburn's translations were taken over almost verbatim from Coverdale, establishing a pattern which was to be repeated again and again in successive attempts to render Luther's hymns into English: Each new translator began with the work of those who had preceded him. Thus when Robert Wisdome came to translate *Es woll uns Gott genädig sein*, a version that was included in an English metrical psalter of 1560, he clearly had both Coverdale's and Wedderburn's versions in front of him: "God be mercyfull unto us."[8]

An independent translator was Richard Cox, one of the English Protestant exiles in Straßburg during the reign of Catholic Mary. He made a complete translation of Luther's *Vater unser im Himmelreich* that first appeared in print in the English psalter, *Psalmes of David in Metre*, published for the English exiles in Wesel in 1556. The first stanza of Cox's translation runs:

Our Father which in Heaven art
and makes us all one brotherhood
to call upon thee with one heart,
our heavenly Father and our God:
graunt we pray not with lips alone,
but with hearts deepe sigh and grone.[9]

The hymn was later incorporated into the Elizabethan Sternhold and Hopkins (Old Version) psalter, as well as in later editions, where it appeared with Luther's associated melody, though usually known as OLD 112TH, since it was also used as the tune for Psalm 112 in the English psalter.[10] But although the text of the English version of Luther's Lord's Prayer hymn was sung to Luther's tune, these English singers had no idea that they were singing a hymn by the German Reformer.

There was another Luther hymn that was translated by an English Marian exile. It too was fairly widely sung by later generations of English worshipers, and, like Cox's translation of Luther's *Vater unser*, the singers were totally unaware that they were singing a hymn by the Wittenberg Reformer. This was Robert Wisdome's "Preserve us, Lord, by thy dear Word," a translation of Luther's *Erhalt uns, Herr, bei deinem Wort*, which first appeared in John Day's 1561 psalter and later incorporated within the Elizabethan Sternhold and Hopkins psalter.

1. Preserve us Lord by thy deere word,
   from Turk & Pope defend us Lord:
   which both would thrust out of his throne
   our Lord Jesus Christ thy dear Son.

2. Lord Jesus Christ showe forth thy might
   that thou art Lord of Lords by right:
   thy poor afflicted flocke defend,
   that they may praise thee without end.

3. God holy Ghost our comforter,
   be our patron help and succour:
   Give us one minde and perfect peace,
   all gifts of grace in us increase.[11]

Like Cox's translation of *Vater unser*, Wisdome's version of *Erhalt uns, Herr* was sung to Luther's associated melody. Much criticism was later heaped upon this hymn found in the Sternhold and Hopkins psalter, but none of the critics apparently realized that the real author was Luther![12]

Most of the sixteenth-century versions are generally imitations rather than strict translations; many of them limp rather badly in their English form, which may help to explain why the seventeenth century hardly saw a Luther translation. Although Wedderburn's *Gude and Godlie Ballates* were reprinted at least twice in the first quarter of the century, the atmosphere in both England and Scotland had become strongly Calvinist, and Lutheran hymns that were not strictly scriptural paraphrases were regarded with suspicion.

Seventeenth- and Eighteenth-Century Translators

Towards the end of the seventeenth century the substance of Luther's *Ein fest Burg* was rendered into English, not as a singable hymn but incorporated into a prose paragraph illustrating Luther's theology. The original source was the Latin history of the Reformation based on documentary sources by Joannes Sleidanus, first published in Straßburg in 1555, with additional material being added in later years: *De statu religionis et republicae, carolo quinto, caesare, commentariorum.* Edmund Bohun prepared a complete translation,[13] published as *The General History of the Reformation of the Church . . . from the year 1517 to the year 1556* (London, 1689). Toward the end of Book XVI Sleidanus effectively includes the whole of Luther's famous hymn, which Bohun expresses thus in English:[14]

> When the Emperor [Charles V] . . . held a Diet at *Augsburg* [1530], a fearful Storm seemed then to threaten . . . ; but he [Luther], in the mean time, both privately and publickly comforted all his friends. And applying the 46th *Psalm* to the present juncture, « [st. 1] *God*, said he, *is our refuge and strength, &c.* That old Enemy of Mankind, is now, indeed, busie at work, applying all his Engines: [st. 2] and our power is but weak, nor can we long withstand so great a force: But that Champion whom God himself chose, hath taken up Arms and fighteth for us: if you ask who that is; know that it is *Jesus Christ*, who must needs conquer and triumph: [st. 3] Though the whole World swarm also with Devils, we are therefore not dismayed, but with assured confidence expect a joyful issue: and though *Satan* foam and rage, yet shall he be able to do nothing against us: for he is judged, and the Word alone makes all his Arms to fall: [st. 4] that Word our adversaries shall not rob us of, but whether they will or no, shall leave it with us: for the Lord is in our Camp and in our Battels, and defends us by his spiritual gifts and graces: if they take away thy Goods, Children, and

Wife, bear it patiently: for they get nothing thereby, and to us there is an immortal Kingdom prepared.» That Psalm which, as I said, he applied to those sad and dismal times, he paraphrased also into *Dutch* [= Deutsch = German] Rhyme, and set a Tune for it, very agreeable to the Subject, and proper to excite and elevate the mind: therefore, since that time, it is frequently sung amongst the other Psalms [= hymns] [in Germany].[15]

Interest in the hymns of Luther was revived in England at the beginning of the eighteenth century with the coming of the Hanoverian kings. Although George I conformed to the Church of England he was permitted to have a Lutheran court chaplain and maintain a German chapel at St. James's Palace in London. John Christian Jacobi was the officially designated "Keeper" of this Royal German Chapel. Jacobi turned his hand to translating German hymns. Between 1722 and 1732 his hymn book, *Psalmodia Germanica*, was issued three times. The first hymn in the collection is Jacobi's version of *Nun komm, der Heiden Heiland*:

1. Now the Saviour comes indeed,
   Of the Virgin-Mother's seed,
   To the Wonder of Mankind,
   By the Lord himself design'd.

2. Not begot like Men unclean,
   But without the Stain of Sin:
   In our Nature God was born,
   Us to save, who were forlorn.
   . . . .

4. From his Chambers forth he went;
   Left the Glorious Element;
   And, at once both God and Man,
   He his blessed Course began.
   . . . .

7. Lord, thy Crib shines bright and clear,
   Chasing Darkness every where,
   Let no Sin o'ercloud this Light,
   That our faith be always bright.[16]

In 1765 another edition appeared, fifteen years after Jacobi's death, which included a supplement of further translations. The same year it appears to have crossed the Atlantic and was reprinted in New York.[17] This collection became the first English hymn book used in Lutheran congregations in the New World, and Jacobi's translations of Luther's hymns were sung by several generations of American Lutherans.

In England a number of Jacobi translations of Luther were sung among the Moravians; indeed, the English Moravians made their own translations of the hymns of the reformer; however, most of them are very paraphrastic and fragmentary. John Gambold—friend of the Wesley brothers, John and Charles, and a Church of England vicar in Oxfordshire who resigned his Anglican orders to join the Moravians—was Zinzendorf's translator when the Moravian leader was in England in the 1740s. Gambold translated a number of German hymns, among them a few by Luther. For example, he translated the seventh stanza of *Christ unser Herr zum Jordan kam* for a small collection of hymns in 1743, which was later included in his massive *Collection of Hymns of the Children of God in all Ages* (London: "Printed, and to be had at all the Brethren's chapels," 1754), and later Moravian hymn books:

> The eye sees water, nothing more,
> How it is poured out by men;
> But faith alone conceives the pow'r
> Of Jesu's blood to make us clean:
> Faith sees it as a cleansing flood,
> Replete with Jesu's blood and grace,
> Which heals each wound and makes all good,
> What Adam brought on us his race,
> And all that we ourselves have done.[18]

Another friend of the Wesleys, who like Gambold resigned his Church of England parish to become a Moravian, was Charles Kinchen. He translated some German hymns including some of Luther's. His somewhat free translation of *Gelobet seist du, Jesu Christ*, which first appeared in 1742, was in use well into the nineteenth century, for not only was it included in successive Moravian hymn books but also in the 1780 hymn book of the Countess of Huntingdon's Connection, which was reprinted numerous times during the following century or so:

1. Jesus, all praise is due to Thee,
   That thou was pleas'd a man to be!
   A Virgin's womb Thou didst not scorn,
   And angels shout to see Thee born. Hallelujah![19]

Nineteenth-Century Translators

During the nineteenth century there was a renewed interest in Luther's hymns, and many turned their hand to translating them. Among the earliest was Arthur Toser Russell, an Anglican vicar who translated a number of German hymns at the request of Baron Bunsen, the Prussian Ambassador in London,[20] for the 1848 Dalston Hospital hymn book. They later appeared, sometimes revised, in his collection, *Psalms and Hymns* (Cambridge, 1851), together with further translations. His version of *Vater unser im Himmelreich* was published in both collections of 1848 and 1851:

8. Deliverance from all evil give,
   for yet in evil days we live.
   Preserve us from eternal death,
   give comfort with our latest breath:
   O grant us all a blissful end,
   then with thy hand our spirits tend.

9. Amen—our prayer be verified—
   our faith with constant strength supplied;
   that we may ne'er distrustful be
   in what we thus implore of thee;
   but asking by thy name and word
   may say a true Amen, O Lord.[21]

Richard Massie, an Anglican vicar, was also an admirable translator of German hymns, among them many by Carl Johann Philipp Spitta, and all—as far as he knew them—by Luther. His edition of *Martin Luther's Spiritual Songs* appeared in 1854 and has been gratefully used by successions of hymn book editors.[22] His success is due to his basic respect for Luther's muscular Christianity. In the preface to the collection he wrote: [in these hymns] "there is no originality of thought, no splendid imagery, no play of fancy calculated to attract the reader, whose taste has been formed on the productions of the nineteenth century; but there is a simple beauty, a homely strength and plainness of language, and above all, a scriptural truth, which found their way to every heart in that less refined age."[23]

The greatest translator of German hymns in the nineteenth century is undoubtedly Catherine Winkworth.[24] She was able to catch the spirit and thought of the German originals and express them in a truly authentic English style. We are still singing with profit her memorable translations, such as "Now thank we all our God" and "Praise to the Lord the Almighty, the King of Creation," among others. But the hymns of Luther created problems for her. It was not their strong theological content but rather their rough-hewn directness that created the difficulty. She had firm ideas about smoothness and correctness of style, meter, and vocabulary. She wrote: "Luther's hymns are wanting in harmony and correctness of metre to a degree which often makes them jarring to our modern ears, but they are always full of fire and strength, of clear Christian faith, and brave joyful trust in God."[25] Six translations of Luther made their debut in the first series of *Lyra Germanica* (1855); one was never used again in her later collections, and of the four which re-appeared in *The Chorale Book for England* (1863), only one was reproduced basically unchanged—the others were either altered or re-written; and one had a short life, appearing only in the first edition of 1855. This was her version of Luther's *Ein feste Burg*. Miss Winkworth was unhappy with her translation, so she withdrew it from the second edition (also 1855) and substituted William Gaskell's version, which she thought much superior to her own:[26]

Ein feste Burg

Catherine Winkworth

1. God is our stronghold
     firm and sure,
Our trusty shield and weapon,
He shall deliver us, whate'er

Of ill to us may happen.
Our ancient Enemy
In earnest now is he,
Much craft and great might
Arm him for the fight,
On earth is not his fellow.

. . . .

4. The word of God they
     cannot touch,
Yet have no thanks therefore,
God by His Spirit and His gifts,
Is with us in the war.

William Gaskell

1. A sure stronghold our
     God is He,
Our trusty shield and weapon;
Our help He'll be and
     set us free

From every ill can happen.
That old malicious foe
Intends us deadly woe;
Arm'd with the strength of hell
And deepest craft as well,
On earth is not his fellow.

. . . .

4. Still shall they leave that
     Word His might
And yet no thanks shall merit,
Still is He with us in the fight
By His good gifts and Spirit.

Then let them take our life,	E'en should they take our life,
Goods, honour, children, wife,	Goods, honour, children, wife–
Though nought of these we save,	Though all of these be gone,
Small profit shall they have,	Yet nothing have they won,
The kingdom ours abideth.[27]	God's kingdom ours abideth.[28]

In the preface to the second series of *Lyra Germanica* (1858), Catherine Winkworth excused herself from translating any further texts of Luther since "all his hymns are accessible . . . in the excellent translation of Mr. Massie."[29]

Other women translators who contributed one or more versions of some of Luther's hymns in their various collections include: Francis Elizabeth Cox, *Sacred hymns from the German* (London: Pickering, 1841);[30] Caroline Fry (Mrs. Wilson), *Hymns of the Reformation by Dr. Martin Luther, and others, from the German* (London: Gilpin, 1845); Jane Borthwick (Mrs. E. Findlater), *Hymns from the Land of Luther* (Edinburgh: Kennedy, 1862);[31] and Mrs. Rundle Charles, *The Voice of Christian Life in Song: or, Hymns and Hymn-writers of Many Lands and Ages* (London: Nisbet, 1858).[32]

These were not the only translators of Luther's hymns in the nineteenth century. There were others, such as John Anderson and John Hunt, who translated the whole corpus of Luther's hymns in 1846 and 1853 respectively.[33] But, as Ulrich Leopold, the editor of volume fifty-three of the American Edition of *Luther's Works: Liturgy and Hymns,* has written, such translators "frequently . . . changed irregular verse forms into more accepted meters. Usually they aimed at a more polished and elegant style than was really justified in view of Luther's angularity. They tried to make him speak in the mellifluent accents of a Victorian churchman, with the result that both the literal sense and the original style were often lost."[34]

Not so the translations of George MacDonald, which were issued in 1876.[35] Leupold chose the work of this rugged Scotsman as the basis for the translations to be included in the fifty-third volume of *Luther's Works.* MacDonald certainly rendered the bluntness of Luther into obtuse English, which is also their weakness. They may be generally faithful to Luther's original, but in English the bluntness interrupts the flow of meaning. However, Macdonald is always faithful to the spirit of Luther even if his English staggers under the load. He wrote that his "paramount desire" was "to preserve first the spirit and next the meaning."[36] But that does not mean that he would not borrow a phrase or a couplet from Massie's translations.

In order to celebrate the 400th anniversary of Luther's birth Leonard Woolsey Bacon brought out a collected edition of Luther's hymns, which also included musical settings by Praetorius, Schein, and J. S. Bach, among others: *The Hymns of Martin Luther Set to their Original Melodies* (New York: Scribner, 1883). The original German texts were given with English translations, which were mostly modified versions of Massie, but also included others by Russell, Miss Cox, and Miss Winkworth. But where Bacon was not satisfied with earlier translations, he supplied his own.[37] As he explains in his introduction, this was done reluctantly but out of necessity, providing an appropriate English rendering for the frequently difficult German.

Others struggled with the bluntness of Luther, especially in attempting to render *Ein feste Burg* into English. There must be a hundred or more different translations of his magnificent hymn— and all of them deficient in some way or other![38] One of the most durable is Thomas Carlyle's *A safe stronghold our God is still*, dating from 1831, in that it has formed the basis for the versions in a good many British hymn books. Another long-lasting translation is that by Frederick H. Hedge, of 1852, which appears in many American hymnals: "A mighty fortress is our God, | a bulwark never failing."[39]

Those Anglicans who followed the ideals of the Oxford Movement did not care much for Luther's hymns, but they did like some of his sturdy tunes. Thus, Sir Henry W. Baker, for the first edition of the Tractarian *Hymns Ancient and Modern* of 1861, wrote this hymn on the isometric form of Luther's melody *Ein feste Burg*:

1. Rejoice today with one accord,
    sing out with exaltation;
    rejoice and praise our mighty Lord,
    whose arm hath brought salvation;
    his works of love proclaim
    the greatness of his name;
    for he is God alone
    who hath his mercy shown;
    Let all his saints adore him.

2. When in distress to him we cried,
   he heard our sad complaining;
   O trust in him, whate'er betide,
   his love is all-sustaining;
   triumphant songs of praise
   to him our hearts shall raise;
   now every voice shall say,
   "O praise our God alway";
   Let all his saints adore him.[40]

Twentieth-Century Translators

The struggle to find adequate English translations of Luther's craggy hymn, *Ein feste Burg*, continued in the twentieth century. Honor Mary Thwaites supplied a new version, clearly based on older models, for *The Australian Hymn Book* (1975), and Michael Perry provided a paraphrastic impression for *Hymns for Today's Church* (1982), both of them using the later isometric form of the melody.[41]

Somewhat earlier Martin H. Franzmann was inspired to write a hymn based on both the text and melody of *Vater unser im Himmelreich* to be used on occasions when Luther's original nine stanzas were thought too long. It appeared in the *Worship Supplement* (1959) and is another fine example of how Luther's hymns have inspired later hymn writers to walk in his footsteps:

1. O thou, who hast of thy pure grace
   Made shine on us a Father's face,
   Arise, thy holy name make known;
   Take up thy power and reign alone;
   On earth, in us, let thy sole will
   Be done as angels do it still.

2. O King and Father, kind and dread,
   Give us this day our daily bread;
   Forgive us, who have learned to bless
   Our enemies, all trespasses;
   Spare us temptation, let us be
   From Satan set forever free.

3. Thine is the kingdom, unto thee
   Shall bow in homage every knee;
   And thine the power; no power shall be

That is not overcome by thee;
The glory thine, by every tongue
Thy praise shall be forever sung.[42]

F. Samuel Janzow, in collaboration with musicians Carl Schalk, Richard Hillert, and Paul Bunjes, produced a translation of the whole corpus of Luther's hymns.[43] He admits that the attempt to translate them "involves frequent sacrifice of the original semantic and syntactic patterns. . . . For example, since the hymns of Luther were assumed to be inseparably wedded to their melodies, the meter is not open to choice, and the frequent feminine rhymes—much less graceful in English than in German—had to be retained."[44] The character of Janzow's translations can be judged from his words of explanation: ". . . the translator felt free to handle Luther's subordinate ideas and imagery with considerable freedom. One will therefore find transpositions of order, paraphrased expressions in place of literal reproductions, the selection of certain values in a given poetic image to the necessary neglect of some others, and sometimes even the substitution of entirely different images. In no instances, however, is the intention to alter the biblical and Reformation concepts in Luther's hymns; the Church delights to be captive to the Word also in its hymnody."[45] But even Janzow, with all his new and challenging translations, is grateful to use the work of his predecessors. For example, a comparison of his version of *Vater unser im Himmelreich* with that of Catherine Winkworth will show that he has taken over some of the lines and rhyming patterns of the earlier translation.[46]

A Conclusion

In reviewing the translations of these marvelous hymns one is always aware of the conflict between the letter and the spirit. In attempting to represent Luther's vocabulary accurately and faithfully in English, the translator's danger is to fall into pedestrian and lifeless verse, the spirit is killed by the letter, and Luther is made unforgivably dull and unchallenging. In attempting to catch the spirit of Luther's hymns the opposite danger is to treat his texts with too much freedom and a paraphrase results; the letter is overwhelmed by the spirit, and the translator's figs appear in the place of Luther's thistles. The ideal, of course, is for the translator to represent faithfully both the letter and the spirit of Luther's texts. Since the English language is not static but always changing and evolving, there will always be the need to try to create new translations that more effectively convey Luther's theology and spirituality. What is still surprisingly lacking is a modern edition of Luther's hymns in which the translated texts are given in parallel with their German originals and with all melodies assigned to them in the hymnals published during Luther's lifetime.

What we do have, however, is a commonality of purpose among the English translators of Luther's hymns, old and new: all of them accepted the difficult task because they were convinced that the English-speaking world should not be denied the vigor and profundity of these expressions of faith in song. Thus this distinctive voice from the past continues to sing powerfully in our contemporary world.

NOTES

1   An earlier version was given as a paper at Lectures in Church Music at Concordia University, River Forest, Illinois, in October 1983, the 500th anniversary year of the birth of Martin Luther. The invitation to give the paper, of course, came from Carl Schalk. John S. Andrews' book, *A Study of German Hymns in Current English Hymnals* (Berne: Lang, 1981), only discusses various translations of Luther's *Ein feste Burg*. The reason is that "English" in his title means the country rather than the language, and *Ein feste Burg* is the only Luther hymn commonly found in hymnbooks in use in English churches. Andrews' methodology is based on usage rather than development, on German hymns found in current hymnals rather than representative English translations in historical perspective, which is the approach here.

2   George Joye produced a lay prayer book in the vernacular, *Ortulus anime: The garden of the soule*, published in Antwerp in 1530. He included Office hymns in a mixture of prose and rudimentary English verse. Two of his hymns are close in content to Luther's *Nun bitten wir* and *Nun freuet euch, lieben Christen gmein* respectively; see Robin A. Leaver, *"Goostly psalmes and spirituall songes": English and Dutch Metrical Psalms from Coverdale to Utenhove 1535–1566* (Oxford: Clarendon, 1991), 60–61.

3   On the background, see Leaver, *"Goostly psalmes and spirituall songes,"* esp. 66–81.

4   Calvin did much the same thing a few years later when he created his first metrical psalter in Strasbourg, *Aulcuns pseaulmes et cantiques mys en chant* (Strasbourg, 1539); he accepted the metrical pattern of the psalms sung in the German congregations, so that he could use the same melodies, but then created his French metrical psalms directly from Scripture rather than translating from the German metrical versions.

5   *Remains of Myles Coverdale containing Prologues to the translation of the Bible . . . . Letters, Ghostly Psalms and Spiritual Songs*, ed. George Pearson (Cambridge:

Parker Society, 1846), 569-70; see also Erich Althoff, *Myles Coverdales "Goostly Psalmes and Spirituall Songes" und das Deutsche Kirchenlied: Ein Beitrag zum Einfluß der deutschen Literatur auf die englische im 16. Jahrhundert* (Bochum: Pöppinghaus, 1935), 87–89.

6 For the background, see Robin A. Leaver, "Coverdale's 'Goostly psalmes' and the English Prayer Book of 1549," *IAH Bulletin*, 13 (1985): 23–35; also Leaver, *"Goostly psalmes and spirituall songes,"* 133-34.

7 *A Compendious Book of Godly and Spiritual Songs commonly known as "The Gude and Godlie Ballatis," Reprinted from the Edition of 1567*, ed. A. F. Mitchell (Edinburgh: Scottish Text Society, 1897; reprint, New York: Johnson, 1966), 49–51.

8 Wisdome translated Luther's *Erhalt uns, Herr, bei deinem Wort* (see below) and also, apparently, the church year sermons of Antonius Corvinus, *A postill or collection of moste godly doctrine upon every gospell through the year* (London: Wolfe, 1550). Corvinus' sermons were originally published in German in 1535, with a preface by Luther: *Kurze Auslegung der Evangelien* (Wittenberg, 1535); see John Julian, *A Dictionary of Hymnology*, 2nd ed. (London: Murray, 1907; reprint, New York: Dover, 1957), 862.

9 Thomas Ravenscroft, *The Whole Booke of Psalmes: With the Hymnes Evangelical and Songs Spirituall. Composed into 4. parts by sundry Authors, to such severall Tunes, as have been and are usually sung in England, Scotland, Wales, Germany, Italy, France, and the Netherlands* (London: Company of Stationers, 1621), 264.

10 Ibid., Ravenscroft describes it as a "High Dutch Tune," where "Dutch" = Deutsch = German.

11 Ibid., 272. Luther's melody is here also called a "High Dutch Tune."

12 The following are representative examples. Richard Corbet, Bishop of Norwich, wrote a satyrical poem, "To the Ghost of Robert Wisdome," in which he calls the disembodied spirit of Wisdome to come from his tomb in Carfax Church, Oxford, where he was buried, and show him how to write versifications the way Wisdome did in the previous century. But Corbett warns the ghost that he should beware, since he might be frightened by Pope or Turk and thus return to his grave:

> Thou once a body, now but ayre,
> Arch-botcher of a psalm or prayer,
>   From Carfax come!
> And patch us up a zealous lay,
> With an old *ever and for ay*,
>   Or *all and some*.
> Or such a spirit lend me,
> As may a hymne down sende me
>   To purge my braine:
> But Robert, looke behind thee,
> Lest Turk or Pope doe find thee,
>   And goe to bed again.

Robert Corbett, *Certain Elegant Poems* (London: Crooke, 1647), 49. In the following century Thomas Warton wrote: Wisdome "is chiefly memorable for his metrical prayer intended to be sung in the church, against the Pope and the Turk, of whom he seems to have conceived the most alarming apprehensions"; Thomas Warton, *History of English Poetry* [1774–1781] (London: Tegg, 1824), 3: 454.

13 An earlier translation was *A famouse cronicle of oure time, called Sleidanes Commentaries, concerning the state of religion and common wealth, during the raigne of the Emperour Charles the Fifth* . . . , trans John Daus (London: Day, 1560).

14 The editorial marking « » indicates the beginning and end of the hymn text.

15 Johannes Sleidanus, *The General History of the Reformation of the Church, from the Errors and Corruptions of the Church of Rome, Begun in Germany by Martin Luther with the Progress thereof in all parts of Christendom from the year 1517 to the year 1556* . . . , trans. Edmund Bohun (London: Jones, Swall and Bonwicke, 1689), 363–64; italics original.

16 *Psalmodia Germanica: or the German Psalmody* (New York: Gaine, 1765), 1-2. On the date of the New York imprint, see the following note.

17 The New York imprint gives the year as 1756: *Psalmodia Germanica: or the German Psalmody, Translated from the High Dutch, Together With their Proper Tunes, and Thorough Bass* (New York: Gaine, 1756). It was an incomplete reprint of a London edition of *Psalmodia Germanica* containing the translations of Jacobi. The title page follows *verbatim* the London edition, even though this New York edition did not include the "Proper Tunes" with "Thorough Bass." The year on the title page, "1756," has been taken at its face value by bibliographers and church music historians alike. They include: Charles Evans, et al, *American Bibliography: A Chronological Dictionary of All Books, Pamphlets, and Periodical Publications Printed in the United States of America from the Genesis of Printing in 1639 Down to and including the Year 1800*, 14 vols. (Chicago: Evans, 1903–1959), No. 7772; Edward C. Wolf, "Lutheran Hymnody and Music Published in America 1700-1850: A Descriptive Catalog," *Concordia Historical Institute Quarterly*, 50 (1977): 166; and Carl Schalk, *God's Song in a New Land: Lutheran Hymnals in America* (St. Louis: Concordia, 1995), 53-56 (and especially the material in note 4 on p. 194). Schalk is correct when he states some English-speaking Lutherans began singing from an early London edition of *Psalmodia Germanica*—just one copy to begin with—under the direction of Henry Melchior Muhlenberg, but incorrect—with everyone else!—in stating that the New York reprint was issued in "1756." True, this is the year that occurs on the title page but it is a typographical error for "1765." The *Psalmodia Germanica* issued in London in 1765 included an appendix of additional hymns that had not appeared in an earlier edition; these supplementary hymns are also to be found in the New York edition (pp. 189–279), which must therefore have been published at the earliest in 1765, though it is possible that it might have been a year or two later. As indicated above, the title page pedantically follows the London edition, even though it contains no music, and therefore it is possible that the typesetter intended to copy exactly the "1765" on the title page of the London edition he was using, even though it might have been sometime later, and by mistake transposed the last two numbers and made it "1756," thereby misleading generations of researchers; see Robin A. Leaver, *Catherine Winkworth: The Influence of Her Translations on English Hymnody* (St. Louis: Concordia, 1978), 3 (and note 16 above).

18 *A Collection of Hymns, for the Use of the Protestant Church of the United Brethren* (London: "Printed: and sold at the Brethren's Chapels," 1789), No. 547.

19 *A Select Collection of Hymns to be Universally Sung in All the Countess of Huntingdon's Chapels* (London: Hughes & Walsh, 1780), No. 209.

20 Bunsen encouraged others to translate German hymns into English, including Richard Massie, Frances Elizabeth Cox, and Catherine Winkworth.

21 *Hymns for Public Worship and Private Devotion: For the Benefit of the London German Hospital, Dalston* (London: Hatchard, 1848), No. 121.

22 Richard Massie, *Martin Luther's Spiritual Songs* (London: Hatchard, 1854).

23 Ibid., v.

24 For a discussion of Winkworth as a translator of German hymns, see Leaver, *Catherine Winkworth*, 47–72, esp. 59–62, for her translations of Luther's hymns.

25 Catherine Winkworth, *Lyra Germanica: Hymns for the Sundays and Chief Festivals of the Christian Year, Second edition* (London: Longmans, 1855), x.

26 Ibid., xviii.

27 Winkworth, *Lyra Germanica . . . , First edition* (1855), 175–76.

28 Winkworth, *Lyra Germanica . . . , Second edition* (1855), 175–76.

29 Catherine Winkworth, *Lyra Germanica: Second Series: The Christian Life* (London: Longmans, 1858), ix.

30 It was later revised and expanded and issued as *Hymns from the German* (London: Rivingtons, 1864).

31 The translations were originally issued in a series of four parts between 1854 and 1862.

32 The fifth revised and enlarged edition was issued as *Te Deum laudamus, Christian Life in Song: the Song and the Singers* (London: SPCK & New York: Young, 1897).

33 John Anderson, *Hymns from the German by Dr. Martin Luther* (Edinburgh: Johnstone, 1846); John Hunt, *The Spiritual Songs of Martin Luther* (London: Hamilton, Adams, 1853).

34 Martin Luther, *Liturgy and Hymns*, ed. Ulrich S. Leupold, Luther's Works: American Edition, vol. 53 (Philadelphia: Fortress, 1965), 199.

35 George MacDonald, *Exotics, A Translation of the Spiritual Songs of Novalis, the Hymn-Book of Luther, and Other Poems from the German and Italian* (London: Strahan, 1876).

36 Cited Luther's Works, vol. 53, 201.

37 The volume is available in electronic format, but without the musical settings, from Project Gutenberg, University of Illinois: http://www.gutenberg.net/.

38 See, for example, Bernhad Pick, *Luther's Battle Song, "Ein feste Burg ist unser Gott": Its History and Translations* (New York: Kaufmann, 1917); Charles Berend Foelsch, *The English Versions of Martin Luther's "Ein feste burg" and Notes on his Other Hymns* (Pittsburgh: [s.n.], 1924).

39 For a discussion of the Carlyle and Hedge versions, see Andrews, *German Hymns in Current English Hymnals*, 15–19.

40 *Hymns Ancient and Modern for Use in the Services of the Church with Accompanying Tunes* (London: Novello, [1868]), No. 237.

41 *The Australian Hymn Book* (Sydney: Collins, 1977), No. 8; *Hymns for Today's Church* (Londond: Hodder & Stoughton, 1982), No. 523. *Hymns for Today's Church* also includes a new text by Christopher Idle, which, like Henry Baker's hymn referred to above, uses Luther's sturdy melody, *Ein feste Burg*, No. 522.

42 See Robin A. Leaver, ed., *Come to the Feast: The Original and Translated Hymns of Martin H. Franzmann* (St. Louis: MorningStar, 1994), 69, 102–3.

43 *Hymns of Martin Luther*, trans. F. Samuel Janzow; musical settings by Paul Bunjes, Richard Hillert, and Carl Schalk (St. Louis: Concordia, 1978–82).

44 Janzow, *Hymns of Martin Luther*, "Notes on the Translations," [21].

45 Ibid.

46 See Leaver, *Catherine Winkworth*, 162–63, 165–67.

The *Cantica sacra* (Hamburg, 1588) of Franz Eler: Latin Chant and German Chorales for the Lutheran Liturgy

Martin Luther's love for and understanding of music prompted the development of new musical repertories for the young Lutheran church within a mere seven years after his posting of the Ninety-five Theses in 1517.[1] Preeminent in this regard is the creation of vernacular congregational song (the chorale), with the earliest collections appearing in 1524.[2] No less important was the first collection of polyphonic settings of chorales, Johann Walter's *Geystliche gesangk Buchleyn*, which appeared in the same year.[3] Luther himself took a keen interest in developing both of these repertories, in the process establishing for the Lutheran branch of the Reformation a distinctive musical receptivity that would welcome vernacular congregational song, polyphony in both German and Latin, Latin monophonic chant from the Catholic heritage, and instrumental participation (though the latter was limited during the earlier sixteenth century, compared to the more prominent use of instruments in Lutheran worship during the seventeenth and eighteenth centuries).

With respect to vernacular congregational song, Luther wrote in his *Formula missae* (1523): "I also wish that we had as many songs as possible in the vernacular which the people could sing during mass, immediately after the Gradual and also after the Sanctus and Agnus Dei."[4] In the same year Luther wrote to Georg Spalatin to seek his assistance in providing German-language texts for singing: "[Our] plan is to follow the example of the prophets and the ancient fathers of the church, and to compose psalms for the people [in the] vernacular, that is, spiritual songs, so that the Word of God may be among the people also in the form of music."[5] Luther saw the German-language hymn as a means to bring the Word of God to the people, music thus playing an important role in proclamation of the Gospel and catechesis. That the people did not necessarily take quickly to singing in church caused Luther some frustration. Joseph Herl has translated excerpts from sermons of 1526 and 1529 in which Luther criticized the people for not singing the German hymns that he had envisioned as integral to their Christian formation.[6]

In the case of sacred polyphony, Luther's enthusiastic admiration for Josquin des Prez and Ludwig Senfl as gifted composers of polyphony is well known.[7] His work with and encouragement of Walter resulted in the 1524 collection of polyphonic settings, for which Luther wrote the preface, emphasizing again the importance of hymns in proclaiming the Gospel and the value of sacred polyphony for the young:[8]

> Therefore I, too, in order to make a start and to give an incentive to those who can do better, have with the help of others compiled several hymns, so that the holy gospel which now by the grace of God has risen anew may be noised and spread abroad. . . . And these songs were arranged in four parts to give the young—who should at any rate be trained in music and other fine arts—something to wean them away from love ballads and carnal songs and to teach them something of value in their place, thus combining the good with the pleasing, as is proper for youth.

While chorales and polyphony have received much scholarly attention, comparatively less work has been devoted to the Latin monophonic repertories that continued to be sung in the context of the Mass, Matins, and Vespers in the Lutheran church, especially in cities and towns with Latin schools. In the *Formula missae* Luther's references to the continued use of Latin chant are both implicit and explicit,[9] and in the context of his introductory comments to the *Deutsche Messe* of 1526 Luther also referred to singing Latin chants.[10] In short, he was an advocate for the continued presence of Latin chant in the church—in part because he wanted the young to learn Latin.[11]

From 1545 to 1589 a succession of publications provided extensive Latin chant repertories for use in Lutheran services:[12]

1545 (Magdeburg)
Johann Spangenberg
Cantiones ecclesiasticae/Kirchengesenge Deudsch[13]

1553 (Nuremberg)
Lucas Lossius
Psalmodia, hoc est cantica sacra veteris ecclesiae selecta[14]

1573 (Wittenberg)
Johannes Keuchenthal
Kirchen Gesenge Latinisch und Deudsch

1587 (Leipzig)
Nikolaus Selnecker
Christliche Psalmen, Lieder und Kirchengesenge

1588 (Hamburg)
Franz Eler
Cantica sacra[15]

1589 (Wittenberg)
Matthäus Ludecus
Missale (2 vols.)
Vesperale et matutinale (1 vol.)
Psalterium Davidis (1 vol.)[16]

Of these extensive sixteenth-century sources of Lutheran liturgical music, Lossius's volume was perhaps the most widely known, being reprinted in 1561, 1569, 1579, 1580, and 1595.[17] Lossius's volume is devoted almost exclusively to Latin chant, the index listing only nine "*Deudsche Gesenge*." By contrast, Spangenberg's volume is actually two books in one, each with its own title page. *Cantiones ecclesiasticae Latinae* provides Latin monophonic music for the Mass, while the second part, *Kirchengesenge Deudsch*, provides German monophonic music for the Mass.[18] Similarly, Eler's volume combines an extensive repertory of Latin chant for Vespers, Matins, and the Mass with a separate second section of German chorales. Thus, in Eler's volume the cantor found repertories of both Latin chant and German chorales for the principal services of the Lutheran church throughout the church year.

This study, necessarily preliminary in scope, aims to provide an overview of Eler's volume. While *Cantica sacra* has received brief treatment in various works devoted to the history of church music in Hamburg, there has been no overview of the entire volume in terms of what it offered the Lutheran cantor and teacher in the late sixteenth and the seventeenth centuries.[19] A more complete study would include a full repertorial inventory of the volume, an edition of the music, and repertorial and musical comparisons with other sixteenth-century sources, especially those identified above.

Hamburg Predecessors of *Cantica sacra*

In addition to printed volumes such as those by Spangenberg and (especially) Lossius, there are two Hamburg manuscripts that precede Eler's 1588 volume and likely exerted an influence on his choices of Latin chant for the Lutheran liturgy. Only one year prior to the publication of *Cantica sacra* the Hamburg organist Hieronymus Praetorius copied a manuscript volume entitled *Cantiones sacrae choralis*, a volume that contains monophonic Latin liturgical music for Vespers, Matins, and the Mass on Sundays and major festivals of the church year.[20] Comparing this manuscript to Eler's volume, Frederick K. Gable characterizes the latter as "an almost identical printed volume of liturgical music, but including orders of services and a Low German chorale collection."[21] In discussing the relationship between these two volumes of 1587 and 1588, Jeffery T. Kite-Powell notes that "The precise relationship of the two works must remain unknown, as neither author mentions the other."[22] In a second repertorial link, Hieronymus Praetorius's volume shows a relationship to his father Jacob's (c. 1530–1586) *Cantilenae sacrae* of 1554, a manuscript collection of chants and chorale melodies.[23] Of these three compilations, however, only Eler's was printed, and it is Eler's volume that continued to exert an influence in Hamburg as late as 1685.[24]

Organization of *Cantica sacra*

Eler organizes his volume in two large parts, each beginning with its own title page and ending with its own index. The first—and largest—part of the volume is entitled *Cantica sacra*, which is the collection of Latin chant, organized (much like the twentieth-century *Liber usualis*) by separate sections of Ordinary chants and Proper chants, the latter according to the liturgical year. The second part of the volume is entitled *Psalmi D. Martini Lutheri* and contains 103 chorales. For the most part, tunes are provided—with the text of the first stanza underlaid; subsequent stanzas are given below the tune (the chorale texts being in Low German).

The three pages preceding the beginning of the Latin chants (i.e., the last three pages of the prefatory material) contain orders of service for Matins, Vespers, and the Mass.[25] The section of Ordinary chants begins with two versions of the Te Deum—one in Latin and one in German, *O Gott, wir loben dich*, both set to the same chant melody. Luther's *Herr Gott, dich loben wir* follows, for two antiphonal choirs.[26] In a manner parallel to the Te Deum, two versions of the Creed come next—one in Latin and one in German, *Ich glaube in Gott Vater* being set to essentially the same chant as used for the Latin version.

Eler provides a section containing various chant versions of the Kyrie and Gloria, followed immediately by a similar section containing various versions of the Sanctus and Agnus. The first of these two sections (pp. 13–23) contains:

Kyrie Summum	[the troped Kyrie "fons bonitatis"]
Kyrie Magne Deus	
Kyrie O Christi pietas	[with Gloria]
Kyrie Apostolicum	
Kyrie Martyrum	[with Gloria]
Kyrie Majus Virginum	[with Gloria]
Kyrie Paschale	
Kyrie Majus Dominicale	[with Gloria]
Kyrie Dominicale	[with Gloria]

Following immediately after this section of Kyrie and Gloria settings is the section containing Sanctus and Agnus settings (pp. 24–29), which Eler links to the previous Kyrie and Gloria settings by name. Thus, for example, the first Sanctus/Agnus pair is labeled: "Sanctus & Agnus ad Kyrie Summum, Kyrie Magne Deus, & Kyrie Paschale." The subsequent pairings are:

Sanctus & Agnus ad Kyrie O Christi pietas
Sanctus & Agnus ad Kyrie Apostolicum
Sanctus & Agnus ad Kyrie Martyrum
Sanctus & Agnus ad Kyrie Majus Virginum
Sanctus & Agnus ad Kyrie Majus Dominicale
Sanctus & Agnus ad Kyrie Dominicale

On what basis are these pairings linked? On the title page of *Cantica sacra*, Eler conspicuously notes his interest in the twelve-mode system of Heinrich Glarean (1488–1563): "*ad duodecim modos ex doctrina Glareani accomodata.*" Throughout the entire volume—Latin chants and German chorales—he consistently indicates the mode for each chant and chorale (sometimes by number only, other times by number and name of the mode). Thus, it is not unreasonable to inquire whether he links Sanctus/Agnus pairings to Kyries and Kyrie/Gloria pairings on the basis of common modalities. In fact, this seems to be the case in only two instances:

> Kyrie O Christi pietas — modes 11 and 12
>
> Sanctus & Agnus ad Kyrie O Christi pietas —
> modes 11 and 12
>
> Kyrie Apostolicum — mode 2
>
> Sanctus & Agnus ad Kyrie Apostolicum — mode 1

Other pairings show widely divergent modalities. Nor, of course, would it necessarily have been customary to unify the sung Ordinary on the basis of modality. Eler doubtless accomplished the pedagogical purpose of teaching the modes simply by indicating on a consistent basis the mode of each piece in the collection.

Following the (Latin) Sanctus/Agnus pairs are German settings of the Sanctus and Agnus: the chorale *Jesaia dem Propheten*, a very brief four-voice setting of the acclamation *Heilig ist Gott der Herre Sabaoth*, and *Christe, du Lamm Gottes*. Completing this first section of Eler's volume are the Proper Prefaces that precede the singing of the Sanctus. He provides prefaces for Christmas, Epiphany, the Purification of Mary, Easter, Ascension, Pentecost, Holy Trinity, and one marked "Quotidiana"—the common, general, or everyday Preface that would be used for all occasions other than the seven festivals for which he provided a specific Proper Preface.

By far the bulk of Eler's volume is devoted to Proper chants for Vespers, Matins, and the Mass (pp. 29–227), arranged in the following church year order:

> First–Fourth Sundays of Advent
> Christmas
> St. Stephen
> St. John the Evangelist
> Sunday within the Octave of Christmas
> Circumcision

Sunday within the Octave of Circumcision
Epiphany
First–Fifth Sundays after Epiphany
Purification of Mary
Septuagesima
Sexagesima
Quinquagesima
Invocavit
Reminiscere
Oculi
Laetare
Passion Sunday/Judica
Annunciation of Mary
Palm Sunday
Maundy Thursday
Good Friday
Holy Saturday
Easter
    Feria secunda
    Feria tertia
First–Fifth Sundays after Easter
Ascension
Sunday within the Octave of Ascension
Pentecost
    Feria secunda
    Feria Tertia
Trinity
First–Twenty-sixth Sundays after Trinity

Interspersed within the post-Trinity Sundays are the following feasts:

Birth of John the Baptist
Visitation of Mary
St. Michael

For each Sunday or feast day Eler provides Latin Proper chants for Saturday Vespers, Sunday Matins, Sunday Mass, and Sunday Vespers. Advent 1 will serve here as a case study for examining the chants and rubrics provided for a given liturgical occasion.

For Saturday Vespers Eler provides chant for the Psalm Antiphon *Ecce nomen Domini venit*. The following rubric specifies

"Psalmi: Benedictus 143. 144" (i.e., Psalms 144 and 145). Eler's volume provides neither Psalms nor Psalm tones, thus the Psalms would have been learned and chanted from another volume. Next he gives the chant for the Responsory *Ecce dies veniunt*. A rubric specifies the Vespers hymn as *Veni Redemtor* [*sic*] *gentium*, though he does not indicate that the text and tune for this hymn are found on page 243 of *Cantica sacra*. Finally, he provides the chant of the Antiphon for the Magnificat: *Qui venturus est veniet*. The rubric "Benedicamus Apostolicum" signals the end of the section devoted to Saturday Vespers.

For Sunday Matins Eler begins by providing chant for the Psalm Antiphon *Scientes quia hora est*. The following rubric specifies "Psalmus, Confitemini. 117" (i.e., Psalm 118). The Responsory *Salvatorem expectamus* follows. A rubric specifies "*Te Deum laudamus, latine*," but without reference to pages 1–3 of this volume. Again, the rubric "*Benedicamus Apostolicum*" is the signal that the section devoted to Matins is complete.

The Introit *Ad te levavi* is the only chant provided for the Mass on Advent 1.[27] It is followed by a rubric specifying: "Kyrie Apostolicum, pag: 16. Loco Sequentiae, Vater unser im etc. Sanctus Apostolicum, pag: 25. Pro conclusio: Da pacem & c." The Kyrie Apostolicum is one of three Kyries not paired with a Gloria, thus appropriate for the season of Advent when the Gloria is often omitted. He chooses the Sanctus and Agnus pair specified for the Kyrie Apostolicum, the former in Dorian mode, the latter in Hypodorian. As a Sequence or Gradual hymn he specifies *Vater unser im Himmelreich*, one of the chorales included in part two of his volume.

Eler closes his section of Propers for Advent 1 by providing two chants for Sunday Vespers: the Psalm Antiphon *Dicite filiae Sion* and the Antiphon for the Magnificat, *Ne timeas Maria*. A rubric specifies the Psalms as "Dixit Dominus. 109. Confiteor. Beatus vir" (i.e., Psalms 110, 111, and 112).

These chants and rubrics for the Proper of Advent 1 occupy four pages, with the bulk of the material relating not to the Mass but to the Offices. Blankenburg notes that Eler "joined the staff of the Johannes Gymnasium in Hamburg after 1529,"[28] and it may be that the emphasis on Vespers and Matins in *Cantica sacra* relates to Eler's role as a music teacher, and the typical role of the boys singing Latin chant within the Offices as part of their education.[29]

The overall pattern shown by the Propers for Advent 1 is largely consistent throughout much of *Cantica sacra*, though there are interesting variants. In Advent 2, for example, Eler suggests the chorale *Ach Gott, vom Himmel sieh darein* as an alternative to the Latin Introit *Populus Sion*. For the conclusion of the Mass on Advent 2 he specifies the chorale *Es wollt uns Gott genädig sein*. Similarly for Advent 3 the concluding chorale is *Wär Gott nicht mit uns diese Zeit*. For Advent 4 the chorale alternative to the Introit *Memento nostri Domine* is *Herr Christ, der einig Gottes Sohn*, and the concluding chorale is *Erhalt uns, Herr, bei deinem Wort*. Thus, he provides the possibility for chorales additional to the one invariably specified as a Sequence hymn.

Festivals often show additional musical elements that enrich this basic pattern. For Christmas, Eler provides the song *Dies est laetitiae* to be sung immediately following the Gloria.[30] He also provides a Latin Alleluia, *Dies sanctificatus illuxit nobis,* and the Sequence *Grates nunc omnes*.[31] Christmas Vespers includes the German carol *Joseph, lieber Joseph mein*. As is the case for other major feasts, Epiphany includes the Alleluia *Vidimus stellam*, and the Feast of the Purification of Mary includes the Alleluia *Virga Jesu floruit*.

For the Feast of the Annunciation of Mary, Eler provides somewhat more elaborate music than he typically does. For the Introit he specifies as performing forces: "organ," "chorus," and "pueri" (i.e., boy choir). The use of varied performing forces for this Introit was not new with Eler. Lossius had specified a similar, though not identical, alternation in his *Psalmodia* (see 192v–194v). While Eler (p. 106) uses the word "Organ," Lossius uses "organum." In his *Dictionary of Ecclesiastical Latin*, Leo F. Stelten notes the meaning of "organum" as "musical instrument, organ."[32] Thus, "organ" in Eler likely refers to the instrument rather than implying a single musician ("organicus"), as opposed to a chorus. Herbert Gotsch cites various pieces of evidence that document the use of the organ specifically at the Introit.[33] The Augsburg pastor Wolfgang Musculus described a service in Wittenberg on May 28, 1536, noting that the organ was used at the Introit.[34] Gotsch provides a second bit of evidence from a manuscript addition to Lossius's *Psalmodia* by a cantor of the Laurentiuskirche in Halle-Neumarkt, whose written instructions state that in a Latin service the organist began the Introit and alternated with the choir and the boys.[35] Gotsch also cites two sixteenth-century church orders that refer to the use of organ with the Introit.[36] Ulrich Leupold cites further evidence from a rubric in the 1537 church order that Nicholas Medler compiled for the Wenzelskirche in Naumburg:

> In public worship all the German songs are sung alternately, i.e., the boy's choir sings one verse and the congregation (having its own cantor) the others. But if the organ is played, three choirs are formed [i.e., the organ forms one choir, the boys the second, and the congregation the third] and the organ always begins, except for the *Et in terra* when the . . . boys begin, then the organ, and then the people. [37]

While Medler speaks specifically here to "German songs," his reference to the alternation of three choirs is pertinent to the Latin Introit in Eler's Proper for the Annunciation. What Medler makes clear is that the organ was considered an equal participant in alternation practice involving two groups of singers—in Naumburg the boy choir and the congregation, in Eler the boy choir and another choir. Cleveland Johnson's catalogue of organ tablatures 1550–1650 testifies to the use of organ specifically with the Introit text *Haec est dies quam fecit Dominus*,[38] though the Visby tablature from Hamburg does not provide an organ setting for this Introit.

Within this Introit for the Annunciation, Eler specifies three instances in which the boys are to sing the phrase "*Hodie Deus homo factus*." While they may do so in the monophonic Latin chant provided, Eler also gives as a performance option two three-part versions for the two repetitions of this phrase. The first three-part setting is homophonic, the second polyphonic.[39] To add further splendor to the music for this feast he refers back to page eighty for the Alleluia (*Virgo Jesu floruit*) that he had provided for the Feast of the Purification. For the Annunciation he also provides the Sequence *Ave praeclarum mundi lumen*.

For Easter Mass, Eler provides the customary Alleluia (*Pascha nostrum immolatus est*) and a particularly interesting version of the Easter Sequence *Victimae paschali laudes*. He specifies that the Sequence be sung phrase by phrase, into which he signals the interpolation of entire stanzas of Luther's chorale *Christ lag in Todesbanden*, using all stanzas in the course of singing the Sequence.[40] A rubric specifies the *Sanctus Summum* (p. 24) and the chorale *Jesus Christus unser Heiland*, after which he provides an additional Latin chant *Laetemur in Christo redemptore*. The feasts of the Annunciation and Easter both provide a window into Eler's work as teacher and church musician, revealing the use of varied performing forces, varied textures (monophonic and polyphonic), and the juxtaposition of related German and Latin texts.

Other festivals also show the pattern of providing both the Alleluia and Sequence for the Mass: Ascension, Pentecost (with its choice of two Sequences: *Sancte Spiritus ad sit nobis gratia* or *Veni sancte Spiritus*), Trinity, and John the Baptist (where Eler provides the Latin Sequence *Psallite regi nostro* and suggests the chorale *Christ unser Herr zum Jordan kam* as an alternative). The Feast of the Visitation of Mary provides two forms of the Magnificat for Saturday Vespers—Latin chant and the *Magnificat Germanice—Meine Seele erhebt den Herren* sung to the *Tonus peregrinus* (p. 181).

Latin Hymns in *Cantica sacra*

Noteworthy in *Cantica sacra* is a set of Latin monophonic hymns, which traditionally played a prominent role in the Vespers liturgy. These hymns are found toward the end of the Latin portion of the volume (on pages 243–54)—after the large section devoted to the Latin Proper for the church year, and after the "*Cantiones funebres*," a Sequence for Mary Magdalene (*Laus tibi Christe*), and the Litany. Eler includes the following hymns (listed here in the order they were printed, which is, for the most part, in church year order):

Hymn	Feast
Veni Redemptor gentium	Advent
A solis ortus cardine	Christmas and Purification of Mary
Herodes hostis impie	Epiphany
Dies absoluti praetererunt	Septuagesima–Quinquagesima
Christe qui lux es et dies	Invocavit–Laetare
Vexilla regis prodeunt	Judica (Passion Sunday) Palm Sunday Holy Saturday
Rex Christe factor omnium	Maundy Thursday Good Friday
Festum nunc celebre	Ascension
Vita sanctorum, decus angelorum	Easter

Veni Creator Spiritus	Pentecost
Fit porta Christi pervia	Annunciation of Mary
Aeterno gratias patri[41]	John the Baptist
Aeterne gratias tibi	Visitation of Mary
O lux beata Trinitas	Trinity Sunday and various Sundays after Trinity
Dicimus grates tibi	
Christe sanctorum decus angelorum	St. Michael
Te lucis ante terminum	Epiphany 2 and various Sundays after Trinity
Lucis Creator optime	Epiphany 3–5 and various Sundays after Trinity
Jesu Redemptor saeculi	various Sundays after Trinity
Deus Creator omnium	Epiphany 2–5 and various Sundays after Trinity
Jesu nostra Redemptio	various Sundays after Trinity

Eler's repertory of Latin hymns for Vespers relates closely to a well-established fifteenth-century German tradition of polyphonic hymns, which has been traced by Tom R. Ward.[42] This traditional set of feasts and hymns in polyphonic repertories of German provenance extends into the sixteenth century, as, for example, in Ludwig Senfl's polyphonic settings in Munich, Bayerische Staatsbibliothek, Mus. Ms. 52.[43] The Latin hymns in *Cantica sacra* demonstrate that this long tradition also played a role in shaping a Lutheran repertory of *monophonic* hymns for Vespers. The hymn texts for Advent, Christmas, Epiphany, Lent, Easter, Ascension, Pentecost, and Trinity in *Cantica sacra* are an exact match with the fifteenth-century German tradition traced by Ward, thus showing the kind of long-term stability that is so characteristic (on so many different levels) of the Western liturgy. Distinctive aspects of Eler's practice are apparent primarily in the Sundays after Epiphany and the Sundays after Trinity, where he draws on six hymn texts (*O lux beata Trinitas*, *Te lucis ante terminum*, *Lucis Creator optime*, *Jesu Redemptor seculi*, *Deus Creator omnium*, and *Jesu nostra Redemptio*) to provide variety from Sunday to Sunday—especially in the lengthy post-Trinity season.

The importance of Latin hymnody within Hamburg Vespers services is further attested by the Visby organ tablature, which contains settings of the following Latin hymns—settings likely used in *alternatim* performance of these hymns within Hamburg Vespers (the hymns are listed here in the order they appear in the tablature, i.e., not in liturgical year order):[44]

> *Christe qui lux es et dies* (3 settings)
> *Vita sanctorum, decus angelorum*
> *Veni Redemptor gentium*
> *Dies absoluti praetererunt*
> *Rex Christe factor omnium*
> *Vexilla regis prodeunt*
> *Aeterno gratias patri*
> *Jesu Redemptor saeculi*
> *Aeterne gratias tibi*
> *Festum nunc celebre*
> *Lucis Creator optime*
> *Deus Creator omnium*
> *Herodes hostis impie*
> *Te lucis ante terminum*
> *Veni Creator Spiritus* (2 settings)
> *O lux beata Trinitas*
> *A solis ortus cardine*
> *Jesu nostra Redemptio* (2 settings)
> *Fit porta Christi pervia*

Only two hymns from Eler's collection, *Dicimus grates tibi* and *Christe sanctorum decus angelorum*, do not find an organ setting in the Visby tablature. Thus, it is not only in the extensive section of Latin Propers for Vespers, Matins, and the Mass, but also in this set of Latin monophonic hymns that Eler's *Cantica sacra* demonstrates a continuing high regard within Lutheranism for Latin monophonic chant.

German Chorales in *Cantica sacra*

Appendix 1 lists the content of chorales (according to their order of appearance) in the second part of Eler's volume—the *Psalmi D. Martini Lutheri*. This Appendix also provides context for this chorale repertory by comparing it to that of the 1545 Babst hymnal—perhaps the most influential Lutheran hymnal of the sixteenth century, and to the 1604 Hamburg *Melodeyen Gesangbuch*, a collection of four-part cantional settings by the organists of the four principal churches in Hamburg: Hieronymus Praetorius, Joachim Decker, Jakob Praetorius, and David Scheidemann.[45] Of

these three collections, Eler's contains the largest number of chorales: 103 chorales in the second part of the volume. Four German
texts are coupled with parallel Latin texts: *Puer natus in
Bethlehem/Ein Kind geboren zu Bethlehem*, a four-part setting
of *Surrexit Christus hodie/Erstanden ist der heilige Christ*,
Ascendit Christus hodie/Gefahren ist der heilige Christ (to be sung
to the same setting as *Surrexit Christus hodie*), and a four-part
setting of *Spiritus sancti gratia/Des heilgen Geistes gnaden*. By
contrast, the 1604 Hamburg hymnal contains 88 chorale texts,
two of them paired with Latin texts: *Puer natus in Bethlehem/
Ein Kind geboren zu Bethlehem* and *Surrexit Christus hodie/
Erstanden ist der heilig Christ*. Of these 88 chorales, only 16 were
not included in Eler's volume, with 7 of the 16 appearing in print
for the first time *after* 1588 (their dates, and number in volume 5
of Wackernagel, are given in parentheses):[46]

Aus tiefer Not laßt uns zu Gott	
Christ, der du bist der helle Tag	
Christe, du Lamm Gottes	
Der Herr ist mein getreuer Hirt	(1598; no. 535)
Hats Gott versehn, wer wills wehrn	(1597; no. 510)
Herr Gott, du bist unsre Zuflucht	(1598; no. 537)
Herzlich tut mich erfreuen	
Hilf Gott, wie gehts so ungleich zu	
Ich armer Mensch unselig zwar	(1596; no. 447)
In dich hab ich gehoffet Herr	
Nun laßt uns Gott, dem Herren	
Selig der Mann zu preisen ist	(1592; no. 448)
Von Gott will ich nicht lassen	
Wachet auf, ruft uns die Stimme	(1599; no. 395)
Wir danken dir, Herr Jesu Christ	
Wie schön leuchtet der Morgenstern	(1599; no. 394)

Comparative study of chorale repertories reveals, of course,
both change and continuity. Comparing the *Melodeyen
Gesangbuch* (1604) to Eler (1588) shows the addition of new chorale texts deemed worthy by Lutheran musicians in Hamburg. It is
instructive, for example, to see the addition of Philipp Nicolai's
(1556–1608) two great chorales, *Wachet auf, ruft uns die Stimme*
and *Wie schön leuchtet der Morgenstern*, a mere five years after
their publication in 1599. Of equal interest is the existence of a
common core of chorales found in Babst (1545), Eler, and the 1604

Hamburg hymnal. Those chorales are listed in Appendix 2, again by the order of their appearance in Eler, this time with seasonal, textual (in the case of Psalms), or topical designations when these are either apparent or stated. Appendix 2 reveals at a glance the continuity of this repertory from 1545 to 1604, showing how this group of chorales found their place not only in the Wittenberg hymnal of 1545 but also in two later books from the north of Germany.

In the end, Eler's volume is mostly about continuity. It shows the continuing use of Latin chant in an urban center of Lutheranism, a monophonic repertory useful, not only in the education of the young, but a repertory also valued for its long tradition of texts and melodies, and for the sheer beauty of the music. The use of a standard repertory of Latin Vespers hymns connects with a specifically German tradition that has been documented from the fifteenth century, illustrating clearly the continuing respect within Lutheranism for historic Catholic repertories. It is easy to take for granted in Eler's volume that these Latin repertories exist rather naturally with an extensive repertory of German chorales, but to do so is to overlook the achievements of Franz Eler and (earlier in the century) Johann Spangenberg. Like composers of chorales and polyphony, these cantors and editors also played an important role in shaping musical practice—both Latin and German repertories—during the first century of Lutheran church music.

APPENDIX 1

Chorales in Eler *Psalmi D. Martini Lutheri* [pt. 2 of *Cantica sacra*]

Chorales are listed by the order in which they appear in Eler. Titles of the chorales are stated (for the most part) in modern German, rather than the Low German of Eler's publication. To provide perspective on this repertory of chorales, the content of Eler's volume is correlated with the Babst *Geystliche Lieder* (1545) and with the Hamburg *Melodeyen Gesangbuch* (1604).

Hymn	1545	1604
Nun komm, der Heiden Heiland	x	x
Christum, wir sollen loben schon	x	x
Gelobet seist du, Jesu Christ	x	x
Vom Himmel hoch, da komm ich her	x	x
Vom Himmel kam der Engel schar	x	x
Was fürchst du Feind, Herodes	x	x

Hymn	1545	1604
Ein Kindelein so löbelich		x
In dulci jubilo		
Puer natus in Bethlehem/Ein Kind geboren zu Bethlehem	x	x
Mit Fried und Freud ich fahr dahin	x	x
Ach wir armen Sünder		x
Da Jesus an dem Kreuze stund		x
Hilf Gott, daß mir gelinge	x	x
O Mensche will gedanken		
O Mensch bewein dein Sünde groß		
Christ lag in Todesbanden	x	x
Jesus Christus unser Heiland, der den Tod	x	x
Christ ist auferstanden	x	x
Surrexit Christus hodie/Erstanden ist der heilige Christ (S,A,T,B)		x
Jesus Christus, wahr' Gottes Sohn		x
Der heiligen Leben thut stets		
Christ fuhr gen Himmel	x	
Ascendit Christus hodie/Gefahren ist der heilige Christ		
Komm, Heiliger Geist, Herre Gott	x	x
Nun bitten wir den Heiligen Geist	x	x
Gott der Vater wohn uns bei	x	x
Allein Gott in der Höh sei Ehr		x
Der du bist drei in Einigkeit	x	
Dies sind die heilgen zehn Gebot	x	x
Mensch, willst du leben seliglich	x	x
Wir glauben all an einen Gott	x	x
Vater unser im Himmelreich	x	x
Ach Vater unser, der du bist im Himmelreich (two melodies)		x
Christ unser Herr zum Jordan kam	x	x
Jesus Christus unser Heiland, der von uns	x	x
Gott sei gelobet und gebenedeiet	x	x
O Lamm Gottes unschuldig		x
O Christ wir danken deiner Güte		
Aus tiefer Not schrei ich zu dir	x	x
Erbarm dich mein, o Herre Gott	x	x
O Herre Gott, begnade mich	x	x
Allein zu dir, Herr Jesu Christ	x	x
Von allen Menschen abgewandt		x
Durch Adams Fall is ganz verderbt	x	x
Es ist das Heil uns kommen her	x	x
Herr Christ, der einig Gottes Sohn	x	x
Ach hilf mich Leid und sehnlich Klag		x
Fried gib uns, lieber Herre		x
Nun freut euch, lieben Christen gemein	x	x
Nun lob, mein Seel, den Herren		x
Fröhlich wollen wir halleluia singen	x	x
Was kann uns kommen an für Not		x
Was lobes solln wir dir, o Vater		x
Wohl dem, der in Gottes Furcht steht	x	x
Kommt her zu mir, spricht Gottes Sohn	x	x

Hymn	1545	1604
Ich ruf zu dir, Herr Jesu Christ	x	x
Es sind doch selig alle		x
Vergebens ist all Müh und Kost	x	
Wo wohl gar viel der Bösen sind		
An Wasserflüssen Babylon	x	x
Ein neues Lied wir heben an	x	
Mag ich Unglück nicht widerstahn	x	x
O Gott, verleih mir dein Gnad	x	
Ach Herr, mit deiner Hilf erschein		
Wenn wir in höchsten Nöten sein		
Ach Gott, vom Himmel sieh darein	x	x
Es spricht der unweisen Mund wohl	x	x
Ein feste Burg ist unser Gott	x	x
Es wollt uns Gott genädig sein	x	x
Wär Gott nicht mit uns diese Zeit	x	x
Erhalt uns, Herr, bei deinem Wort	x	x
Verleih uns Frieden gnädiglich	x	x
Sie ist mir Lieb, die werte Magd	x	x
Wo Gott der Herr nicht bei uns hält	x	x
Hilf Gott, wie geht es immer zu	x	x
O Herre Gott, dein göttlich Wort	x	x
Mitten wir im Leben sind	x	x
Herr Jesu Christ, wahr Mensch und Gott		
Was mein Gott will, das geschäh allzeit		x
Wenn mein Stündlein vorhanden ist		x
Mag ich dem Tod nicht widerstan		
Nun laßt uns den Leib begraben	x	x
Ihr lieben Christen freut euch nun		
Wacht auf, ihr Christen alle		x
Nun willet nicht vorsagen		
Ich dank dir, lieber Herre	x	x
Steht auf ihr lieben		
Christe, der du bist der Licht		
Christe, der du bist Tag und Licht	x	x
O Gott, wir danken deiner Güte		x
Herr Gott nun sei gepreiset		
Singen wir aus Herzensgrund		x
Nun schlaf mein liebes Kindlein		
Litany: Gott Vater in dem Himmelreich		
Spiritus sancti gratia/Des heilgen Geistes gnaden		
Gott hat das Evangelium		
Nun lasst uns Christen fröhlich sein		
Warum betrübst du dich, mein Herz		x
Wohl in guter Hofnung will		
So wahr ich leb, spricht Gott der Herr		
Gott Vater der du deine Sohn		
Dancksagen wir alle Gott		
Lasst uns nun alle danksagen dem Herrn Christ		

APPENDIX 2

Chorales common to Babst (1545), Eler (1588), and *Melodeyen Gesangbuch* (1604)

Feast, text, or topic	*Hymn*
Advent	*Nun komm, der Heiden Heiland*
Christmas	*Christum, wir sollen loben schon*
Christmas	*Gelobet seist du, Jesu Christ*
Christmas	*Vom Himmel hoch, da komm ich her*
Christmas	*Vom Himmel kam der Engel schar*
Christmas	*Was fürchst du Feind, Herodes*
Christmas	*In dulci jubilo*
Christmas	*Puer natus in Bethlehem/*
	Ein Kind geboren zu Bethlehem
Song of Simeon	*Mit Fried und Freud ich fahr dahin*
Passion	*Hilf Gott, daß mir gelinge*
Easter	*Christ lag in Todesbanden*
Easter	*Jesus Christus unser Heiland, der den Tod*
Easter	*Christ ist auferstanden*
Pentecost	*Komm, Heiliger Geist, Herre Gott*
Pentecost	*Nun bitten wir den Heiligen Geist*
Trinity	*Gott der Vater wohn uns bei*
Ten Commandments	*Dies sind der heilgen zehn Gebot*
Ten Commandments	*Mensch, willst du leben seliglich*
Creed	*Wir glauben all an einen Gott*
Lord's Prayer	*Vater unser im Himmelreich*
Baptism	*Christ unser Herr zum Jordan kam*
Communion	*Jesus Christus unser Heiland, der von uns*
Communion	*Gott sei gelobet und gebenedeiet*
Psalm 130	*Aus tiefer Not schrei ich zu dir*
Psalm 51	*Erbarm dich mein, o Herre Gott*
Psalm 51	*O Herre Gott, begnade mich*
Confession	*Allein zu dir, Herr Jesu Christ*
Justification	*Durch Adams Fall ist ganz verderbt*
Justification	*Es ist das Heil uns kommen her*
Redeemer [Epiphany]	*Herr Christ, der einig Gottes Sohn*
Justification	*Nun freut euch, lieben Christen gemein*
Psalm 117	*Fröhlich wollen wir halleluia singen*
Psalm 128	*Wohl dem, der in Gottes Furcht steht*
Redeemer	*Kommt her zu mir, spricht Gottes Sohn*
Prayer	*Ich ruf zu dir, Herr Jesu Christ*
Psalm 137	*An Wasserflüssen Babylon*
	Mag ich Unglück nicht widerstahn
Psalm 12	*Ach Gott, vom Himmel sieh darein*
Psalm 14	*Es spricht der unweisen Mund wohl*
Psalm 46	*Ein feste Burg is unser Gott*
Psalm 67	*Es wollt uns Gott genädig sein*
Psalm 124	*Wär Gott nicht mit uns diese Zeit*
Word of God	*Erhalt uns, Herr, bei deinem Wort*
Close of service	*Verleih uns Frieden gnädiglich*
Church	*Sie ist mir Lieb, die werte Magd*
Psalm 124	*Wo Gott der Herr nicht bei uns hält*

Psalm 2	*Hilf, Gott, wie geht es immer zu*
Word of God	*O Herre Gott, dein göttlich Wort*
Death/Eternity	*Mitten wir im Leben sind*
Burial	*Nun laßt uns den Leib begraben*
Morning	*Ich dank dir, lieber Herre*
Evening	*Christe, der du bist Tag und Licht*

NOTES

1   For a recent consideration of Luther and music see Robin A. Leaver, "Luther as Musician," *Lutheran Quarterly* 18 (Summer 2004): 125–83.

2   These collections include the so-called "Achtliederbuch" (Nuremberg, 1524) and two hymnals published in the same year in Erfurt, each entitled "Enchiridion." A facsimile of the "Achtliederbuch" was published as an insert to *Jahrbuch für Liturgik und Hymnologie*, 2 (1956).   A facsimile of the Erfurt hymnals was published as *Das Erfurter Enchiridion*, Documenta Musicologica, Erste Reihe: Druckschriften-Faksimiles, no. 36 (Kassel: Bärenreiter, 1983).

3   A facsimile was published as Johann Walter, *Das geistliche Gesangbüchlein "Chorgesangbuch,"* Documenta Musicologica, Erste Reihe: Druckschriften-Faksimiles, no. 33 (Kassel: Bärenreiter, 1979).

4   Martin Luther, *Liturgy and Hymns*, ed. Ulrich S. Leupold, Luther's Works: American Edition, vol. 53 (Philadelphia: Fortress, 1965), 36 (hereafter cited as "Luther's Works, vol. 53").

5   Martin Luther, *Letters II*, ed. Gottfried G. Krodel, Luther's Works: American Edition, vol. 49 (Philadelphia: Fortress, 1972), 68.

6   Joseph Herl, *Worship Wars in Early Lutheranism: Choir, Congregation, and Three Centuries of Conflict* (New York: Oxford, 2004), 14–15.

7   See Leaver, 152–61; for a summary see Carl F. Schalk, *Luther on Music: Paradigms of Praise* (St. Louis: Concordia, 1988), 21–24.

8   Luther's Works, vol. 53, 316.

9   See, for example, Luther's Works, vol. 53, 36.

10   Ibid., 62–63, 68–69.

11   Ibid., 63.

12   These collections are enumerated by various writers, e.g., Walter Blankenburg in his articles on "Eler, Franz" and "Ludecus, Matthäus" in *The New Grove Dictionary of Music and Musicians*, 2d ed. (2001), and Herl, *Worship Wars*, 104.

13   A facsimile is forthcoming from Olms.

14   A facsimile is available in the series Faksimile Heilbronner Musikschatz, no. 12 (Stuttgart: Cornetto-Verlag, 1996).

15   A facsimile is available: Hildesheim: Georg Olms, 2002.

16   Blankenburg lists the *Vesperale* and the *Psalterium*, cf. his entry on "Ludecus," *New Grove* (2001), vol. 15, 277.

17   See *Das deutsche Kirchenlied: Verzeichnis der Drucke von den Anfängen bis 1800*, ed. Konrad Ameln, Markus Jenny, and Walther Lipphardt, RISM B/VIII/1 (Kassel: Bärenreiter, 1975). Lossius's volume has received the most extensive scholarly scrutiny; see Werner Merten, "Die 'Psalmodia' des Lucas Lossius," *Jahrbuch für Liturgik und Hymnologie*, 19 (1975), 1–18; 20 (1976), 63–90; 21 (1977), 39–67.

18 For an overview of Spangenberg's volume see Daniel Zager, "Music for the Lutheran Liturgy: Johann Spangenberg's *Cantiones ecclesiasticae/Kirchengesenge Deudsch* (1545)," in *This Is the Feast: A Festschrift for Richard Hillert at 80*, ed. James Freese (St. Louis: MorningStar, 2004), 45–60 . A more extensive study is Robin A. Leaver, "Johann Spangenberg and Luther's Legacy of Liturgical Chant," *Lutheran Quarterly* 19 (Spring 2005): 23–42.

19 A brief consideration of *Cantica sacra* is found in Hugo Leichsenring, *Hamburgische Kirchenmusik im Reformationszeitalter*, Hamburger Beiträge zur Musikwissenschaft, Bd. 20 (Hamburg: Verlag der Musikalienhandlung Karl Dieter Wagner, 1982), 50–57. Though published in 1982, Leichsenring's study is, in fact, his 1922 dissertation (Berlin). Another brief, but recent, perspective on Eler's volume is found in *Dedication Service for St. Gertrude's Chapel, Hamburg, 1607*, ed. Frederick K. Gable, Recent Researches in the Music of the Baroque Era, 91 (Madison, Wis.: A-R Editions, 1998), xiii–xv.

20 See Leichsenring, 39–50, for lists of the contents of the 1587 collection by Hieronymus Praetorius.

21 Gable, xiv.

22 Jeffery T. Kite-Powell, *The Visby (Petri) Organ Tablature: Investigation and Critical Edition*, 2 vols., Quellen-Kataloge zur Musikgeschichte, 14 (Wilhelmshofen: Heinrichshofen's Verlag, 1979), 1:21.

23 See Leichsenring, 28–35, for lists of the contents of the 1554 collection by Jacob Praetorius.

24 Gable, xiv.

25 For a transcription and translation of the order of service for the Mass, see Gable, xiv–xv.

26 The 1545 Babst hymnal had earlier provided *Herr Gott, dich loben wir* for two choirs. A facsimile of this influential book was published as *Geystliche Lieder* (Kassel: Bärenreiter, 1929).

27 The Hamburg liturgy was drawn up by Johannes Aepin (1499–1553) in 1539 and officially approved in 1556. In outlining the Mass, he stated that the Latin Introit should be retained. See Kite-Powell, 17.

28 Walter Blankenburg, "Eler, Franz" in *The New Grove Dictionary of Music and Musicians*, 2d ed. (2001): vol. 8, 113.

29 Regarding Vespers and Matins, see Herl, 62–65. Herl notes that "in the Lutheran churches, Matins was held only where there were schoolboys capable of singing in Latin," 65.

30 Lossius provides this song as well (26v–27) but not following the Gloria; rather, it follows Second Vespers for Christmas and a series of ferial Antiphons. Lossius groups it with other Latin Christmas songs: *In dulci jubilo*, *Puer natus in Bethlehem*, and *Resonet in laudibus*. The 1545 Babst hymnal followed a similar procedure: see nos. 52–57.

31 This Alleluia/Sequence pair is also found in Spangenberg (18v–19v) and in Lossius (17v–18).

32 Leo F. Stelten, *Dictionary of Ecclesiastical Latin* (Peabody, Mass.: Hendrickson, 1995).

33 Herbert Gotsch, "The Organ in the Lutheran Service of the 16th Century," *Church Music* 67.1 (1967): 7–12.

34 Ibid., 7. A transcription of this report by Musculus, as given in the 1883 *Analecta Lutherana*, is found in Georg Rietschel, *Aufgabe der Orgel im Gottesdienste bis in das 18. Jahrhundert* (1892; reprint, Buren: Frits Knuf, 1979); see pp. 19–21,

especially fn. 12 on p. 20, where the report from Musculus begins: "Primum Iudebatur Introitus in organis succinente choro latine . . . ." On p. 21 Rietschel argues that in this context the word "succinere" means "to respond to" rather than "to accompany."

35 Gotsch, 8. A transcription of the primary source document is found in *Handbuch der deutschen evangelischen Kirchenmusik*, 1. Band, 1. Teil, Einführung, *Der Altargesang* (Göttingen: Vandenhoeck & Ruprecht, 1940), 62*.

36 Gotsch, 9.

37 Ulrich S. Leupold in Luther's Works, vol. 53, 185–86. I am grateful to Robin Leaver for bringing this passage to my attention.

38 Cleveland Johnson, *Vocal Compositions in German Organ Tablatures, 1550–1650: A Catalogue and Commentary* (New York: Garland, 1989), 304. For *Haec est dies quam fecit Dominus*, Johnson lists organ intabulations of compositions by Jacob Handl, Johannes Knöfel, Claudio Merulo, and Philipp de Monte.

39 In the analogous instance, Lossius provided three settings for the boys: a duo, a trio, and a four-part setting (see 194r–194v of his *Psalmodia*).

40 By contrast, both Spangenberg and Lossius present *Victimae paschali laudes* without the chorale interpolations.

41 Eler notes the authorship of this hymn, as well as the hymns *Aeterne gratias tibi* and *Dicimus grates tibi*, as being by Philipp Melanchthon.

42 Tom R. Ward, *The Polyphonic Office Hymn, 1400–1520: A Descriptive Catalogue*, Renaissance Manuscript Studies, 3 (Rome: American Institute of Musicology, 1980), 17. Ward traces distinctive Italian and German traditions of polyphonic Vespers hymns (feasts and texts), traditions that continued to be observed in the sixteenth century.

43 For a correlation of Senfl's settings with the German tradition of polyphonic hymns, see Daniel Zager, "The Polyphonic Latin Hymns of Orlando di Lasso: A Liturgical and Repertorial Study" (PhD diss., University of Minnesota, 1985), 15.

44 For an inventory of the hymn section of the Visby Tablature see Kite-Powell, 1:24–25. His edition of the hymns is found at 2:120–227. Another edition of these hymn settings is found in Hieronymus Praetorius, *Sämtliche Orgelwerke/ Complete Organ Works*, Teil 2/Part 2, ed. Klaus Beckmann, Meister der Norddeutschen Orgelschule/Masters of the North German Organ School (Mainz: Schott, 2003). On p. 110 Beckmann provides a complete list in church year order of the Latin hymns specified by the 1587 *Cantiones sacrae chorales*.

45 The *Melodeyen Gesangbuch* (Hamburg: Rüdinger, 1604), originally published in a choirbook format, is available in a modern edition in keyboard score: *Melodeyen Gesangbuch, Hamburg 1604*, ed. Klaus Ladda and Klaus Beckmann (Singen: Bodensee-Musikversand, 1995).

46 Philipp Wackernagel, *Das deutsche Kirchenlied*, vol. 5 (1877; reprint, Hildesheim: Olms, 1990).

Johann Krieger's Musical Contrast of Law and Gospel in the Cantata *Danksaget dem Vater*

Textual contrasts often gave composers of the Baroque era opportunity to apply their inclination to contrast elements of musical style. The cantata *Danksaget dem Vater* (Give thanks to the Father) gave Johann Krieger such an opportunity, which he grasped with amazing skill and insight.

Johann Krieger

As a native of Nuremberg, Johann Krieger (1652–1735) grew up in a city well-known for music performance, composition, instrument making, and music publishing. His musical contemporaries in his early years there included his older brother, Johann Philipp Krieger (1649–1725) and Johann Pachelbel (1653–1706). Throughout his life, Krieger maintained close ties to his older brother, Johann Philipp, the long-time Kapellmeister in Weißenfels and one of the most prominent German musicians in the generation before Johann Sebastian Bach. Johann Philipp helped the younger Krieger obtain his various appointments as court organist in Bayreuth (1673–78), court Kapellmeister in Greiz (1678–81) and Eisenberg (1681–82), and civic director of choral music as well as organist in Zittau (1682–1735). In addition, the catalog of repertoire that Johann Philipp and his son Johann Gotthilf maintained for the Weißenfels court is the single most important source describing the extent of Johann Krieger's oeuvre. This catalog lists over two hundred sacred vocal works by Krieger, including motets, cantatas, concertos, Mass movements, and Magnificats.[1] Unfortunately, only twenty of Krieger's concerted sacred works are extant today.[2]

In the eighteenth century, Johann Krieger's reputation as a composer was not based on his vocal music but rather on the two collections of keyboard music published during his lifetime, the *Sechs musicalische Partien* and the *Clavier-Übung*.[3] The latter publication was especially well respected, and important figures such as Johann Mattheson and George Frideric Handel lauded Krieger's contrapuntal abilities. In *Der vollkommene Kapellmeister* (1739) Mattheson referred to Krieger as one of "the best and most thorough contrapuntists of this century."[4] Mattheson prefaced this discussion with a direct message for J. S. Bach: "I . . .would rather wish to see something in the same manner [as Krieger's fugues] put forth by the famous Herr Bach in Leipzig, who is a great master of the fugue."[5] Interestingly, *Der vollkommene Kapellmeister* was published in 1739, and Bach wrote parts of *The Art of Fugue* (BWV 1080) only a short time later (in the early 1740s). Bach would surely have known of Mattheson's challenge, due to the latter's fame as a writer about music; if so, Bach would have therefore seen Krieger's music in *Der vollkommene Kapellmeister* and known of his contrapuntal ability.

Krieger worked for over fifty years as the leading musician in Zittau, a wealthy city located at a strategic mountain pass between Prague and Saxony. Krieger's performers in Zittau included the best singers from a famed Gymnasium that attracted pupils from a wide area of German-speaking lands. His instrumental musicians, who were civic employees, also possessed a high level of skill, for Zittau had the economic resources to invest heavily in the arts. It is telling that figures such as Andreas Hammerschmidt and Johann Krieger worked in Zittau, that Wilhelm Friedemann Bach and Carl Philipp Emanuel Bach applied for positions there, and that Gottfried Silbermann built one of the largest organs of his late career for Zittau's primary church, St. John.[6] Even though Krieger was hired as an organist, his position also included the duties of *Director chori musici* (civic director of choral music), which gave him oversight of the musical life for the entire city. This responsibility usually fell to cantors in cities and towns of central Germany at this time, but in Zittau the cantor handled the day-to-day music duties in the Gymnasium, thereby giving Krieger more time for performing, composing, and teaching the best pupils. This arrangement more closely approximated the employment situation in cities such as Lübeck and Nuremberg, and it also bore some parallels to

Krieger's earlier positions as a court Kapellmeister. Thus, Zittau's economic resources gave Krieger the time and musicians to develop sacred vocal music there to a high level.

The theological climate of Zittau, which was strongly orthodox, also lent support for a high level of musical artistry in the city. Zittau had rejected Roman Catholicism in 1521, only four years after Luther posted his Ninety-five Theses in Wittenberg. Saxony, overall a leading center of orthodoxy throughout the seventeenth and early eighteenth centuries, was also home to opposing theological ideas. Pietism, for example, had strong supporters in Halle, Dresden, and Herrnhut, a village located only ten miles north of Zittau. Perhaps because of this proximity to Herrnhut, in addition to its long history as a Lutheran city, Zittau remained staunchly Orthodox throughout Krieger's lifetime. Given the city's theological leanings, its clergy almost certainly would have followed Luther's directives to preach the doctrines of Law and Gospel. These theological concepts provide a dichotomy of images:

> The Law contains commandments of what we are to do and not to do and how we are to be; the Gospel reveals what God has done and still does for our salvation. The purpose of the Law is to serve as a curb, mirror, and rule; the purpose of the Gospel is to forgive sins and give heaven and salvation as a free gift.[7]

In his cantata *Danksaget dem Vater*, Krieger displays the Lutheran concept of Law and Gospel through the use of contrasting musical styles that represent these two ideas and their interrelationship. *Danksaget dem Vater* is the only extant vocal work by Krieger that contains more than one style: *stile antico*, typical of his motets, and *stile concertato*, the most common type of writing in his biblical cantatas.

Krieger's Motets

In 1706 Martin Fuhrmann defined the motet in Germany as " . . . a church harmony, four voices strong (sometimes more) without instruments, set according to Hammerschmidt's standard, in which the voices make fugues and concertize only a little or not at all."[8] In 1646 Hammerschmidt himself described his motets as "full-voiced" (for several singers) and indicated that they could be performed with or without *basso continuo*.[9] Thus a motet written in the German lands during the late seventeenth century was a sacred work for four or more voices written in continuous counterpoint with an optional basso continuo accompaniment.

Krieger's extant motets are the *Magnificat a 4* (1687), the *Sanctus a 4* (1699), and *Laudate Dominum omnes gentes* (n.d.).[10] Krieger would certainly have been well aware of the music and style of Hammerschmidt, his famous predecessor at St. John, and these three works follow some aspects of "Hammerschmidt's standard" quite closely—sacred texts, four or more vocal parts, optional basso continuo accompaniment, and imitative counterpoint. In addition to these style characteristics, Krieger's three surviving motets also feature *stile antico*, Latin texts, and motives with a restricted range (usually a fourth or fifth).[11]

All three motets contain non-chordal passages for the basso continuo at the beginning of sections. In these passages the keyboard player doubles the voices for their entrances and resumes chordal playing after at least three of the singers have entered. In two of Krieger's motets (the *Magnificat a 4* and *Laudate Dominum*), the only instrumental part is the basso continuo, which doubles the bass voice exactly.

Krieger composed his motets in the *stile antico* tradition, with motet-style imitative counterpoint. This type of writing, with points of imitation for each short phrase of the text, creates a homogenous style and texture across the entire work. Each phrase of text usually receives its own motive, with a new point of imitation beginning when the next textual phrase begins.[12] Each motive is strictly imitated in the successive voices, but there is no countersubject (i.e., the material following the head-motive differs between the voices). Entrances of each motive usually occur alternately in the tonic and dominant of the current key.

Krieger's three motets are predominantly written with half and whole notes ("white" notation), which is typical of *stile antico*. The time signature of *Laudate Dominum* is ¢, with the descriptive term "Alla breve" appearing repeatedly in the work. Many of the vocal and organ parts of the *Sanctus a 4* are notated with ¢. The *Magnificat a 4* is not in ¢, as would be expected, but other features of this work indicate that alla breve should be used. For example, even though the *Magnificat a 4* is in common time (c), the title page and first page of music prominently include the words "Alla breve." Thus, all of Krieger's motets should be performed in ¢, as was customary for motets in the late seventeenth century.

Krieger's Biblical Cantatas

Krieger's extant biblical cantatas are *Halleluja Lobet den Herrn* (1685), *Danket dem Herrn* (1687), *Dies ist der Tag* (1687), *Danksaget dem Vater* (1688), *Gelobet sei der Herr* (1689), the *Magnificat a 10* (1689), *Dominus illuminatio mea* (1690), and *Rühmet den Herrn* (n.d.).[13] These works are distinguished from his four extant concertos by their separation into distinct movements, rather than continuous sections. The biblical cantatas are also quite different in text and style from Krieger's later madrigal and mixed madrigal cantatas, of which five examples survive. All of Krieger's biblical cantatas have only one type of text (biblical) and are usually written in *stile concertato*. The mixed madrigal cantatas contain multiple types of texts, mostly not biblical. The texts of the madrigal and mixed madrigal cantatas are set primarily as recitatives, arias, and choruses.

Most of the movements in Krieger's biblical cantatas are scored for several voices and tutti instruments, usually strings and basso continuo without wind or brass instruments. Krieger employs two violins in most of these works, but the number of violas varies from zero to three, with three being the most common. The viola parts usually double the soprano, alto, and tenor parts, while the two violin parts are independent of the voices. Passages featuring two obbligato violins with rhythmically independent parts are common in Krieger's music and that of his contemporaries; this type of writing, however, is not seen in Krieger's motets and is rare in his concertos and late cantatas. In almost all of Krieger's works in any genre, the bass voice is doubled by the basso continuo, making it a *basso seguente*.

Krieger employed a great deal of *stile concertato* in his biblical cantatas, with ample contrasts between blocks of sound. This includes contrasts between different groupings of singers (e.g., individual soloists vs. full vocal ensemble) and between singers and instruments. Differences in dynamics are an inherent result of changes in forces, but Krieger at times also uses dynamic markings (*f* and *p*) to further underline these contrasts. The accompaniment varies, so that sometimes only basso continuo is heard, but more often a fuller instrumentation is present. In addition, the instruments often play introductions for the work as a whole (sometimes labeled Sonata or Symphonia), while instrumental interludes and postludes are more often seen in interior movements.

Besides *concertato* writing, the other predominant style feature in Krieger's biblical cantatas is counterpoint. His music is most strongly characterized by invertible counterpoint, motet-style imitative writing, and head-motives that are followed by varying material. Invertible counterpoint, in which the music of a previous section is presented with the voice parts exchanged, received great praise from many authors and composers in the late seventeenth and early eighteenth centuries. Mattheson's term "double fugue" thus refers to any fugue with invertible counterpoint, including double, triple, and quadruple fugues, each of which is progressively more difficult to write. For example, Mattheson describes the skill required to write double counterpoint, which was his term for invertible counterpoint:

> Double counterpoint and the double fugues that derive
> from it are . . . appropriate for composers who possess
> substantial powers of judgment by nature, who are of
> great, indefatigable intellect and diligence, [and] who
> also deeply understand the powers of harmony. . . .[14]

In Mattheson's *Critica Musica*, he specifically mentioned Krieger in a passage about composers of invertible counterpoint: "Among the old, brave masters, I know of no one who surpassed Herr Kapellmeister Johann Krieger in Zittau."[15] Krieger's use of invertible counterpoint can be seen in the conclusions of *Danksaget dem Vater* (six-voice double counterpoint) and *Gelobet sei der Herr* (six-voice triple counterpoint).

Krieger's contrapuntal texture is often based on motet-style imitative writing, with successive points of imitation used to set the phrases of text. This technique, which is very evident in his *stile antico* motets, is also found in contrapuntal sections or movements within the biblical cantatas. Rather than using the "white" notation seen in the motets, however, the idiom in the biblical cantatas is more modern with its smaller note values ("black" notation) and in its combination with *concertato* writing. For example, Krieger sets a phrase of text to a specific motive with which it appears each time a new voice part enters.[16] The voices enter in turn, usually at the fifth or the octave, as in a fugal exposition. After they come together homophonically and eventually cadence, the next phrase of text receives a different motive, and the whole process begins again. The motives are usually presented with staggered entrances at the fifth or octave, and only rarely do the themes overlap.

Krieger's fugal writing is usually monothematic and often does not include countersubjects.[17] For example, it is common for Krieger's subjects to have a head-motive followed by free counterpoint (e.g., *Danksaget dem Vater*, mvts. 1, 3, and 4; and *Gelobet sei der Herr*, mvt. 3). While this material is always based on motives in the subject, its variety from entrance to entrance keeps it from being considered a countersubject.

Danksaget dem Vater

The compositional date of Krieger's biblical cantata *Danksaget dem Vater* is not known, but the first record of a performance comes from Weißenfels in 1688.[18] According to the only manuscript source that is not a holograph (i.e., copied by Krieger), the cantata is scored for "Canto, Alto, Tenore, Basso," two violins, three violas, and "Continuo."[19] This work, unlike Krieger's more continuous concertos, is clearly delineated into four movements, all of which end with whole notes, fermatas, and double bars. The text, which is the only setting of an Epistle reading among Krieger's extant vocal works, is taken from Colossians 1:12–14:

> [Movement 1:] Give thanks to the Father
> [Movement 2:] who has qualified us to share in the
>   inheritance of the saints in light.
> [Movement 3:] He has delivered us from the dominion of
>   darkness and transferred us to the kingdom of his
>   beloved Son,
> [Movement 4:] in whom we have redemption, the
>   forgiveness of sins.[20]

The cantata opens with a thirty-nine-measure setting of the words *"Danksaget dem Vater"* (Give thanks to the Father). The music for this movement is written in motet-style imitative counterpoint for four equal voice parts (SATB) with exact doubling by three violas (Example 1). The basso continuo part is a *tasto solo*

Example 1. *Danksaget dem Vater:* mm. 1-19.

passage until the third voice enters, after which the keyboard player begins chordal playing. The predominant note value is the half note, and the music is marked "Alla breve." Even though obbligato violins are employed later in the cantata, they are omitted in the first movement. The voices enter in turn on the first and fifth scale de-

grees, as in a fugal exposition. The text is set with a monothematic
head-motive, and since the material after the motive varies, there
are no distinct countersubjects.

For the second movement of the cantata, Krieger set the text in
stile concertato, with abundant contrasts between chorus and soloists, and between voices and instruments. This entire movement,
with its more modern style, differs sharply from the *stile antico* of
the first movement. The text of the second movement is the phrase
"*der uns tüchtig gemacht hat zu dem Erbtheil der Heiligen im
Licht*" (who has qualified us to share in the inheritance of the saints
in light). The music is homophonic, using "black" notation and
featuring obbligato violins (Example 2). The movement ends with
an eleven-measure passage for instruments alone.

The third movement begins with a long passage in *stile antico*
(mm. 65–128), but it concludes in *stile concertato* (mm. 129–76).
The opening is musically similar to the first movement, with a few
exceptions. Unlike the first movement, the third movement has

Example 2. *Danksaget dem Vater*: mm. 40-49.

two themes, with the second one motivically derived from the first (Example 3). The second theme initially appears to be a two-measure motive that is repeated as a sequence, but a comparison with the first theme confirms its derivation, since the notes that define the underlying harmony are identical. The first theme is reserved for the words "*Welcher uns errettet hat*" (who has delivered us), while the second theme accompanies the words "*von der Obrigkeit der Finsterniß*" (from the dominion of darkness). The themes are not combined, but appear only when their respective texts are used. Another major difference between the styles of the first and third movements is the use of instruments. While the third movement begins with voices accompanied only by basso continuo, two obbligato violins enter in measure ninety-one and are soon joined by

Example 3. *Danksaget dem Vater*: mm. 71-74 (Soprano) and mm. 84-87 (Soprano).

the violas, which double the voices. Lastly, the *stile antico* portion of this movement cadences with a homophonic passage (mm. 116–28) containing *concertato* elements (e.g., the soprano against the tutti, and the voices against the strings). The third movement then concludes with a *concertato* setting of the words "*und hat uns versetzt in das Reich seines lieben Sohns*" (and transferred us to the kingdom of his beloved Son). This section contains abundant contrasts between soprano and chorus, and between voices and instruments.

The fourth and final movement begins with a primarily homophonic section (mm. 177–94) for all voices and instruments on the phrase "*an welchem wir haben die Erlösung*" (in whom we have redemption). The movement's conclusion (mm. 195–214) is based on two themes that are masterfully written in double counterpoint as a lengthy six-voice stretto.[21] For the first time in the cantata, two themes are used to set the same text: "*die Vergebung der Sünden*" (the forgiveness of sins). The words "*die Vergebung*" are always set with one of the two themes (i.e., head-motive), while the words "*der Sünden*" vary each time the themes enter. The two head-motives are completely different in style (Example 4). The first one is a simple ascending line of half notes, which is typical of *stile antico* or "white-note" writing. The second head-motive is a busy combination of eighth- and sixteenth-notes, which is characteristic of *concertato* or "black" notation.

Example 4. *Danksaget dem Vater*: mm. 195-96 (Alto) and mm. 197-198 (Alto).

The combined use of *stile antico* and *stile concertato* within the same work is a unique feature of the cantata *Danksaget dem Vater* compared to Krieger's other extant vocal works. His choice of two different styles for this work seems directly related to the liturgical occasion for which it was composed. In 1688, *Danksaget dem Vater* was performed in Weißenfels on the Feast of the Reformation and repeated there in 1699, also for Reformation.[22] Even though the Colossians passage was not the appointed pericope for Reformation Day, its themes are nonetheless appropriate for this celebration. For example, this text includes contrasts between "Father" (Old Testament and Law) and "Son" (New Testament and Gospel), which are intermingled with metaphors of darkness and light. Reformation, a celebration of freedom from the law of Rome, was an especially suitable time to emphasize traditional Lutheran teaching on Law and Gospel. Additional Reformation themes can also be found in this passage in the following phrases: "inheritance of the saints," and "redemption, the forgiveness of sins." Luther himself included some of these ideas in his sermon on this passage from Colossians (1:3–14), designated for the Twenty-fourth Sunday after Trinity. For example, Luther's description of verses twelve through fourteen (the text set in Krieger's cantata) includes abundant binarisms:

> Such is the doctrine of the Gospel, and so is it to be declared. It shows us sin and forgiveness, wrath and grace, death and life; how we were in darkness and how we are redeemed from it. It does not, like the Law, make us sinners, nor is its mission to teach us how to merit and earn grace. But it declares how we, condemned and under the power of sin, death, and the devil, as we are, receive by faith the freely-given redemption and in return show our gratitude.[23]

Luther continues his discussion with more Reformation themes, such as comparing the Jews' emphasis on the Law and the Christians' concern for the Gospel, and exhorting his listeners to avoid compromise with papists.[24]

Krieger set the textual contrasts of this biblical passage with different styles of music. The *stile antico* passages, which were known musically as old-fashioned, academic renditions of the musical "laws" of counterpoint, reflect the Old Testament concepts in the Colossians passage.[25] This style is directly associated in the cantata text with three different ideas—Father, darkness, and sins. In Luther's sermon on this text, several further concepts are also implied—wrath, death, law, devil, Old Testament, Jews, and papists. The sections in *stile concertato*, with their abundant contrasts and modern connotations (for Krieger's day), are used to set passages related to the Son, light, forgiveness, and redemption; additional ideas reflected in Luther's sermon include grace, life, Gospel, Christ, New Testament, Christians, and (more specifically) Lutherans.

This cantata contains various ways of combining the two styles, with their interrelationship increasing over the course of the work. The first and second movements are set completely in *stile antico* and *stile concertato*, respectively. The third movement, the longest in the cantata, includes both styles in succession; its presentation of contrasting ideas and musical styles lies at the heart of the whole work. The fourth movement, which is relatively short, serves to draw together both the textual and musical ideas of the work. This synthesis is achieved by combining *stile antico* and *stile concertato* through the simultaneous use of two themes, one in each style, on the words "*die Vergebung der Sünden*" (the forgiveness of sins).

This juxtaposition of styles reflects the theology of the text. The first movement is a motet setting of the words "*Danksaget dem Vater*" (Give thanks to the Father), and the monothematic writing emphasizes the text's mention of the Father alone. The use of *stile antico* refers to God the Father as the giver of the Law (Ten Commandments). The second movement is solely in modern *stile concertato*, reflecting the New Testament connotations of the phrase "*der uns tüchtig gemacht hat zu dem Erbtheil der Heiligen im Licht*" (who has qualified us to share in the inheritance of the saints in light).[26] The third movement makes reference to redemption with the words "*Welcher uns errettet hat*" (who has delivered us). The subject of this passage ("he") can be interpreted as either the Father or the Son; from a strict grammatical view, the text points to "he" as the Father, but from a theological standpoint, it is Jesus who delivered salvation through his crucifixion and resurrection. Krieger underscores these two possibilities by using two themes, one derived from the other, which appear successively and not in combination. Thus, the first theme (for "Father") is the source of the second theme (for "Son"), just as Jesus was "begotten" of the Father. The themes also appear separately, which is possibly a reference to the Incarnation, which made Jesus physically distinct from the Father.

Finally, in the fourth movement the same textual phrase— "*die Vergebung der Sünden*" (the forgiveness of sins)—is set to two different themes, which underlines the theological significance of these words. The concept "forgiveness of sins" combines both Old Testament and New Testament ideas (sins and forgiveness, respectively), and therefore Krieger used simultaneous themes in two styles (*stile antico* and *stile concertato*) to represent these concepts. "Sins" and "forgiveness" are closely related, since forgiveness is impossible unless sin has first occurred. The interdependence of these two ideas is reflected in Krieger's conclusion to the cantata, with its intricate six-voice stretto in double counterpoint. The text of *Danksaget dem Vater*, with its combination of concepts, gave Krieger an excellent opportunity to employ opposing musical styles throughout the work and then combine them in a final masterful passage that is both theologically appropriate and musically satisfying.

NOTES

1 Klaus-Jürgen Gundlach, ed., *Das Weissenfelser Aufführungsverzeichnis Johann Philipp Kriegers und seines Sohnes Johann Gotthilf Krieger (1684–1732): Kommentierte Neuausgabe* (Sinzig: Studio Verlag, 2001), 279–98.

2 The number of Krieger's sacred vocal works that survive is three motets (including one *Magnificat* and one *Sanctus*), four concertos (including three settings of the *Sanctus*), eight biblical cantatas (including one *Magnificat*), one madrigal cantata, and four mixed madrigal cantatas.

3 Johann Krieger, and Johann Philipp Krieger, *Sämtliche Orgel- und Clavierwerke*, eds. Siegbert Rampe and Helene Lerch, 2 vols. (Kassel: Bärenreiter, 1999). Krieger's sacred vocal music, with the exception of his *continuo Lieder*, was not published during his lifetime.

4 "... die besten und gründlichsten Contrapunctisten dieses Jahrhunderts ...." Johann Mattheson, *Der vollkommene Kapellmeister* (Hamburg: Christian Herold, 1739; reprint in Documenta Musicologica, Erster Reihe, V, ed. Margarate Reimann, Kassel: Bärenreiter, 1954), 442.

5 "Ich ... sondern vielmehr wûnschen môgte, etwas dergleichen von dem berühmten Herrn Bach in Leipzig, der ein grosser Fugenmeister ist, ans Licht gestellet zu sehen." Mattheson, *Der vollkommene Kapellmeister*, 441. This translation is taken from Johann and Johann Philipp Krieger, *Sämtliche Orgel- und Clavierwerke*, 1:xxx.

6 The two Bachs applied to work in Zittau in 1753, almost twenty years after Krieger's death. See Carl Philipp Emanuel Bach, *Briefe und Dokumente: Kritische Gesamtausgabe*, ed. Ernst Suchalla, 2 vols. (Göttingen: Vandenhoeck & Ruprecht, 1994), 1:21–33. For information on the Silbermann organ, which was destroyed in 1757, see Ulrich Dähnert, *Historische Orgeln in Sachsen: Ein Orgelinventar* (Leipzig: VEB Deutscher Verlag für Musik, 1983), 280–81.

7 "Law and Gospel," in *Lutheran Cyclopedia*, ed. Erwin L. Lueker (St. Louis: Concordia, 1975), 463.

8 Martin Fuhrmann, *Musicalischer-Trichter* (Frankfurt an der Spree [Berlin], 1706); translated in Kerala Snyder, *Dieterich Buxtehude: Organist in Lübeck* (New York: Schirmer, 1987), 153–54. The emphasis on fugues in this passage ("the voices make

fugues") does not imply strict fugal form; rather, Fuhrmann is suggesting a homogeneous contrapuntal texture instead of the contrast typical of *concertato* writing.

9 Snyder, *Dieterich Buxtehude*, 153.

10 For the location of the manuscripts of these works, see Mary Benson Stahlke, "Johann Krieger and Sacred Vocal Music in Zittau, 1682–1735" (Ph.D. diss., University of Southern California, 2002), 533–34, 536.

11 Hammerschmidt's works represent a different stream of writing that eventually led to motets with primarily homophonic textures and German texts. This trend was most prevalent in central Germany. See Daniel Melamed, *J. S. Bach and the German Motet* (Cambridge: Cambridge University Press, 1995), 15–16.

12 The text and its motive are almost always linked, so that if two phrases of text are set simultaneously, the two motives are also heard at the same time (e.g., *Laudate Dominum*, mm. 15ff).

13 For the location of the manuscripts of these works, as well as a listing of modern editions of *Danket dem Herrn* and *Gelobet sei der Herr*, see Stahlke, "Johann Krieger," 529–35. For a recent edition of *Halleluja Lobet dem Herrn*, see Johann Krieger, *Halleluja, lobet dem Herrn in seinem Heiligtum: 1685*, ed. Karl-Heinz Schickhaus (St. Oswald [Austria]: Tympanon, 2002).

14 "Der doppelte Contrapunct, und die von ihm herstammenden Doppel-Fugen gehören . . . für solche Componisten, die von Natur eine starcke Urtheils-Krafft besitzen, von grossem, unermüdeten Nachdencken und Fleiß sind, auch die Kräffte der Harmonie oder Vollstimmigkeit tief einsehen. . . ." Mattheson, *Der vollkommene Kapellmeister*, 415. This translation is found in Laurence Dreyfus, *Bach and the Patterns of Invention* (Cambridge, Mass.: Harvard University Press, 1996), 142. For more information on the high status of invertible counterpoint in this era, see 141–60.

15 "Von alten braven Maitres wüste ich keinen der den Herrn Capellmeister Johann Krieger in Zittau darinn überginge." Johann Mattheson, *Critica Musica*, 2 vols., (Hamburg, 1722–25; reprint, Amsterdam: Frits A. M. Knuf, 1964), 1:326. Mattheson mentions only one other composer known for double fugues (Handel).

16 In most of Krieger's works, regardless of genre, the text always appears with its motive no matter how often it is repeated in the piece.

17 In the cases where he wrote double or triple counterpoint, however, the second and third themes are usually treated as countersubjects.

18 Gundlach, *Das Weissenfelser Aufführungsverzeichnis*, 280.

19 *Danksaget dem Vater*, Berlin, Staatsbibliothek, Preussischer Kulturbesitz, Mus. ms. 12153 (no. 5).

20 [Movement 1:] *Dancksaget dem Vater*

[Movement 2:] *der uns tüchtig gemacht hat zu dem Erbtheil der Heiligen im Licht.*

[Movement 3:] *Welcher uns errettet hat von der Obrigkeit der Finsterniß und hat versetz in das Reich seines lieben Sohns,*

[Movement 4:] *an welchem wir haben die Erlösung durch sein Blut nehmlich die Vergebung der Sünden.*

The spelling of this text is taken directly from the manuscript of Krieger's *Danksaget dem Vater*. The English translation is taken from the Bible, Revised Standard Version.

21 The six parts are SATB and two obbligato violins, while the other string instruments do not have independent parts.

22 Gundlach, *Das Weissenfelser Aufführungsverzeichnis*, 280. Because Johann Krieger wrote this work, it likely received its premiere in Zittau. This author, however, has only found information about its performance and liturgical use in Weißenfels, not in Zittau.

23 Martin Luther, *Luther's Epistle Sermons: Trinity Sunday to Advent*, trans. John Nicholas Lenker, Luther's Complete Works, vol. 9 (Minneapolis: Luther Press, 1909), 377. Interestingly, if Easter falls early in the year, the Twenty-fourth Sunday after Trinity takes place on or near Reformation Day.

24 Ibid., 368, 375.

25 For example, Andreas Werckmeister stated that invertible counterpoint is *"ein Spiegel der Natur und Ordnung Gottes"* (a mirror of nature and God's order), which are concepts analogous to the Law. Andreas Werckmeister, *Harmonologica musica* (Quedlinburg, 1707), [v]; quoted in David Yearsley, *Bach and the Meanings of Counterpoint* (Cambridge: Cambridge University Press, 2002), 20.

26 J. S. Bach's use of contrasting styles can also reflect theological and structural concepts (e.g., the 'Confiteor' in the "Symbolum Nicenum" of the *B minor Mass* [*BWV* 232]). See John Butt, *Bach: Mass in B Minor* (Cambridge, England: Cambridge University Press, 1991), 79–80; and Christoph Wolff, "Bach and the Tradition of the Palestrina Style," in *Bach: Essays on his Life and Music* (Cambridge: Harvard University Press, 1991), 92–93, 102–3.

EVANGELINE RIMBACH

The Sacred Vocal Music
of Johann Kuhnau

Background

I t remains as true today as it was almost forty years ago that
Johann Kuhnau is remembered chiefly as a keyboard composer.
There is good reason for this in that his keyboard works continued
to be published after his death, whereas his vocal works were never
published. It was not until the twentieth century that a few of the
sacred vocal works were printed in both scholarly and practical
editions.

Among the first vocal works to be published were the four
church cantatas, which were printed in *Denkmäler deutscher
Tonkunst, Bd. 58/59,* edited by Arnold Schering. They are:

> *Wie schön leuchtet der Morgenstern*
> *Gott sei mir gnädig nach deiner Güte*
> *Wenn ihr fröhlich seid an euren Festen*
> *Ich freue mich in Herrn*

Max Seiffert edited one cantata for the *Organum* series—*Ich habe
Lust abzuscheiden.* It is now considered a doubtful work.

In the 1960s a number of cantatas appeared in practical editions. *Ich hebe meine Augen auf* was edited by Harald Kümmerling
and published by Verlag Edmund Bieler in Köln. It is now considered a doubtful work. Horace Fishback III edited two cantatas in
the 1960s: *How Brightly Shines the Morningstar* (H. W. Gray, 1961)
and *Christ lag in Todesbanden* (J. Fischer, 1966). And more recently I edited two works for practical editions: *Magnificat* (A-R
Editions, 1980) and *Lobe den Herrn* (Bärenreiter, 1995).

Another vocal work of Kuhnau has received a lot of attention
through the years, namely, the motet *Tristis est anima mea,* which
also is considered spurious. It is interesting to note that it is still

sung and even recorded with attribution to Kuhnau. The Netherlands Bach Society in its recent tour of the United States sang *Tristis est anima mea* and the cantata *Gott sei mir gnädig nach deiner Güte*, and listed the motet as a work by Kuhnau without any question as to its authenticity.

The *Magnificat* has recently been receiving more attention by professional choirs. Two fine recordings of the *Magnificat* exist. The Rheinische Kantorei recorded it in 1992 for EMI along with *Magnificats* of Antonio Caldara and J. S. Bach. This recording is notable because of the insertion of the *Laudes: Freut euch und jubiliert, Gloria in excelsis Deo, Vom Himmel hoch,* and *Virga Jesse floruit*. The Christmas *Laudes* will be discussed later. The other recording of the *Magnificat* was made in 1998 by the Bach Collegium Japan. This recording also includes two additional *Magnificats*, one by Jan Zelenka and one by J. S. Bach.

The only recent recording of Kuhnau cantatas was made in 1998 by The King's Consort directed by Robert King. It contains six numbers—five cantatas and the spurious motet *Tristis est anima mea*. Two of the five cantatas were printed in *DdT* years ago: *Wie schön leuchtet der Morgenstern* and *Gott sei mir gnädig nach deiner Güte*. The other three have never been published: *Ihr Himmel jubilirt von oben, Weicht ihr Sorgen aus dem Hertzen,* and *O heilige Zeit*.

An earlier LP recording of *Wie schön leuchtet der Morgenstern* was made by the Norddeutscher Singkreis in 1963 on the Archive label.

An interesting concert of church cantatas for Christmas and New Year by the Balije Consort and Choir took place in December 1992 in Alden Biesen, Belgium. They performed three works of Kuhnau: *Wie schön leuchtet der Morgenstern, Vom Himmel hoch,* and *Das Alte ist vergangen*. They had become acquainted with the publication of the Kuhnau *Magnificat* and were interested in other Kuhnau works. They used my dissertation editions of *Vom Himmel hoch* and *Das Alte ist vergangen* for their performance.

All this more recent interest in Kuhnau's vocal works shows that "these pieces are worthy of comparison with Bach's (early) Mühlhausen cantatas. . . . Indeed, just as Kuhnau is the most significant link between Schütz and Bach, he might also be the only German composer who was of immediate influence on the development of both Bach and Handel."[1]

What is known about the life of Johann Kuhnau? He was born on April 6, 1660, in Geising in the Saxon Erzgebirge on the border of the Czech Republic not far from Dresden. The church records state that a son, Johannes, was born to Barthel Kuhn on the sixth of April about 7:00 a.m., and he was baptized on the eighth of April. The family name was always listed as Kuhn in Geising, except for the notice of Johann's mother's death on December 27, 1709, when it appeared as Kuhnau. The first reference to the name in its new form of "Kuhnau" was in the Leipziger *Ratsprotokollen* on October 3, 1684, at the time of Kuhnau's election as organist of the Thomaskirche. Two years earlier, on September 26, 1682, Johann's name was given as Cuno in the competition for the organ post at the Thomaskirche. Earlier that same year he was listed as a student in the Zittau Gymnasium under the name of Kuhn.

Johann's father was a carpenter by trade. His mother was the daughter of a tailor. There were seven children in the Kuhn family, three of whom became musicians. Johann was the third child and the second of five sons. Two other sons also became musicians and cantors: Gottfried and Andreas.

One of the godparents at Johann's baptism was Andreas Schelle, in all probability a relative of Johann Schelle, Kuhnau's predecessor at the Thomaskirche in Leipzig and also a native of Geising, the hometown of the Kuhnaus. Family ties were known to exist between the Schelles and Kuhnaus.

A prominent musical relative of the Kuhnaus was Salomon Krügner, a court musician in Dresden. The chronicler Christoph Sicul calls Krügner a cousin of the Kuhnau family. It is probable that the three Kuhnau brothers received their singing positions at the Kreuzschule in Dresden through the influence of Krügner.

Johann entered the Kreuzschule on February 2, 1671. Since Heinrich Schütz died in November 1672, it is entirely possible that Johann was one of the boys who sang at his funeral. Johann's organ teacher at the school was Alexander Heringk, a student of Schütz. Another of Johann's teachers in Dresden was the Hofcapellmeister Vincenzo Albrici, who in 1680 became the organist at the Thomaskirche in Leipzig.

When the plague hit Dresden in 1680, Kuhnau went to Zittau to join a fellow classmate, Crucianer Erhard Titius, who had taken over the cantorate in Zittau in September 1680. Moritz Edelmann, the organist at the Johanniskirche in Zittau, who had succeeded Hammerschmidt in 1676, died suddenly in December 1680. His death afforded Kuhnau the opportunity of temporarily playing the organ in the Johanniskirche.

In May 1681 Kuhnau's friend Titius died, and Kuhnau was commissioned to write music for the funeral. The resulting composition was a five-voice aria-motet *Ach Gott, wie lästu mich erstarren*. This aria-motet is the earliest known work by Kuhnau and the only piece of his sacred vocal music to be published during his lifetime.

Kuhnau had come to Zittau for the main purpose of completing the Prima class at the Gymnasium. When Titius died, Kuhnau filled the cantorate vacancy until a successor was elected. Following Titius's death, Kuhnau lived in the home of the city recorder, von Hartig, a well-educated and well-traveled man who played both clavier and lute and had studied music in Italy and France.

Early in 1682 Johann Krieger began his service in Zittau as organist and Director Chori Musici. Shortly after this, Kuhnau left the city for study in Leipzig. He entered the law faculty of the University of Leipzig where his brother Andreas had already matriculated the previous year.

Shortly after his arrival in Leipzig, Kuhnau was introduced to Professor D. Johann Adam Schertzer, who offered him free board in his home. When Albrici resigned his organ position at the Thomaskirche after scarcely a year of service, Schertzer encouraged Kuhnau to apply for the position. However, he lost that election to Gottfried Kühnel, the Hofcapellmeister in Zeitz.

In 1683, the twenty-three-year-old Kuhnau received "an unusual compliment, that he had no equal in the field of music" after the performance of his *drama per musica* when Elector Johann Georg III visited Leipzig to celebrate the victory over the Turks at Vienna.[2]

In October 1683 Kühnel died, and Kuhnau again applied for the position of Thomaskirche organist. This time he was elected unanimously. Simultaneously with the beginning of this job, he began his regular study of law at the university. During the first two and one-half years at the university, he studied philosophy, logic, and music. In 1688 he was qualified to practice law upon the publication of his dissertation *De Juribus circa Musicos Ecclesiasticos*. In 1692 he successfully passed a new exam required of all lawyers and continued his law practice.

In 1689 Kuhnau married Sabine Elisabeth Plattner, the daughter of a Leipzig burger and leather worker, in the Thomaskirche. Six daughters and two sons were born to the couple, but only three daughters survived their father.

All of Kuhnau's well-known clavier compositions were written and published during the period of his tenure as Thomaskirche organist. They include:

1. *Clavier-Übung, I Teil*, Leipzig, 1689 (2nd ed. 1695)
2. *Clavier-Übung, II Teil*, Leipzig, 1692 (eds. 1695, 1703, 1726)
3. *Frische Clavier-Früchte oder Sieben Sonaten*, Leipzig 1696 (eds. 1700, 1710, 1719, 1724)
4. *Musicalische Vorstellung einiger biblischer Historien in 6 Sonaten*, Leipzig, 1700 (2nd ed. 1710)

None of Kuhnau's organ compositions was published during his lifetime. Early in the twentieth century Karl Straube published two of the chorale preludes in his *Choralvorspiele alter Meister*. Two preludes and fugues plus a toccata appeared in the *Organum* series, Vol. IV, No. 19, edited by Max Seiffert.

The last decade of the seventeenth century was a successful and happy time in the life of Kuhnau. Besides the publication of his clavier works, a number of his literary works appeared. Mattheson's *Ehren-Pforte* lists the following treatises and novels: *Der Schmied seines eigenen Unglück* (The Smithy of his own Misfortune), *Das Fühlen* (the first volume of a series on the moral use of the five senses), *Der lose Causenmacher, Der musikalische Quacksalber,* and *Musicus curioses.* There were also several Latin treatises: *De Tetrachorda seu Musica antiqua ac hodierna, Disputatio de Triado harmonica,* and *Fundamentum compositionis.* The most famous of the literary works is *Der musikalische Quacksalber,* a satirical novel about a pseudo-Italian Baroque musician who travels about posing as a scholar and deceiving people.

When the Thomas Cantor Johann Schelle died in March 1701, Kuhnau applied for his position. He was unanimously elected and began his cantorate in April 1701. As a condition of his appointment, he had to give up his law practice.

His duties as Thomas cantor consisted of the general instruction of the four upper classes and instruction in scholarly studies of the Tertia and Quarta classes at the Thomasschule. Of course, his main duty was to direct the church music in the Thomaskirche and Nicolaikirche. After 1711 he also had to direct the music at the Peterskirche and on high feasts at the Johanniskirche. In addition, he had the supervision of the organs in the Thomaskirche and

Joh. Kuhnau Musicus

Nicolaikirche and was supervisor of the *Stadtpfeiffer* and *Kunstgeiger*. As the Director Chori Musici of the university, Kuhnau had to supply music for the quarterly orations and university festivals at the Paulinerkirche. After 1711 regular services were held at that church.

One interesting innovation Kuhnau introduced to Leipzig was the practice of publishing the texts of the church music for Sundays and feast days. The historian Sicul in his *Neo Annalium Lipsiensium, Continuatio II*, states:

> This *figural-musik*, especially that for high feasts, which is listened to with all the more devotion, usually lasts a long time, so the Cantor has published beforehand the texts under the title, "Church Music," which from one high feast to the other will be set to music so that each one can read and re-read them.[3]

Kuhnau's tenure at the Thomaskirche and Schule was plagued with problems. There were discipline problems with students, and the quality of the boys' voices at the school was poor. Kuhnau was continually losing student singers to the opera. Then there was also competition with Telemann, who had come to Leipzig in 1701 as a law student. Telemann was composing operas for both Leipzig and Weissenfels and had founded his own *Collegium musicum* among the students. In 1704 Telemann became the organist and music director at the Neuen Kirche. He was very popular with the students and the townspeople, and the city council encouraged his activities. Kuhnau protested to the council against the work of the "new organist who composes operas," but his pleas remained unanswered. Kuhnau, himself, composed at least two operas, but evidently they were unsuccessful. The critic Scheibe refers to Kuhnau's theatrical work:

> The famous Kuhnau, Bach's worthy predecessor in the cantorate at Leipzig, was a scholar and experienced in all knowledge pertaining to theoretical and practical music, and was in his time very eminent. Not forgetting his great deserving, one knows very well how unsuccessful he was when he undertook the task of setting a *Singspiel* to music and staging it.[4]

Kuhnau protested against opera and its corrupting effects in many petitions to the city council. He believed the use of recitative and da capo aria in church music had a secularizing effect. He was convinced that, as a true and faithful servant of the church, he had to fight against it.

Kuhnau suffered bouts of illness that became another burden for him. In 1703 he was so ill that people believed he was on his deathbed. In fact, the city council was ungracious enough to propose Telemann as a successor to him at this time. It is thought his disease was tuberculosis, since mention is made several times that he suffered a severe cough.

Kuhnau died on June 5, 1722, most probably as the result of tuberculosis. He was survived by his wife and three daughters. Preceding him in death were three of his children, two daughters and a son.

A number of Kuhnau's students became prominent musicians. They include Johann David Heinichen, an assistant and copier for Kuhnau, Christoph Graupner, and Johann Friedrich Fasch. In 1722–23 Graupner was chosen to succeed Kuhnau as Thomaskantor when Telemann declined the post. However, his Landgrave rejected his resignation, and the position was given to J. S. Bach.

During his lifetime Kuhnau carried on a correspondence with Johann Krieger in Zittau and Johann Mattheson. Some of the correspondence of the year 1717 on the occasion of the Buttstedt-Mattheson battle over solmization can be found in Mattheson's *Critica Musica* of 1725. Kuhnau met Bach a number of times. One occasion was in 1714 when Bach came to Leipzig, played at the Thomaskirche, and directed a performance of his cantata *Nun komm der Heiden Heiland*. In 1716 both men, together with Christian Friedrich Rolle, examined the new organ in the Liebfrauenkirche in Halle.

Kuhnau was a man of many talents. He was a classical scholar, a linguist, a jurist, a writer, as well as a musician. Telemann attested that he had learned counterpoint and fugue mainly through a study of Kuhnau's compositions.[5] Mattheson extolled him as a great organist, a learned man, a great musician, composer, and choral director above all his contemporaries.[6]

In the mid-eighteenth century, Jacob Adlung states: "I do not know whether or not he brought more honor to the ranks of musicians or to other scholars. He was a learned man in theology, in law, in rhetoric, in poetry, in mathematics, in foreign languages, and in music.[7]

Extant Sacred Vocal Works
Latin Sacred and Secular Works

1. *Bone Jesu, chare Jesu, ne me tu desere, a 3.* 2 violins, soprano solo, continuo. Parts MS. Dom. 13 Trinit. 1690. (Sächsische Landesbibliothek, Dresden).

2. *In te domine. Ps. 31:1-6, a 6.* 2 violins, bassoon, soprano solo, continuo. Parts MS. Dominica 23, Tr. 1690. (Sächsische Landesbibliothek, Dresden).

3. *Laudate pueri, a 4.* 2 violins, trombone or viola da gamba or violoncello, tenor solo, continuo. Full score MS. (Staatsbibliothek, Berlin).

4. *Magnificat.* 5 voci, 3 clarini, timpani, 2 oboes, 2 violins, 2 violas, continuo. Full score MS. (Staatsbibliothek, Berlin).

5. *Missa-F dur.* 2 violins, viola, bassoon, bass solo, continuo. Full score and Parts MS. (Stadtkirchenarchiv, Mügeln).

6. *Spirate clementes.* 2 violins, 2 sopranos, bass, continuo. Full score MS. (Staatsbibliothek, Berlin).

7. *Tristis est anima mea.* Motetto *a* 5 voci. Full score MS (spurious). (Staatsbibliothek, Berlin).

German Church Cantatas

1. *Ach Herr, wie sind meiner Feinde so viel.* Ps. 2. 2 clarini, 2 violins, trombone, bassoon, soprano, bass, continuo. Full score MS. (Staatsbibliothek, Berlin).

2. *Christ lag in Todesbanden, a 9.* 2 cornetti ad placitum, 2 violins, 2 violas, violone, soprano, alto, tenor, bass, organ. Full score MS. (Staatsbibliothek, Berlin).

3. *Daran erkennen wie, dass wir in ihm verbleiben.* In Festum Pentec. Feria. I. Joh. IV:13. 2 clarini, timpani, 2 violins, 2 oboes, 2 violas, bassoon, 2 sopranos, alto, tenor, bass, organ. Full score MS. (Staatsbibliothek, Berlin).

4. *Das Alte ist vergangen, siehe es ist alles neu geworden.* 2 clarini, timpani, 2 violins, viola, bassoon, soprano, alto, tenor, bass, continuo. Full score MS. (Bibliothèque Conservatoire Royal, Brussels).

5. *Ende gut und alles gut.* violin, soprano, continuo. 27th Sunday after Trinity. Parts MS. (Nicolaikirchenarchiv, Luckau).

6. *Erschrick mein Hertz von dir.* 14th Sunday after Trinity. 2 violins, violetta, bass solo, soprano, alto, tenor, bass, organ. Parts MS. (Musikbibliothek, Leipzig).

7. *Es steh Gott auf.* Ad festum Paschatos, *a* 13. 2 clarini, tamburi, 2 violas, 3 trombones, 2 sopranos, alto, tenor, bass, 5 voci in ripieno, continuo. Parts MS. (Doubtful) (Sächsische Landesbibliothek, Dresden).

8. *Frohlocket ihr Volker und jauchzet ihr Heiden.* 4 voci, 3 clarini, timpani, 3 violins, organ. (Staats-und Universitätsbibliothek, Hamburg).

9. *Gott der Vater, Jesus Christus, der heil'ge Geist wohn uns bey a* 10. oboe or tromba da tirarsi, 2 violins, viola, soprano, alto, tenor, bass, continuo. Full score MS. (Staatsbibliothek, Berlin).

10. *Gott sei mir gnädig nach deiner Güte a* 9. 2 violins, 2 violas, bassoon, soprano, alto, tenor, bass, 4 voci in Ripieno, continuo. Parts MS. (Sächsische Landesbibliothek, Dresden). Quinquagesima 1705, Sexagesima 1716, Misericordia 1722.

11. *Ich freue mich im Herrn und meine Seele ist fröhlich. Isaiah 61:10.* Second Sunday after Epiphany; 20th Sunday after Trinity. 2 violins, viola, soprano, alto, tenor, bass, continuo. Parts MS. (Sächsische Landesbibliothek, Dresden).

12. *Ich habe Lust abzuscheiden.* Feast of the Purification of Mary, *a* 9 voci. oboe, 2 violins, viola, bassoon, violoncello, soprano, alto, tenor, bass, 4 voci in ripieno, continuo. (Doubtful and MS now lost).

13. *Ich hebe meine Augen auff.* Psalm 120. alto solo, 2 violins, violono, organ. Parts MS. (Doubtful) (Musikbibliothek, Leipzig).

14. *Ihr Himmel jubilirt von oben.* For Ascension Day. 3 clarini, timpani, 2 violins, 2 violas, 2 flauti, 2 sopranos, alto, tenor, bass, continuo. Full score MS. (Musikbibliothek, Leipzig). (Example 1).

15. *Lobe den Herrn meine Seele. a* 6. oboe (Anglois), violin, alto, bass, organ. Parts MS. (Sächsische Landesbibliothek, Dresden).

16. *Lobe den Herrn meine Seele, a 15.* 2 violins, 2 violas, bassoon, 2 cornetti, 3 trombones, 2 sopranos, alto, tenor, bass, continuo. Full score MS. (Staatsbibliothek, Berlin).

17. *Lobet, ihr Himmel, den Herrn.* Feast of the Ascension of Christ, *a* 12. 2 clarini, timpani, 2 oboes, 2 violins, viola, soprano, alto, tenor, bass, organ. Full score MS. (Staatsbibliothek, Berlin).

18. *Mein Alter kommt, ich kann nicht sterben, a 10.* 2 violins, 2 violas, bassoon, 2 sopranos, alto, tenor, bass, continuo. Parts MS. (Sächsische Landesbibliothek, Dresden).

19. *Muss nicht der Mensch auf dieser Erden.* tenor solo, clarino, violin, bassoon, organ. Parts MS. (Nikolaikirchenarchiv, Luckau).

20. *Nicht nur allein am frohen Morgen.* For Second Christmas Day. 2 clarini, timpani, 2 violins, viola, corni, soprano, alto, tenor, bass, continuo. Full score MS. (Musikbibliothek, Leipzig).

21. *O heilige Zeit, wo Himmel, Erd und Lufft.* 2 violins, 2 violas, soprano, alto, tenor, bass, continuo. Full score MS. (Staatsbibliothek, Berlin).

22. *O heilige Zeit, wo Himmel, Erd und Lufft.* soprano, bass, 2 oboes, 2 violins, viola, continuo. Full score MS. (Doubtful) (Musikbibliothek, Leipzig).

23. *Schmücket das Fest mit Meyen.* 2 violins concertati, 2 violins ripieni, 2 flauti dolci, violetta, soprano, alto, tenor, bass, continuo. Full score MS. (Staatsbibliothek, Berlin).

24. *Singet dem Herrn ein neues Lied.* 2 trombe, timpani, 2 violins, viola, bassoon, soprano, alto, tenor, bass, organ. Full score MS. (Staatsbibliothek, Berlin).

25. *Und ob die Feinde Tag und Nacht.* 23rd Sunday after Trinity. soprano solo, violin, organ. Parts MS. (Musikbibliothek, Leipzig).

26. *Vom Himmel hoch.* 2 clarini, timpani, 2 violins, viola, violoncello, soprano, alto, tenor, bass, continuo. Parts MS. (Musikbibliothek, Leipzig).

27. *Was Gott thut das ist wohlgethan.* oboe, bassoon, 2 violins, viola, soprano, alto, tenor, bass, continuo. Parts MS. (Sächsische Landesbibliothek, Dresden).

28. *Weicht ihr Sorgen aus dem Hertzen.* 7th or 15th Sunday after Trinity. soprano solo, 2 violins, 2 violas, organ. Parts MS. (Nicolaikirchenarchiv, Luckau).

29. *Welt adieu, ich bin dein müde.* 24th Sunday after Trinity. 2 corni, 2 oboes, flauto, 2 violins, 2 violas, 2 sopranos, alto, tenor, bass, continuo. Incomplete parts MS. (Musikbibliothek, Leipzig).

30. *Wenn ihr fröhlich seid an euren Festen.* 5 voci, 5 voci in ripieno, 2 clarini, trombone, principale, tamburi, 2 violins, 2 violas, bassoon, organ. Parts MS. (Sächsische Landesbibliothek, Dresden).

31. *Wie schön leuchtet der Morgenstern.* For Christmas Day. 2 corni grande, 2 violins, 2 violas, 2 sopranos, alto, tenor, bass, continuo. Full score MS. (Staatsbibliothek, Berlin).

One additional work is not present in the above listing. That is the aria-motet written for the funeral of Titius in Zittau in 1681. The title of that work for five voices is *Ach Gott, wie lastu mich erstarren.*

The cantata *Was Gott thut das ist wohlgethan* does not appear in the *MGG* listing of Kuhnau's works. This manuscript was obtained years ago from the Sächsische Landesbibliothek in Dresden. The manuscript copy is in the hand of J. G. Schicht, an early nineteenth-century cantor at the Thomaskirche. Also of note is the fact that *The New Grove Dictionary of Music* (1980) incorrectly states that the *Missa* in Mügeln is lost. There were two Masses originally in that town; one is lost, but the *Mass in F* is still in the church archives. In addition, the cantata *Frohlocket ihr Volker und jauchzet ihr Heiden* is not listed in *The New Grove* but is listed in the new *MGG*.

The Church Cantatas

A. Texts of the Church Cantatas

The majority of church cantatas in the seventeenth and eighteenth centuries existed only in manuscript sources. However, from the beginning of the eighteenth century, texts were published for the use of the congregation. As stated previously, Kuhnau was the first Leipzig composer to have his cantata texts printed for the congregation. The texts were often written by people in the vicinity (theologians, court poets, teachers) or by the composer himself. Many composers made use of the same text compilations. Kuhnau in 1709–10 states that he compiled the texts of only two cantatas for that church year and a friend did the remainder.[8] Altogether, Kuhnau published nine volumes of cantata texts during the years 1707–21. This helps to explain why there are many more cantata texts extant than music manuscripts.

Six different categories of texts of cantatas by Kuhnau may be distinguished: 1) biblical cantatas (chiefly Psalm texts), 2) biblical-ode cantatas (scriptural texts with poetic interpolations), 3) chorale cantatas, 4) cantatas of mixed forms, which include chorale texts with poetic interpolations and texts with chorales appearing at the end of the cantata or at the end of the first part of the cantata, 5) madrigal cantatas (usually poetic paraphrases of the assigned Gospel text, and 6) extant Latin cantatas.

1. Biblical Cantatas
   a. *Singet dem Herrn ein neues Lied.* Psalm 98.
   b. *Lobe den Herrn meine Seele* (choir and soloists). Psalm 103:1–10.
   c. *Lobe den Herrn meine Seele* (alto and bass soloists). Psalm 103:1–10.
   d. *Ich hebe meine Augen auff.* Psalm 121. Now considered doubtful.
   e. *Gott, sie mir gnädig nach deiner Güte.* Psalm 51:1–8.

2. Biblical-ode Cantatas
   a. *Ach Herr, wie sind meine Feinde so viel.* Psalm 3:1–9. Two aria duets use free poetry.
   b. *Daran erkennen wir.* I John 4:13. Solos use lyrical poetry.
   c. *Das Alte ist vergangen.* II. Cor. 5:17, Galatians 3:27, Isaiah 26:8, Luke 10:20.
   d. *Es steh Gott auff.* Psalm 68:2. Solos use lyrical poetry. Now considered doubtful.
   e. *Ich freue mich in Herrn und meine Seele ist fröhlich.* Isaiah 61:10. Solos use lyrical poetry.
   f. *Lobet ihr Himmel den Herrn.* Psalm 148:1,2, Psalm 150:6, Psalm 47:6, II Timothy 2:3. Solos use lyrical poetry. Also has closing chorale (Stanza 3 of *Herzlich lieb hab' ich dich, O Herr*).
   g. *Muss nicht der Mensch auf dieser Erden.* Job 7: 1. After first arioso, remainder of cantata uses lyrical poetry.

h. *Schmücket das Fest mit Meyen.* Psalm 118:27, Song of Solomon 4: 17, Song of Solomon 2:10–12, John 14:23, Song of Solomon 2:8 and 5:2, II Cor. 4:6. Closing chorale a paraphrase of Verse 3 of *Wie schön leuchtet der Morgenstern.*

3. Chorale Cantatas

   a. *Gott der Vater.* Chorale by Luther.

   b. *Was Gott thut, das ist wohlgethan.* Chorale of six verses by Samuel Rodigast.

   c. *Welt adieu.* Chorale of seven stanzas by Johann G. Albinus.

4. Mixed-form Cantatas

(Chorale Texts with Poetic Interpolations)

   a. *Christ lag in Todesbanden.* The opening chorus uses stanza 1 of the chorale. The following chorus and solo portions are in madrigal poetry. The closing chorus returns to stanza 6 of the chorale.

   b. *Vom Himmel hoch.* Four chorale choruses make up this work: *Vom Himmel hoch, Freut euch und jubiliert, Gloria in excelsis,* and *Virga Jesse floruit.* These choruses were most probably meant to be inserted in the *Magnificat* just as Bach had indicated in the earlier of the two extant manuscripts of his *Magnificat.* This tradition of inserting German chorales or other Latin texts between the verses of the *Magnificat* goes back at least to Praetorius.

   c. *Wie schön leuchtet der Morgenstern.* Chorale by Phillip Nicolai. First chorus text is stanza 1 of the chorale; second chorus is based on Isaiah 9:6; and the final chorus uses stanza 6 of the chorale. The solos use madrigal poetry.

(Cantata Texts with Closing or Mid-point Chorales)

   a. *Ich habe Lust abzuscheiden.* First chorus uses Philippians 1:23; second chorus uses I Kings 19:4; and third chorus uses Revelation 14: 13. Solos use madrigal poetry. Closing chorus is stanza 1 of Luther's *Mit Fried und Freud ich fahr dahin.*

   b. *Nicht nur allein am frohen Morgen.* Free poetical text except for the final chorus which uses stanza 4 of Luther's *Gelobet seist du, Jesu Christ.*

5. Madrigal Cantata Texts:
   a. *Ende gut und alles gut.* Text by Erdmann Neumeister in his *Fünffache Kirchen-Andachten* of 1716.
   b. *Erschrick mein Hertz vor dir.* Author unknown.
   c. *Ihr Himmel jubilirt von oben.* Author unknown.
   d. *Mein Alter kommt.* Author unknown.
   e. *O heilige Zeit.* Text by Erdmann Neumeister in his *Fünffache Kirchen-Andachten* of 1716.
   f. *Und ob die Feinde.* Text by Erdmann Neumeister in his *Fünffache Kirchen-Andachten* of 1716.
   g. *Weicht ihr Sorgen aus den Hertzen.* Text by Erdmann Neumeister in his *Fünffache Kirchen-Andachten* of 1716.
   h. *Wenn ihr fröhlich seid an euren Festen.* Author unknown.
6. Extant Latin Cantatas:
   a. *Bone Jesu, chare Jesu, ne me tu desere.* Author unknown.
   b. *In te domine.* Psalm 31:1–6.
   c. *Laudate pueri.* Psalm 113.

B. Musical Style of the Church Cantatas

The predominant stylistic feature exhibited in all the church cantatas is that of concertato. Contrast was pre-eminent: contrast between voices and instruments, solo voices and choirs, low and high voices, string instruments and brass, homophonic texture and contrapuntal texture, soli and tutti, statement and echo, voice and continuo, recitative and aria, forte and piano, allegro and adagio.

Three types of movements are found in the cantatas: choral movements, solo movements, and instrumental movements. In choral movements four styles are used: 1) concerto, 2) fugue, 3) chorale prelude, and 4) cantional. The concerto style was most prominent. The cantional (simple chordal style) was least important.

Five styles are found in the solo movements: 1) solo concerto, 2) song (*Strophen-lied*), 3) recitative, 4) arioso, and 5) aria. The solo concerto was marked by irregular phrases, a variety of note values, changing meters, melismas, musical rhetorical figures, and faithfulness to the grammatical accent of the text. Some movements in song style are often designated "aria." However, these so-called "arias" are more like stanzas of a strophic song. The emphasis is on the rhymed meter of the text. It is characterized by its tunefulness, continuous melody, regular phrases, and little use of repetition or imitation. All solo movements in cantatas before 1680 are solo concertos; later they are in song style. The recitative form was first used by the Kriegers in Nuremberg and Kuhnau in Leipzig. The arioso, often characterized by a walking bass line, had only continuo accompaniment. Pachelbel and the Kriegers were the first Nuremberger composers to write da capo arias. Kuhnau was the first Leipzig church composer to do so.

Instrumental movements include the opening sinfonias or sonatas and ritornellos. Some sinfonias are like the Venetian opera overture, with a chordal *grave* section followed by a lively contrapuntal section. Ritornellos are usually contrapuntal and lively.

Instrumental accompaniment may be *per chorus*, that is, a series of alternating instrumental and vocal blocks; it may double the vocal parts, it may follow an obbligato scheme, or it may present a harmonic background.

Choral movements in the cantatas make use of the four different styles mentioned above. The final movement of the solo cantata for bass, *Erschrick mein Hertz vor dir*, ends with a four-voice chorus in cantional style broken by solo passages for soprano and alto. The solo cantata for tenor, *Mein Alter kommt,* also has a closing chorus, but with a five-voice choral opening in homophonic style before proceeding to a central fugal section; it ends with a return to the homophonic section. A number of Kuhnau's choruses form this kind of da capo or ABA form (e.g., the first chorus of the cantata *Christ lag in Todesbanden, "Alleluia es ist Victoria"*). The final chorus of this same cantata is similar to a choral prelude with points of imitation at the beginning of each phrase, and then the chorale is treated in homophonic style.

Often choruses will show a mixture of homophonic and fugal styles, as, for example, the first chorus of *Das Alte ist vergangen*. The second chorus of this same cantata is a true fugue without any homophonic sections. It contains two complete expositions of its fugal subject. The following two choruses in *Das Alte ist vergangen* are in strict cantional style, while the final chorus is like the first with its mixture of homophonic and fugal writing. The most extended fugue in all the extant cantatas is the final chorus of *Wenn ihr fröhlich*.

Example 1. Beginning of *Ihr Himmel jubilirt von oben.* (Ms. reads: In Nomine Jesu. M. April 1717. In Fest. Ascens. Domini. Johann Kuhnau.)

A practice Buxtehude and others followed is found in the Easter cantata *Es steh Gott auf*, in *Lobe den Herrn* (the five-voice setting), and in *Was Gott thut*. The opening sonata and chorus are repeated at the end of the cantata.

Closing chorales appear in four cantatas. A chorale in four-voice cantional style concludes the cantata *Ich habe Lust abzuscheiden*. It is Luther's chorale *Mit Fried und Freud ich fahr dahin*. The continuo accompanies the simple chordal setting in steadily moving eighth-notes. The Ascension Day cantata *Lobet ihr Himmel* closes with stanza 3 of Schalling's *Herzlich lieb ich dich, o Herr*. The continuo accompanies in steadily moving eighth-notes, while the oboes and strings present short interludes between each phrase of the chorale. The fourth stanza of Luther's chorale *Gelobet seist du, Jesu Christ* concludes the Christmas cantata *Nicht nur allein am frohen Morgen*. Again Kuhnau writes the continuo part in constant moving eighth-notes, while the chorale melody proceeds in half-notes. A secular paraphrase of the chorale *Wie schön leuchtet der Morgenstern* closes the wedding cantata *Schmücket das Fest mit Meyen*. The textual paraphrase turns the chorale into a love song. Strings double the voice parts, while solo violins have an obbligato part with bustling sixteenth-notes. Instrumental interludes separate the chorale phrases.

Kuhnau wrote both secco recitatives and accompanied recitatives. Sometimes the solos contain elements of both aria and recitative, as, for example, the first bass solo in *Ach Herr, wie sind meiner Feinde*. There are also examples of a solo combining *recitativo secco* and *recitativo accompagnato* styles, as in several recitatives in the bass solo cantata *Erschrick mein Hertz vor dir*. An early solo cantata for tenor, *Mein Alter kommt*, has recitatives that are more extended in length than in any other cantata. In general, recitatives tend to be more important in the solo cantatas than in the choral cantatas. This is in contrast to the very short recitatives in the choral cantata *Schmücket das Fest mit Meyen*—for example, the four-measure soprano recitative "*Mein Freund komme in seinen Garten.*"

Usually recitatives separate arias, but, in one case at least, two recitatives follow one another without an interruption. In the wedding cantata mentioned above (*Schmücket das Fest mit Meyen*) an unaccompanied recitative for soprano is followed by an unaccompanied recitative for bass.

Kuhnau's arias fall mainly into two categories: the *Strophenlied* (i.e., a stanza from a strophic song) and the da capo aria. He was one of the first German composers to use da capo arias in his church cantatas and the very first Leipzig composer to do so.

The instrumental accompaniment to the arias will often feature a concertizing solo instrument that carries a repeated motive throughout the aria. One good example is the *wiegen* (rocking) motive in the alto aria, *"Klingt ihr Sterbeglokken"* from *Ich habe Lust abzuscheiden.*

The instrumental introductions to arias will most frequently present the main theme of the vocal line. On the other hand, the material presented in the introduction is used in ritornelli several times during the aria and at the close and may bear no relation to the soloist's material (e.g., the final aria in *Ende gut und alles gut*). There are also some arias that begin without any introduction whatsoever (e.g., *Ich hebe meine Augen auff*).

Kuhnau's da capo arias are not elaborate but are really miniatures of this vocal form. If Section A is in a minor key, Section B will modulate to the relative major key. Like the Italian cantata composers, Kuhnau favors the 3/2 meter for his arias. There are a few examples of 6/8 siciliano rhythm being used in arias. One such example is *"Wir haben die reinen und seeligen Lehren"* from the cantata *Und ob die Feinde*. A few arias contain coloratura passages (e.g., the opening aria in *Ich hebe meine Augen auff*).

Examples of strophic arias are found in the early cantatas, such as the tenor solo cantata *Muss nicht der Mensch*, in which two verses of a strophic song are separated by a recitative. A good example of the old *Strophenlied* form is also found in the cantata *Christ lag in Todesbanden*. Here the soloists sing the different stanzas of the Easter chorale or paraphrases of the chorale.

In the cantata *Lobet ihr Himmel* a larger da capo form is created by oboe and soprano. An oboe solo precedes and follows a soprano aria, *"Kommt ihr Engel,"* thus creating a large da capo form of oboe solo, soprano solo, and oboe solo.

The arias abound in examples of text painting. The cantata *Singet dem Herren*, a setting of Psalm 98, offers a colorful text, especially in the bass solo with 'Drommeten und Posaunen... das Meer brause ... die Wasser ströme froh locken.' Much of the text painting is the type that the Germans call *Augenmusik* (eye music). Examine, for example, the falling tears (*'mit Wehmuts Thränen fliessen'*) in the alto aria *"Ach denk ich zwar mein liebster Jesu"* from the cantata *O heilige Zeit* (Example 2). An expressive coloratura passage is used to portray the word *schmertzen* (grieve) in the soprano aria from *Weicht ihr Sorgen* and also later in the aria *"Mein Hoffen und mein Sehnen"* there is an expressive setting of the word *Sehnen* (longing).

Example 2. Alto Aria, *"Ach denk ich zwar mein liebster Jesu,"* in Cantata *O heilige Zeit*, mm. 16–19.

Violins, flutes, and oboes are the favorite concertizing instruments used in arias. More rare are clarini, which are used in a number of "triumph" arias. The final bass solo in the cantata *Es steh Gott auff*, *"Wolan er lebt . . . er triumphirt,"* is one example which calls for two clarini and continuo.

Instrumental sonatas open sixteen of the extant cantatas. Often they begin with a slow, stately section and conclude with an allegro section; sometimes this latter section is in fugal style. One of the opening sonatas is in the style of a chorale prelude (*Gott der Vater*). Other cantatas will begin with several measures of instrumental introduction leading directly into the first chorus or aria.

Kuhnau created the basic structure of the church cantata as used by Bach in his Leipzig years. He defined the role of the recitative and aria and freed the melody of the old *Strophenlied* so that in the new da capo aria it became a more flowing, lyrical outpouring of song. He was the first Leipzig composer to use the da capo aria form in the church cantata. Although Kuhnau criticized the recitative and da capo aria for having secularizing effects upon church music, it was he who gave them a secure position in the Leipzig church cantata. He also initiated the tradition in Leipzig of closing a cantata with a chorale.

Before leaving the subject of the German church cantatas, a few words must be said about the lost Passion. Kuhnau wrote one setting of the Passion story, that according to St. Mark. Only a sketch of the *St. Mark Passion* was said to exist in the early part of the twentieth century in a copy made by Burgermeister in 1729. This manuscript was in the university library in Königsberg, Prussia, and during World War II Königsberg was heavily bombed and the university destroyed. After the war Königsberg became Kaliningrad and a part of the Soviet Union. It still belongs to Russia today.

The text of the *Markus Passion* came from the fourteenth and fifteenth chapters of the Gospel of Mark. The work was in two parts and called for numerous soloists, including an Evangelist and choir. Chorales and lyrical meditations in the form of arias, duets, and trios appeared throughout. There were a total of twenty arias and nineteen chorales. The work opened with an instrumental sonata and the old invitation "*Höret an das Leiden....*" The choral movements were short and only comprised a few measures most of the time. It was first performed on Good Friday 1721 and repeated the following year on Good Friday at the newly established Vespers service in the Thomaskirche.[9]

The Latin Works

After the Protestant Reformation in some regions of southern Germany, the Latin order of worship was completely suppressed by the end of the sixteenth century. In other regions, especially Leipzig and Nuremberg, it was preserved up into the eighteenth century. The Kyrie, the Gloria, sometimes the Credo and the Sanctus, the Magnificat, some Vesper hymns, and occasionally even an Introit in Latin, continued to be composed into the eighteenth century—here and there, even into the nineteenth century.[10] There is hardly anyone among the Lutheran musicians of the later seventeenth century who did not occasionally write a Latin Mass, a Magnificat, or a couple of Latin songs, hymns, or responsories.[11]

The Magnificat

The Latin liturgical song continuously held in high esteem and widely distributed was the Magnificat. Georg Rhau, the prominent music publisher of the Reformation era, published Latin Magnificats organized either for the seven days of the week or according to *de tempore*. Within these collections of Magnificats, the arrangement was according to the succession of church modes. The number of Protestant Magnificats exceeds that of all categories of

Latin liturgical texts. Among the more prominent Lutheran composers of Magnificats are Leonhard Lechner, Andreas Raselius, Erhard Bodenschatz, Christoph Demantius, Hieronymous Praetorius, Melchior Vulpius, Bartholomäus Gesius, and Michael Praetorius.

Orlande de Lassus, with his collection *Magnificat octo tonorum* (1567), became the authorative figure for Magnificat composers to follow. The first verse was intoned to a Psalm tone. This was followed by the alternation of verses in plainsong and polyphony. Either the even-numbered verses or the odd-numbered verses were set polyphonically.[12]

Another form of Magnificat composition was the through-composed setting of the entire text, including the introduction and *Gloria Patri*. In almost all cases the formula of one of the Psalm tones formed the musical foundation. The completely free compositional style of Magnificats appeared with the concertato style about 1620. These were written for either small or large ensembles.

Beginnings of the concertato sectional construction are seen in the Magnificats of Monteverdi's *Vespers* of 1610. The *Magnificat* of Schütz (SWV 468) is a notable example of this sectional style.

As the Baroque period progressed, this concertato sectional style gradually evolved into a sequence of self-contained numbers (arias, choruses, etc.). The most important contribution to the catalogue of early German Baroque Magnificats was by Michael Praetorius. His *Megalynodia Sionia* of 1611 contains fourteen Magnificats, eleven of which are motet, madrigal, and chanson parodies, and three of which are evidently original compositions. Inserted into the first two Magnificats are German Christmas songs and into the third one, German Easter songs. This custom prevailed until the first setting of J. S. Bach's *Magnificat* (BWV 243a).[13] These insertions may also be found in the Magnificats of Gesius and Kuhnau.

It is interesting to note that the German Magnificat gained favor beginning about 1600. One masterful example of this is in Melchior Franck's *Laudes Dei Vespertinae* (1622). Neither German nor Latin Magnificats supplanted the other.

Later German Baroque composers continued to set the Latin text. Here we can list Schütz, Schein, Buxtehude, Johann Philip Krieger, Kuhnau, J. S. Bach, and Telemann.

The *Magnificat* of Kuhnau is his largest extant vocal work. It calls for four soloists, a five-voice choir, and a festival orchestra of three clarini, timpani, two oboes, two violins, two violas, and continuo. The manuscript in the Deutsche Staatsbibliothek in Berlin is the only known source of this work. The manuscript is a full score in the hand of Gottfried Heinrich Stölzel, who was the Hofkapellmeister in Gotha and composer of numerous cantatas and other works. The manuscript bears no date. There is no indication of the occasion for which the *Magnificat* was written, although it may have been composed for the Christmas season, especially since Kuhnau's so-called cantata *Vom Himmel hoch* contains the four choruses traditionally inserted into the Magnificat. It is probably a late work of the composer, and it contains some of his best vocal writing.

After a brief, twelve-measure instrumental introduction, solo voices state the first phrase of the opening chorus (the single word '*Magnificat*'). Then the tutti chorus repeats the opening phrase. The remainder of the text of the first chorus is treated homophonically. A da capo of the opening instrumental section appears at the end of the chorus. The second chorus ("*Quia fecit*") opens with a short fugato. The fugal writing is of short duration, and by the time all the voices have entered, the fugato comes to an end. The middle chorus ("*Fecit potentiam*") opens with a short brass fanfare creating a martial atmosphere that expressively portrays the meaning of the text. A fugato opens the chorus "*Sicut locutus*" as well as the final chorus "*Sicut erat.*" Here again, there is alternation of solo and tutti sections—the solo voices indicated at the opening of the fugato. Kuhnau's facility in writing double counterpoint is exhibited in this final chorus.

The first soprano aria, "*Et exultavit,*" has a flowing siciliano rhythm. It is a motto aria with a da capo of the nine-measure instrumental introduction occurring at the close. This plan of instrumental introduction and da capo is followed in the two tenor arias, "*Et misericordia ejus*" and "*Suscepit Israel.*" On the other hand, the alto aria, "*Quia respexit,*" has no instrumental introduction, no motto beginning, and no da capo form. Here, the voice enters after one downbeat chord in the strings and proceeds with some use of melodic sequence in through-composed style.

The duet for soprano and bass, "*Deposuit,*" illustrates Kuhnau's imitative treatment of the two solo voices as well as some typical text painting on the word '*deposuit.*' The duet for soprano and alto,

"*Esurientes,*" that follows the "*Deposuit*" without pause uses the accompanying strings in ritornello fashion.

Kuhnau's setting of the "*Gloria Patri*" is unique in that it makes use of both soloist and chorus. Whereas in most Baroque settings the full chorus sings the entire *Gloria Patri, Gloria Filio, Gloria Spiritui* text, here the composer writes a setting of these words for bass solo; the chorus does not enter until the words 'Sicut erat.' Kuhnau may have been influenced by Johann Krieger's *Magnificat* of 1685 that has the same arrangement.[14]

Originally, a performance of Kuhnau's *Magnificat* would have included the insertion of the four choruses from the so-called cantata *Vom Himmel hoch.* As noted earlier, this work contains four Christmas hymns: *Vom Himmel hoch, Freut euch und jubiliert, Gloria in excelsis,* and *Virga Jesse floruit.* These four choruses are textually the same as the four choruses Bach had originally included in his *Magnificat* (BWV 243a) of 1723. The four choruses of *Vom Himmel hoch* are all in the key of C major, the key of the Kuhnau *Magnificat,* and could well be inserted between certain movements, as in the Rheinische Kantorei recording cited earlier.

It is interesting to compare Kuhnau's setting of the Magnificat with one of Johann Krieger's many *Magnificats* and Bach's *Magnificat.* It is quite possible that each composer knew about the existence of at least one of these settings besides his own. The earliest of these settings is the one written by Johann Philip Krieger in 1685. Four sections of the text are set for chorus: "*Magnificat,*" "*Fecit potentiam,*" "*Sicut locutus,*" and "*Sicut erat.*" The remaining verses are set for solo voices, including a trio ("*Deposuit*") and a duo ("*Suscepit*"). Kuhnau's *Magnificat,* written sometime after Krieger's, shows great similarity to it in its distribution of choruses and arias. With one exception, an additional chorus for the verse beginning "*Quia fecit,*" he sets the same textual portions for chorus as Krieger did.

Bach's *Magnificat* (BWV 243a), written in 1723, shows similarity to Kuhnau's setting, and hence also to Krieger's, in its choice of choruses and arias. He has five choruses, just as Kuhnau did, but his second chorus uses the "*Omnes generations*" text instead of the "*Quia fecit*" text. Bach sets the "*Quia fecit*" for bass solo. Moreover, Bach sets the entire "*Gloria Patri*" text for chorus, whereas Kuhnau sets only the second portion ("*Sicut erat*") for chorus. Thus we can deduce that Kuhnau was most probably acquainted with and influenced by Krieger's *Magnificat* and Bach with Kuhnau's *Magnificat.*

Latin Cantatas

The first three Latin cantatas listed in the catalogue of vocal works are sacred cantatas. *Bone Jesu, chare Jesu, ne me tu desere* is a soprano solo cantata with accompaniment of two violins and continuo. *In te Domine speravi* is a setting of Psalm 31 and was written for the Twenty-third Sunday after Trinity. It calls for solo voice, two violins, two violas, bassoon, and continuo. *Laudate pueri* is a cantata for tenor solo with two violins, trombone or viola da gamba, and continuo. It is a setting of Psalm 113. Taking a look at the last-named cantata, we see that the first three verses of the Psalm text are treated in arias with some coloratura passages on expressive words such as *'excelsis'* and *'gloria.'* It is not until verses five and six that we have two accompanied recitatives. The final two verses of the Psalm are again treated in an aria. The cantata ends with a festive "Alleluia" aria.

The one extant secular chamber cantata by Kuhnau is *Spirate clementes, O Zephyri amici* (Blow gently, O zephyrs, friends). It is written for two sopranos and bass accompanied by two violins and continuo. An interesting feature of this cantata is a duet for first soprano and bass over a ground bass. This is the only example we have of Kuhnau writing an aria on a ground bass. The four-measure bass theme is repeated fifteen times. Its *'lamento'* (chromatic) descending theme is a very fitting setting for the text: "Ye sad waves, ye deep floods, ye seas and fountains that flow to the nations; do not be niggardly, rather extinguish the torch of my love and give peace back to my grieving heart."

Masses

As stated earlier, there is hardly any Lutheran musician who did not occasionally write a Latin Mass. According to Albert Schering's listing of Kuhnau vocal works in *DdT,* Bd. 58/59, which dates from the early twentieth century, there were two manuscripts of Masses extant: a *Missa* MS of full score and parts in the church in Mylau and a *Missa a 4* in the church archives in Mügeln. *MGG* lists two Masses for the town of Mügeln, one of them now lost. Attempts at securing any of these Masses during the Communist DDR days proved unsuccessful. With the re-unification of Germany and the advent of the Internet, it was recently possible to obtain a photocopy of the one extant *Mass* from Mügeln. The *Mass* originally in Mylau is also now lost. It is interesting to note that the Stadtkirche in Mylau has in its archives a *Tablaturbuch* from around 1730 that contains some organ pieces by Kuhnau. The Mylau church is the proud owner of a Silbermann organ.

The Mügeln *Mass* is a *Kurzmesse* (short mass) containing just the Kyrie and Gloria. Short two-movement Masses consisting of Kyrie and Gloria, seldom with Credo or Sanctus, were written either in concerto style or in the older polyphonic style. The use of these short Masses may have been brought about by the separation of the sermon from the celebration of Holy Communion and the substitution of the Credo by the creed chorale (*Wir glauben all*). Even so, there was no specific Lutheran type of Mass composition. Eight of the ten Masses in Gesius' *Missae ad imitationen cantionum Orlandi* (1611) are short Masses. In contrast, one finds in Hieronymus Praetorius's *Liber missarum* (1616) complete Mass compositions in Hamburg. The same happens in the eastern part of Saxony in Masses by Jacob Schedlich and Christoph Demantius. In another part of Saxony we have composers Stephan Otto, Andreas Hammerschmidt, and J. Jeuschel writing three-movement Masses consisting of Kyrie, Gloria, and Sanctus.

Early in the seventeenth century a special development can be found in Michael Praetorius's *Polyhymnia caducciatrix* (1619), in which two German Masses call for polychoral forces and independent instrumental parts. Samuel Scheidt and Thomas Selle undertook the development of this type of Mass composition. This style culminated in the Masses of Johann Rosenmüller. In the Austrian-South German area a type of concerto Mass for few solo voices was developed by Andreas Rauch in his solo concerto Masses that were composed in an expressive monodic style.[15]

In the latter part of the seventeenth century most of the Protestant Masses were short Masses. Among the most important composers in this genre are Sebastian Knüpfer, Christoph Bernhard, Johann Theile, Friedrich Zachow, and Johann Philipp Krieger. However, in larger churches Masses in the old contrapuntal style were performed along with those in the brilliant style of the concerto for large ensemble. Johann Philipp Krieger is said to have composed more than a hundred Masses and Mass settings of all kinds and lengths, culminating in his festive *Mass* for fifty-eight voices in Roman style, written for the dedication of the chapel at the castle of Weissenfels (1682).[16] Nothing of this composition has survived.

Turning to Kuhnau's *Mass in F*, we find that it is a solo Mass for bass voice with the accompaniment of two violins, viola, bassoon (French bassoon in B-flat), and continuo. (As noted

Example 3. Kyrie from *Mass in F* for 2 violins, viola, vocal bass solo, and continuo (bassoon and organ).

previously, *The New Grove* (1980) states, incorrectly, that this *Mass* is lost.) The *Mass* opens with the *"Kyrie eleison"* section in duple meter without any instrumental introduction (Example 3). There is an inconsistent treatment of the word *'eleison.'* Sometimes it is broken up into four syllables, i.e., *e-le-i-son*; sometimes it is divided into three syllables, i.e., *e-lei-son*. The *"Christe eleison"* is set in 3/2 meter and modulates to the dominant key of C major. The *"Kyrie"* is indeed a short movement—the *"Kyrie eleison"* section is just thirteen measures in length; the *"Christe eleison"* section is sixteen measures long.

The *"Gloria"* returns to F major and begins with the setting of the words, *'Et in terra pax,'* in duple meter accompanied by the strings, which have repeated sixteenth-notes. The words *'in terra pax'* are repeated many times. The next section of the *"Gloria"* is in the relative key of D minor and begins with the words *'Gratias agimus.'* *"Domine Deus rex coelestis"* returns briefly to F major. It is in duple meter and quicky modulates to D minor and then G minor. Again, the voice is accompanied by strings in sixteenth-notes in a broken-chord pattern. The *"Qui tollis"* section in B-flat major has a pulsing eighth-note rhythm in the continuo part. This brings us to the last major section of the *"Gloria,"* the *"Quoniam tu solus"* section, which returns to triple 3/2 meter and the key of F major. The *"Amen"* returns to duple meter.

This rather simple setting of the short *Mass* seems to have been an early work of Kuhnau. The writing for both voices and instruments is not demanding and is mainly in homophonic style.

In conclusion, although the majority of Kuhnau's vocal works have been lost, the few that are extant show him to be a talented composer caught in the middle of two worlds of church music—the old traditional style of the seventeenth century and the new operatic style of the eighteenth century. Although he criticized the influences of the operatic style on church music, he did incorporate recitatives and da capo arias into his mature cantata compositions. In his interest in expounding the Word, he began the practice of printing the texts of his cantatas for the congregation. As a theologian, as a linguist, as a poet, as a writer, as well as a musician, he was truly a Renaissance man living in the Baroque era.

Addendum

Since writing this essay, it has come to my attention that Roberrt King of The King's Consort in London has produced a number of performing editions of Kuhnau cantatas. These are available only online from The King's Consort.[17]

NOTES

1 John Butt, "Sacred Music by Johann Kuhnau," line notes on Hyperion CDA67059, p. 7.

2 Richard Münnich, *"Kuhnau's Leben," Sammelbände der Internationalen Musikgesellschaft* (1901/1902), 505.

3 Arnold Schering, "Johann Kuhnau," *Denkmäler deutscher Tonkunst,* Bd. 58/59, xli.

4 Münnich, 515.

5 Johann Mattheson, *Grundlage einer Ehren-Pforte* (Hamburg, 1740), 359.

6 Ibid., 159.

7 Jacob Adlung, *Anleitung zu der musikalischen Gelahrheit* (Erfurt, 1758), 195.

8 Berhard F. Richter, *"Eine Abhandlung Johann Kuhnau's," Monatshefte für Musik-Geschichte,* XXXIV (1902), 147.

9 Friedrich Blume et al., *Protestant Church Music: A History* (New York: Norton, 1974), 303.

10 Ibid., 234.

11 Ibid., 235.

12 Ibid., 177.

13 Ibid.

14 See *DdT, 1 Folge,* Bd 53/54, 16-23.

15 Peter Ackermann, *"Messe,"* in *Musik in Geschichte und Gegenwart,* Sachteil, BD. 6, 209-10.

16 Arnold Schering, *Musikgeschichte Leipzigs* (Leipzig, 1926), Zweiter Band, 24.

17 The following cantatas are available in Robert King's performing editions: *Gott, sei mir gnädig nach deiner Güte; Ihr Himmel jubiliert von oben; O heilige Zeit; Weicht ihr Sorgen aus dem Hertzen;* and *Wie schön leuchtet der Morgenstern.* King has also produced his own performing edition of Kuhnau's *Magnificat* (The King's Consort, 34 St. Mary's Grove, Chiswick, London W4 3LN; www.tkcworld.com).

CHRISTOPH WOLFF

Bible and Hymnal in Johann Sebastian Bach's Music: A Commentary on Three Cantata Movements

One of the most influential and long-term achievements of the sixteenth-century Lutheran Reformation was the creation of a most meaningful and inseparable pair of books: Bible and hymnal. Putting these companions in the hands of the people changed forever the practice of worshippers as well as Christian culture in general. People could now read the Holy Scripture in the vernacular and sing hymns at church or at home, both for spiritual edification and in praise of God.

The first hymnals from Wittenberg and Erfurt, the so-called *Achtliederbuch* of 1523–24 and the *Enchiridion* of 1524, were extremely modest in size, containing no more than eight and twenty-six hymns, respectively. However, they initiated a movement that for a long time could hardly keep pace with the rapidly increasing practice of congregational singing and the fast growing production of lyrics in order to meet an unprecedented demand. By 1600, the numerous regional hymnals that sprung up had grown to a size of several hundred songs—"chorales" in Lutheran terminology. They presented a repertoire ranging from translations of early medieval hymns such as *Nun komm der Heiden Heiland*, Martin Luther's poetic translation of the Ambrosian hymn *Veni redemptor gentium*, to other genres and categories like catechism and didactic chorales, narrative hymns (on the Passion of Christ and other biblical stories), songs for special occasions (weddings, funerals), chorales on the conduct of Christian life, and so forth.

For a long time to come, the hymnal along with the Bible supplied Protestant composers with enormously rich and varied resources. While the hymnbooks provided melodies and poetry, the Bible offered exclusively text, and mainly prose. Within the scripture, key verses from the New Testament became particularly important as they offered manifold possibilities for musically underscoring the central message in the prescribed Epistle and Gospel for the Sundays and festivals of the ecclesiastical year. These were usually called *Kernsprüche* (core verses) or *Kraft- und Saftsprüche* (powerful and juicy verses) and provided the basis for innumerable polyphonic motets, often gathered and published in anthologies or cyclical collections for use throughout the year. Luther himself had argued that "*Deus praedicavit evangelium etiam per musicam*" (God preaches the Gospel also through music.)[1] and thereby firmly established one of the fundamental principles of Protestant church music.

Despite the inevitable liturgical pairing of Bible and hymnal and their general complementary relationship, the use of and emphasis on the two varies a great deal among composers. Heinrich Schütz, for example, rarely based his compositions on chorale texts or melodies. His *Musikalische Exequien* of 1637 is one of his works that includes chorales. On the other hand, Schütz made particularly extensive use of biblical texts of various kinds. His contemporaries, Johann Hermann Schein and Samuel Scheidt, however, turned much more frequently to the hymnal than to the Bible. Then, roughly a century later, Johann Sebastian Bach appears on the scene as a composer who balances the two cornerstones of Protestant church music in a manner that has neither precedent nor parallel. His cantatas and other sacred compositions give the role of Bible and hymnal a new meaning, not only because of the volume and unique musical quality of his works devoted to biblical texts and chorales, but also because of the depth of thought and profound theological reflections applied to these compositions.

Bach's genuinely scholarly approach towards both Bible and hymnal is that of a true book man. We are particularly well informed about his theological library, whose inventory has survived[2] and which informs us that he was particularly interested in exegetical literature.[3] Moreover, he possessed three different editions of Martin Luther's complete works, among them the important Altenburg edition of 1661=64. The Thomascantor seems to have frequented book-shops and visited booksellers, and no place offered more and better opportunities than Leipzig, the publishing capital of Germany. Bach apparently attended book auctions, too, as we know from a pertinent note in Bach's own hand, which reads:

These *Teutsche und herrliche Schriffen des seeligen Dr. M. Lutheri* (which stem from the library of the eminent

Wittenberg general superintendent and theologian Dr. Abraham Calov, which he supposedly used to compile his great German Bible; also, after his death they passed into the hands of the equally-eminent theologian Dr. J. F. Mayer), I have acquired at an auction for 10 thlr., anno 1742, in the month of September. | Joh: Sebast: Bach.[4]

The document tells us that Bach was not just interested in the contents of his books but even in their provenance. Of particular importance to him in this case was the fact that he owned the most famous publication of this distinguished author, Calov's three-volume Bible with extensive critical commentary—a work he consulted heavily, as his annotations and marginalia indicate.[5]

Bach also owned a considerable collection of hymnals. However, hymnbooks with melodies were, like the other genuine musical items in his library, not inventoried in his estate catalogue. An exception in this regard is his copy of the most authoritative hymnological source book of his time, Paul Wagner's eight-volume *Gesang-Buch* of 1696, printed without melodies.[6] But while Bach's own copy of this work has never been traced, his exemplar of the hymnal of the Bohemian Brethren, edited by Michael Weisse, in its first German edition of 1538, did survive.[7] Incidentally, the far-ranging selection of Lutheran hymns throughout Bach's sacred works demonstrates that the composer had a clear preference for the older, classic repertoire of chorales. That is, the hymns and hymn melodies from the early sixteenth century through the generation of Paul Gerhardt in the mid-seventeenth century are dominant. Only rarely did Bach make use of more contemporary kinds of hymns.

Bach's regular pre-compositional activity of reading, comparing, and trying to understand and interpret texts becomes immediately evident in his musical treatment of hymns. First and foremost, he shows great respect for his sources, a highly developed sense of textual and literary detail, and a curiosity for background and contextual information. One of the most impressive examples in dealing with biblical text can be seen in his autograph fair copy of the *St. Matthew Passion*—in both external and internal respects. There he consistently wrote the biblical text underlay in red ink, and also switched from Gothic to Latin script for citations from the Old Testament. Musically he differentiated even more strongly, for example, between the general treatment of the Evangelist's recitatives as opposed to the words of Christ (enhanced by the use of string accompaniment) and, within the latter, between plain narrative and more emphatic phrases. Hence, we find highly expressive instrumental underpinnings in the accompaniment to Jesus' reply to Judas' question, "Master, is it I?" when he simply states, "Thou hast said." At this point the string accompaniment does much more than provide harmonic support; its declamatory style reflects the emotional dimension of Christ's deep disappointment about his betrayer. Immediately following this scene, Bach switches to the elevated liturgical style for the institution of the Lord's Supper.

Bach also demonstrates substantial sophistication in the simple four-part chorale harmonizations ordinarily found in the Leipzig cantatas, Passions, and oratorios. However, despite their surface simplicity, Bach's four-part chorales typically represent subtle contrapuntal polyphony; most notably, they regularly trace in their delicate compositional elaboration the meaning of the text—a feature recognized as something special by Bach's contemporaries in their references to the particular expressiveness of his chorale settings.

Ordinarily, Bach the composer is a faithful follower of his librettos, someone who pays close attention to the precise meaning of his given church texts, which usually consist of a combination of biblical prose, sacred poetry, and strophic hymns. There are instances, however, where the composer does more than merely set a single given text to music. Three cantatas from the first few months after Bach's Leipzig appointment have opening movements that are based on a biblical dictum, but to which the composer added an instrumental chorale melody—an element not provided by the original libretto. Scripture and chorale do not stand side by side in sequel as usual. In these movements they are presented simultaneously on different, yet interrelated levels. The biblical text is spelled out in the text underlay of the vocal score and sung by the choir, whereas the chorale is prominently embedded within the instrumental accompaniment. Its words remain unpronounced, but they are familiar to the congregation. Here Bach makes use of a possibility no verbal sermon, but only music, could offer: the simultaneous interpretation of one text, with words openly sung, by another text, with words tacit yet clearly understood.

Cantata *"Du sollt Gott, deinen Herren, lieben"* (BWV 77)

This cantata, first performed on August 22, 1723, and written for the Thirteenth Sunday after Trinity, is based on a libretto by an unknown author. The cantata text relates closely to the Gospel prescribed for this Sunday, Luke 10:25=37 (The Good Samaritan). The opening sets to music the Gospel's central passage (Luke 10: 26=27), which focuses on the main words of Jesus but leaves out the preceding short dialogue:

> *Du sollt Gott, deinen Herren, lieben von ganzem Herzen, von ganzer Seelen, von allen Kräften und von ganzem Gemüte und deinen Nächsten als dich selbst.*

[Jesus said unto him, "What is written in the law? how readest thou?" And he answered]:

> Thou shalt love the Lord thy God with all thy heart, and with all thy soul, and with all thy strength, and with all thy mind; and thy neighbor as thyself.

The biblical dictum presented a problem for the composer, for it is hard to bring this text to life musically. It is neutral in its stark, commanding tone; it offers no imagery nor does it contain any words that evoke strong *affects*. However, Bach does not treat the dictum from the libretto as an isolated, self-contained statement. He knows its biblical context and understands that Christ's words represent an interpretation of the First Commandment. Therefore, he decides to let Martin Luther's Ten-Commandment song of 1524, *Dies sind die heilgen zehn Gebot,* run parallel to the Gospel text, an instrumental quotation of a particularly well-known, immediately recognizable chorale.

The contemporary listener would easily identify the famous song, but not necessarily associate its melody with the second stanza that specifically paraphrases the First Commandment:

> *Ich bin allein dein Gott und Herr,*
> *Kein Götter sollt du haben mehr,*
> *Du sollt mir ganz vertrauen dich,*
> *Von Herzensgrund lieben mich.*
> *Kyrieleis.*

> I alone am your God the Lord.
> You are to have no other gods.
> You should trust me completely,
> and love me from the depths of your heart.
> Kyrie eleison. [8]

The phrases *"lieben von ganzem Herzen"* from the dictum and "von Herzensgrund lieben" from the chorale relate directly to each other and show the thoughtfulness of Bach's choice. But Bach's interpretation and, thereby, intensification of the biblical text does not end here. For the way he introduces the instrumental chorale melody adds another dimension to the setting. The *cantus firmus* is introduced line-by-line, beginning in measure eight, by the trumpet (*tromba da tirarsi*) in quarter-note values. The *cantus firmus* is also presented, line-by-line and beginning in measure nine, by the basso continuo in half-note values. Bach constructs an augmentation canon that impressively frames the choral-instrumental score throughout the entire cantata movement. Canonic technique, the most rigorous type of traditional polyphony, which follows the law of strict imitation, serves to draw the question preceding the interpretation of the First Commandment, "What is written in the law?", into the picture as well.

The musical structure of the movement, then, consists of three layers that complement one another, enhancing and expanding on the words of Jesus, the primary layer: a New Testament reading of Old Testament law. The second layer adds Luther's interpretation of the First Commandment by way of the melody and implied text of the Ten-Commandment hymn. Finally, the third layer holds it all together by way of the canonic frame that represents the law as such and underscores the centrality of the First Commandment in its enlarged New Testament version.

Cantata *"Es ist nichts Gesundes an meinem Leibe"* (BWV 25)

The following Sunday, August 29, 1723, saw the first performance of a work whose opening movement was designed in a similar fashion. However, the cantata text for the Fourteenth Sunday after Trinity, again written by an unknown librettist, does not begin with a quote from the Sunday's Gospel, Luke 17:11=19 (Jesus cleanses ten lepers). Instead, the librettist chose a well-fitting passage from the Old Testament by turning to verse four from Psalm 38:

> *Es ist nichts Gesundes an meinem Leibe vor deinem Dräuen und ist kein Friede in meinen Gebeinen vor meiner Sünde.*

There is no soundness in my flesh because of thine anger; neither is there any rest in my bones because of my sin.

Very different from the previous cantata, this text lends itself to an effective translation into musical ideas. The imagery of the sick and feeble people offers rich possibilities for an expressive musical treatment and, indeed, Bach makes use of an array of motives that depict the poor, suffering, sighing, and limping lepers as they approached Jesus and called upon him, "Master, have mercy on us."

These words are, of course, not set to music. But the composer can assume that his listeners knew the story that, after all, was refreshed by the Gospel immediately preceding the cantata performance. By working a chorale into the setting Bach lets the lepers cry for mercy, without words, by way of one of the best-known hymns from the later sixteenth century by Cyriacus Schneegaß. The chorale *Ach Herr, mich armen Sünder* of 1597, with one of the most well-known and most-frequently used melodies of the day, *Herzlich tut mich verlangen*, is performed by an instrumental ensemble in Bach's cantata movement.

But it is obviously the second stanza that Bach has in mind for the metaphorical choir of lepers representing the people attending worship. (Similarly, the words from Psalm 38 were chosen by the librettist in order to generalize and actualize the story of the lepers):

Heil du mich, lieber Herre,
Denn ich bin krank und schwach,
Mein Herz betrübet sehre,
Leidet gross Ungemach.
Mein G'beine sind erschrocken,
Mir ist sehr angst und bang,
Mein Seel ist auch erschrocken,
Ach du Herr, wie so lang!

Heal me, dear Lord,
for I am sick and weak.
My heart is very troubled
and suffers great adversity.
My bones are terrified;
I am very worried and alarmed;
my soul is also terrified,
O Lord, for so long.[9]

The chorale is presented as a four-part setting, in line-by-line sections, in a scoring of extraordinarily sad and somber quality (soprano played by *cornetto* plus three recorders in the upper octave; alto, tenor, and bass played by three *sackbuts*, an instrumental sonority that stresses the depth of the highly emotional plea). But it is not only the text of the second stanza that counts, but the multi-strophic hymn as a whole, which the Leipzig hymnal lists as a "prayer for the refreshment of an anxious soul." Bach broadens the impact of the chorale citation by letting it function as an element of consolation.

Bach stresses the significance of the chorale as a defining element and a crucial interpretive companion to the Psalm text of the opening movement by introducing the first line of the chorale in augmented note values at the very beginning of the movement (mm. 1-5, repeated in mm. 21-25) in the basso continuo, the fundamental part of the musical score.

Cantata *"Ich elender Mensch, wer wird mich erlösen"* (BWV 48)

The third cantata of our group, a work composed for the Nineteenth Sunday after Trinity and first performed five weeks after BWV 25 on October 3, 1723, also begins with the setting of a biblical text not taken from this Sunday's prescribed Gospel, Matthew 9:1–8 (Jesus heals a palsied man). Nevertheless, the New Testament text, Romans 7:24, chosen by the unknown librettist correlates very closely with the content of the Gospel for the day:

> *Ich elender Mensch, wer wird mich erlösen vom Leibe dieses Todes?*

> O wretched man that I am! Who shall deliver me from the body of this death?

Again, the grim, desperate anxiety asserted in the text as such offers the composer a starting point sufficient for developing the proper musical *affect*. Yet, Bach apparently wants to be more specific in finding the most fitting musical vehicle for this short biblical sentence. Thus, he turns to the related Gospel text in Matthew 9 and considers the words Jesus spoke to the man afflicted with the palsy: "Son, be of good cheer; thy sins be forgiven" (verse 2) and "Arise, take up thy bed, and go unto thine house" (verse 6). Bach then links these words to Bartholomäus Ringwaldt's chorale *Herr Jesu Christ, du höchstes Gut*, originally published in 1588 under the heading "A good song for the remission of sins" and a classic hymn for this topic ever since:

1. *Herr Jesu Christ, du höchstes Gut,*
    Du Brunnquell aller Gnaden,
    Sieh doch, wie ich in meinem Mut
    Mit Schmerzen bin beladen,
    Und in mir hab der Pfeile viel,
    Die im Gewissen ohne Ziel,
    Mich armen Sünder drücken.

7. *Ach Herr, mein Gott, vergib mirs doch*
    Um deines Namens willen,
    Und tu in mir das schwere Joch
    Der Übertretung stillen,
    Daß sich mein Herz zufrieden geb,
    Und dir hinfort zu Ehren leb
    In kindlichem Gehorsam.

1. Lord Jesus Christ, you highest good,
    you fountain of all mercy.
    Behold how my spirit
    is burdened with pain.
    I have many arrows in me
    which oppress me, a poor sinner,
    without measure in my conscience.

7. O Lord, my God, forgive me
    for your name's sake, and quiet
    the heavy yoke of transgression
    in me so that my heart is at peace
    and lives to your honor
    with childlike obedience.[10]

Bach's score reflects the two-layered musical imagery of the palsied man taking up his bed and walking—unsteadily, but with the assurance that his sins are forgiven. The principal layer of the G-minor score (strings and choral parts) dedicated to the biblical text depicts in halting phrases of two-measure length and limping basso continuo underpinning, and with emphatic dissonances on the downbeat, "the wretched man" facing death (from Romans 7) and the "the poor sinner, burdened with pain" (from the hymn, first stanza). The second layer, on the other hand, presents a steady and stabilizing force throughout the movement. Two instrumental treble parts (*tromba* and oboes I/II) perform the chorale melody in a strict canon, stressing the firm resolve of Jesus' words, "that ye may know that the Son of man hath power on earth to forgive sins" (verse 6). The theological implications of the entire chorale, in particular its first and seventh stanzas, are as obvious as the close interrelationship of the text sources. Bach's music makes their complementary association perfectly transparent.

Conclusion

The three cantata movements of 1723, Bach's first year in his Leipzig office, provide striking examples of the new Thomas cantor's intense, multi-directional reading and study practice in preparing himself for the challenge of composing a cantata in its function as a musical sermon. The remarkable results of his efforts demonstrate in particular how well he knew to make use of Bible and hymnal as rich resources for his task as a musical interpreter of theological messages. Hence, the opening movements of the cantatas BWV 77, 25, and 48 reveal how Bach's ingenious combination of two layers with mutually elucidating texts add a dimension to his music that is equally powerful in its theological allure, musical imagination, and expressive magnetism.

A faithful servant of his church, Bach is determined to follow the Lutheran principle of "preaching the Gospel through music" and, even more than that, of invoking God's presence through music. This is established by one of the most informative autograph annotations in the margins of his Calov Bible:[11]

> NB. Bei einer andächtigen Music ist Gott allezeit mit seiner Gnadengegenwart.

> With a devotional music God is always present in his grace.

Bach's comment deals with the invisibility of God and refers to the text of 2 Chronicles 5:13–14, a passage describing an incident of 120 priests making music in Solomon's Temple: "When they lifted up their voices with trumpets and cymbals and instruments of music, and praised the Lord . . . , then the house was filled with a cloud; . . . for the glory of the Lord had filled the house of God." For Bach, God's presence was not, as suggested by the He-brew Bible, in a cloud or in a fire. For him, God was invisible but not inaudible since "with a devotional music God is always present with his grace."

Hence, for Bach the act of composing and performing a piece of sacred music offered a way of invoking the presence of the Divine.[12] But what constitutes "devotional music"? On Bach's terms, this is nothing less than a composition that listens to, understands, transforms, and projects the biblical message; a composition that enhances, clarifies, and elevates the biblical word by the singing and playing of hymns.

NOTES

1   Martin Luther, *Table Talk*, ed. Theodore G. Tappert, Luther's Works: American Edition, vol. 54 (Philadelphia: Fortress, 1967), no.1258.

2   Hans T. David and Arthur Mendel, eds., *The New Bach Reader: A Life of Johann Sebastian Bach in Letters and Documents*, rev. and expanded by Christoph Wolff (New York: Norton, 1998), no. 279. (Cited hereafter as NBR.)

3   Robin A. Leaver, *Bach's Theological Library: A Critical Bibliography* (Neuhausen-Stuttgart, 1983). 22–27.

4   NBR, no. 228. Bach acquired by auction the Altenburg edition of Luther's collected works, 10 parts in 7 volumes.

5   NBR, no. 165.

6   NBR, p. 254.

7   Given in 1772.by C. P. E. Bach as a memento to Charles Burney. See Christoph Wolff, *Johann Sebastian Bach: The Learned Musician* (New York: Norton, 2000), 499.

8   Trans. in Mark S. Bighley, *The Lutheran Chorales in the Organ Works of J. S. Bach* (St. Louis: Concordia, 1986), 72.

9   Trans. in Bighley, 264.

10 Trans. in Bighley, 288.

11 NBR, no. 165.

12 See also Christoph Wolff, 338–39.

Dancing Before the Lord:
Dance Rhythms in Bach Cantatas

Dance and dance rhythms have energized and invigorated music for thousands of years. In fact, the Greeks described the concept of rhythm as an *activity* inherent not only in bodily movement, but also in poetry and music. We "rhythm" notes and harmonies in order to give them organization, shape, form, and a distinctive life. The excitement and passion in dance music has been captured by principles of form and design and labeled with specific titles in pieces of prescribed length and shape.

Dance rhythms have also permeated countless compositions in which composers have not labeled the specific rhythm or rhythms. It is indeed surprising that despite the voluminous body of research describing the music of the Baroque, and in particular with that of J. S. Bach, a serious discussion and detailed analyses of his extant titled dances, numbering over 230, was not undertaken until the last decade of the twentieth century.[1] And now, musicians of the twenty-first century are able to appreciate not only the extent and importance of these dances in Bach's creative thinking, but also the degree of permeation and influence of dance rhythms in his other works.[2]

The rhythms of Bach's popular and sometimes highly stylized titled dances (bourées, gavottes, minuets, passepieds, sarabandes, loures, forlanas, and various types of gigues/gigas), which characterize many of his instrumental works, are also found in pieces that do not have dance titles. To date, 193 examples have been discussed and undoubtedly more will be discovered. Examples are found in organ fugues, the *Well-Tempered Clavier*, preludes and fugues, sinfonias, concertos, the *Musical Offering*, sonatas (solo and chamber), chorale preludes, the *Goldberg Variations*, and inventions. But surprisingly, the compositions in which Bach incorporated dance rhythms most frequently are vocal works; they outnumber the instrumental examples almost three to one. The majority of these vocal pieces are in the cantatas, both sacred and secular, but examples do occur in Masses, oratorios, Passions, and the *Magnificat*. One may ask, as interesting as all of this is, what does it mean for the performer; of what value is it to know that the rhythm of piece X is based on that of dance Y? To put it bluntly, so what?

The answer is both profound and complex, but deals fundamentally with the concept of *affect* or characterization that is *essential* to a musical performance of a composition whether the dance title is present or not. Johann Philipp Kirnberger (1721–1783), a student of Bach and devoted follower and advocate, writes:

> The term *Gemüthsbewegung*, which we Germans give to passions or affections, already indicates their analogy to tempo. In fact, every passion and every sentiment— in its intrinsic effect as well as in the words by which it is expressed—has its faster or slower, more violent or more passive tempo. This tempo must be correctly captured by the composer to conform with the type of sentiment he has to express.
>
> Thus I must admonish the aspiring composer above all that he study diligently the nature of every passion and sentiment with regard to tempo, so that he does not make the terrible mistake of giving the melody a slow tempo where it should be fast, or fast tempo where it should be slow. However, this is a field that is not limited to music, and that the composer has in common with the orator and poet.
>
> Furthermore, he must have acquired a correct feeling for the natural tempo of every meter, or for what is called *tempo giusto*. This is attained by diligent study of all kinds of dance pieces. Every dance piece has its definite tempo, determined by the meter and the note values that are employed in it.[3]

In order to understand the *tempo giusto* of a dance, the performer must first be able to identify its unique rhythm, which is key to realizing the ramifications for performance. Since there are many dance types in Bach's vocal works, this essay will use only a few selected examples from the bourée, gavotte, minuet, sarabande, and various gigue types.

Baroque dance rhythms are organized in a hierarchy of varying degrees of motion and repose (arsis and thesis) that are of a prescribed length and shape and recur with a frequency capable of characterizing a particular dance type. In addition, each dance type bears its own *affect* and tempo, and is further characterized by distinctive melodic figures. However, it is beyond the scope of this article to discuss this last feature.[4]

Example 1,[5] the bourée dance phrase, is eight beats in length (four measures) preceded by an upbeat, and in 2 or ¢ meter with the half-note as the beat. Beat 7 and the first half of 8 constitute the primary repose or thesis; beat 3 and the first half of 4 provide a preliminary resting point or secondary thesis. The bourée is a relatively fast dance (faster than the gavotte) with the beat at the level of the half-note. Its character is variously described as gay or joyful, and it should be performed lightheartedly.

Example 1. Overture in the French Style in B Minor (BWV 831), *Bourée* **1, mm. 1-4.**

Clearly, the suggested articulations in the examples that follow highlight the bourée dance rhythm. Now it is possible to recognize this rhythm in a piece of music not so titled. But a word of caution: the level of the beat in a titled dance may not be the same as in an untitled example. For example, in the organ *Fugue in C Minor* (Example 2) the half-note is the beat; but in the organ *Fugue in G Minor* (Example 3) the beat is the quarter note and the dance pattern is extended.

Example 2. *Fugue in C Minor* **for organ (BWV 537), mm. 1-4, articulation added.**

Example 3. *Fugue in G Minor* **for organ (BWV 542), mm. 1-4, articulation added.**

Among the many cantatas that utilize bourée rhythms is Cantata 140, *Wachet auf, ruft uns die Stimme*. Both the superb duet, *"Mein Freund is mein"* (Example 4), and the chorale setting, *"Zion hört die Wächter singen"* (Example 5), are characterized by the bourée dance rhythms in which the quarter note in each case is the beat.

Example 4. Cantata *Wachet auf, ruft uns die Stimme* (BWV 140), mvt. 6, mm. 9-12.

Bach's use of the dance rhythm is unique in each piece. In the former example the bourée rhythm dominates the singers' duet, and Bach often splits the rhythmic phrase between them. In the latter, the bourée rhythm floats above the chorale. Here we need another word of caution. One might be tempted to label almost every dance-like aria or chorus with a dance title. But there are

Example 5. Cantata *Wachet auf, ruft uns die Stimme* (BWV 140), mvt. 4, mm.13-15.

specific characteristics for each dance as we have seen, and the text must provide further insight into its *affect* and character; it must support the basic premise of a dance rhythm, not be extraneous to it. Not only do both examples follow the bourée dance pattern with little deviation, but their texts also reflect joy and happiness; in the duet (Example 4) happiness and eventual bliss in the bond between the Soul and Christ; in the chorale (Example 5) the watchmen sing joyfully and eagerly in anticipation of Christ's arrival.

The conductor and singers now have useful performance information. For the duet (Example 4) a rather fast tempo is appropriate, as well as stressing the most thetic beats (appoggiatura on *"sein"* and slight *inégale* on the appoggiaturas on *"scheiden"*). In the oboe solo that begins the duet (not present in Example 4) slurs over groups of four, slurs over neighbor-note groups of twos, and a clear break for the upbeat of two sixteenth-notes immediately signal the bourée dance rhythm. Of course there are some overlapping rhythmic patterns and imitative interplay in the duet, but the rhythmic inflections of the dance should be present.

For the chorale (Example 5) a brisk tempo is also appropriate. The counter-melody in the strings begins ahead of the chorale and establishes the characteristic joyful, lighthearted affect of the bourée. This will certainly dissuade the singers from getting bogged down in a ponderous, slow tempo.

The gavotte (Example 6), a much older dance than the bourée, reached a high point in popularity during the 1720s and 1730s when Bach wrote most of his gavottes. The metric structure of the gavotte is identical to that of the bourée (see above); however, it is quite a different dance because of its balanced, rhyming phrases and its often slower tempo. The grouping of beats by twos crosses bar lines and the phrase is divided in the middle after the fourth beat. Beat 8 is the primary thetic point and beat 4 a secondary thesis. The gavotte could express a variety of *affects* including graceful, joyful, and pastoral; sometimes it is tender and slow. Though contrasting, all are moderate, not extreme. The aria for tenor and flute, *"Lass, o Fürst der Cherubinen"* from Cantata 130,5 (not shown here), is a good example of these characteristics and shows clearly balanced phrases within a pastoral *affect*.

Example 6. *French Suite V in G Major* (BWV 816), *Gavotte*, mm. 1-4.

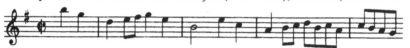

Two gavotte-like pieces, notated differently than Example 6, are from Cantata 32, *Liebster Jesu, mein Verlangen* and the *Magnificat in D* (BWV 243), in both of which the beat is the quarter-note. In the duet *"Nun verschwinden alle Plagen"* from Cantata 32 (Example 7) the phrase begins on beat 2 of a four-beat measure, and the whole phrase is 16 beats long, not eight. The trills emphasize the thetic beats, but they should not all be performed with the same emphasis. The strings must be careful to play the intricate thirty-second-note diminutions lightly—not an easy task. The *affect* of the text, which expresses joy in which trouble and pain must vanish, is enhanced by the dance rhythm. The conductor should understand the "vivace" directive by Bach to mean lively, not as fast as possible.

Example 7. Cantata *Liebster Jesu, mein Verlangen* (BWV 32), mvt. 5, mm. 1-5, reduced score.

Another wonderful vocal example of the gavotte is the bass aria *"Quia fecit mihi magna"* from the *Magnificat in D* (BWV 243,5; Example 8). The gavotte rhythm serves as an ostinato and, as in the previous example, begins on beat 2 of the measure. Its stateliness underlines the thought that God has done great things for us.

Example 8. *Magnificat in D* (BWV 243), mvt. 5, mm. 1-6.

A unique example for our discussion is the famous soprano aria *"Mein gläubiges Herze"* from Cantata 68 (Example 9), which appears to feature two dance rhythms going on at the same time, but operating at different metric levels. The violincello piccolo begins in gavotte rhythms and the soprano enters in bourée rhythms! Furthermore, the character of the text is compatible with both dance *affects*.

The minuet (Example 10) was the most famous of all the French dances. It was a popular social dance at court at least by the 1680s and remained an important ingredient in all types of music into the late eighteenth century. Bach reserved the elegant minuet rhythm almost exclusively for vocal pieces within his untitled dance-like music The minuet dance rhythm consists of a harmonic-rhythmic phrase 4 beats (measures) in length with a thesis on beat four. The four-measure phrase is normally balanced or answered by a second four-measure phrase with a greater sense of arrival on measure eight. The meter sign in the instrumental music is normally 3/4, but in the vocal works the meter is almost always 3/8 as in the Italian style. The beat in 3/4 meter is the dotted half-note, and in 3/8 the dotted quarter. The minuet is moderate in character like the gavotte and is not given to extremes of passion like the sarabande. Examples abound but two will be sufficient to give the reader a feel for this dance. The aria *"Unser Mund und Ton der Saiten"* (Example 11) from Cantata 1, *Wie schön leuchtet der Morgenstern*, illustrates Bach's ingenuity with dance rhythms.

Example 9. Cantata *Also hat Gott die Welt geliebt* (BWV 68), mvt. 2, mm. 1-6.

Example 10. *Brandenburg Concerto I* (BWV 1046), *Menuetto*, mm. 1-4.

This elegant song of praise and honor to God is 267 measures long, in which rhythmic subtleties unfold in a moderate tempo within an overall sense of balance, which is the hallmark of the minuet. The performers might want to highlight the hemiolia figure of sixteenth-notes grouped in 3s in the violin parts so that the vocal entry grouping of 4+2 sixteenth-notes in measure 29 produces lovely cross-rhythms. The second pulse syncope is also a common feature of the minuet rhythm.

Example 11. Cantata *Wie schön leuchtet der Morgenstern* (BWV 1), mvt. 5, mm. 1-4, reduced score.

Example 12. *Magnificat in D* (BWV 243), mvt. 2, mm. 13-16.

A particularly lovely example of the minuet rhythm is found in *"Et exultavit spiritus meus"* from the *Magnificat in D* (Example 12). Mary's intimate song of quiet joy is simply and beautifully set as a minuet, which could accompany ballroom dancing but for two truncated phrases, one in measure 51 and the other in measure 81. The stately and noble setting of this text by Bach speaks volumes about the attention he paid to the union of text, music, and *affect*. This poignant aria is all the more effective because it follows the boisterous exuberance of the opening chorus.

Example 13. *French Suite VI* in E Major (BWV 817), *Sarabande*, mm. 1-4.

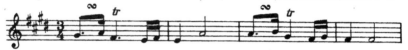

The sarabande (Example 13) had a long and colorful history before it was transformed into its noble form at the French Court. Its dance rhythm consists of a phrase of 12 beats (four measures) in 3/4 meter in which the thesis, or release from tension, occurs on beat 10 (beginning of measure four) and diminishes going into beat 12. Balance is important, and phrases that are not four or eight measures long occur only rarely. This rhyming phrase structure also appears in the gavotte and minuet, but the sarabande is much older, and this simplicity of phrase structure led composers to experiment with various rhythmic figures and soloistic techniques. Typical features include the syncope on the second beat, (also not uncommon to the minuet, and not, by itself, the defining feature of the sarabande dance), hemiolia figures, dotted rhythms as in the French Overture style, and solo passages with elaborate ornamentation. The sarabande tempo is slow, and the *affect* is noble, majestic, and sometimes passionate.

The beautiful opening chorus of Cantata 6, *Bleib bei uns, denn es will Abend werden* (Example 14), incorporates the sarabande dance rhythm in its first 80 and last 20 measures. The middle section, with a change of meter to ¢, proceeds in motet style until measure 114, where the sarabande rhythm returns with the simple words, *"Bleib bei uns."* The persistent drone in the strings may represent Christ's constancy.

The third aria, *"Christen müssen auf der Erden"* (Example 15) from Cantata 44, *Sie werden euch in den Bann tun*, is a rather grim reminder that Christ's true disciples will undergo torture and pain before they will be blessedly delivered. The pulse-level triplets that begin in the third measure are a common type of elaboration in Bach's titled sarabandes. Performers will want to resolve the duplet figures, dotted eighth- and sixteenth-notes, to the more pervasive triplet figures. The dissonances in measures 55–79 intensify the text, particularly on the words, *"Marter, Bann und schwere Pein"* (torture, ban, and grievous pain), which are also lengthened in duration. A fairly slow tempo will make this alto aria truly tormented and passionate.

Both of Bach's unsurpassable Passions use the rhythm and character of the sarabande in their last great choruses: *"Ruht wohl, ihr heiligen Gebeine"* (Example 16) from the *St. John Passion* (BWV 245) and *"Wir setzen uns mit Tränen nieder"* from the *St. Matthew Passion* (BWV 244). Although the second beat syncope is an important part of the latter chorus, it does not play an important role in the *St. John Passion, "Ruht wohl."* However, it is cast in balanced phrases throughout, some very long, and has wrenching

Example 14. Cantata *Bleib bei uns, denn es will Abend werden* (BWV 6), mvt. 1, mm. 1-4.

melodic turns and a frequently chromatic bass line. The texts of both choruses are serious and passionately pray that the crucified body of Christ will rest in peace.

Bach's gigues, or as they are sometimes called, giga, jig, jigg, gique, in time signatures as diverse as 3/8, 6/8, 12/8, 12/16, 9/16, C, and Ø, lead us into a variety of styles, types of upbeat, and *affect*. Our present research, based on an analysis of metric structures, establishes the grouping of gigues into three types: French gigue, giga I, and giga II[6] (See Example 17). However, more sub-groups may still be identified.

Example 15. Cantata *Sie werden euch in den Bann tun* (BWV 44), mvt. 3, mm. 1-8.

Example 16. *St. John Passion* (BWV 245), mvt. 67, mm. 1-4, instruments only.

Example 17. Three types of gigue in the music of J. S. Bach: a. French gigue, from *French Suite II* in C Minor (BWV 813); b. Giga I, from *French Suite V* in G Major (BWV 816); c. Giga II, from *French Suite VI* in E Major (BWV 817).

Bach composed only six titled French gigues, so we assume it was not his favorite dance. The constant use of the *sautillant* figure (dotted eighth, sixteenth, eighth) was perhaps not interesting enough for an extended work. At any rate, this "bouncing" rhythmic figure is easily recognizable and does not need a printed example here. (See the early cantata aria *"Bereitet die Wege, bereitet die Bahn"* [BWV 132,1].)

The Giga I dances fall into two groups that can be called the "complex style" and the "balanced style." The so-called "Jig Fugue" for organ (BWV 577) is a good example of the complex style. This type of giga has a rather exuberant *affect*, is moderately fast, has long and unbalanced phrases, often with fugal construction, relentless movement, and "jigging" rhythms (short-long, short long). Example 18 from Cantata 30, a da capo aria for soprano, *"Eilt Stunden, kommt herbei,"* has some of the characteristics of a Giga I.

Example 18. Cantata *Freue dich, erlöste Schar* (BWV 30), mvt. 10, mm. 1-4.

The balanced style of the Giga I features a joyful affect, moderate to moderately fast tempo, phrases often balanced with extensions, homophonic texture, and jigging rhythms. The aria for soprano, *"Wie freudig ist mein Herz,"* from Cantata 199, illustrates the style (Example 19).

Finally, the Giga II is the most problematic of all the giga types. Not only is its history clouded in mystery, but its metric structure, when it is 3/8, is identical with that of both the minuet and passepied. However, the Giga II *affect*, which is joyous and intense, along with contrapuntal texture and long phrases, is not compatible with either of the aforementioned French dances. It is also true that there are a wide variety of pieces which embody the Giga II characteristics (some the same as the Giga I), but it is the only one in which the ternary figures are divided into binary groups. Example 20, the duet from Cantata 28, *Gottlob! Nun geht das Jahr zu Ende,* is one such piece.

Example 19. Cantata *Mein Herze schwimmt im Blut* (BWV 199), mvt. 8, mm. 10-11.

Example 20. Cantata *Gottlob! Nun geht das Jahr zu Ende* (BWV 28), mvt. 5, mm. 1-10.

Musical examples from *Dance and the Music of J.S. Bach*, expanded ed., by Meredith Little and Natalie Jenne (Bloomington, Indiana: Indiana University Press, 2001).

Perhaps this brief "dance" through some of the incomparable vocal works of Bach will embolden performers of this repertoire to approach them with a greater understanding and appreciation of the rhythmic possibilities inherent in the music.

NOTES

1   Meredith Little and Natalie Jenne, *Dance and the Music of J.S. Bach* (Bloomington: Indiana University Press, 1991).

2   Ibid., expanded edition (2001).

3   Johann Kirnberger, *Die Kunst des reinen Satzes in der Musik, aus sicheren Grundsätzen hergeleitet and mit deutlichen Beyspielen erläutert*, vol. 2 (Berlin and Konigsberg, 1776-79), English trans. David Beach and Jurgen Thym as *The Art of Strict Musical Composition* (New Haven: Yale University Press, 1982), 376.

4   The definitions of all the dances discussed in this essay were arrived at by an extensive study of descriptions from the period, dance choreographies, examples of tonguings, bowings, meter signification, time-words, articulation marks, fingerings, text prosody and breath marks, ornamentation, use of *notes inégales*, and of prime importance, use of harmony.

5   All examples, complete or in part are used by permission of the publisher and are taken from Little and Jenne, ibid., given in the order in which they appear in the body of this article: 35, 206, 207, 212,215, 47, 219, 214, 62, 225, 226, 92, 242, 239, 249,144, 268, 272, 282.

6   Ibid., 143–84.

Part Two

The Lutheran
Musical Heritage
and Worship in the
Twenty-first Century

Seven Habits of Highly Effective Liturgies: Insights from the Sixteenth through the Eighteenth Century

One of my colleagues has a cartoon on his office door with the caption "Seven habits of highly effective people," a reference to the best-selling book. Pictured are seven people wearing nuns' habits. The humor, of course, derives from the double meaning of the word "habit."

Unexpected uses of words can be enlightening. Habits, for example, are normally considered traits of people, not of things. One does not usually speak of the habits of liturgy. But the word's common meaning of "a customary practice acquired through frequent repetition" is perfect to describe the recurring features that allow liturgies to be effective in proclaiming the Word of God and offering in response the praise and thanks of his people. Let us consider here seven of these "habits" found in Lutheran liturgies from the sixteenth through the eighteenth century that are instructive for us today.

Number 1: The Primacy of the Word

In a 1545 letter to Martin Luther, Prince Georg of Anhalt inquired whether it would be proper for him to establish a set form of liturgical ceremonial and require its use throughout his realm. Luther replied that a more urgent matter was to provide for the Word to be purely and richly taught and to appoint learned and competent ministers who were of one heart and soul in the Lord. Then it would be easy, he wrote, to bring ceremonies into conformity with each other.[1]

For Luther, there was no true worship without the Word. So that the Word could be readily heard, he insisted that the Mass be sung audibly by priest and choir rather than mumbled by the priest alone, as was common during the late Middle Ages. He also allowed the Mass to be held in the language of the people. To be sure, the Latin Mass was retained in many larger towns, partly out of tradition, partly out of a need to educate boys in that universal language, and partly out of an appreciation for the familiar Latin chants. But even where Latin was retained, certain parts of the liturgy were sung in German, including the lessons (which were sometimes read in both languages), the Lord's Prayer and the eucharistic consecration, plus several hymns. Luther's German Creed was also sung in most places, either in addition to or in place of the Latin Creed.

The sermon was also in German, as it had been before the Reformation. In medieval Germany, the liturgical placement of the sermon varied from place to place, and it was frequently held as a separate service apart from the Mass. Lutherans restored it to a place of prominence within the Mass, where it had been in early Christian liturgies. What is interesting, though, is that these early Lutheran sermons did not necessarily contain a clear proclamation of the Gospel of salvation. Today we expect to hear both Law and Gospel clearly preached from Lutheran pulpits. But one can read sermons of Luther and find such content lacking more often than not. This is not to say that the sermons were not scripturally based. They were. But they tended to be catechetical rather than kerygmatic, and Luther was not averse to attacking social evils with a ferocity that would shock most present-day Lutherans, often offering specific remedies as well.

Even when it was lacking in the sermon, though, the Gospel message was to be found in other parts of the Mass. It was present in the Mass Ordinary, in the readings, and in the collects. It was present in the German hymns. It was present in the words of consecration, which Luther in the *German Mass* of 1526 deliberately set to the same chant tone as the Gospel. It was most notably present in the exhortation to the communicants, which appeared before the communion liturgy in many Lutheran Mass orders and which explicated in a nutshell Lutheran teaching concerning justification and the Lord's Supper.

Luther understood the liturgy to have two functions: a sacramental one, with God speaking to his people, and a sacrificial one, with the people responding to God's action. He said this in so many words in a sermon for the dedication of the palace church in Torgau in 1544, in which he exhorted the assembly to take heed that "the purpose of this new house may be such that nothing else may ever happen in it except that our dear Lord himself may speak to us through his holy Word and we respond to him through prayer and praise."[2] If we accept Luther's formulation, then it follows that one may judge each aspect of the liturgy according to whether it helps or hinders God's Word and our response.

It is not always easy to judge whether something is helpful or not. Music is usually said to be beneficial to the liturgy because it can make a text more memorable (its sacramental function) and add emphasis to the people's praise (its sacrificial function). But the same music can be detrimental if it is sung or played badly. It can be distracting if the tune or style is unfamiliar. And for a strict Zwinglian—who would allow no singing in the liturgy at all out of concern that it might draw attention away from God's Word—any music, no matter how well performed, would be downright idolatrous.

German Lutherans of the late seventeenth and early eighteenth centuries raised this issue in regard to a new style of music that had been imported from the south; namely, concerted music in the style of Michael Praetorius, Schütz, Schein, Buxtehude, Telemann, and Bach. Originating in Italy, this style combined both voices and a small instrumental ensemble to produce sacred concertos, oratorios, cantatas, and the like, which were performed for a listening congregation as for an audience. Such music met with vociferous criticism from a number of Lutherans, who objected that it obscured the text and merely tickled the ears with sound. Many noted with dismay its connection with opera, whose style it closely resembled.

Several influential eighteenth-century musicians defended the new style, noting that the purpose of such music in church was to move the emotions of the listeners and so direct them to God.[3] Because the new style of music could produce more emotion in listeners than could the old motet-style polyphony, it was therefore deemed to be more suitable for use in church, provided, of course, that the emotions so produced were the right ones, ones that, in the words of Johann Adolph Scheibe, could "arouse an audience to devotion in order to awaken in them a quiet and holy fear toward the Divine Essence."[4] According to one of the most enlightened Lutheran musicians of the eighteenth century, therefore, the purpose of music in church was to manipulate people into having a religious experience.

For what purpose do we make music in church today? Is it to carry the Word of God? Is it to allow the people to respond to that Word? Is it to produce a mood of religious devotion? Are these goals mutually exclusive? When does an attempt to create a mood cross over into a sentimental manipulation of emotions?

I would argue that the answer has to do with the priority given to the Word. Much of the concerted church music composed during the seventeenth and eighteenth centuries is deservedly forgotten today, and some of the criticisms leveled against it may indeed have been justified. What redeems the best of it is not only its superior musical creativity and craftsmanship but also its intimate connection with the Word, and in particular with the lectionary. The well-known church cantatas of Bach, for example, had texts that responded to and expanded upon the Gospel for the day, and churchgoers could purchase books with the texts to read while the music was being performed. The general mood of the music and devices of musical rhetoric highlighted portions of the text. Hymn stanzas were frequently interspersed, and the rest of the cantata text connected them with the Gospel. The cantatas, therefore, served a devotional purpose: they embedded the day's theme more deeply into the hearts of the hearers and invited them to reflect on it.

The first habit, therefore, of an effective liturgy is that the music, and indeed everything that happens, points to and elevates God and his Word.

Number 2: The Centrality of the Lord' Supper

The 1572 church order for the duchy of Kurland gave explicit instructions on how to clean the chalice after communion. It is not done, the order stated, in the papistic manner; that is, by licking it out with the tongue. Rather, a bit of unconsecrated wine is poured into the chalice, swished around, then the last communicants drink what remains.[5] This practice allowed the last bit of the blood of Christ to be consumed rather than discarded.

Such careful attention to the conduct of the sacrament is typical among early Lutherans. For them, the Lord's Supper was the center around which all other services revolved. Except for a few areas in the south that were influenced by the Swiss Reformation, the Supper was offered every Lord's day and holy day throughout Lutheran Germany. Several practices highlighted the importance of the sacrament:

1. Private confession before each reception of the sacrament was required in nearly all Lutheran territories. Günther Stiller reports that in eighteenth-century Leipzig there were so many penitents that confessional stations had to be set up in the church on Saturdays and eves of holy days from 8:00 in the morning until late afternoon.[6] This practice not only assured the pastor that communicants were prepared for the sacrament, but also enabled him to count the communicants before consecrating the bread and wine. Thus the problem of what to do with the body and blood of Christ that remained after all had communed was avoided, as only enough for the announced communicants was consecrated.

2. The traditional vestment for Mass, the chasuble, was retained in many Lutheran churches.

3. With few exceptions, the Consecration, as it was called in the sixteenth century, was always sung. This practice was new with Luther; prior to his time in western Christianity, the priest said the Consecration softly so the people could not hear it.

4. Many Lutherans retained the Elevation, in which the priest raised the consecrated body of Christ aloft for the people to view.

5. In many Saxon churches, according to a contemporary report, the ringing of the Sanctus bell at the consecration of the bread and cup was retained into the eighteenth century.[7]

6. Only ordained pastors distributed the sacrament.

7. Some churches used a houseling cloth to catch any crumbs that might fall from the host while it was being distributed. It was carried by an assistant and held underneath the chin of each communicant.

I list these practices only to demonstrate the importance that early Lutherans attached to the sacrament, not to suggest that we should uncritically adopt them. They did not, alas, automatically guarantee a healthy sacramental life. This has to do partly with history. Prior to the Reformation, it was common for most people to commune only at Easter. The very devout might have communed three or four times a year. This tradition, coupled with the expectation that parishioners would attend confession prior to communing, meant that attendance at Communion was often sparse in Lutheran churches. The reformers therefore made accommodation, with Lutheran church orders stating that when there were no communicants the Communion liturgy was to be omitted. The wording of this, "when there are no communicants," is informative: it assumes that Communion will be offered at every opportunity unless no one wishes to commune. Today, both *Lutheran Book of Worship* and *Lutheran Worship* state that "when there is no Communion, the service continues [below]."[8] The assumption here is that churches may plan not to offer Communion, something that would have surprised sixteenth-century Lutherans.

Twentieth-century liturgical research has shown that the Eucharist was the normal Sunday service as far back as we can trace. This was the case in Lutheran churches until people lost interest in communing. If we wish to restore the centrality of the Lord's Supper in our churches, then the first step is to offer it whenever it seems likely that people will desire it. It is true that the liturgical movement has convinced many of our churches to offer Communion more frequently. But except in a few places, we are not yet at a point where one can go to church on Sunday and expect to commune. The Eucharist is not yet the center around which other services revolve. In many larger churches in America with more than one service, Communion is offered at the early service one week and at the late service the next week. This is an improvement over times past, but it means that the Eucharist is still not viewed as normative, but rather as an option.

If this is to change, then our pastors must be convinced that it needs to happen. In the old Lutheran church orders, whenever there were no communicants, the pastor was frequently instructed that he should exhort the people to commune more often. Today, some pastors may simply decide that Communion will be offered every week, and that is that. Others may be concerned that the people must first be educated. I know one pastor who, during the first part of his ministry at a parish, never preached a sermon without somewhere in it pointing to the altar and extolling the benefits of the sacrament. After several years of this, the people were begging for more frequent Communion. Today that church has three services every weekend, all with Communion.

Number 3: The *de tempore* Principle

In the preface to his 1631 hymnal, David Gregor Corner told the story of a minister secretly holding Calvinist beliefs who had been invited to preach in a Lutheran church. It was the third Sunday of Advent, and the preacher began to sing the Easter hymn "Christ is arisen." The congregation, related Corner, could barely contain its laughter, and few were inclined to sing along. But after the sermon, when the hymn "Savior of the nations, come" was begun, the people sang enthusiastically, for, as Corner wrote, the latter was a hymn *de tempore;* the former was not.[9]

The Latin term *de tempore,* meaning "of the time," refers to liturgical time; specifically, the season of the church year. Lutherans are a *de tempore* people. One of the first things one notices in early Lutheran liturgies is how they structured time according to the day, the week, and the year.

Nearly two hundred liturgical agendas appeared in Lutheran Germany during the sixteenth century alone. They differed from each other in varying degrees of detail, but their schedule of services was remarkably similar.[10] Each day Matins and Vespers were sung in city churches by a choir of schoolboys. Each weekend a set of services was held, beginning with Vespers on Saturday evening. After Vespers private confession was offered to those planning to commune the following day. Early on Sunday, Matins was held in the cities, but was omitted in small villages. The Communion service followed (which was commonly called the Mass, a term Lutherans retained for at least a century after the Reformation). On Sunday afternoon Vespers with sermon was held, usually combined with catechism instruction for children. In larger towns, sermons were also preached on one or more weekdays, and Mass was held daily when there were people who wished to commune.

Holy days were frequent. All the apostles' days, plus a handful of additional saints' days, were commonly observed with Mass in the morning. Most feasts of our Lord (including Circumcision, Epiphany, Presentation, Annunciation, Ascension, Visitation), plus St. John the Baptist and St. Michael, were observed with both morning Mass and afternoon Vespers. The three highest festivals—Christmas, Easter, and Pentecost—were generally observed for two and a half days, with Mass and Vespers on the first two days and Mass on the third day. Workers had all these days (or half days) off, and so the life of the community revolved around the feasts of the Lord and of his apostles.

It is hard for us to imagine what it must have been like to be constantly reminded of one's Christian faith through the ebb and flow of the liturgical day, week, and year—to be carried, as it were, in the womb of the liturgy. Our society today is simply not attuned to this. We church musicians feel that we have moved a mountain if we can convince our people to wait until Christmas to sing Christmas hymns. Is it possible today to create the kind of liturgical awareness that existed in the sixteenth century?

I believe it is, at least to an extent. Of course most of our employers are not going to give us the morning off for the Beheading of St. John. We cannot control what goes on outside the church, but we can provide better opportunities within the church for our people to worship. A good first step is the determination to hold services on important holy days, such as the Epiphany, the Annunciation, and the Ascension, even if few people are present. Churches in the more populated areas can go a step further and offer daily services. During the first centuries after the Reformation, it was common in larger cities to be able to hear a sermon nearly every day at one church or another (the schedule was so arranged that no individual parish would be responsible for more than one weekday sermon). Would this work today? Would anyone attend?

It might also be profitable to offer said or sung Matins (before work) and Vespers (after work). We can learn from our brothers and sisters in Christ in this regard. In the town where I used to live, Morning Prayer and Evening Prayer were read every day in the Episcopal church by lay persons licensed to do this. Sometimes others in the parish attended, sometimes not; but it was always done, and there was a certain comfort in knowing that the prayer of the Church continues even when one cannot be physically present. In the same town, Mass was held twice a day in the Catholic church, at 7:00 a.m. and 12:10 p.m. Knowing that official Catholic policy has discouraged private Masses in recent years, I asked a parishioner who attended daily Mass what was done if no one showed up. She was taken aback momentarily by the question, then answered that to her knowledge it had never happened. Each Mass normally had about forty people present, she reported, although she recalled that once during a blizzard there were only a handful. Where is this sort of devotion present among Lutherans? If we never give our people the opportunity for daily corporate worship, is it any surprise that they turn to such substitutes as Christian radio (which is often slanted toward American evangelicalism) or books such as the *Left Behind* series?

If the preceding ideas seem too innovative to implement, those dealing with the church year are much easier and more likely to be readily accepted. How do our churches encourage awareness of the liturgical year? Are the seasons clearly distinguished through appropriate liturgical texts and music, visual elements, and so on? Do our churches' schools teach and make evident the church year in classes, chapel services, bulletin boards, and artistic and musical activities? Are resources made available to families to help them observe seasons and holy days with special foods and other customs?[11]

One time of the year that many Lutherans still observe with some liturgical uncertainty is Holy Week, especially the Triduum; that is, the three days beginning with Maundy Thursday evening. The same Episcopal church mentioned above has a most memorable Triduum. When the altar is stripped on Holy Thursday, all its furnishings are taken to a temporary chapel in the parish hall. The chapel is fragrant with flowers, and chairs with kneelers are set up facing the temporary altar. A nearby table contains various devotional books. Members of the parish keep a vigil there through the night until noon on Friday, with at least two people signing up for each hour-long block. Those who experience it frequently describe it as a highlight of their year as Christians, second only to the Easter Vigil. The Vigil is held at 10:00 p.m. on Saturday, and it is celebrated in such a way that it is clearly the most important event of the year. At its conclusion around 1:00 a.m., a dessert feast is held in the parish hall, with lots of hors d'oeuvres, fruit, vegetables, sandwiches, cheeses, pastries, and chocolates, all beautifully laid out and served on the church's finest china, plus punch and wine. People gather around, eat, and talk for an hour or more.

Advent and Lent are times of liturgical distinction; and most of our churches, at least in the Lutheran Church–Missouri Synod, still have Wednesday evening services during those seasons. My current church uses Evening Prayer from the hymnal on Wednesdays during Advent. It is most carefully prepared, and the leaders are trained in the way they should carry themselves, gesture, speak, and sing, all with the goal of allowing the congregation to focus on

God rather than on the leader. The organ provides an unobtrusive accompaniment to the canticles so that the music does not overshadow the text. The organ is not used at all until the first Psalm (the entire service of light is sung without accompaniment). The appointed silences are substantial. The result is an Office in which the people can focus on God and his Word with very little to distract them. I would like to try, but have not yet had the opportunity, to do something similar on Wednesday evenings in Lent. I'd like to begin the service with Evening Prayer as described above, then retire to the parish hall for a simple supper (soup and bread, perhaps). During or immediately after supper a sermon would be preached, and then everyone would return to the church for Compline.

Creative engagement with the liturgical year can be a wonderful way to help strengthen our people in their lives as Christians. Most of the time they are receptive to such things, but sometimes it can seem like an uphill battle. I teach at a Lutheran university, and fully half our students are preparing for full-time church work. Each year the university makes a daily appointment calendar available for students to purchase, which includes the dates and times of sporting events, concerts, and other activities held on campus. A couple of years ago I suggested that the calendar also include an identification of each Sunday in the church year, along with the holy days observed by Lutherans. I was told that this would take too much space and that students would not be interested in it anyway. I argued, to no avail, that many students would indeed be interested; and even if they were not, it is still our responsibility to set before them those things that are important to our faith. Lutherans are a *de tempore* people. This is worth remembering.

Number 4: Pavlov's Liturgy

Just over a hundred years ago Russian physiologist Ivan Pavlov carried out a series of experiments that were to make his name a household word. Investigating the digestive processes of dogs, he discovered that they would begin to salivate even before they had been presented with any food; for they had learned that certain events, including the ringing of a bell, would always accompany feeding time. Soon they began to salivate upon hearing the bell, even if no food was presented. The dogs had been conditioned to equate the bell with food, and their salivation was a *conditioned reflex*.

Conditioned reflexes are a part of good liturgy. Someone once observed that you are not really dancing if you are still counting the steps. In the same way, it is difficult to be truly involved in the liturgy if you are constantly trying to figure out what comes next. With few exceptions, the liturgies for any given Lutheran territory changed little between the introduction of the Reformation and the late eighteenth century. And so several generations of Lutherans learned to do the liturgy the same way. Whatever else changed in the church and the world, the liturgy was a constant.

Today confusion reigns. The 1982 *Lutheran Worship* is one of the chief offenders in this regard. Where does the offering come? Is it after the prayers as in the Divine Service? Or immediately after the sermon as in the truncated Divine Service (also known as the Service of Holy Communion without Communion)? Or perhaps before the sermon as in Morning and Evening Prayer? What is the response to "This is the Word of the Lord"? Is it "Thanks be to God" as in Divine Service I? Or is it silence as in Divine Service II? What is the response to "The Lord be with you"? Is it "And with your spirit" (Divine Service I) or "And also with you" (Divine Service II)? Incredibly, I am told that this dual response to "The Lord be with you" will be perpetuated in the forthcoming *Lutheran Service Book.*

Some churches, trying to bring order into the confusion, make matters worse by using audible rubrics. By audible rubrics I mean those service directions given verbally by the pastor or other worship leader: "You may be seated to sing the hymn, which is number 123 in the blue *Lutheran Worship* hymnal found in the pew rack in front of you," or "We respond with the Nicene Creed, which is printed in the service folder immediately following the item you currently have your eyes glued to." Usually such prompting is given by a well-meaning pastor under the guise of helpfulness to visitors. But its unintended effect is to drive faithful parishioners up the proverbial wall. "We know, we know!" they cry in their hearts, but to no avail.

Perhaps an analogy would help to explain just why this is a problem. One pastime I enjoy whenever I have the opportunity is traditional English and American country dancing accompanied by live music. Each dance consists of certain steps or figures set to a tune of a fixed length that is repeated several times. The dances are first walked through so the dancers can learn the figures. Then, the first few times through a dance the leader briefly announces each figure to jog the dancers' memory. But as soon as it is apparent that the dancers know the dance, a good leader will drop out and allow the music to guide the dancers. Why? Because as the dancers attune themselves to the music, the steps become cleaner, the timing better, and everyone is more relaxed. Sometimes inexperienced leaders feel they must announce the figures throughout the entire dance. The result is usually choppy figures, with people dancing behind the beat as they listen to the leader rather than to the music.

Something similar happens in the liturgy. When it is allowed to flow without interruption, the participants get into a "groove," and nothing matters to them except the work of the liturgy itself. But when it is constantly interrupted by directions to sit, turn to a particular page, and so on, then they are jolted out of their participation in that work as their attention shifts from God's Word to human words.

This is not to say that helping visitors through the liturgy is unimportant. But there are better ways to do it. Written instructions in the service folder should be as clear as possible. Church members should be taught to be alert to anyone sitting near them having difficulty with the service. Even when a large portion of the congregation is unfamiliar with a particular liturgy, for example, when it is being introduced, it should still be possible to do it without undue interruption. In such cases I have frequently placed "ringers" near the front of the congregation. They have specially marked copies of the service telling them exactly when to sit and stand. They do so without further direction, and the rest of the congregation follows them. When these simple steps are taken, it should be possible to eliminate nearly all audible rubrics from the service. I guarantee, once you have become accustomed to doing it this way, you will never want to go back to relying on audible directions.

This brings to mind a related concern, one I hesitate to raise because it means accusing certain pastors of violating the seventh commandment. I am sure they know the Lord's command, "You shall not steal," but somehow they manage to ignore it or (to give them the benefit of the doubt) to justify their actions in spite of it. Their crime has to do with the fact that there are several parts of the liturgy that properly belong to the people and to no one else.

The one that occurs most frequently is the response to every prayer; namely, the little word "Amen." In bringing forth their "Amen" the congregation is saying, "I agree; this is my prayer, too." So often, however, just as grandma is getting ready to speak the word, the pastor comes running up, grabs it from the tip of her tongue, and rushes back to the front of the church so swiftly that most people don't even notice anything amiss. But the evidence is right there in plain view, for in the next split second comes the booming voice of the pastor in microphone-induced magnificence: "AMEN!" The next time this happens, I recommend that parishioners follow the dictates of Matthew 18, which directs, "If your brother sins against you, go and tell him his fault, between you and him alone." Just ask gently as the pastor shakes your hand at the back of the church, "Why did you steal my Amen?" If your pastor has a sense of humor and a modicum of liturgical sensitivity, then the two of you can have a good laugh together.

Once the Amen has been restored to the people, you can concentrate on other responses that ought to be as quick and as sure as salivating when the bell rings: "Bless we the Lord." *"Thanks be to God."* "Lord, in your mercy: *hear our prayer."* "This is the Word of the Lord." *"Thanks be to God"* (even when it's *not* printed). "This is the Gospel of the Lord." *"Praise to you, O Christ."* "The Lord be with you." *"And also, uh, with you or, uh, your spirit."* (The last one could use a little work.)

Good liturgy is like good drama: it is worth doing, everyone has a part, and nothing interrupts its flow. In this regard we can learn something from Rome. The Constitution on the Sacred Liturgy of the Second Vatican Council (1962–65) decreed that "the rites should be distinguished by a noble simplicity; they should be short, clear, and unencumbered by useless repetitions; they should be within the people's powers of comprehension, and as a rule not require much explanation."[12] This is precisely what one sees in early Lutheran liturgies, and it is a worthy goal for our liturgies today.

Number 5: The Role of the Choir

While it is true that the texts of Lutheran liturgies changed little between the sixteenth and eighteenth centuries, church music changed considerably. In the sixteenth century the choir's role was liturgical. It sang the parts of the liturgy assigned to it, and the thematic unity of the liturgical Proper texts gave a focus to the service. The liturgy and hymns were sung mostly by the choir in unison or polyphonic settings, with the organ (if present) introducing individual items and playing alternate verses. The congregation sang well in a few places, especially during the first years after the Reformation; but the role of the people became less significant toward the end of the century as the choir sang more polyphony, displacing the congregation's song. In some places it was several generations before the common people became accustomed to singing in church.

By the second half of the eighteenth century the people, accompanied by organ, were singing the liturgy and hymns, and by all accounts singing them well. The choir had assumed a new role: that of performing extraliturgical religious music for the listening congregation. This is the role it retains today in most of our churches.

In the liturgical renewal of the 1960s and 1970s there were calls for the choir to assume once again its task of leading liturgical song, bringing into focus the day's theme. Church publishers produced volumes of Introits, Graduals, Responsories, Verses, Offertories, and hymn concertatos for this purpose. Some churches used them regularly; many did not. Today, most such choral settings are in filing cabinets gathering dust. Hymn concertatos are still being published, but their performance is often limited to special occasions. What happened, and why did a renewed liturgical role for the choir fail to take root in our churches?

One reason, certainly, is that it is hard to buck tradition. With no authority to enforce liturgical renewal, many churches saw no need for it or perhaps never even heard of it; and pastors, accustomed to doing the liturgy in their own comfortable manner and knowing the limits of their education and skill in the matter, often lacked the will and insight to make significant changes. A second reason is that having the choir sing principally hymn stanzas and liturgical Propers can leave choir members feeling unchallenged, especially if the music consists mostly of easy unison settings, which was frequently the case. Third, choirs often prefer learning the classics of church choral literature, or simply music that is more fun to sing. Fourth, people today are accustomed to thinking of music in terms of entertainment rather than of ritual, and so congregations are not used to hearing music that lacks a catchy tune. A fifth reason has to do with the three-year lectionary and its impact on the liturgy.

The three-year lectionary was originally developed by Roman Catholics after the Second Vatican Council in an attempt to familiarize churchgoers with more Scripture. It was adopted by North American Lutherans and various other churches in the 1970s, and today it has almost completely displaced the traditional one-year cycle that had been in use since the early ninth century. The one-year cycle did have one significant disadvantage: whereas in early Lutheranism pastors preached every year on the appointed Gospel, by the mid-twentieth century pastors frequently chose to substitute other biblical texts to provide variety in their preaching, and so the whole idea of a lectionary was lost. But the three-year lectionary also has some notable disadvantages. One is that the annual repetition of the Gospel appointed for the day has been lost. In the old days, people knew what theme to expect for every Sunday of the church year, especially if the pastor maintained tradition and preached on the Gospel every week. Now, except for festivals and a few other Sundays in the year, the readings are repeated only once every three years, which is too long for congregational memory to be effective. Add to this the fact that pastors today will frequently preach on one of the other readings, and every Sunday seems new and different.

A second disadvantage of the three-year lectionary is that the other Propers—Introit, Gradual or Psalm, Alleluia, Offertory, and hymn of the day—are still on a one-year cycle. This makes it difficult to tie all the Propers together so they reinforce one another, as the readings will match the other Propers at most once every three years. Of course a three-year series of Propers is conceivable and, barring a return to the one-year lectionary, which seems unlikely, is arguably the best solution (and will, I understand, be implemented in the new *Lutheran Service Book*). But it has the disadvantage of requiring the choir to learn three times as much music, making it even less likely that they will actually sing the Propers. And while it is fairly simple to come up with a three-year cycle for most Propers, it is more difficult for the hymn of the day, because good hymns are harder to write. Even if we had a lectionary-based hymn for every Sunday of the three-year cycle, they could not all be included in a hymnal, at least not if we have any hope of fitting it into our pew racks.[13]

A third negative impact of the three-year lectionary is the limited amount of choral music available for it. Composers have had over a thousand years to produce music for the traditional lectionary, but only about thirty for the new one. One might think that church publishers would move quickly to produce new music, but in fact the very opposite has happened: less lectionary-based music is available now than ever before. The reason is simple: publishers do not make money by selling music that will be used only once in three years. What sells is music with general texts that can be used on more than one occasion during a single year. The result has been a further fragmentation of the liturgy, with the Gospel pointing in one direction, the sermon frequently in another, each of the other Propers in another, and the supporting music for choir in yet another.

In this environment, it is difficult to produce a coherent liturgy, one where everything points in the same direction and all the people leave knowing the focus of the day. Difficult, but not impossible. It just takes more work and a deeper knowledge of available music. In Bach's day, cantata texts that were based on the Gospel for every Sunday in the church year were available from various authors. They were not mere restatements of the Gospel, but rather devotional commentaries on it. Because this sort of text is rarely available in today's choral music, it will require a new conception of church music that moves beyond the organ and SATB choir. It is one in which the Word predominates and the musical forces are flexible, responding to the liturgical needs of the day. Ideally, the Propers and extra music point to, reflect on, or respond to the Gospel for the day. This includes pre-service music, which may well be vocal rather than instrumental. Depending on the Gospel, some contemporary Christian songs may be effective here. (I make a distinction between the performance-oriented contemporary Christian song, some of which has solid lyrics that go well with particular readings, and the praise and worship songs intended for congregational use, whose texts are by and large not specific enough to use in this way.)

Also useful for this purpose is the Gospel-based music for soloist and for small ensemble composed by seventeenth- and eighteenth-century German Lutherans, only some of which is available in English. I have also found success with English choral music from the Tudor period. One difficulty here, though, is that many of these texts simply restate the Gospel. Although there certainly is value in allowing worshipers to reflect once more on the Gospel, it would be better, in my opinion, if the texts went further, applying the biblical readings to real life. I hope that creative and resourceful poets and church musicians will take up this challenge.

A lectionary-based repertoire will require a change in the way music directors select music. Last summer I attended a reading session for Lutheran choir directors at which music from various publishers was presented. The session was billed as a review of music suitable for the fall's services, so I was all prepared with my list of lectionary readings so I could match up what was presented with appropriate Sundays. It was, alas, not to be. Some of the music was admittedly quite attractive, but only one or two of the pieces were based on the lectionary, and those were not from the fall's readings, so I didn't find anything I thought I could use. It would have been more useful to me if the presenter had said, "This is the Gospel for the umpteenth Sunday after Pentecost, and here are two pieces that relate to it."

Many churches have several different ensembles that participate in services, and the music director properly asks them to keep the Gospel or the season in mind as they select music. That is a start, but it doesn't go nearly far enough. In fact, in a lectionary-based system such an approach is backwards. One should rather *start* with the Gospel, then select music on the basis of its relationship to the Gospel or another reading, and finally schedule the needed musicians. There is also the important step of consulting with the pastor to find out where the sermon is headed. Ideally this should be done early, before the choir season starts. Pastors who persist in planning at the last minute can at least look at the hymns and other music to give them ideas on where to go with the sermon. It would help if the pastor can be convinced always to preach on the Gospel, especially during the festival half of the church year and during the period when this musical planning system is being developed. In any case, if the hymns, Propers, and other music are truly unified, all pointing in one direction, then it will be the off-topic sermon that sticks out, not the music. I should add parenthetically that it is *not* necessary for all the congregational hymns to point to the day's readings. Hymns have differing functions; some will reflect the readings, but others may be chosen for another reason, such as a hymn of invocation preceding a confessional service, Communion hymns during the distribution, and the like.

The scenario I have just presented is an ideal one. Now we should say a few words about real life. It sometimes happens that a perfect text for an occasion is set to mediocre music, while a piece of great music has a text that is only slightly connected with the Gospel. This is a problem, because good musicians do not like to perform mediocre music. Confronted with this situation, more often than not I will choose the piece with the great music and hope that people will make the connection. If I doubt that they will, I may place a note in the bulletin explaining how the music responds to the Gospel. Occasionally, because of the particular readings or the available performing forces, I may be unable to find usable music related to anything in the readings. In that case, I usually place it as far from the readings as possible, such as during the Communion, reasoning that if it cannot support the day's readings, at least it can avoid distracting from them.

We have centuries of music for worship to draw upon, but it isn't nearly enough to cover the texts in our lectionary. It may take centuries more before this happens. In the meantime, we do as well as we can, always putting the Word first.

Number 6: City and Village

Most territorial Lutheran liturgical orders from the sixteenth century have separate provisions for services in cities and in villages. In cities, there were often Latin schools with boychoirs capable of singing a Latin Mass, which was done with as much ceremony as was customary in the region. At times the liturgy was done in German. In villages, where there was no choir, the Mass was paraphrased in German and sung (at least ideally) by the people, who were led by the schoolmaster or parish clerk.

There is good reason today to distinguish between larger and smaller churches, for the latter often lack the musical leadership needed to sing the liturgy adequately. It does not help that most of the musical settings in our hymnals require instrumental accompaniment, and in many communities competent organists and pianists are increasingly difficult to find. Churches have tried all sorts of ways to deal with this problem; one obvious solution is to speak the entire liturgy, including the hymns. But in my experience, this solution is eminently unsatisfying, and congregations tire of it quickly. There is another alternative that has much to commend it, but is hardly ever used: singing the liturgy unaccompanied.

Of course this requires both a setting that works without accompaniment and one or several singers with pleasing voices who can lead the singing, but it may be easier to find these than a well-trained pianist or organist.

There are two settings in our current hymnals that work well unaccompanied: the third communion setting in the *Lutheran Book of Worship* (LBW), which is mostly in unison plainchant, and the sole setting in *The Lutheran Hymnal* of 1941, which is a mixture of styles, including Anglican chant and harmonized plainchant, and which is quite lovely sung unaccompanied in four parts. As nice as these settings are, though, I would prefer more options. It seems to me that several of the simpler items from the standard Gregorian Mass Ordinaries, translated into English, would fit the bill nicely. They are attractive and not too difficult, they require no accompaniment, and they wear well. Such a setting could find wider use as well. Eugene Brand, who directed the development of the LBW, has in recent years called for a chant setting as the preferred mode for normal Sunday use, with the other settings reserved for occasional and festival use. In a recent article, he notes that a chant setting such as LBW, Holy Communion Setting Three, serves to illuminate the text without forcing a particular interpretation on it, as do the other LBW settings. As example, he cites the Sanctus, asking whether its mood is hushed and mystical or gloriously triumphant. In chant, he concludes, it can be either. With more interpretive settings, the mood is determined by the music, and so the music begins to draw attention to itself and away from the text. He hastens to add, however, that he does not mean to impugn interpretive settings such as LBW, Settings One and Two:

> Occasional use of these settings can be exhilarating and refreshing, and provide necessary diversity. Such occasional use is not destructive because the every-Sunday chant has bored the text deep into people's consciousness. But regular use of such settings diminishes the impressive power of the texts and soon may lead to the thirst for even more such settings.[14]

These comments match my own experience with liturgy. I am not so naive as to think that smaller churches would welcome an unaccompanied liturgy with open arms. But in the right place, with the right leaders, it could work well; and such a church could serve as a model showing how it could be done. It would be an interesting twist if smaller churches were to adopt unaccompanied chant settings of the liturgy successfully, for they might well be the envy of larger churches.

Number 7: "And the children shall lead"

Of all the books by Carl Schalk, *First Person Singular* (MorningStar, 1998) may not be the best known; but it is, I think, my favorite. In it he presents his own thoughts on various matters concerning worship, and some of the most earnest and compelling parts of the book are those dealing with children. He believes that children are more capable, musically speaking, than we give them credit for; and he would like to see them more actively participating in the church's worship.

This is hardly a new idea. During the period we are considering, in places that had schools, the school choir was the church's choir. The liturgy and hymns were all sung by boys from the school, sometimes only by them, as the congregation in some places sang poorly or not at all. Of course it helped that boys' voices, on average, did not change until age 17 or 18 (this was true until the twentieth century), so they had an extended period serving as trebles in the choir. As choirs began to sing more polyphony in the second half of the sixteenth century, older boys and men were needed to sing the lower parts; but most of the burden was still carried by schoolboys.[15]

How was this possible? Quite simply, these children were taught to sing and to read music. On average, four hours per week were spent in music instruction through most, if not all, of a child's time in school. This includes time for singing and music fundamentals only; any time spent learning an instrument was extra. Now I have examined several of the school music textbooks from the period. While they present the material in a systematic manner to aid learning, it is nonetheless apparent that we have discovered much since then about how children learn, and in particular how they learn music. It ought to be possible today to spend fewer hours and accomplish similar results. How many hours is anybody's guess, but I have no doubt that if every Lutheran elementary school devoted just two half-hours per week in each grade to general music instruction—that is, instruction in music fundamentals and singing, not playing an instrument—then we would see a huge improvement in the quality of music making in our schools and, in the long term, in our churches as well.

There is one caveat. I alluded above to modern methods of music instruction. In order to achieve this dream, teachers of music must be familiar with these methods. It has been a long tradition in our Lutheran schools that classroom teachers handle general music instruction. It is, to be sure, a good and worthy practice for all teachers to sing with their students. But their education has, by necessity, prepared them to teach reading, math, science, social studies, and so on. Few have specialized education in music instruction methods. Many people think that anyone who knows a bit about music can teach the subject, and they can to a certain extent; but very few have the musical knowledge, the vision of how much children are capable of in music, and the familiarity with modern methods of music education to really pull it off. It is therefore advisable for schools to have on staff, either full-time or part-time, a specialist in elementary music education. Very few professional musicians would be qualified to teach music in an elementary school, because they have not learned the methods. Elementary music specialists know how to do it.

How much can we expect children to learn? A few years ago, I was privileged to visit Immanuel Lutheran School in Valparaiso, Indiana, and sit in on music classes taught by William Ickstadt. At 8:30 a.m., the sixth to eighth grade choir rehearsed. It had sixty members, and the director told me that he had had 99 percent perfect attendance at services and performances during the previous year. They rehearsed hymns for the next Sunday and three choral pieces, including Vivaldi's *Laudamus te* and Benjamin Britten's difficult *Ceremony of Carols* for three-part treble chorus; and they sang them well, with a purity of vowels that would put most of our adult choirs to shame. Later in the morning the fifth grade music class met, and they were reading music at sight without hearing it played or sung first. The third grade class was up at the chalkboard writing music notation.

An exception, you say? Hardly. Schoolchildren all over the country are doing this, although the practice is more common in public than in Lutheran schools. It isn't so hard as some might think. There are twenty-six letters in the alphabet, and most children learn to read, write, and use them to make words and sentences by the time they complete elementary school. There are only seven notes in the scale. Is it harder to learn seven notes than twenty-six letters? We just need someone to teach them.

A reader might wonder why I have said nothing thus far about the desire for children to learn a musical instrument. It is true, I admit, that learning an instrument is useful; but it is even more useful *for our purposes as Lutherans* that children learn to sing and read music. Why? Because realistically, only a few of our children will continue to play an instrument after they graduate from high school or college, while all of them (we hope) will continue to sing in church every Sunday for the rest of their lives. I have to admit I have an ulterior motive here: as a church musician, I would love to have a church full of people who can read and sing any new hymn I put in front of them. And the kicker is, it's easier than most people think, and I know many children who can attest to that.

Is there any place, then, for instrumental music in our Lutheran schools? Absolutely. When I lived in Germany, our parish church had a brass choir that assisted the organ in accompanying hymns. To make it easier for both adults and children to participate, the instruments were owned by the church, and anyone could check one out, learn to play it, and join the ensemble. The children learned from the adults in the choir. Something similar could work in our churches and schools. There are, to be sure, good reasons for having a traditional band in an elementary school, not the least being that band music is readily available. But if a school wanted to explore new paths and find a way for children to be truly useful in a church service, it might establish a wind, brass, or string ensemble and have it learn to accompany the liturgy and hymns and play a piece or two for a postlude. The key is to integrate church and school music in a way that the music of the children is not just well done and attractive, but is also vital to the church's liturgy.

As I write these words, I have just returned from a Sunday church service. The congregational singing was strong and the choral and instrumental music inspiring. As I left the church, I heard someone exclaim what a wonderful service it was. But there was something missing. There was no Communion, and I left unfulfilled. The liturgy, which was printed in the service folder, followed the same order as in the hymnal; but the words were changed just enough to be annoying, and I couldn't say any of it without reading it. The sermon was quite good, but it was unrelated to any of the readings. The choir sang no Propers, and the choral music was unrelated to either the readings or the sermon. The liturgy, such as it was, was punctuated by constant verbal instructions. As a result, even now I cannot recall the theme of the service, if there was one. I suppose I shouldn't be surprised that some people thought that the service was wonderful, for they may never have known anything better. But we know better. Let's make it happen.

NOTES

1   Letter to Georg of Anhalt, 10 July 1545, in *D. Martin Luthers Werke: kritische Gesamtausgabe* (Weimar: Böhlau, 1883–), series 4 ("Briefwechsel"), vol. 11, 132–34. Not in the American edition of Luther's works.

2   *D. Martin Luthers Werke* (as above), series 1, vol. 49, 588; also in Luther's Works, American Edition, vol. 51 (Philadelphia: Fortress, 1958–86), 333.

3   See, for example, Gottfried Ephraim Scheibel, *Zufällige Gedancken von der Kirchen-Music, wie sie heutiges Tages beschaffen ist* (Frankfurt and Leipzig, 1721), 23, 29; Heinrich Bokemeyer, "Melodischer Vorhof," in *Critica musica*, ed. Johann Mattheson, vol. 2 (1725), 297–98; Johann Mattheson, *Der musicalische Patriot* (Hamburg, 1728; reprint Kassel: Bärenreiter, 1975), 105; Johann Adolph Scheibe, *Critischer Musikus* (Leipzig, 1745), 161–62.

4   Scheibe (1745), 162.

5   *Kirchenordnung, wie es mit der lehre göttliches worts, austheilung der heiligen hochwirdigen sacrament, christlichen ceremonien, ordentlicher ubung des waren gottesdiensts, in den kirchen des herzogthums Churland und Semigallien in Liefland, sol stetes vermittelst göttlicher hülf gehalten werden* (Rostock, 1572); reprinted in Emil Sehling, *Die evangelischen Kirchenordnungen des XVI. Jahrhunderts* (Leipzig, 1902–13; Tübingen, 1955–), vol. 5, 90.

6   Günther Stiller, *Johann Sebastian Bach and Liturgical Life in Leipzig*, trans. Herbert J. A. Bouman, Daniel F. Poellot, and Hilton C. Oswald; ed. Robin A. Leaver (St. Louis: Concordia, 1984), 45.

7   Christian Gerber, *Historie der Kirchen-Ceremonien in Sachsen* (Dresden and Leipzig, 1732), 455.

8   *Lutheran Book of Worship* (Minneapolis: Augsburg, 1978), p. 75; *Lutheran Worship* (St. Louis: Concordia, 1982), p. 167.

9   *Groß Catholisch Gesangbuch*, 1631; reprinted in Wilhelm Bäumker, *Das katholische deutsche Kirchenlied in seinen Singweisen* (Freiburg i. B., 1886–1911), vol. 1, 228.

10 See the details in Joseph Herl, *Worship Wars in Early Lutheranism: Choir, Congregation, and Three Centuries of Conflict* (New York: Oxford, 2004), 37–39.

11 For creative ideas on observing the liturgical year, see three books by Peter Mazar, all published by Liturgy Training Publications in Chicago: *To Crown the Year: Decorating the Church Through the Seasons* (1995); *Winter: Celebrating the Season in a Christian Home* (1996); and *School Year, Church Year: Customs and Decorations for the Classroom* (2001). See also *Teaching and Celebrating Advent* by Patricia and Donald Griggs, rev. ed. (Livermore, Calif.: Griggs Educational

Service, 1974); *The Art of Tradition: A Christian Guide to Building a Family* by Mary Caswell Walsh (Denver: Living the Good News, 1998); and *Unplug the Christmas Machine: a Complete Guide to Putting Love and Joy Back into the Season* by Jo Robinson and Jean Coppock Staeheli, rev. ed. (New York: William Morrow, 1991).

12 *Constitution on the Sacred Liturgy,* § 34; quoted in *The Liturgy Documents: A Parish Resource,* rev. ed., ed. Mary Ann Simcoe (Chicago: Liturgy Training Publications, 1983).

13 I am simplifying somewhat, for the sake of the argument, the role of the hymn of the day. In early Lutheran churches, it was usually a German hymn substituted for the Latin Gradual and often reflected the appointed Gospel only on festivals. At other times, the hymn was selected because it was a traditional hymn for the liturgical season or because it reflected the general idea of a season. This helped to establish within Lutheranism a set of hymns, which, with regular repetition, achieved "classic" status. Today, part of the difficulty in assigning hymns of the day is balancing these classic hymns with more recent hymns, often non-Lutheran in origin, that may be beloved by our people and that may even better reflect the readings for a given day.

14 *CrossAccent: Journal of the Association of Lutheran Church Musicians* 11/3 (Fall 2003): 26.

15 Early Lutheran documents contain scattered references to schoolgirl choirs, but apparently this was quite rare, with such choirs singing only plainchant, not polyphony.

BARBARA J. RESCH

"A New Song Here Shall Be Begun:" Reformation-era Hymnody for Twenty-first Century Children

M artin Luther's first hymn may be the least well known of all his hymns. It is a ballad about the first two martyrs of the Reformation, two young men who were burned at the stake in 1523 for refusing to recant their faith. It starts with these words: "A new song here shall be begun—the Lord God help our singing!"[1]

This couplet summarizes the remarkable era that was about to begin, a period in which Luther and others presented an amazing number of new hymns to a church that was unused to singing. These hymns encapsulated Reformation theology, taught the believers what God had done for them, and gave them words to sing back to God. They were a crucial ingredient in the spiritual growth and nurture of these Reformation Christians.

This body of stalwart hymnody, now hundreds of years old, continues to be a rich source of spiritual nourishment for today's young people whose needs are not very different from those of the youth who first sang these hymns nearly 500 years ago. To learn theological truths, to be a part of the worshiping community, to study and enjoy the art of music, and to find words to express their faith—these were salutary goals for students during the time of the Reformation that remain appropriate today.

A number of teachers contributed their thoughts to the development of this paper. All of them have taught Reformation-era hymnody to twenty-first century Lutheran children, and all are confident in the belief that the melodies, the theology, and the rationale of that body of music are not only accessible but also actually appealing to modern children. Their experiences, along with those of the writer, provide a body of anecdotal evidence, often in the words of the children themselves, that the hymnody of the Reformation is not simply an artifact but an active and vital treasure ready and waiting to be used.

Learning Theological Truths

The scope and significance of the teaching that took place during the Reformation cannot be overestimated. Luther's conviction about the importance of teaching, combined with Melanchthon's wisdom and experience in education, established a thorough and effective plan for people of his time to learn and understand God's Word. The *Small Catechism* served as an efficient textbook, presenting key elements of Reformation faith in understandable statements, in a question and answer format that lent itself well to classroom teaching. But wise teachers also know that a text carried by an interesting melody will work its way into the memory even more effectively, and thus the hymns based on the *Catechism* became valuable tools to help people learn and remember Reformation theology.

An interesting example is "These are the holy ten commands" ("Here is the tenfold sure command," *Lutheran Worship,* No. 331), a twelve-stanza hymn that explicates the Ten Commandments, with a text set by Luther to a thirteenth-century hymn tune. Ulrich Leupold points out that the Wittenberg church order of 1533 directs the choir boys to sing this hymn before catechism sermons,[2] suggesting that it was indeed considered an appropriate hymn for children to sing at that time in history.

A skeptic might wonder how this hymn could possibly be helpful to modern day children. It has many verses, its tune originated over 700 years ago, its metrical text nearly 500 years ago, and it is based on a set of commandments that are largely ignored by current society. Contemporary educational thought takes a dim view of shaking the finger of the Law at children. Postmodern society has little use for a hymn that reiterates all of those "thou shalts and shalt nots."

Yet some corners of the church still recognize the critical importance of catechesis, of teaching children the tenets of their faith, including the "shalts and shalt nots" laid out in the Law. One Lutheran teacher whose young students sing this hymn with great energy uses it to teach the *Catechism*. Each stanza of the hymn is an answer to the question, "What does this mean?" She spends a week or two on each stanza, making sure that the children understand the vocabulary and the implications of the text. ("Nor foul your tongue with calumny"does warrant some explanation.) This tune has been described by children as "bouncy," a reference to the characteristic eighth note/quarter note pickup rhythm that is found in so many of Luther's hymns, and they love it. She reports that they clamor to sing this hymn so much that, once they have learned it, they like to play a game where they write the number of each stanza on a slip of paper and then choose a slip at random from a box to determine which one they will get to sing from memory.

Comparable to the Ten Commandments hymn in its role as a teacher of the faith is *Wir glauben all* ("We all believe in one true God," *Lutheran Worship,* No. 213). But unlike the relatively simple structure of "Here is the tenfold sure command," Luther's hymn based on the Creed has an angular and far-reaching melody with ten dissimilar phrases, a melodic range of a tenth and several melismas that tempt the singer to end the word early. This melody carries three stanzas of text, each one paraphrasing one of the three articles of the Nicene Creed. The hymn is what my students call "a three-pager," and is both musically and textually challenging.

The teacher mentioned previously takes the time to discuss and explain each phrase of this hymn text and then has the students create a picture or symbol that represents each phrase. The resulting chart of icons serves as a "cue card" for singing, freeing the children from the printed page of the hymnal and letting them sing "by heart" in the fullest sense of that term. More importantly, this process of working to restate the meaning of the text in a picture ensures that the students have a deeper understanding of these words.

My students once calculated that it takes three times longer to sing "We all believe in one true God" than it does to speak the Nicene Creed. While musing on this discovery, one of them concluded that singing the hymn "lets you think about the words, plus you have to concentrate more because it's harder to sing than to talk." This is a profound statement about the power of music to engage the whole brain and deliver a text to both the memory and the understanding of a singer. We speak thousands of words easily and sometimes thoughtlessly throughout the day, but the extra effort necessary to sing, placing the right word on the right note at the right time, intensifies the potency of the sung text. Surely the Reformers realized this and were careful to frame versifications of the *Catechism* that were authentic, knowing that these words would remain with the singers.

Other examples of didactic Reformation hymnody abound. "Our Father, who from heaven above" (*Lutheran Worship*, No. 431) functions similarly to elucidate and expand on the explanation of the Lord's Prayer in the *Catechism*. Leupold refers to another of Luther's hymns, "Dear Christians, one and all rejoice" (*Lutheran Worship*, No. 353), as the "ballad of the believer's justification,"[3] a gradually unfolding narrative that presents the full story of salvation. Children love stories, and this hymn could be taught as an ongoing lesson, a stanza per week, until the whole tale has been told.

In Geneva John Calvin was also overseeing the versification of the Psalms and canticles, putting God's Word into the mouths and hearts of the Reformation people. The tunes by Louis Bourgeois and others typically used rhythmic combinations of only two or three note values and are engaging in their strength and buoyancy. Like Luther, Calvin understood both the necessity of placing the Scriptures into people's hands and the power of music to make those words even more memorable.

Too often the songs that are given children to sing in modern times are not these authentic expressions of the faith. Carl Schalk has written:

> The church has failed children by simply neglecting to teach those songs which best nourish and nurture the faith. . . . One of the most significant things the church can do to pass on the faith to the coming generation is to teach them a basic core of hymns which the church uses to confess and celebrate the faith.[4]

The need for confessional teaching to a new generation is as great now as it was in the Reformation era, and the hymnic tools provided by the Reformers are as appropriate now as they ever were.

Joining the Worshiping Community

Both Calvin and Luther were intent on teaching children to become a part of the worshiping community. Theirs was not a culture that established a schedule of separate services for children or a separate body of hymnody for children. The instructive nature of the new body of congregational song was appropriate for both adults and children, and people were encouraged to sing their faith in all corners of their lives. Calvin advocated the singing of psalms not only in church but "even in our rooms and in the fields."[5] And the well-known painting of the Luther family singing at the table accompanied by their father is a clear illustration of intergenerational singing at home.

Many Reformation-era hymns, in fact, are composed in a way that allows for shared participation by a range of ages. Whether or not this was by design, to include children who had not yet learned to read words or music as well as adults who were not literate, it is a happy circumstance that provides for inclusive singing. For example, the "Leisen" hymns with the refrain "Kyrie eleison"[6] can be sung with the non-readers joining in on the "Lord, have mercy," listening and waiting for their cue, and beginning to learn the rest of the words in the process. The "Alleluia" at the end of each section of *Christ ist erstanden* ("Christ is arisen," *Lutheran Worship*, No. 124) is another shared response. Hymns from other times and places also offer this opportunity, among them *Gelobt sei Gott* ("O Lord, we praise you," *Lutheran* Worship, No. 238) and *Lasst uns erfreuen* ("A hymn of glory let us sing," *Lutheran Worship*, No. 149).

Vacation Bible School (VBS) is seldom a site where Reformation hymnody is taught, at least in part because the time is short and the age span of the children is wide, typically including a large number of preschoolers. One pastor who was determined to teach "A mighty fortress" to the VBS children was able to convey the imagery and melody to the older children and primed the youngest ones to listen for the question "Ask ye, Who is this?" at which point they joined in with a very energetic "Jesus Christ it is!" The level of involvement is age-appropriate—manageable for young children—while focusing all attention on the heart of the Gospel message expressed at that point in the hymn.

Another Luther hymn that encourages shared participation by the entire gathering of worshipers is one that adults consider difficult but that children love to sing: "Isaiah, mighty seer, in spirit soared" (*Lutheran Worship*, No. 214), the song of Isaiah. This one is a "four-pager," but those four pages are full of brilliant sensory imagery—sights, sounds, and smells—that stimulates a child's imagination. Once while leading a group of children ages four through thirteen in a choir camp devotion using this hymn, I taught the "Holy is God, the Lord of Sabaoth" phrase to everyone, so those who could read sang the whole hymn but even the youngest children joined that full-throated three-fold Sanctus. The children sang enthusiastically and accurately, and several of them cited this as their favorite song of the week.

One older girl told me, "There are two things I love about the Isaiah song. One is when we sing the word 'heaven' on the highest note. The other is that I always get chills when we sing 'Holy is God, the Lord of Sabaoth!' because I feel like I am singing with the angels." Hers is a superb insight. As a member of the Holy Christian Church she was singing in a choir that spanned both time and place, repeating words sung by saints and angels on a timeless continuum. For twenty-first century children, who witness a lot of "living for the moment," this experience folds them into a community of believers who have preceded them and who will follow them, as well as those who surround them in the present.

Experienced teachers will testify that children are generally more open to new musical experiences than adults. Calvin and Luther wisely advocated the formation of children's choirs for the purpose of leading congregations, unaccustomed to taking an active singing role in the service, in the newly-composed congregational music. Rather than being relegated to a place of insignificance in the service, the children thus became leaders of the church's song in the worshiping communities of the Reformation. Calvin's strategy included:

> Selecting children and teaching them to sing in a clear and distinct fashion, so that people, listening with attention and following with the heart what was sung by the mouth, might, little by little, become accustomed to sing together.[7]

Apparently this kind of musical leadership by the choir was necessary because the congregation was handicapped by an inability to read music and thus could not sing the new tunes. Sternfeld cites this memorable Christmas service in Geneva:

> Indeed, on December 25, 1561, the Geneva congregation was ordered to abstain from accompanying the songmaster and the students in the singing of new psalm tunes because, to the horror of visitors, many of the congregation sang along with the new songs haphazardly, without knowing the melody.[8]

Church musicians who have survived the process of introducing a new hymnal to a parish will recognize the crucial role the choir plays in teaching the congregation. As in the Reformation example described earlier, the choir can model the new hymn or portion of the liturgy by singing clearly and confidently while the people listen and participate as they are able. A choir of children, while not providing a huge body of sound, can still offer a musical example for the congregation to follow. They may sing the new hymn first as a choral voluntary or lesson response before it is given to the congregation to sing. My own children's choirs have taken this leadership responsibility seriously, often introducing a new hymn by singing the first stanzas alone and then trying hard to help their fellow worshippers as they joined in. On more than one occasion, members of the congregation commented on the process and remarked, "I figured that if the kids could sing it, I could probably learn it too."

Striving for Musical Literacy

Another goal at the time of the Reformation that is shared by educators in modern times was the implementation of a comprehensive music education. Although school music teaching existed in Germany before the Reformation, evidence suggests that it was not consistent or effective. Andreas Ornithoparcus wrote in 1517, "Germany nourishes many cantors but few musicians," and that cantors were chosen "by the shrillness of their voice, not for their cunning in that art, thinking that God is pleased with bellowing and braying."[9] Good singing became an important goal of music instruction. One document cites letters to classroom teachers in which the cantor was advised that the chorus was "to sing, not to shout, that too broad pronunciation of vowels and diphthongs were be to avoided, and flexible voice production to be aimed at."[10] Luther's well-known remark that "a schoolmaster must know how to sing or I would not allow him to teach" also points up the importance attached to good singing, especially among those in positions of teaching children, and the supporting relationships between the church, school, and community in the newly reformed German educational system.[11]

The necessity for singing that was not only accurate but also artful grew out of the aforementioned need for musical leadership provided by the choirs as they introduced and supported congregational singing. The program of music instruction supported by both Luther and Calvin encompassed more than singing, however. In the course of the school day there might be time for devotional singing or instruction in sacred songs during religion classes, but music instruction included theoretical as well as practical study and was a required part of the school curriculum.

In the schools of Germany music classes were always held the first hour after lunch, from noon to 1:00 p.m., perhaps for dietary reasons; Agricola noted the physiological importance of music as a "restorative against fagged minds and bodies."[12] Melanchthon's directions were that "the first hour after noon every day all the children, large and small, should be practiced in music."[13] In the Lateinschulen "large and small" meant all students ages eight through eighteen. All schools, even those with only two teachers, had a cantor on the staff, and in some schools no student was admitted without being examined in music by the cantor.[14] Schools in Geneva also provided daily instruction in music, generally during the hour from 11:00 a.m. to noon.

Textbooks specifically for music instruction were developed to address the need for systematic and thorough music instruction. Georg Rhau's *Enchiridion* (1517) and Martin Agricola's *Rudimenta musices* (1539) were among the most widely used examples. These books were in Latin because that was the language of instruction in Lutheran schools, but Agricola and others also produced music textbooks in the vernacular for adult learners. Rhau's book made reference to musical and literary material from antiquity, the medieval period, and current sources, and included musical examples of both plainsong and polyphony. It was widely used and published in several editions over a thirty-six year period.[15]

Students in Genevan schools used psalmbooks as one source for their music reading practice, but also studied from a textbook by Louis Bourgeois, *Le droict chemin de musique* (1550), which was written in the vernacular and included instruction for both beginning and more advanced learners. In the preface to this book Bourgeois noted that he had purposely departed from medieval teaching methods to find an approach to music learning that was "simpler and shorter;" he introduced a sol-fa system and wrote in a patient style that guided the student through the learning process. He also acknowledged that those with considerable musical training had perpetuated the art of music faithfully for many years, but that their training had taken as long as a medical doctor's or lawyer's. Clearly he believed that a more attainable degree of musical preparation was beneficial and appropriate for the task at hand.[16]

Both Calvin and Luther were aware of the idea carried on from the Greeks that music has the power to elevate or debase the spirit. Calvin wrote in the preface to the Genevan Psalter of 1543:

> It must always be looked to that song be not light and frivolous but have weight and majesty, as Saint Augustine says; and there is likewise a great difference between the music one makes to entertain men at table and in their houses, and the psalms which are sung in the church. . . .
>
> Now among the things proper to recreate man and to give him pleasure, music is either the first or one of the principal, and we must think that it is a gift of God for that purpose. For which reason we must be careful not to abuse it . . . that it should not be the occasion of our giving free reign to dissoluteness or of making ourselves effeminate with disordered pleasures and that it should not become the instrument of lasciviousness.[17]

Calvin's caution in such musical choices meant that the practice of church music in Geneva did not include polyphonic choral music whose elaborate settings might obscure the text, and it did not include accompaniment by organ or other instruments. The responsibility for singing fell to the congregation as led by the choir and established the irrefutable need for general music instruction in all of the schools. Nonetheless, this restriction of opportunities for the creation and production of other musical genres in the church service meant that the scope of music education was also limited and focused on the reading and understanding of musical notation to support the learning of congregational song.

Luther's contrasting view was to encourage the arts, and especially that of music, to thrive in the service of the One who has created and given it. He drew on the rich musical heritage of the past and made sure that the music of the Reformation church contributed to and continued that musical tradition instead of ignoring it or bringing it to a halt. He offered church music to young people as an enjoyable alternative to less seemly musical options:

> And these songs (hymns) were arranged in four parts to give the youth, who should at any rate be trained in

music and the other fine arts, something to wean them away from love ballads and carnal songs and to teach them something of value in their place, thus combining the good with the pleasing as is proper for youth.[18]

A look at Lutheran music education in the twenty-first century suggests that many of the issues facing the Reformers have returned to challenge us. The repertoire of new congregational song has become limited by the inability of the average churchgoer to read music. The plague of simplistic praise songs with repetitive melodies that can be learned quickly by rote is often attributed to the congregation's helplessness to sing anything more complex. The outlook for "the singing Church" is perilous if its singing is restricted in this way.

Defensive explanations may be raised to explain why the Lutheran day school has not followed the Reformation pattern of an hour of sequential music instruction every day after lunch: The children already sing in their classroom devotions and in chapel services; there is no time for a special class after we teach all of the core subjects; we can't afford to hire someone with a music degree, and the classroom teachers are not comfortable teaching music. Imagine Luther's response to these statements, including his assertion that the discipline of music is also a core subject, not an optional add-on. The example he set centuries ago by insisting on universal musical education for German students has been credited for the dominance of German music in the centuries that followed. The musical legacy of the current educational establishment will be a paltry one if greater precedence is not given to music instruction today.

Enjoying the Art of Music

Although few Lutheran schools teach music with the rigor modeled by the schools of the Reformation, one musical benefit that modern children are able to glean easily from the hymnody of that time is the pleasure of involvement with well-crafted music. The experience of singing music that is aesthetically pleasing is seldom granted to the young, to whom modern culture typically offers music that is trivial and banal. Research shows that an individual's enjoyment of music grows with the complexity of the piece: the more complex it is (up to a point), the more we like it and the longer we like it. Children can be motivated to master musical challenges, and will work hard to learn a difficult hymn. Many hymns of the Reformation are robust, rhythmically interesting, and melodically appealing—all musical features that engage young people in the learning process.

Of all of the Reformation-era hymns that colleagues and I have taught to children, the one that emerges as an unexpected but overwhelming favorite is the previously mentioned "We all believe in one true God" (*Wir glauben all an einen Gott*). I have vivid memories of a middle school choir rehearsal when I announced that we would be singing hymn 212 in *Lutheran Worship* (a simpler creedal hymn in isorhythmic style from the seventeenth century), and the group rose up in protest and began to chant, "Let's sing 213! Two-thir-teen! Two-thir-teen!" The very idea that my choir was out of control because they wanted to sing *Wir glauben* was incomprehensible to me, until I heard of a child at another school who told her mother that when she got her first car, she wanted to have "*LW* 213" on her license plate because that was her favorite hymn.

When asked what they liked about *LW* 213, one adolescent boy said, "I love it when you turn the page and there's that high part." Others said, "It's cool," "It's not cheesy," and "It's hard, but you feel good when you finally learn it." These are not necessarily well-formulated statements of aesthetic theory but they do indicate an inherent sense of participating in a musically satisfying event. Surrounded each day by music that is alternately raucous and inane, children and teens do respond to music of quality when someone makes the effort to teach it to them.

Fundamental to the success of that teaching effort is the teacher. The colleagues who contributed anecdotes to this paper are dedicated teachers who care passionately about the theology and music of the Reformation and exude that passion in their classes. In addition, they are good musicians who are able to convey the spirit of each hymn with confidence. Each one teaches this hymnody unapologetically, with enthusiasm and conviction, and their twenty-first century children capture and share that enthusiasm.

Expressing the Faith

A final justification for teaching children texts that are centuries old is that every generation needs to find the words to express its faith. These old hymns (as well as many hymns of other eras) are succinct, well-crafted statements of belief, and they give both children and adults a means of articulating what they know to be true.

Luther did write two hymns specifically for children. *Vom Himmel hoch da komm ich her* ("From heaven above to earth I come," *Lutheran Worship,* No. 37) was probably written for his own children for a Christmas celebration at home. It is pleasant to conjure up the image of the Luther family taking the parts of the angels and the observers and perhaps joining together to sing the final stanza: "Glory to God in highest heaven." This hymn must have been sung by countless children over the years on Christmas Eve, its form folk-like and accessible, its stepwise melody set so well for young voices, its reflective stanzas framing a childlike response to the birth of the Christ child.

The hymn entitled "A Children's Hymn" in Luther's day is a different matter. The original text, *Erhalt uns, Herr, bei deinem Wort* ("Lord, keep us steadfast in your Word," *Lutheran Worship,* No. 334), was written in 1541 or 1542 for the boys' choir to sing during particularly difficult times for both the empire and the church. The political situation was dangerous on several fronts, and many of the Roman Catholic principalities were prepared to use violence against Lutheranism; in fact, the second phrase of this hymn originally asked for protection from both the Turks and papists. The Elector requested that the people pray for divine protection.[19] Luther may have included this hymn for the children to sing in a special prayer service, even though the text hardly seems "childlike" in its pleas for the Church's defense, peace and unity on earth, and support in our final strife.[20]

In the fall of 2001 I chose a version of this hymn for my middle-school choir to sing in church on Reformation Sunday. In this arrangement, the three stanzas of "Lord, keep us steadfast" are followed by another hymn, "Grant peace, we pray, in mercy, Lord," as was often the case in Reformation-era churches:

> Grant peace, we pray, in mercy, Lord;
> Peace in our time, oh, send us!
> For there is none on earth but you,
> None other to defend us.
> You only, Lord, can fight for us. Amen.[21]

We had begun learning this work early in September, so it was in our folders already when we met for the first time after the terrorist attack of September 11, 2001, on New York City. We sang it, knowing that the words went to the heart of every child. We rehearsed it each week and sang it on Reformation, our voices echoing the prayers sung by children who were frightened and confused by war almost 500 years earlier.

There was a great deal of talking about the reactions of children after that terrorist attack, about their need to express their emotions and to feel secure. At one point, a child psychologist on a radio talk show stated cautiously that "we don't have a monopoly on tragedy, you know," suggesting that horror and fear have stalked children all over the world for centuries. This hymn from the 1540s provided children at that time the opportunity to name the enemy—deceit, sword, strife—and to courageously implore God for protection. Thank God that those words are still available for fearful children in the twenty-first century.

The period of the Reformation gave the Church a wealth of new songs—songs that were new to the people of that time and that taught and encouraged them in their faith. Centuries later there is still a newness in the engaging melodies and confessional texts that can nurture children of our time. It is not easy being a child or raising a child in the twenty-first century, but neither was it easy in the sixteenth century. The hymns written for that generation still serve us well. The Lord God help our singing!

NOTES

1   Martin Luther, *Liturgy and Hymns*, ed. Ulrich S. Leupold, Luther's Works: American Edition, vol. 53 (Philadelphia: Fortress, 1965), 211–16.

2   Ibid., 277.

3   Ibid., 217.

4   Carl Schalk, "Teaching the Songs of Faith," in *First Person Singular* (St. Louis: MorningStar, 1998), 71.

5   Iain Fenlon, "Education in Music," in *The New Grove Dictionary of Music and Musicians* (1980), vol. 6, 10.

6   Some well-known examples are: "To God the Holy Spirit let us pray (Lutheran Worship, No. 155), "O Lord, we praise you" (Lutheran Worship, No. 238), and the hymn on the Ten Commandments (Lutheran Worship, No. 331).

7   Bernharr Rainbow, *Music in Educational Thought and Practice* (Aberystwyth: Boethius Press, 1989), 53.

8   Frederick Sternfeld, "Music in the Schools of the Reformation," *Musica Disciplina* 2 (1948), 102.

9   Andreas Ornithoparcus, cited in Rainbow, 52.

10 Sternfeld, 117

11 Fenlon, 10.

12 Sternfeld, 101.

13 Rainbow, 51.

14 Sternfeld, 112.

15 Fenlon, 11.

16 Rainbow, 54.

17 Jean Calvin, in Oliver Strunk, *Source Readings in Music History* (New York: Norton, 1950), 345–47.

18 Leupold, 316.

19 Leupold, 304-305.

20 See Carl Schalk, "No Fleecy Clouds and Little Lambs," in *First Person Singular* (St. Louis: MorningStar, 1998), 59–60.

21 Text as it appears in *Lutheran Worship*, No. 219.

No Special Doctrinaire Schemes[1]

Doctrinaire Schemes

Protestant and Roman Catholic

Friedrich Blume, in his study of church music as it developed in the sixteenth century under the influence of Martin Luther's reforming activity, made this comment: "... the inherent overall tendency of Protestant church music [was] to absorb contemporary, living musical expression and to create for itself no special doctrinaire schemes."[2]

The dictionary defines "doctrinaire" as 1) "dogmatic" or 2) "merely theoretical; impractical." "Protestants" have been taught that Roman Catholics are doctrinaire in both of these senses. Roman Catholics are burdened, so the rhetoric goes, by medieval hierarchical pretensions, and their music follows the same path. Documents like *Annus qui* of Benedict XIV in 1749 and the *Motu proprio* of Pius X in 1903 are regarded as dogmatic and impractical, understood to carry unwarranted authoritarian pretensions that rule out some styles and rule in others.

This interpretation can appear to work until you get to Vatican II and the "Constitution on the Sacred Liturgy" in 1963. Then the whole matter of liturgical inculturation, which it becomes clear is not of recent vintage but is an integral part of the church's entire history, stops such an interpretation in its tracks. Suddenly you are forced to ask whether the Roman Catholic tradition and its documents are about doctrinaire schemes, or whether their underlying point is that the church has not, as Vatican II says, "adopted any particular style of art as her very own [but] has admitted fashions from every period according to the natural talents and circumstances of people."[3]

Once this question arises, a second one quickly follows, namely, whether the essence of the Roman Catholic musical tradition is any different from ". . . the inherent overall tendency of Protestant church music to absorb contemporary, living musical expression and to create for itself no special doctrinaire schemes." But Protestants have had almost five hundred years now to convince themselves that they are right and Roman Catholics are wrong, undoing Luther's and many other reformers' underlying intentions. In the process Protestants have been blinded to their own "special doctrinaire schemes." It's time to take the blinders off. This does not mean denying legitimate critical capacities. It simply means taking them seriously enough to realize they apply across the board.

So what about Protestants? Is Calvin's unison singing without polyphony or instruments a doctrinaire scheme? Maybe, but one could easily argue it is not really at issue any more and has been superseded long ago. What about Pietism and its propensity dogmatically to shut out certain kinds of music? Maybe one could say that it too is not at issue anymore, though the case here is harder to make. Pietistic strictures against music that might be considered high art, for example, are in some places still pretty strong. But let us assume those strictures are also things of the past. What about our day? Have Protestants left behind all doctrinaire schemes, even if they once had them?

Megachurches have become one of the strongest influences in many Protestant circles and are considered by some to be quintessentially "Protestant." In what is often considered good Protestant fashion, the megachurch model has "ignored or dismissed traditional forms of Christian liturgy."[4] That may well be regarded as not doctrinaire or dogmatic, but, as John Witvliet observes, this perspective has its own "self-conscious pattern, or *Ordo,* for worship" with a "decisive split between a time for worship and a time for teaching. Music is typically prominent in the first part of the service."[5]

How is music used there? It ushers the worshiper from "'the outer courts' into the 'holy of holies' of God's presence." Music "is the means for encounter with God." It is "sacramental," as Witvliet says. He suggests "it is often as stark and highly charged as medieval eucharistic theology." The language is "almost . . . *ex opere operato,* the phrase used to convey the perceived efficacy of the priest's words to effect the transubstantiation of the elements in the medieval Mass."[6] Or one could compare music's use here to that of medieval indulgences.

"As soon as the coin in the coffer rings,
The soul from purgatory springs,"

said Tetzel as he sold his letters of indulgence.[7] The language of our generation about church music is not likely to be as crass as that, but the logic is the same. As soon as the "palpable experience"[8] of music takes place, one is in the presence of God. When the song leader tells congregations she hears the Holy Spirit in their song or when the Holy Spirit is said to "ride on the guitar," the same posture is present. It is as doctrinaire in the sense of dogmatic as *ex opere operato* and indulgences ever were.

What about the second definition of doctrinaire, "merely theoretical; impractical"? That definition of "doctrinaire" fits neither the medieval Roman Catholic model nor the modern Protestant megachurch. Both are pre-eminently practical, consumerist endeavors. Both have attracted large crowds and raised lots of money. But now we have another problem. Protestants have rightly and regularly raised serious questions about *ex opere operato* and indulgences. (So have some Roman Catholics.[9]) For Protestants to embrace the theology and practice they have opposed, even if it is worked out with different means, is at the very least contradictory and more than a little curious.

Eugene H. Peterson, retired Presbyterian pastor and professor of spiritual theology, places the megachurch phenomenon in the American consumerist context. He says, first, that Christian spirituality, unlike American spirituality, is not about us, but about God.[10] Secondly, he says the American culture of acquisition has in some places turned the congregation "into a consumer enterprise . . . . A consumer church," he says, "is an anti-Christ church, not the way to develop . . . a life in which the Jesus way and the Jesus truth are congruent, where 'kingfishers catch fire, dragonflies draw flame.'"[11]

There is an unavoidable conclusion here: neither Roman Catholics nor Protestants have been free from denying the very gospel they presume to confess. And an unavoidable implication follows: rather than throwing stones at one another or attacking each other from behind superficial and stereotypical ramparts, it would be far more helpful for the church and the world if we constructively asked together what music "without doctrinaire schemes," "according to the natural talents and circumstances of people," might look like.

More Doctrinaire Schemes

Before we get to that question, four more doctrinaire schemes need to be isolated in order to clear the board of what church music is not.

1. *The church's music, at least at worship, is not a museum piece.* The church has, as the "Constitution on the Sacred Liturgy" of Vatican II noted, "in the course of centuries . . . brought into being a treasury of art."[12] That treasury is open for use by the church. Sometimes it may even be used in concerts and may in some sense then be regarded as a museum piece, but for worship there is no concert or museum about it. To use music as a concert or museum at worship turns it into doctrinaire dogma.

2. *The church's music is not a reflection of the culture.* It lives in the culture and responds to the culture, but it is not a reflection of the culture. For us in our period that means the church's music is not a manipulative means to sell Christianity. Our culture assumes that everything and everybody are for sale, and that music is the means to do the selling. This assumption is as doctrinaire and dogmatic as any assumption could possibly be. Christianity, however, breaks out of the dogma. Christianity is not for sale. It has nothing to sell. Grace is free for the taking. The church proclaims grace from God who in Christ through the Holy Spirit gives away the very self of God's Trinitarian being. As soon as the church submits to the culture's norm of sales, two things happen. First, the church returns to the bondage from which it is freed, and it tries to control other people by putting them in bondage. Second, music is turned into what is of dubious quality. In place of the finest crafting of God's gift of music, music is fashioned as a momentary enticement for money.

3. *Church music is not an emotional drip.* Its purpose is not to drug people and insulate them from the world's pain and needs. Church music is not fundamentally about feelings or emotions, another of our age's dogmatic cultural assumptions about music. Christianity breaks out of this doctrinaire dogma and faces the world as it is with the gift of music as part of the church's honest confession.

4. *Church music is not about one style.* Music to sell and music as emotional drip lead to the tyranny of a very narrow dogmatic stylistic grid. Church music breaks out of that dogma and ranges across many styles from many times and places, all broken to Word, font, and table.

Church Music Without Doctrinaire Schemes

If the church's music is stripped of doctrinaire schemes, how might it be defined? Here are some clues:

Celebration and Lament

1. *There is a victory in Christ to be celebrated.* Church music celebrates it, as in Martin Luther's hymn, "Christ Jesus lay in death's strong bands."[13] One death swallows up another. Death's sting is lost forever. We keep the festival and sing, "Hallelujah!"

2. *There is brokenness and suffering in our individual lives and in the world.* It is taken up in Christ, to be sure, but it still has to be acknowledged. Church music voices the lament, as in Luther's hymn, "Out of the depths I cry to you,"[14] and Albert Bayly's hymn, "Lord, whose love in humble service."[15] We cry out in our personal distress and rebellion; we know children still wander homeless, the hungry still cry for bread, and captives long for freedom. We sing all of that in the light of Christ's grace, compassion, and call to service.

Around Word, Font, and Table

3. *The song of victory and lament in Christ is sung around Word, font, and table.* There, with all other cultural artifacts, it is set next to the Gospel, broken to the Gospel, and made new by the Gospel. There a new song is sung, not the song of our novelty whether old or new, but the song of a new creation in Christ.

Gift of God

4. *Music is the gift of God.* Humanity is called to craft the gift of music, but the gift itself is not of humanity's making. It comes from God. Music is the raw material that the signature of the harmonic series unveils as the sounding form of the universe. It overflows creation's goodness. Like the rest of the creation it can be perverted and misused, but it remains God's gracious gift.

Old and New

5. *Church music is old and new.* It is not a museum piece, though the gift has been well-crafted into a remarkable treasury by many who have gone before us. Their music still speaks with vitality. We continue to use it with gratitude and benefit. Church music is not identifiable with the culture either, though the gift can continually be crafted anew in response to God in every time and place. We who are alive at any given moment are called to do the crafting as well as possible.

Folk Art and High Art

A most remarkable thing about church music is this: It is both unrehearsed folk art and rehearsed high art, not one or the other, but both one and the other.

6. *Church music is unrehearsed folk art.* At its heart church music is the folksong of the people of God, the song of the baptized—that is, not just the song of trained musicians, but of human beings made new in Christ who sing around Word, font, and table. The baptized as a whole don't practice like a choir or instrumental group, but they sing hymns, settings of the liturgy, canticles, and Psalms. Their song is the folk ballad of the church, conceived congregationally for assemblies of men, women, and children from all walks of life and all segments of society.

7. *Church music is rehearsed high art.* The church has realized its message calls into play groups that rehearse, for two reasons: a) so that the people have musical leadership, and b) so that the music the people cannot sing and play finds expression. An amazing repertoire of mostly choral music, but organ and other instrumental music as well, has naturally developed. With this music trained singers and players (who may be amateurs as well as professionals) introduce music for the congregation, lead the congregation, alternate with the congregation, and sing and play what the congregation cannot. This music began in connection with worship, and it continues to have its intrinsic relation to worship. But it has also spilled out beyond worship, for example, into an oratorio tradition that is a gracious gift to the world from the church. It joins the world's finest musical heritage.

Vocal and Verbal

8. *Church music is first of all vocal.* In the West instruments have in recent centuries been admitted, but the practice of the early

church and of much of the church thereafter—the Orthodox, sixteenth century Calvinists, and Lutherans with their characteristic unaccompanied song of the congregation—points to the central thing, the human voice.

9. *Words are central.* The church sings words that bear the Word of God. Instruments have of late been welcomed, but they do not substitute for the centrality of sung words. They play around the verbal center.

Glory, Edification, Sanctification, and Pleasure

Whenever the nature of church music comes up for discussion in either Roman Catholic or Protestant circles, it invariably includes the glory of God, edification, sanctification, and pleasure.

10. *Church music is for the glory of God.* We cannot add to or subtract from God's glory, the *kabod Yahweh,* that the priest and prophet Ezekiel, among others, teaches us about. It is so splendid and brilliant that we cannot get near it and live, so Ezekiel can only speak of it at several steps removed, as the "appearance of the likeness of the glory of God."[16] God's glory for the Christian is finally known in Christ, and we sing that glory as our "bounden duty." We give God the glory God already has, and we do it partly with music.

To glorify God with music is to use the gift of music rightly, to acknowledge the order between creator and creation, and to sing a song of new creation in Christ. This means that Pius X was right when he said in the *Motu proprio* of 1903 that music has to possess sanctity, goodness, excellence of form, and universality, though the way he construed that in musical syntax—essentially through chant and sixteenth-century polyphony—may have been too narrow and doctrinaire. It means Calvin was right when he said music has to have weight and majesty, though the way he construed that in musical syntax—through unison congregational song without choirs or instruments or polyphony—may have been too narrow and doctrinaire. The central notion in both cases was right, however, that music in worship has to have *gravitas*[17] and relates in some way to the splendor and perfection of beauty that shines forth out of Zion.[18]

11. *Church music is for the edification of people.* Here the direction is reversed, from God to humanity. Music is part of the church's task of proclamation and teaching. The church seeks

faithfully to proclaim to the whole world the glory God imparts to humanity in Christ and to teach us about it. This task is carried out partly with music. J. S. Bach addressed his *Orgelbüchlein* to the glory of God and the instruction of the neighbor.[19] By instruction of the neighbor he meant partly the purely musical craft related here to the organist, but it is not accidental that he tied this notion to settings of congregational chorales, which in his sketch of intentions constituted "virtually the entire 'classic' Lutheran hymn repertory up to about 1675."[20] What was this repertory about? Partly the glory of God, but also the edification of the neighbor.[21]

12. *Church music is for the sanctification of people.* God invites humanity to share God's very glory. God chooses to sacrifice God's self in the self-offering of the Son. "The Word became flesh, lived among us, and we beheld his glory as of the only Son from the Father, full of grace and truth."[22] We get to sing this glory, and, lo and behold, God turns the song upside down and not only edifies us, but blesses us and sanctifies us. The incarnate Word is carried by words, and, in a mystery Luther found remarkable, those words about the Word can be carried in song.[23] This means, as Bach and his librettist knew, the Word is carried in our voices[24] and in our lives.

13. *Church music is in part about pleasure.* This component lives in the woodwork of the last three points, though it is not always mentioned. It includes music's play. In connection with the glory of God, edification, and sanctification it is healthy—not only healthy but inevitable, delightful, and wonderfully good, especially in light of the Incarnation. It can get out of hand, however, in one of two directions. If you deny and repress the pleasure of music, it will pop up to bite you when you least expect it. If you embrace pleasure on its own, you wind up wallowing in sectarian idolatry, submerged in self-absorbed isolation from God's glory. There is a healthy balance at work when pleasure and play are rightly construed in relation to God. Creator and creation are then understood in their right and salutary relationship, and incarnation is lived out with bodily vigor and vitality.

Praise, Prayer, Proclamation, Story

When you parse all these characteristics out and ask what music does, you discover it bears the church's praise, prayer, proclamation, and story.[25]

14. *Church music bears the church's praise.* God acts, and "from inner material necessity," as Karl Barth says, we respond in praise.[26] This song is expressed at worship through the congregation's voice, the choir which helps lead the congregation and sings what it cannot sing, and instruments which may be seen as standing in for the whole creation. This song is sung in a variety of past and present styles from around the globe, appropriate to a given time and place with all the resources at a community's disposal, from the simplest to the most complex.

15. *Church music bears the church's prayer.* This takes shape in dialogues with leaders of worship; in lamentation and thanksgiving; for peace, justice, the common good, the world's leaders, in intercession for the whole world, and for individual needs. The simplest prayer responses, the most artistic motets, and the most anguished wail of instruments and voices are all part of this prayer.

16. *Church music bears the church's proclamation.* That's what singing of lessons, medieval sequences, Schütz motets, Bach cantatas, and some hymns are about. Here, though the congregation's song includes this motif, the musical forces which practice have an especially important role because they can exploit the polyphonic possibilities of music where themes can be woven together and the breadth of the proclamation expressed in ways that are not possible for any other medium. Bach's *Christmas Oratorio* provides a prime example. There the PASSION CHORALE associated with Lent takes on an Easter *Christus Victor* text, and the whole story from death to resurrection is proclaimed with proleptic breadth at the manger.

16. *Church music bears the church's story.* This story moves from creation to consummation—from the morning stars at the birth of the world through the exodus, prophets, priests, and kings, to the central event of Christ and the church in the world, and on to the eschaton. That's what Psalms, canticles, and hymnody taken as a whole are about. This facet includes music's unique relation to time and its capacity to articulate the time of worship and the procession of Christian pilgrimage.

According to the Natural Talents and Circumstances of People

18. *Church music bears all these things "according to the natural talents and circumstances of people."* That brings us to a central question: how does music with all its multivalent responsibilities

get worked out in a specific time and place? There are two ways to get at this question.

One is to assume we as the church know all the answers as well as all the questions, or to assume we know the answers even before we hear the questions. This is the mind-set of those who regard music either as a museum piece or a reflection of the culture. The musical choices of these two perspectives may differ, but they are the same in that everything is resolved in doctrinaire boxes. This is bondage, not grace. It is more allied to civil religion than to Christianity. It shuts out lots of things, among them the most honest music of our period by the finest composers who reflect that honesty. It denies the Christian Gospel.

There is another option more allied to the essence of the Christian faith. It lives with the honest questions of our day and welcomes the work of the finest composers. This answer is at once simple and complicated just like life and the Christian faith. It does not mean anything goes, however, because at worship music has to be broken to Word, font, and table.

a. At the congregational level what the people are given to sing has to be what they *can* sing. If Bela Bartok is right, there is no such thing as an atonal folk song.[27] Folk song gravitates to a tonic or a modal final, and the song of the congregation is folk song. Its rhythm cannot be complex eye rhythms either, but has to be able to live in the ears of people who are not trained as musicians. A challenging tune by Hugo Distler, Jan Bender, or Richard Dirksen is surely possible and welcome, but a tune without the coherence of an idiom people can comprehend is off limits, not for doctrinaire reasons, but for pastoral ones.

b. At the choral, organ, and instrumental level of music that alternates with a congregation or is an independent unit not tied to the congregation's song (a motet at Communion, for example), the musical possibilities are much greater. All sorts of twentieth-century and other compositional devices can be used. Psalm 88 can be set in anguished ways that are honest to the composer's time and place. Questions, pain, and prophetic words are not foreign to the Christian tradition. They stand in the center of the Psalms and canticles, for example. But this does not suggest chaos. Music has to be broken to the Gospel, font, and table. Life is not just one thing after another in a meaningless succession. Life has a purpose known in Christ that leads somewhere—for others, and to an eschatological endpoint. It is possible to use all sorts of music at worship, maybe even the chance music of John Cage. It may be possible to figure out musically in worship how to embrace what chaos theory reveals about chance in the universe, but the church's confession is not about chance or chaos. It is rather about God who goes with us into the chaos and can be trusted throughout it. Music at worship fits into that context.

Examples

Are all of these clues to the nature of the church's music about theoretical pie-in-the-sky, or are there examples from the church's actual practice that give them some flesh? My suspicion is that the church's music for virtually every tradition in some way breaks out of doctrinaire schemes and constraints. It is surely also constrained by any number of forces in different ways at different times. There is no doubt about that. But I suspect in every tradition it also breaks free of doctrinaire constraints into a discipline of creativity. I would invite people of various traditions to test out that hypothesis in their own respective traditions to see if it is true or not. What I want to do here is to utilize the Lutheran tradition as a test case, especially since the quotation from Blume applies specifically to the Lutheran tradition that, if Blume is right, consciously presumes to oppose doctrinaire schemes. Has music in the Lutheran tradition in fact been characterized, at least in some ways and times, by freedom from doctrinaire schemes?

Luther and Bach

Martin Luther and J. S. Bach are perhaps the best examples of "no doctrinaire schemes" lived out in the paradox of discipline and creativity. Here's what Luther says:

> God has [the Gospel] preached also through the medium of music; this may be seen from the compositions of Josquin, all of whose works are cheerful, gentle, mild, and lovely; they flow and move along and are neither forced nor coerced and bound by rigid rules, but, on the contrary, are like the song of the finch.[28]

Luther expresses the paradox. He cites Josquin Des Prez (a Roman Catholic) as an example of music that is free, not forced, not coerced. He would surely have said the same thing about J. S. Bach (a Lutheran) had he been alive to hear Bach's music. Bach is the logical musical outcome of Luther's point of view. The music of Josquin and Bach is free, not "forced or coerced and bound by rigid and stringent rules," yet here is the interesting thing: both of these composers hardly avoided the "rules." If any composers understood and followed the logic and "rules" of harmonic and polyphonic complexity of the past lived out in the currents of their own periods, it was Josquin and Bach.

The paradox is that composers who most enter into the discipline of their craft—that is, follow its rules by learning from and being stimulated by both old and new—are precisely the ones who are not controlled by doctrinaire schemes, not coerced nor bound by dogmatic rules. Their music explores the dimensions of sound with which God has gifted the creation for the people of a given time and place. Their music explores the gift of God's creation under the arc of God's grace. In so doing freedom from doctrinaire schemes breaks out.

Between Luther and Bach

If Carl Schalk is right in his book, *Music in Early Lutheranism*,[29] other composers in the Lutheran stream also point to freedom from doctrinaire schemes. Schalk sketches an overview of Lutheran music history from the Renaissance to the Baroque and then details the lives of seven Lutheran church musicians who lived between 1524 and 1672, musicians who link Martin Luther and J. S. Bach. Johann Walter and Heinrich Schütz are the first and the last of this group. Between them come Georg Rhau, Hans Leo Hassler, Michael Praetorius, Johann Hermann Schein, and Samuel Scheidt.

Schalk delineates five insights that these early Lutheran musicians provide: They were all highly trained musicians, all were involved to some degree in secular music, all of them after Walter and Rhau wrestled with "new" musical styles, all of them found the liturgy the most natural context for their music, and all of them were teachers. The three inner insights get at our concern here. These musicians were involved in secular music, wrestled with new musical styles, and found the liturgy the most natural context for their music.

1. Involvement with secular music meant that these musicians were acquainted with and engaged by the serious musical currents

of their day. They did not retreat to a doctrinaire musical stance provided by some presumed official authority of the church or other agency, but took up the study and understanding of the musical developments around them. They participated in and contributed to these developments as part of their being as musicians and church musicians.

2. They wrestled with new musical styles, absorbing "contemporary musical expression," as Blume said. "Their solution, simply stated," according to Schalk, "was to cautiously experiment with the new without rejecting the old."[30] Heinrich Schütz may be the most obvious example. He linked the Renaissance and the Baroque, the Italian and the German. In *The Psalms of David* of 1619 he brought to Germany Giovanni Gabrieli's new Venetian techniques, with polychoral and instrumental splendor; yet near the end of his life in 1665 and 1666 he wrote unaccompanied Passions modeled on older Gregorian traditions. The ancient style of the Passions, however, was itself influenced by newer Florentine operatic monody and the German Lied.

Without doctrinaire schemes, with respect for both the old and the new—and with the chorale the "pivotal point, which kept the two in balance"[31]—these composers were creatively stimulated. Indeed, says Schalk, their "greatest contributions [are] to be found precisely in those aspects of their work in which they pressed beyond the boundaries of the 'old'."[32]

3. These composers found the liturgy the most natural context for their music. This is most telling. It means that their music was disciplined by Word, font, and table, with the chorale their "pivotal point." This was not a dogmatic doctrinaire scheme, but a discipline that freed them to welcome the old and the new, and to unlock their creativity. Igor Stravinsky, in a completely different context, points to the paradoxical reality of what he calls restriction and liberty, which might also be termed discipline and creativity. In discussing the imposition of "a certain convention" when he was composing *Oedipus*, he says:

> The need for restriction, for deliberately submitting to a style, has its source in the very depths of our nature, and is found not only in matters of art, but in every conscious manifestation of human activity. It is the need for order without which nothing can be achieved, and upon the disappearance of which everything

disintegrates. But one would be wrong to regard that as an impediment to liberty. On the contrary, the style, the restraint, contribute to its development and only prevent liberty from degenerating into license.[33]

Carl F. Schalk

What do we learn from a study like this? The church of God—whether Protestant or Roman Catholic—when it has affirmed its birthright has broken out of "doctrinaire schemes." We who are the church in our time and place have this very same calling, not to sing the dogma of oppression and tyranny in Caesar, but the song of the church, the song of liberation in Christ, without "doctrinaire schemes," adapted "to the natural talents and circumstances of people," around Word, font, and table.

We have an example among us of one who has lived out this calling. The calling is not only evident in church musicians who lived faithfully in past centuries, though we learn much from them. It is also a thing of the present, and we learn much from those who live it out faithfully among us. Carl Schalk, for whom this *Festschrift* is prepared, is one of them. He has embodied among us in our time and place what he has articulated about other faithful church musicians in theirs. Those of us who have been privileged to know and learn from him owe him our deepest gratitude and appreciation. So does the rest of the church and the world, for faithfully carrying out his calling as a church musician in his study, writing, conducting, playing, composing, and teaching—without doctrinaire schemes, but with craft and relish, living fully, station carefully hewn and lovingly keen.

NOTES

1   Part of this article is adapted from Paul Westermeyer, "What About Church Music?" for the Kyrkomusikaliskt kädslag 2004 i Lund under temat: Vad will vi med all kyrkomusik? (11 March 2004) and from The Northcutt Lecture, Baylor University, Waco, Texas, April 15, 2004.

2   Friedrich Blume, rev. Ludwig Finscher, trans. F. Ellsworth Peterson, "The Period of the Reformation," *Protestant Church Music: A History* (New York: Norton, 1974), 80.

3   "Constitution on the Sacred Liturgy," *Documents of Vatican II* (New York: Guild Press, 1966), 175.

4   John Witvliet. *Worship Seeking Understanding* (Grand Rapids: Baker Academic, 2003), 255.

5   Ibid.

6   Ibid.

7   Roland Bainton, *Here I Stand: A Life of Martin Luther* (New York: Abingdon, 1950), 78.

8   Witvliet, 256.

9   See, for example, Geoffrey Robinson, "Confirmation: A Bishop's Dilemma," *Worship* 78:1 (January 2004): 58.

10 Quoted from a *Christian Century* lecture by Eugene H. Peterson in Martin E. Marty, *Context* 36:3 (March 2004, Part B): 1.

11 Ibid., 2.

12 "Constitution on the Sacred Liturgy," *Documents of Vatican II*, 175.

13 *Lutheran Book of Worship* (Minneapolis: Augsburg, 1978), No. 134.

14 Ibid., No. 295.

15 Ibid., No. 423

16 Ezekiel 1:28b.

17 The basic meaning of *kabod* is "weight, importance, consideration," so it is not surprising that the music associated with giving God glory is precisely music that has weight, majesty, and *gravitas*. As the Hebrew *kabod* traveled through the New Testament in the Greek *doxa*, its crown of "splendor" and "brightness" was increased. In English the nuance of "glory" moves toward renown, triumphant exultation, and rejoicing.

18 Psalm 50:2.

19 "*Dem höchsten Gott allein zu ehren, dem nechsten, draus sich zu belehren.*" From the title page, given in Johann Sebastian Bach, ed. Albert Riemenschneider, *The Liturgical Year* [*Orgelbüchlein*] (Bryn Mawr: Oliver Ditson, 1933). A photographic facsimile of the title page is given in Johann Sebastian Bach, ed. Robert Clark and John David Peterson, *Orgelbüchlein* (St. Louis: Concordia, 1984), 23.

20 Christoph Wolff, *Johann Sebastian Bach The Learned Musician* (New York: Norton, 2000), 127.

21 See, "Lord, thee I love with all my heart," stanza 2, *Lutheran Book of Worship*, No. 235.

22 John 1:14.

23 See Oskar Soehngen, "Fundamental Considerations for a Theology of Music," in *The Musical Heritage of the Church*, vol. 6, ed. Theodore Hoelty-Nickel (St. Louis: Concordia, 1963), 15.

24 See J. S. Bach, Cantata, *Ein feste Burg ist unser Gott* (BWV 80), movement 7: "*Wie selig sind doch die, die Gott in Munde tragen*" (how blessed are those who carry God in their mouths). There is a double meaning here. *Mund* means both "mouth" and "tongue." They are blessed, therefore, who carry God on their tongues by singing words about the incarnate Word, and they are blessed who carry God in their mouths by receiving the bread and wine in, with, and under which the body and blood of Christ are present.

25 I have discussed this at greater length in Paul Westermeyer, *The Church Musician* rev. ed. (Minneapolis: Augsburg, 1997), ch. 4, and in an expanded version in Paul Westermeyer, *The Heart of the Matter: Church Music as Praise, Prayer, Proclamation, Story, and Gift* (Chicago: GIA, 2001).

26 Karl Barth, *Church Dogmatics*, IV, Part Three, Second Half, trans. G. W. Bromiley (Edinburgh: T. & T. Clark, 1962), 866.

27 See Elliott Schwartz, ed., *Contemporary Composers on Contemporary Music* (New York: Holt, Rinehart and Winston, 1967), 77.

28 Quoted in Walter E. Buszin, *Luther on Music* (St. Paul: North Central Publishing Co., 1958), 13.

29 Carl Schalk, *Music in Early Lutheranism: Shaping the Tradition (1524–1672)* (St. Louis: Concordia Academic Press, 2001).

30 Ibid., 182.

31 Ibid., 183.

32 Ibid.

33 Igor Stravinsky, *An Autobiography* (New York: Norton, 1936), 131–32.

WILLIAM H. BRAUN

New Life for the Musical Passion: Selected Passions for Liturgical Worship, 1955–2004

Background

The Passion of Christ, the account of his suffering and death, is the narration of the central event in the life of Christ and is of supreme importance to the Christian faith. The singing of the Passion began in the early medieval church as part of the liturgical rites of Holy Week, and composers of later generations continued the practice in a variety of ways. Regrettably, however, over time the musical settings of Christ's Passion became separated from their liturgical moorings; even the greatest of these settings, such as those by Bach, have performed as concert pieces rather than in the liturgical environment for which they were conceived. The genre itself underwent changes after Bach; the words of Scripture were not used exclusively to tell the story, but were paraphrased, often to elicit an emotional response from the hearer.

The middle of the nineteenth century witnessed a restored interest in liturgical church music in general. Herzogenberg's *Die Passion* of 1898, which marked the beginning of a revival of liturgical Passion composition, is an example.[1] Adam Adrio in his essay "Renewal and Rejuvenation" notes how important "the return to biblical texts" was in the revival of liturgical church music in the early part of the twentieth century.[2] This emphasis on biblical texts helped the composers in this revival to place their creative output at the service of the church by writing music that served the liturgy. The emphasis on Scripture in the twentieth century was not limited to liturgical Passions, but can be found in Passion settings that were designed for the concert hall, such as those by Rogers, Martin, Penderecki, Pärt, Tan Dun, Rihm, Gubaydulina, and Golijov. Renewal in liturgical Passion music was manifest before

World War II with groundbreaking settings by Kurt Thomas and Hugo Distler and after World War II with settings by Ernst Pepping and Rudolf Mauersberger.[3]

The output of new Passion settings continued unabated during the latter half of the twentieth century with an increasing diversity in style, form, and use as found in other genres. Various Passions of the past served as models that modern composers continued to use and refashion into structures suited to their own purposes. Some of those models of the past that twentieth-century composers used include the responsorial Passion, the motet Passion, the oratorio Passion (also known as the dramatic Passion), and the *summa* Passion.

In the responsorial Passion the narrative sections of the Gospel, the words of Christ and those of other individual characters of the Passion drama (the *synagoga*) were chanted monophonically, while the utterances of groups of people (the *turba*) were set polyphonically. The motet Passion (also known as the "through-composed Passion") gave the complete text of one Gospel history set polyphonically as an extended motet. The oratorio Passion, influenced by the development of opera, contained reflective arias and choruses that were added to the biblical text. German oratorio Passions often included congregational hymns (chorales) as a means of personalizing or commenting on the biblical message. *Summa* Passions could be in either the responsorial or motet format, but consisted of sections of texts taken from all four Gospels. This piecing together of Gospel texts was most often applied to the seven words of Christ on the cross.

Chorales also played an important role in twentieth-century Passion settings, functioning in the drama as a brief reflective moment or a place to involve the congregation's voice. It is here that one can observe how an American tradition in Passion settings reshaped the older German models. Often contemporary composers replaced the chorales with Negro spirituals, American shape-note hymns, Gospel hymns, or new hymn tunes and texts. At other times the composers expanded their means of expression "by augmenting the denominational desiderata with styles and techniques that they . . . learned from other religious persuasions."[4]

The harmonic language varies greatly from one setting to another demonstrating a variety of styles and techniques. These include mostly simple root position triadic chords (devoid of even

seventh chords), mildly dissonant modal harmonies, harsh and stri-
dent non-functional harmonies, serialism, tape, and electronic
techniques. While early in the twentieth century most of the settings had been modeled after the a cappella ideal, many in the
twentieth century call for a variety of instruments including those
of Carl Orff.

This essay will first survey a select group of liturgical Passion
settings in English from the last half of the twentieth century. These
Passions illustrate the diversity that can be found in modern Passion settings. The second section lists a group of additional settings
of a similar nature that expand the study. Most of the Passions in
both lists were published since the appearance of Friedrich Blume's
landmark study of Lutheran church music, *Protestant Church
Music: A History*.[5] Roman Catholic composers represented on the
lists reflect the influence of the Second Vatican Council (1962-1965),
which was a watershed event for liturgical music in general. Because of the Council, Roman Catholic composers could set Passions
in the vernacular. In this essay the defining criteria for a liturgical
Passion are: 1) a setting designated by the composer as a liturgical
Passion, 2) a setting which, though not designated as liturgical, limits
the text to events of the Passion and comments thereon,[6] and 3) a
setting with a performance time of an hour or less.[7]

The Holy Spirit has blessed the church with many gifts, among
which are Passion settings by musicians who tell the story in a
variety of ways. It is the earnest desire of this author that, by making church musicians aware of the wide variety of settings that are
available, the Passion story set to music may once again become
the common means of proclaiming the Gospel in Holy Week.

Representative Passion Settings
Behold the Man
C. Armstrong Gibbs (1912–1992)
Oxford, 1955
Duration: 55 min.
T-Evangelist, Bar-Christ, Bar-Pilate,[8] SATB choir, full orchestra

Behold the Man is a *summa* Passion with the King James text
compiled by Benedict Ellis. Eric Routley praises the setting for its
effective use of Old Testament passages within the Passion narrative and finds this "biblical Passion on a small scale" worthy to
stand with Charles Wood's well-known *St. Mark Passion.* Routley,

however, is critical of the "somewhat mournfully conventional newly-composed hymns that appear here and there" and suggests that they be replaced.[9] Gibbs, providing for this possibility, states in his preface, "Well-known Passiontide hymns may be substituted for the chorales if it is desired to allow the congregation to take a part."

Gibbs was very much a "people's" composer, producing much useful music for amateurs.[10] *Behold the Man* seems to be designed with that in mind. Gibbs notes in the preface that Christ's part is written well within the range of "any experienced amateur soloist" and that the Evangelist's part, "cast for a tenor of moderate range . . . , is not difficult and could be sung by a high baritone." The narrative recitatives are notated rhythmically, but are very lyrical and are accompanied throughout. Although the work would be most effective when performed with an orchestra, the organ reduction is very playable and adequate for performance when large resources are not available. The harmony is solidly tonal and the choral parts are largely homophonic (Example 1).

Example 1. Gibbs, *Behold the Man*, p. 51.

The opening chorus combines Old and New Testament passages: "How beautiful upon the mountains are the feet" leads into a solo by Jesus, "I am come a light into the world," which, in turn, is followed by Palm Sunday's "Hosanna!" Throughout the entire work various textual passages are intertwined. Because of the brevity of this setting, not all Passion history texts are included. In the closing movement Routley's critique and Gibb's option for substituting another chorale should be observed. Both the text and music of the movement do not live up to the standard set earlier in the work. An alternative hymn, such as "O Darkest Woe" in a simple four-part setting, would better serve the conclusion.

Passion According to Saint Mark

Jan Bender (1909–1994)
Chantry, 1962
Duration: 40 min.
T-Evangelist, Bar-Pilate, B-Christ, SATB choir, harpsichord (optional string bass)

Passion According to Saint Mark was commissioned by Frederick Otto (founder of Chantry Press), a friend of Bender and long-time proponent of liturgical music. The setting is dedicated to the faculty of Concordia Teachers College, Seward, Nebraska. While Bender's previous *Johannes Passion* (1958, but not treated here because it was not published) utilized a large number of instruments, including Orff instruments, this St. Mark setting fits easily into the capabilities of a modest parish, being modeled after the responsorial Passion form as revived by Hugo Distler who was Bender's teacher. The solo parts are notated in an unmeasured chant rhythm, as in Distler's *Passion*. Bender suggests using the string bass or a 16' stop on the organ to accompany the words of Christ. The choral writing displays harmonic daring within a tonal/modal setting typical of Distler and Bender.

The King James Version text does not skip or shorten any part of the Gospel story, unlike many other contemporary Passion settings. The only additional texts are those of the various chorales interspersed throughout; however, they are not suitable for congregational participation. The *Passion* is divided into four major sections:

Part I: Jesus' Anointment and Jesus at the Mount of Olives (Mark 14:1–31)

After the *Exordium*[11] is sung by the choir, Bender's setting continues with the anointment of Jesus by Mary. Although the entry of Jesus into Jerusalem actually occurs earlier in the Mark Gospel, it is noted in the next chorale, "All glory, laud, and honor." During the Last Supper, when Jesus indicates that one of the disciples will betray him, each disciple asks, "Is it I?" Bender personalizes this question, calling for the Soul to also ask, "Is it I?" (Example 2). The chorale "Soul, adorn thyself with gladness" closes the scene. After the disciples vow their loyalty, Part I concludes with the stanza, "Here I will stand beside thee," from the chorale, "O sacred head."

Example 2. Bender *Passion According to Saint Mark*, p. 16.

From *Passion According to St. Mark* by Jan Bender copyright © 1962 Chantry Music. Used by permission.

Part II: Christ at Gethsemane and before the Sanhedrin (Mark 14:32–64)

When Jesus finishes praying in Gethsemane, the choir sings "Thou, ah, thou hast taken on thee" to the tune JESU, MEINES LEBENS LEBEN. After the trial by the Sanhedrin the section closes with a short motet setting of "Behold the Lamb of God."

Part III: Christ Before Pilate (Mark 14:65–Mark 15:19)

JESU, MEINES LEBENS LEBEN appears at the conclusion of the mocking of Jesus by the guards of the high priest. "O sacred head" closes the scene that depicts Jesus being tormented by the soldiers of Pilate.

Part IV: The Crucifixion and Burial (Mark 15:20–46)

Example 3 shows Bender's typical *turba* writing; it also contains the open fourths and fifths so prevalent in his style. The recitative of the "Spongefiller" exhibits a rare madrigalism on the words, "take him down." This scene closes with the chorale "O darkest woe." The *Conclusio*[12] at the end of the *Passion* is identical to the *Exordium*.

Example 3. Bender, *Passion According to Saint Mark*, p. 61.

From *Passion According to St. Mark* by Jan Bender copyright © 1962 Chantry Music. Used by permission.

St. John Passion

Alan Ridout (1934–1996)
Stainer & Bell, 1964
Duration: 22 min.
T-Evangelist, T-Pilate, B-Christ, SATB (*divisi* trebles), choir, organ

Commissioned for the Canterbury Cathedral Choir in 1964 by Allan Wicks, the *Passion* is part of a successful collaboration between Wicks and Ridout that resulted in an abundance of choral works, including an unpublished *St. Matthew Passion*.[13] The *St. John Passion*, which has a King James Version text, opens with the traditional *Exordium* sung by the choir and immediately moves to the abridged narrative of John 18:1. The only extra text added to the John narrative is a brief *Kyrie eleison* (Example 4) that is inserted at four different points: after Peter's first denial, after Peter's third denial, after the crucifixion, and after Christ's death. It is expanded in the last case to form the conclusion of the work.

Example 4. Ridout, *St. John Passion*, p. 13.

The organ is used throughout as accompaniment for both soloists and choir. The narratives are notated rhythmically and are vocally demanding in terms of intervallic relations, rhythmic complexity, and range. Christ's words are always accompanied by a set of five pitches: D-flat, D, D#, G# (A-flat), and A. These pitches are used harmonically in either a perfect fifth that collapses to a perfect fourth or a perfect fourth that expands to a perfect fifth (Example 5). Harmonically, Ridout is eclectic, using techniques that include free tonality with only slight functional implication, polychords, and bitonality.

Example 5. Ridout, *St. John Passion*, p. 6.

St. Mark Passion

Daniel Pinkham (b. 1926)
Peters, 1966
Duration: 33 min.
T-Evangelist, Bar-Pilate, B-Judas, S solo on words of Psalm 22, SATB choir, 2 tpt, 2 hn, 2 trb, timp, perc, db, harp, organ (manuals only)

The St. Mark's School, Southboro, Massachusetts, commissioned this work in 1965 on the occasion of its one-hundredth anniversary. According to Pinkham's foreword, "it is largely fashioned after the musical setting of the North German Reformation composers of the Baroque era." It deviates from Baroque Passion oratorios, developed by Sebastiani and brought to a peak in the Passions of J. S. Bach, because there are no extra-biblical additions or any chorales. The Mark text is considerably abridged, but a large number of Old Testament texts have been added, including eight from the Psalms, two from Isaiah, one from Jeremiah, and two from Lamentations. In general, the King James Version is used, but passages from the Psalms are taken from the Book of Common Prayer.

Example 6. Pinkham, *Saint Mark Passion*, p. 52.

The role of the Evangelist is sung by a tenor in *recitativo secco* (with "dry," i.e., simple accompaniment); however, the part is quite demanding (as are all the solo parts) and would require professional vocal skills, as can been seen from the two versions in Example 6. (Version A is a minor third higher than Version B.) The single utterance of Christ in Mark's Gospel is "Eli, Eli ...," an Old Testament quotation that is sung by the choir and a soprano soloist (Example 7). The chorus, as usual, portrays the crowd parts in the drama, but it also sings passages of commentary, admonition, or contemplation as seen in the opening chorus, "Watch," and the closing chorus, "Wait."

Example 7. Pinkham, *Saint Mark Passion*, p. 49.

St. Mark 15: 35 and Psalm 22: 1

The harmony is sparse and stridently dissonant, characteristic of Pinkham's idiomatic choral and vocal style. The instrumental forces are divided into two ensembles: a small group (organ, harp, and double bass) and a larger group (brass and percussion). The small ensemble is used as a basso continuo for the Evangelist, while the large group is primarily associated with the chorus and the three other soloists. A piano or organ reduction of the orchestral parts is provided in the vocal score, but is not an adequate substitute for an orchestra to effectively render the colors and contrasts Pinkham has written in the full score.

The Passion According to Saint Matthew

Howard Boatwright (1918–1999)
E. C. Schirmer, 1967
Duration: 29 min.
T-Evangelist, Bar-Pilate, B-Christ, SATB choir *divisi*, congregation, organ

Boatwright's *Passion*, first performed on April 28, 1962, at St. Thomas Episcopal Church, New Haven, Connecticut, ranks high among his large choral compositions.[14] It is a responsorial Passion with the Evangelist narrating the events in a combination of unaccompanied chant and accompanied recitative. The chorus portrays the *turba* and sings eleven reflective hymns. The libretto, based on the King James Version, begins with Christ's arraignment before Pilate (Matt. 27:1) and ends with the Centurion's declaration, "Truly this was the Son of God" (Matt. 28:54). Except for the eleven hymns, the *Passion* does not use any text other than the Gospel itself.

Two stanzas of the hymn "Go to dark Gethsemane" sung to the tune PETRA (written for four-part choir or congregation) open this setting, followed by the *Exordium* sung by the Evangelist without accompaniment. At the conclusion of this scene, the hymn "Ah, holy Jesus" is sung to the tune ROUEN rather than the traditional HERZLIEBSTER JESU. Other hymns conclude various scenes:

"Who was the guilty," sung to HERZLIEBSTER JESU
"For sins of heedless word or deed," sung to JERVAULX ABBEY
"All praise to thee," sung to ENGELBERG
"Alone thou goest forth, O Lord," sung to THIRD MODE MELODY
"The royal banners forward go," sung to PUER NOBIS
"O sacred head," sung to PASSION CHORALE
"When I survey the wondrous cross," sung to GUIDETTI
"Jesus, all thy labor vast," sung to SWEDISH LITANY
"Sing my tongue, the glorious battle," sung to DULCE CARMEN

In the early part of the work these hymns are set to simple four-part harmonizations that can be sung either by the choir or the congregation. As the *Passion* continues, however, the settings become more polyphonic (e.g., "Alone thou goest forth") or are set in keys too high for congregational singing (e.g., "The royal banners forward go" in G-flat major). The *turba* passages are never extended, but do involve some *divisi* writing (Example 8).

Example 8. Boatwright, *The Passion According to Saint Matthew*, p. 44.

The harmonic language is tonal or modal with little chromaticism, and the part-writing is very traditional. The simple recitative style is notated rhythmically and utilizes functional harmony. The only melisma present expresses the agony of Christ at the moment of crucifixion (Example 9). The events following the crucifixion are compressed into twenty measures of recitative sung by the Evangelist; the final chorus is a motet-like setting of the centurion's words, "Truly this was the Son of God." The *Passion* closes with "Sing my tongue, the glorious battle," sung by both choir and congregation with a soprano descant.

Example 9. Boatwright, *The Passion According to Saint Matthew*, p. 50.

Excerpts from *The Passion According to Saint Matthew* (examples 8 and 9) used by permission of Helen Boatwright.

Passion According to St. Luke

Keith Bissell (1912–1992)
Waterloo, 1973
Duration: 40 min.
T-Evangelist, Bar-Pilate, B-Christ, S and A solos, SATB choir, optional children's chorus, 2 fl, 2 ob, 2 cl, 2 bsn, 4 hn, 3 tpt, 2 trb, tb, timp, perc, strings, and organ

Bissell's *Passion*, more closely related to the Passion oratorio model than Pinkham's *St. Mark Passion*, is also more challenging than most of the other Passion settings. This is due to a number of factors: 1) greater forces are required, 2) additional texts and hymns have been incorporated into the Gospel narrative, and 3) the harmonic language is more complex.

The individual orchestral parts are moderately difficult in range and technical demands. The organ reduction of the score allows for the performance of the *Passion* without an orchestra. The demands on the soloists are greater than most of the other settings considered in this survey. The vocal ranges are large (the soprano rises to a b-flat'' and the tenor to g') and the parts contain some rhythmic and vocal difficulties. Bissell calls for a children's choir or a gallery choir that is presumably separated from the main *tutti* choir. This part could, however, be sung by a single soprano since it is only a unison line that does not compete with the main choir.

Example 10. Bissell, *Passion According to St. Luke*, p. 43.

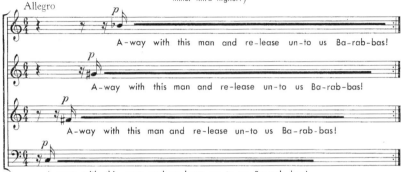

Most of the sung solo parts are notated rhythmically and are accompanied throughout; however, there are parts that are spoken freely over an orchestral accompaniment. The harmony is tonal, but dissonant. Bissell calls for a speech choir, aleatoric speaking, and tone clusters to recreate the mob (*turba*) effects in various passages (Example 10).

The abbreviated King James Luke text is supplemented with additional texts by Oscar Wilde, John Donne, Robert Bridges, Bishop R. Heber, and with the Sussex Mummers' Carol. The *Passion* is divided into seven sections, each either beginning or ending with one of the extra-Gospel texts. It opens with the children's choir (or gallery choir) singing the refrain, "O mortal man, remember well," without accompaniment. The refrain, repeated by the main choir two more times, forms the opening prelude and returns a number of times throughout the narrative. Traditional chorale texts such as "Ah, holy Jesus" appear, but Bissell writes his own melodies and harmonizations. The *Passion* closes with "Sweet Jesu, sleep on." The children's choir intones the Latin text of *Dormi Jesu* to a quasi-Gregorian chant, while the mixed choir responds by singing an English translation of the children's choir text as a four-part chorale accompanied by the orchestra. The effect is similar to the conclusion of Bach's *St. Matthew Passion*, in which the choir responds to the soloists by singing, "*Mein Jesu, gute Nacht!*"

The Passion According to Saint John

Richard Hillert (b. 1923)
Concordia, 1974
Duration: 22 min.
T-Evangelist, Bar-Pilate, B-Christ, SATB choir, vibraphone

Hillert's *Passion* is modeled on the responsorial Passion form established by Schütz: a choral Prolog (*Exordium*), chant-like recitatives for the soloists, a cappella four-part *turba* sections, and a choral Epilog (*Conclusio*) that offers praises to Christ the Savior (*Gratiarum actio*). No chorales, hymns, or extra texts are used (negating any congregational participation); however, the complete text from John 18:1 to 19:42 in the Revised Standard Version is used.

The vibraphone, in a unique application, sounds at various crucial points to help maintain the pitch level of the soloists. The three solo parts each have their own distinctive melodic cadences: The pitch pattern for the Evangelist employs a simple tetrachord, that of Jesus is confined to three notes, and the parts for the *synagoga* comprise a five-note pattern. Hillert provides the starting pitch for each subsequent section, either by the vibraphone or the last note of the previous singer. The harmonies are modal, and the rhythms are simple and straightforward, which should make the *Passion* easily accessible to most parish choirs (Example 11).

Example 11. Hillert, *The Passion According to Saint John*, p. 6.

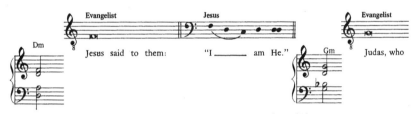

The Passion Gospel According to Matthew

Paul Hamill (b. 1930)
Gemini Press, 1979
Duration: 26 min.
Speaker (no soloists), SATB choir, congregation, organ

In the *Passion* the narrative is spoken with interspersed hymns. While Hamill's writing does not vary from straightforward, traditional four-part hymn settings for the choir, he does sample a wide variety of hymn tunes by contemporary composers that include Duke Ellington, Gordon Young, Roberta Bitgood, and Emma Lou Diemer. The spoken narration is from the *Good News Bible*.

The Passion of our Lord According to John

Lucien Deiss (b. 1921)
North American Liturgy, 1987
Duration: 35 min
3 speakers (or soloists), SATB choir, congregation, organ

Deiss suggests that the *Passion* could be performed in either of two ways. The account could be read by three clerics: The first proclaims the narrative, the second the individual characters and crowd, the third, usually the parish priest, takes the part of Jesus. The alternative is based on the responsorial Passion model and is similar to the Bender and Hillert settings with the parts of the speakers being sung. The choral *turba* parts are distinctly modal with an occasional bit of twentieth-century harmonic spice such as seconds added to a chord to portray deceit or pain, and parallel fifths and octaves to depict falseness or betrayal.

Deiss wants the congregation to be involved in presenting the *Passion*, but feels that the congregation should not be asked to portray the mob crying out, "We want Barabbas!" or "Crucify him! Crucify him!" Historically, however, this participation has been seen as an acknowledgement of our sins in causing Jesus' death. Presenting a Passion is also a reading of an historical event, and the author of this article cautions against changing the perspective.

Since participation of the Christian assembly is at the heart of this *Passion*, Deiss intersperses an acclamation of the assembly ("Remembering, O Lord . . . We acclaim you, the Savior of the world.") at ten places within the Gospel narrative. The middle phrase within each acclamation changes to reflect the various scenes (i.e., "your passion and its glory," "your trial and its judgment," "the denial of Peter," etc.). Deiss provides two differing arrangements of this acclamation, one for a soloist accompanied by the choir and one for the whole congregation singing a simple plainsong refrain.

The *Passion* begins with a prayer to Christ sung by the choir, followed by a prayer of the assembly, also sung by the choir. After this opening a brief *Exordium* leads to the Gospel narrative beginning with John 18:1. The *Passion* concludes with the closing of the tomb and a final acclamation.

Passion of Our Lord According to St. Matthew

John Bertalot (b. 1931)
Augsburg, 1992
Duration: 18 min.
T-Pilate, 2 Bar-Evangelists, B-Christ, SATB choir, congregation, organ

Passion of Our Lord According to St. Mark

John Bertalot
Augsburg, 1993
Duration: 24 min.
Bar-Christ and Pilate, SATB choir, congregation, organ

Passion of Our Lord According to St. Luke

John Bertalot
Augsburg, 1994
Duration: 27 min.
SATB Quartet, SATB choir, congregation, organ

Each of Bertalot's three Passions employs its own set of performers and is cast in its own form, but all involve the congregation and are brief enough to fit into a service of average length. The harmony in each setting is basically tonal with a small amount of chromaticism and an occasional bit of quartal harmony. The organ parts are simple and require few registration changes.

The Matthew account is set as a responsorial Passion but uniquely presents the narrative by having two Evangelists sing individually, in unison, or in harmony (Example 12). The Evangelists' recitatives are unaccompanied, and the choir participates at times as the narrator by singing in harmony parts that are generally reserved for a soloist.

The *Passion* begins with the chorale "Ah, holy Jesus" (Herzliebster Jesu) sung by the choir and congregation in unison with organ, which only accompanies the hymns throughout the work. The story begins at the point where Christ is arraigned before Pilate (Matt. 27:1). The responses of the chief priests are sung by the men of the choir in four-part harmony. This first section concludes with another stanza of the opening chorale for choir and congregation. The trial before Pilate continues in the same manner with the chorale "O sacred head" providing a moment of reflection in which the congregation can participate. During the crucifixion scene the hymns, which include *Pange lingua* and *Vexilla Regis*, are chanted with no accompaniment. After the death of Jesus the choir softly sings the Bach chorale *Es ist genug* as the two Evangelists continue the narration of the Gospel. The closing chorus is a simple motet setting of the words of the centurion. The last two stanzas of "Ah, holy Jesus," sung by the choir and congregation, form the final chorale.

Example 12. Bertalot, *Passion of Our Lord According to St. Matthew*, p. 4.

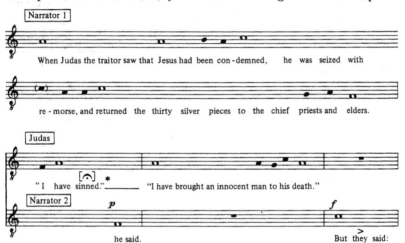

* Lines indicate the length of fermatas, so that two soloists sometimes sing together in harmony.

From *Passion of Our Lord According to St. Matthew* by John Bertalot copyright © 1992 Augsburg Fortress. Used by permission.

The organ is used extensively throughout the *St. Mark Passion*: It accompanies the hymns, provides interludes between scenes, and accompanies the two soloists and choir. The narrative is given to the choir; there is no solo Evangelist part. The trial before Pilate (Mark 15:1) commences after two stanzas of the hymn "Go to dark Gethsemane" are sung by the choir alone. The congregation sings several stanzas of "My song is love unknown" during Christ's trial. It also sings various hymn texts to THE THIRD TUNE throughout the crucifixion scene, as well as the final stanza of "Go to dark Gethsemane" (sung to PETRA) at the death of Jesus. The *Passion* closes with the final stanza of "My song is love unknown" sung by choir and congregation with a soprano descant.

The *St. Luke Passion* features an Evangelist's narrative that is sung mostly by a mixed quartet. The choir joins in at climatic points and also sings *turba* sections. Bertalot agrees with Deiss concerning the negative aspect of having the congregation take the role of the mob. Bertalot explains his view of the congregation's role in his *St. Luke Passion*:

When a congregation is invited to join in the reading of the Passion Gospel for Palm Sunday, it usually is given the part of the crowd: those who were against Jesus and called for him to be crucified. This seems unfortunate, since the faithful are asked to speak words of unfaithfulness. Therefore, in this setting of the *Passion of Our Lord According to St. Luke* the congregation is invited to sing the part of Jesus—to see the story from his viewpoint.

As noted above in the discussion of Deiss' *Passion*, the author of this article repeats his caution about this viewpoint. The congregation's role throughout the *Passion* is limited to a simple two-note chant (Example 13); thus there are no intervening or hymns of reflection.

Example 13. Bertalot, *Passion of Our Lord According to St. Luke*, p. 5.

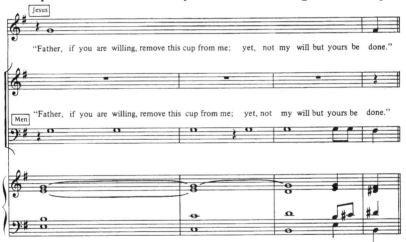

The Passion According to Four Evangelists

Robert Kyr (b. 1952)
E. C. Schirmer, 1995
Duration: 60 min.
S-Mary, A-Mary Magdalene, T-Christ, B-Pilate, SATB choir, 2 fl, ob, Eng hr, 2 cl, 2 bsn, 2 hn, 2 tpt, 2 trb, strings

Using the Revised Standard Version of the Bible as his text, Kyr has written a *summa* Passion with four soloists representing the four evangelists as well as the characters named above. Kyr explains:

In *The Passion According to Four Evangelists*, the story of Christ's death is told from the differing viewpoints of the four Gospel narrators, who join together to present a composite version of it. The roles of Matthew, Mark, Luke, and John are sung by four soloists (soprano, alto, tenor, and baritone, respectively) and the shared parts of the story are set as duos, trios, and quartets. Unexpectedly, the most prominent Evangelist roles (Matthew and Mark) are sung by the soprano and alto, which reverses the oratorio and opera tradition of giving women's roles to men. In addition, each soloist also takes the part of a principal character in the drama: the soprano and alto represent Mary and Mary Magdalene in the *Stabat Mater* (Mary stood weeping); the tenor is Jesus; and the baritone is Pilate. In this way, the Evangelists narrate a story, which they enact, as well.

The *Passion* is divided into three sections: 1) The Judgment focuses on Pilate's decision to crucify Jesus, 2) The Way of the Cross tells of Jesus' ordeal in carrying the cross to Golgotha, and 3) The Crucifixion recounts the seven last words of Jesus on the cross and the lamentation after his death. Throughout the narrative the soloists at times relinquish their storytelling roles and sing an aria of personal reflection. These reflections, however, are not extra-biblical (with the exception of the *Stabat Mater*), all are taken from the book of Psalms (Psalms 22, 69, 22/31, 34, 88, and 130).

The solo vocal lines are lyrical, and the harmonic language is a modern form of tonality, employing a substantial amount of dissonance wrapped into the contrapuntal textures for soloists, chorus, and orchestra. The four solo parts are difficult and require well-trained voices. The choral parts are of moderate difficulty, but could be undertaken by a church or college choir looking for a challenge. If the whole *Passion* is performed as written, it would take over an hour, but judicious cuts were made for the recording of this work that have shortened it to about one hour. Protestant choirs may choose to not include the *Stabat Mater*.

The Passion of Our Lord Jesus Christ

Gilbert Martin (b. 1941)
Sacred Music Press, 1998
Duration: less than 60 min.
Speaker, (no soloists), SATB choir, congregation, organ

Martin's *Passion*, subtitled *A Meditation for Choir, Congregation, Narrator, and Organ*, intersperses congregational hymns and choir anthems throughout the Gospel narrative. The Revised Standard Version text uses selected verses that abridge the narrative. It is a *summa* Passion that is divided into five different sections. It also includes additional readings from other sources, such as those by Crossman and Isaiah. The choral writing uses simple rhythms, is harmonically tonal, and features unison or two-part voicing with some four-part homophonic writing for climaxes and emphasis.

Preparation
Narrator	"My song is love unknown" by Crossman
Congregation	"O love, how deep" (sung to BOURBON)
Choir	"The Call" (text by Herbert)

The Entry
Narrator	Matthew 21:1–3, 6–11
Congregation	"Ride on, ride on in majesty" (sung to St. DROSTANE)
Choir	"So lowly does the Savior ride" (text by Pennewell)

The Upper Room
Narrator	Mark 14:12–20, 22–25
Congregation	"Here, O our Lord, we see you face to face" (sung to LANGRAN)
Choir	"Let us break bread together" (traditional)

The Mount of Olives
Narrator	Mark 14:26, 32, 35–39, 41–46, 48–50
Congregation	"Go to dark Gethsemane" (sung to PETRA)
Choir	"There is a green hill far away" (text by Alexander)

The Crufixion
Narrator	John 19:17–19, 23–30, 38, 40, 42
Choir	"Ah, holy Jesus" (sung to HERZLIEBSTER JESU)
Narrator	Isaiah 53:1–7
Congregation	"Cross of Jesus, cross of sorrow" (sung to CHARLESTOWN)
Narrator	Hymn to God the Father (text by Donne)
Choir	"Were you there?" (traditional)

St. John Passion

John Ferguson (b. 1941)
Augsburg , 1999
Duration: less than 60 min.
Speaker, SATB choir, congregation, organ

The *St. John Passion* was commissioned by the Chancel Choir of Bethany Lutheran Church, Englewood, Colorado, and was conceived for a Good Friday service with an outline similar to the Lessons and Carols order popular at Christmas. It is essentially a cycle of choral responses featuring Passion hymns that are inserted between sections of the account by St. John. Provision is made for the congregation to sing along with two of the hymns.

Ferguson suggests that the spoken words of each character be assigned to different readers to heighten the impact of the *Passion* as was done in the medieval church. The harmony is tonal, and vocal parts are predominantly homophonic with a few polyphonic sections. The stanzas of each hymn receive a varied treatment, including unison singing, men alternating with women, and four-part choral writing (Example 14). The organ part is essential but not difficult, providing introductions, transitions, and support for the choir. The outline of the *Passion* follows:

1. John 18:1–11—Jesus in the garden
   Response: "Jesus, name of wondrous love" (sung to LOUEZ DIEU)

2. John 18:12–27—Jesus denied by Peter
   Response: "When we are tempted to deny your son"
   (text by Romig)

3. John 18:28—19:16a—Jesus before Pilate
   Response: "Ah, holy Jesus" for the congregation
   (sung to HERZLIEBSTER JESU)

4. John 19:1 6b–22—Jesus goes to Calvary
   Response: "Drop, drop slow tears" (sung to SONG 46)

5. John 19:23–25a—Jesus is crucified
   Response: "To mock your reign, O dearest Lord"
   (text by Green)

6. John 19:25b–30—Jesus gives up his spirit
   Response: "Sing, my tongue, the glorious battle"
   (sung to FORTUNATUS NEW)

7. John 19:31–42—Jesus is placed in the tomb
   Response: "My song is love unknown" (sung to LOUEZ DIEU)

8. "When I survey the wondrous cross" for the congregation (sung to HAMBURG)

Example 14. Ferguson, *St. John Passion*, p. 18.

From *St. John Passion* by John Ferguson copyright © 1992 Augsburg Fortress. Used by permission.

Lenten Canticles

John Leavitt (b. 1951)
Brookfield Press, 2001
Duration: less than 60 min.
Speaker, SATB choir, congregation, organ (optional fl, ob, 2 cl, bsn, 2 perc, harp, 2 vn, vla, vc, db)

Lenten Canticles is similar to Ferguson's and Martin's Passion settings; however, Leavitt's accompaniments are more varied rhythmically. The choir sings five anthems with optional congregational participation on three hymns. The setting can be performed with only an organ accompaniment; however, Leavitt provides an optional chamber orchestration for live performance or a ChoirTrax™ CD that provides a professionally recorded accompaniment that can be played over the church's sound system to accompany the musical selections. The order of *Lenten Canticles* follows:

> Reading: Isaiah 52:13–53:12—Prophecy
> Opening Hymn: "Lead me Lord"
>   (based on music by S. S. Wesley)
> First Lesson: John 18:1–11—Jesus in the garden
> Hymn: "Go to dark Gethsemane" (sung to PETRA)
> Second Lesson: John 18:12–27—Peter's denial
> Hymn: "O sacred head, now wounded"
>   (sung to HERZLICH TUT MICH VERLANGEN)
> Third Lesson: John 18:28—19:16a—Jesus is led before Pilate
> Anthem: "Come, my way, my truth, my life"
>   (text by Herbert)
> Fourth Lesson: John 19: 16b–22—Jesus goes to Calvary
> Anthem: "God so loved the world" (music by Stainer)
> Fifth Lesson: John 19: 23–25a—The crucifixion of Jesus
> Anthem: "Jesu, my treasure" (music by Handel)
> Sixth Lesson: John 19: 25b–30—The death of Jesus
> Anthem: "Jesu, joy of my desiring" (music by Bach)
> Seventh Lesson: John 19: 31–42—The burial of Jesus
> Anthem: "Set me as a seal" (text from Song of Solomon 8:6–7)
> Hymn: "In the cross of Christ I glory" (sung to RATHBUN)

The Passion of our Lord Jesus Christ According to John
Christopher Walker (b. 1947)
Oregon Catholic Press, 2002
Duration: 28 min.
Speaker, Bar-Christ, SATB choir, congregation, organ

Walker's *Passion* was written for Father Tom Jones and the New Schola Cantorum of St. Paul the Apostle Church, Los Angeles. It opens with the refrain "There is no greater love than this" (Example 15) sung by the choir and congregation from a reprint sheet that is provided. Walker uses this and three other similar refrains throughout the *Passion* to unify the setting and allow for the congregation's participation. The refrains are to be sung twice at each presentation, first by the choir alone and then with the congregation. The choral writing is no more complex than the refrain and is often doubled in two or three parts.

The choir sings Old Testament quotations to the medieval Gregorian chant *Tonus peregrinus*. The Evangelist's narration is spoken over an organ background as are the parts of the other characters such as Pilate, the Maid, and Peter. Christ's role, the only solo part, is based on three chant-like phrases. A chord based on the Landini cadence signals that Christ is about to speak (Example 15).

Example 15. Walker *The Passion of Our Lord Jesus Christ According to John*, p. 1

William H. Braun ■ 221

Additional Liturgical Passion Settings

The Road to Calvary

J. S. Bach, compiled by John Cozens; Concordia, 1952; Reader, SATB, org. Similar to a "Lessons and Carols" service; intersperses chorales by J. S. Bach between readings of the *summa* Passion narrative.

The Cross of Christ

Donald Rommé; J. Fischer, 1953; S, Bar, B, SATB, org (piano). An abridged Passion narrative with emphasis on *turba* parts and choruses; a responsorial Passion of easy to medium difficulty.

The Passion of Our Lord Jesus Christ According to Saint Mark

Vernon Davis; E.C. Schirmer, 1955; T, Bar, B. A monophonic Passion set to the traditional chant formulas.

On the Passion of Christ

David Williams; H. W. Gray, 1955; S, T, Bar, SATB, org (opt. str). A condensed responsorial Passion from the St. Matthew Gospel; simple tonal writing for soloists, choir, and organ; duration: 30 min.

The Wondrous Cross

Reginald Hunt; Oxford, 1956; T, B, SATB, cong, org. A short responsorial setting; moderately difficult solo and choral parts; includes four well-known hymns.

Passion of Christ

Paul Van Dyke; Flammer, 1960; T, Bar, SATB, org. The choir sings the Evangelist part; medium difficulty; optional SAB youth choir; duration: 40 min.

To Calvary

Everett Titcomb; H. W. Gray, 1960; Speaker, SATB, cong, org. A speaker delivers the Gospel narrative; choir and congregation reflect on the events; very simple part-writing for choir, brief solo arias, and optional youth choir.

The Passion According to St. Mark

Ron Nelson; Augsburg, 1962; Speaker, S, A, T, B, SATB, cong, org/piano (opt. 2 fl, 2 cl, tpt, str). A speaker presents the Gospel narrative over an organ background; soloists sing no character parts, but sing responses to the action, often in Old Testament words; choral parts are of easy to medium difficulty; congregation may sing the nine interspersed hymns.

The Passion

Raymond Warren; Novello, 1964; 2S, A, 2T, 2B, SATB, fl, ob, cl, bsn, hn, piano, perc, str. A responsorial Passion; Evangelist part sung by the choir;

vocal and instrumental parts are challenging; text from *The New Testament in Modern English* by J. B. Phillips; duration: 70 min.

Our Savior's Passion

Virgil Ford; Flammer, 1964; T, Bar, SATB, org. A responsorial Passion set very simply; duration: 30 min.

Christ Crucified

Eugene Butler; Flammer, 1966; A, T, Bar, B, SATB, org. A responsorial Passion; the Evangelist part is divided between a contralto and a tenor; solo, choral, and organ parts not difficult; duration: 30 min.

The Passion of Christ

Desmond Ratcliffe; Novello, 1973; Speaker, cong, org. A Lessons and Carols format with interspersed chorales from both *St. Matthew* and *St. John Passions* by Bach; readings are a poetic paraphrase of the St. Matthew Gospel.

The Passion of Our Lord

Eugene Butler; Bock, 1989; Speaker, 2T, Bar, 2B, SATB, kybd. A responsorial Passion with the narrative divided between the speaker and the soloists singing the Evangelist role; soloists also sing some character roles and a few short arias; easy choral parts.

The Passion of Our Lord According to St. John

Randall DeBruyn; Oregon Catholic Press, 1990; Speaker, 2T, B, SATB, org, (opt. fl, ob, vn). A speaker delivers the entire Gospel narrative with an organ accompaniment; soloists take principal character parts; optional instruments may play the upper organ line for variety; medium difficulty.

Crucifixion

Bryan Kelly; Roberton, 1993; S, T, SATB, org. The setting begins with the arrest of Jesus; the text by Anne Ridler is an abridgement and free paraphrase of St. Mark with added emotionally charged poetry; two soloists sing the narrative, character parts, and arias; music is tonal and mildly dissonant; medium difficulty; duration: 36 min.

The Passion of St. John

Everett Freese; Pastoral Press, 1995; S, B, Bar, SATB, cong, org. A responsorial setting with chant-like cantors' parts accompanied by droning perfect fifths; simple choral parts are also accompanied by fifths; could be sung by a unison choir; congregation sings four responsories, three hymns, and Psalm 130.

Voices from the Passion

Ron Nelson; Egan, 1995; Speaker, S, T, Bar, SATB, org (opt. orch.). A meditation on the words of the characters of the Passion drama; an abbreviated Gospel narrative; choral and instrumental parts are moderately difficult.

What Wondrous Love

Lloyd Larson; Beckenhorst Press, 2000; 2 narrators, SATB, kybd, cong, 2 treble instruments. An abridged, spoken Passion narration with four choir hymns; congregation sings only the final stanzas of two hymns; duration: 15 min.

NOTES

1   Kurt Fischer, "Passion," in *The New Grove Dictionary of Music and Musicians*, 2nd ed. (2001), vol. 19, 209.

2   Adam Adrio, "Renewal and Rejuvenation," *Protestant Church Music: A History*, ed. Friedrich Blume et al. (New York: Norton, 1974), 436.

3   Adrio, 451–61.

4   Elwyn A. Wienandt, *Choral Music of the Church* (New York: Free Press, 1965), 30.

5   Friedrich Blume et al., *Protestant Church Music: A History* (New York: Norton, 1974).

6   A number of recent Passion settings end with the story of the resurrection, which negates their liturgical use in a Palm Sunday or Good Friday service. Examples include: Hamilton's *The Passion of Our Lord According to St Mark* (Presser, 1982) and Harvey's *Passion & Resurrection* (Faber, 1998).

7   Since the length of many worship services today is approximately one hour, Passion settings longer than one hour would not be appropriate in many parishes. For example, *The Passion According to Saint Luke* (E. C. Schirmer, 1965) by Randall Thompson might serve as a liturgical Passion, except that it lasts for over one and one-half hours.

8   The list of soloists required for performance will only name those with substantial parts.

9   Erik Routley, *Twentieth Century Church Music* (New York: Oxford, 1964), 60.

10 John France, "A Conversation with the Composer/Writer Richard Stoker about Cecil Armstrong Gibbs," http://www.musicweb.uk.net/classrev/2003/Nov03/Stoker_Gibbs.htm (accessed August 13, 2004).

11 Following ancient tradition, the E*xordium* announces the Passion and often names the Gospel from which it is taken.

12 A closing section of Passion settings developed during the fifteenth century. The text was not taken from the Gospel but often expressed thanksgiving for Christ's sacrifice.

13 Hugo Cole and Malcolm Miller, "Alan Ridout" in *The New Grove Dictionary of Music and Musicians*, 2nd ed. (2001), vol. 21, 352.

14 Kurt Pahlen, *The World of the Oratorio*, trans. Judith Schaefer (Portland, Oregon: Amadeus Press, 1990), 70.

PAUL BOUMAN

Choral Classics for the Lutheran Church Musician: A Letter to a Young Church Choir Director

Dear Friend,

Congratulations on having decided to become a church musician and choral director.

You have chosen a noble profession with a long and distinguished heritage. I know that you will face many challenges and find many rewards in your career. One of your great joys will be the selection of music for your choir.

I would like to share with you a few thoughts on the choice of music for your church choir, a challenge I found particularly rewarding. Although we represent two quite different generations, I believe that there are lasting solutions to the challenge of selecting worthy choir music for worship that I hope will be of interest to you. Along the way, I will also address some related matters that might help in performing the selected pieces.

In preparing this list for you I decided to limit myself to thirty pieces for mixed choir because I wanted to draw your attention to a few special compositions of excellence that have meant much to me and my singers. This was very difficult for me. To choose one composer over another became a personal matter, and the choice I did make was not always because one was a definite favorite over the other. In fact, over the years I have developed so many favorites that it was almost impossible to select just a few to recommend to you.

As you review this list, you should understand that I see the task of the choir as that of proclaiming the Gospel in worship, not that of entertaining the congregation. I believe that the Word must come through clearly in every composition performed. The music, no matter how beautiful, must not overwhelm or detract from that message.

Next, in congregations I served the compositions were selected to fit into the historic liturgy and its themes. Therefore, I gave preference to the parts of the service traditionally assigned to the choir, especially the Proper of the Holy Communion service. I always began my selection with the many available settings of the Introit and Gradual. (These were later replaced by Alleluia Verses, Offertory Verses, and Psalm settings.) I paid attention also to the hymns to be sung by the congregation and occasionally tried to select appropriate hymn concertatos for congregation and choir, or settings of hymn stanzas that the choir could sing in alternation with the congregation. More recently, I also realized the possibility of occasionally having the choir sing some of the parts of the Ordinary, such as the Kyrie, Gloria in excelsis, or Agnus Dei, in place of the congregation.

After I had selected the specifically liturgical music for each Sunday I thought about special music that could be sung elsewhere during worship. And that brings me to the present list of thirty pieces of special music for worship.

You will note that these pieces come from a variety of periods of music history and originate in various countries. They are also written in differing musical styles. Throughout my career I probably paid most attention to the works of the great Lutheran composers, such as those by Bach, Schütz, Praetorius, and Hassler. For the present list I did not include such obligatory collections as the Bach chorales, the "Becker" Psalms of Schütz, and the Michael Praetorius chorales, although I loved and used all of these many times during my ministry. I did not limit myself to these important composers and selected works from many sources, works that could find a hospitable home in the Lutheran liturgy. For example, you can see that I am especially fond of music of the Anglican Reformation heritage because of its high quality and fidelity to Scripture.

How, then, did I come to choose the ones I ultimately included in this list? I spent much time thinking about and examining the many choral compositions I dealt with in my 65 years as church musician. It became evident to me that in the several congregations I served my choices always seemed to gravitate to music with three qualities: pieces with texts useful for specific worship services, compositions that had high musical quality, and music that was possible for my choral groups to perform well.

First of all, the text of choral music for worship must reinforce the theme of worship of the day. It must support the message of the Gospel or the readings. Most of the best choral texts are taken or are inspired directly by Scripture itself, or from related hymns or other poetry. By contrast, I believe that many of the texts of today that repeat the pious but simplistic encouragement to "praise God," but that offer no additional theological insight, are often missing the opportunity to support the specific theme of worship of the day, or to articulate significant theological truths. Good texts abound. One must simply search for them.

Next, over the years my colleagues and mentors who knew the repertoire and the requirements of Lutheran worship impressed on me the importance of remembering the scriptural exhortation that *everything* that is used in the worship of God has to be of the highest quality. In the Old Testament our Lord stressed that only the finest type of building materials were to be used in the erection of the Temple. People were asked to bring their most precious jewelry to the task. I transferred this example to my choices in musical materials to be used in worship. Granted, tastes change through the years, but some musical compositions seem to have an ageless quality that lifts them out of the ordinary and places them alongside the best products of any age. Having established for myself a set of values for musical quality, I was steered away from much that seemed to be usable and attractive at first but soon began to reveal a triviality that later caused me to lay it aside.

What period of music is the best from which to select choral music for worship? Since examples of textual and musical quality can be found in worship music of nearly every age, it is well to review the early history of Lutheran music for guidance.

Historically, the choir's primary function during and after the Reformation era was to support the singing of the hymns and the liturgy. This was in accord with Martin Luther's desire to involve the laity directly in worship, especially in the singing of the newly-created chorales.

Choirs were also encouraged to sing motets, chorales, and other pieces based on texts of the liturgy and those related to the scriptural message or the theme of the particular service. For this purpose Luther recommended choral compositions of his contemporaries as well as those of an earlier time. He also recognized that talented musicians from the Catholic and Reformed faiths had made notable contributions that were eminently suited for Lutheran worship.

Inspired by this practice you will find in my list examples of worship music of the highest quality and usefulness from the Reformation and post-Reformation periods, the English Tudor period, the Baroque, and the nineteenth and twentieth centuries—examples that include works of Lutheran and non-Lutheran composers. May these few compositions give you the encouragement to build a solid foundation for the development of a distinguished and practical choral library for your congregation. (I've arranged the pieces in alphabetical order for your convenience.)

A Parish Magnificat

Carl Schalk (b. 1929)
Concordia, 1990, No. 98-2887
Unison choir, cantor, congregation, organ

Carl Schalk has a gift for writing simple yet memorable and lyrical vocal lines. It was difficult to decide which of his compositions to include in my list. I chose this one because both choir and congregation are involved in the singing of one of the great canticles of the church. Since the Magnificat is part of the Office of Vespers, this setting may substitute for that usually sung by the congregation alone. A refrain, which may be reproduced in the worship folder for the congregation, is included. The work is accessible for a choir of any degree of proficiency.

A Virgin Most Pure

Carl Halter (1915–1989)
Concordia, 1952, No. 98-1237, print on demand
SATB, organ

This setting of an old English folk carol would bring joy to singers and listeners alike in any Christmas service. The sprightly arrangement of this fine carol calls for careful attention by the choir to choral line and phrasing.

Agnus Dei

Hans Leo Hassler (1564–1612), ed. Walter Ehret
Shawnee, No. A1482
SATB

Hassler composed a number of Masses in the years following the Reformation, of which this Agnus Dei is a very beautiful example. We owe it to our choirs to acquaint them with the polyphonic style of music, for it helps in the training of each voice of the choir to sing independent contrapuntal lines. On occasion the choir might sing this part of the Ordinary of the Holy Communion liturgy in place of the congregation. I urge you to sing this in Latin, after drawing attention of the congregation in the service folder to the English text in the liturgy and the role of the choir in substituting for the congregation at this point.

All Glory Be to God on High

Leonhart Schroeter (c.1532–c.1601), ed. Carl Schalk
Concordia, 1994, No. 98-3114
SATB

Both the text and tune of this wonderful old chorale were composed by Nikolaus Decius (c. 1485–aft. 1546). Several performance possibilities exist: it may be sung as printed, as an anthem, or as the Hymn of Praise in the Holy Communion liturgy. In the latter case the choir would alternate stanzas with the congregation as suggested by the editor. The vocal parts may also be played by instruments, either alone or with the choir. A joyful sound! It also provides an opportunity to extend the heritage of the Lutheran chorale.

All the Ends of the World

William Boyce (1711–1779), ed. Ernest Bullock
Novello, 28.1229 special sales: www.musicroom.com
SATBB

Based on Psalm 22:27, this anthem gives the choir the opportunity to experience the rich timbre of five-part writing. Adding an alto or two to the tenor part is a possibility as well as moving the tenor to the Bass I part. The text is suitable for the Epiphany season.

Ascendit Deus

Peter Philips (c. 1560/61–1628), ed. Peter Le Huray
Oxford, 1965, No. 3520125
SSATB

This stirring motet from the Tudor era is based on Psalm 47:5, and provides a festive contribution to an Ascension service, perhaps as a substitute Offertory Verse. Another good opportunity to sing a Latin text. When singing a foreign language it is necessary to print both the foreign language and the English translation in the worship folder.

Be Filled with the Spirit

Ronald A. Nelson (b. 1927)
Augsburg, 1975, No. 11-1733, print on demand
SA, organ accompaniment

Though listed as SA, it is an excellent teaching piece for both children and adults in that it helps develop independence in part singing. It also gives a very good expression to Ephesians 5:18b–20, which is part of the Epistle for Pentecost 13.

Before the Ending of the Day

Healey Willan (1880–1968)
(Walton, 1937, 1979, No. WEI 1067)
SATB

This British-born composer immigrated to Canada as a young man where he had a long and distinguished career as church musician and as opera, symphony, organ, and choral composer. This hymn-anthem is a lovely example of his appealing choral style. The eighth-century text with its plainsong melody is found in both *Lutheran Book of Worship* (No. 297) and *Lutheran Worship* (No. 489), as well as in the hymnals of a number of other denominations. Although it is traditionally used in the evening Compline liturgy, it is well suited for any evening service.

Call to Remembrance

Richard Farrant (1525-30–1580), ed. Edward Klammer
GIA, 1987, G 3051
SATB

This beautiful and devotional anthem, based on Psalm 25:5–6, is one of the gems from that rich period of church music composition, the Tudor age in England, which extended roughly from 1500 to1625 (the death of Orlando Gibbons). There seems to be a tendency in our day to give choirs overly rhythmic music in a kind of pseudo-sacred popular style to "keep them coming." Meanwhile, deeply devotional texts that give an opportunity for introspection are overlooked. The composer has clothed two verses of Psalm 25 with incomparably beautiful music, giving the choir a musical expression of penitence that should not be denied them. One editor many years ago said, "The whole composition should be sung as if the singers were on their knees, with intense prayerful expression." Psalm 25 is appointed for Advent I in Series C, Pentecost 8 in Series C, and Pentecost 19 in Series A. A word of caution: this popular anthem is often performed in an overly dramatic style that almost completely ruins the penitential message. You must control the performance to keep it simple and unaffected, wherein lies the beauty of this composition.

Cantate Domino (Sing to the Lord, Our God)

Giuseppe Pitoni (1657–1743), ed. James Pruett
G. Schirmer, 1966, No. 50313160
SATB

The text is from Psalm 149:1–2. The Psalm is assigned to both Easter 3 and Holy Trinity, when it could be performed on occasion in place of the congregational singing of the Psalm. This is a text that sings much better in Latin than in English. Although many composers have chosen to set this text to music, I have enjoyed this classic because of its lyrical and buoyant qualities; it was also more readily accessible for some of my choirs.

Christians, Rejoice!

Johann Eccard (1553–1611)
H. W. Gray, 1934, 1962, No. 184
SATB/SATB

Singing a double-choir setting may seem like an insurmountable challenge to many choirs. However, there are ways of overcoming such an obstacle by teaching the choir one of the choral settings and playing the other one on the organ; or the second choir could be a choir of instruments, either brass, woodwinds, or strings, or a judicious combination of whatever is available. Perhaps a vocal quartet could be drawn from your choir to form the second choir. Try a number of ways, but don't give up! I have had this composition in my choir library for many years, and it was loved by children and adults alike. An excellent Easter Sunday Alleluia Verse or Gradual.

For God So Loved the World

Heinrich Schütz (1585–1672), ed. C. Buell Agey
Concordia, 1959, No. 98-1472
SATTB or SATBB, organ

This setting of the beloved John 3:16 text by one of the greatest of Lutheran masters may be sung in English or German. Don't be frightened by the double tenor part; the second tenor line may be sung by a single baritone. Use the organ accompaniment as the composer himself probably did with his limited forces during the hardships imposed by the Thirty Years' War. It is well worth a little extra rehearsal time. The text is part of the Gospel for both Holy Trinity and Lent 4 in Series B. Take the time to examine other works of this master.

He Shall Give His Angels Charge Over You

Richard Hillert (b. 1923)
GIA, 1993, G 3983
Unison choir, organ, oboe or other C instrument

Richard Hillert's choral compositions have a refreshingly contemporary quality that has contributed to their popularity. This gem is an example of a Psalm setting (Psalm 91:9–12; 15–16) that fits well into the service. The entire choir may sing the recurring refrain, "He shall give his angels charge over you to keep you in all your ways," while a soloist or a small group may sing the verses. The work is especially appropriate for Lent 1 with its Gospel on the Temptation of Jesus, when it could be sung as a substitute Offertory.

If Ye Love Me

Thomas Tallis (c. 1505–1585), ed. Peter Le Huray
Oxford, 1972, No. 3521385
SATB

This beautiful little anthem is a must for the Pentecost season. The tenor part goes a bit high, but a little help from an alto or two can save the day! Also, it is historically appropriate to use a light organ accompaniment that would give assurance to the vocally exposed high tenor! Encourage your choir to achieve the intended light, well-blended ensemble tone that is a quality to be sought for in many of these Tudor anthems.

Jesu, Joy of Man's Desiring

Johann Sebastian Bach (1685–1750), ed. David Music
GIA, 1991, G 3470
SATB, organ, string parts available

I have always considered this extended chorale setting a wonderful introduction to the music of J. S. Bach. It is an arrangement of a chorale from his Cantata No. 147. Children and adults are intrigued by the challenge of getting to know the place of their entrances as the lovely accompaniment line flows along so beautifully. It gives the choir a satisfying feeling of accomplishment. This is very effective when sung by children in unison. (There are other similar chorale settings by J. S. Bach, which the curious conductor can discover with a little digging!) This piece is especially appropriate for any Sunday when the Gospel features the ministry of Jesus.

Lamb of God

F. Melius Christiansen (1871–1955)
Augsburg, 1933, No. 0800652592
SATB

This composer, a pioneer in twentieth-century choral development, produced many choir settings of Lutheran chorales, of which this brief example is an absolute gem. Treat it with care! Be careful of over dramatization! The beautiful flow of the music speaks for itself. It may be sung occasionally in place of the congregational Agnus Dei. A word about the pronunciation of the final word "Jesu." This word has provoked an argument for years. Early in my career a highly respected choral conductor encouraged us to say "Yay-zoo" when singing Latin or German and "Jee-zoo" when singing in English. My Webster dictionary supports this latter pronunciation.

Laudate Nomen Domini (Praise the Name of the Lord)

Christopher Tye (c. 1505–before 1573), ed. Eugene W. Ritter
GIA, 1979, G 2234
SATB

This is one of a number of short motets by this Tudor-era composer that deserves to be included in the service. This setting of verses from Psalm 113 is especially worthy! The purity of the harmonization and the movement within the setting give it a delightful spirit. This text is assigned to Epiphany 3 and Pentecost 18 in Series C.

Lo! How A Rose

Hugo Distler (1908–1942)
Concordia, 1967, No. 98-1925
SATB

This twentieth-century German composer is frequently regarded as the present-day counterpart of the seventeenth-century master, Heinrich Schütz. Distler was a master who gave a new sound and new life to the chorales of earlier times. This exquisite setting of a charming old carol ought to be a staple for the Advent season, perhaps alternating with the equally lovely setting of the same tune and text by Michael Praetorius.

Lord, for Thy Tender Mercy's Sake

ascribed to Richard Farrant (c. 1525-30–1580) and
John Hilton (d. 1608), ed. Edward Klammer
GIA, 1987, G 3049
SATB

The uncertain authorship in no way detracts from the value and beauty of this anthem as a highly suitable service resource. It is excellent for teaching independence of part-singing to an inexperienced choir; but it also commends itself very well to a group with professional skills. It is especially useful for any of the penitential Sundays. In the repeated section it is customary to vary the performance. You could, for example, begin the repeat louder and end quieter. The final Amen is a fine example of the exquisite writing style of the Tudor composers. I have another edition of the anthem that is in A-flat. Try any of the anthems of this period in various keys.

O God Be Merciful

Christopher Tye (c. 1505–before 1573), ed. Milsom
Oxford, 1934, No. 3521490
SATB

This motet is sometimes also ascribed to Thomas Tallis. Whoever it was, the composer created a masterpiece within the space of a few pages that has been a great favorite of mine for many years. The text, drawn from Psalm 67, is especially appropriate for several days where the full Psalm is designated: Pentecost 13 in Series A, Epiphany 2 in Series B, or Easter 6 in Series C. However, it is also suitable for many other occasions.

O Holy Child, We Welcome Thee

Carl Halter (1915–1989)
Concordia, 1952, No. 98-1236, print on demand
SATB, organ

This setting of a simple, lovely German Christmas carol is a most appealing arrangement with a tender quality that really touches the heart. The moving upper line of accompaniment of stanzas 1 and 3 could well be duplicated by a violin, oboe, or flute, or by all of them! If you transposed this into B-flat major, the tenor in the second stanza could be sung by a low alto. A cello could support the bass. Whatever you do, keep the *tender* quality.

O Sacred Feast

Healey Willan (1880–1968)
Warner, 1924, 1952, No. GCMR00715
SATB

This beautiful Communion anthem is a perennial favorite because of the composer's masterful choral style. In much of his great output of choral music Willan, a prolific composer, adapted a compositional style from an earlier period but gave it a contemporary flavor. The devotional character of this anthem (typical of much of his music) is especially apparent when it is sung during the distribution of Holy Communion.

O Sing Joyfully

Adrian Batten (1591–1637), ed. Maurice Bevan
Oxford, 1985, No. 3502283
SATB

This classic, polyphonic anthem, based on Psalm 81:1–4, displays the exuberance that characterizes so many Psalm settings of its time. While Psalm 81 is the assigned text for Pentecost 2 (Series B), the anthem could be sung as the substitute Psalm for any Sunday of Easter.

O Taste and See

Ralph Vaughan Williams (1872–1958)
Oxford, 1953, No. 3535114
Soprano solo, SATB, organ intro.

In a few measures Vaughan Williams has created a masterpiece in this setting of Psalm 34:8. You may wish to alter the language to make it more inclusive. The last line could read "bless-ed are they that trust in him." This is a twentieth-century gem, suitable for singing during the distribution at any Holy Communion service. Handle with care, striving to project a pure, light, and clear tone.

Praise to the Lord

Hugo Distler (1908–1942), ed. John Dressler
J. Fischer, 1966, No. FEC09695
SATB

The stirring, sturdy character of this setting of a great chorale is bound to inspire any group of singers and listeners. The work is helpful in the important task of introducing the choir to the sounds of slightly dissonant twentieth-century harmony. The second stanza alone could serve as an alternate choral stanza when the congregation sings this hymn (*LBW,* 543; *LW,* 444).

Psallite—Sing Your Psalms to the Holy Child
Michael Praetorius (1571–1621)
Concordia, 1962, No.98-1869
SATB

This composition was found among the works of Praetorius and is usually ascribed to him, but it has not been established who the actual composer was. Nonetheless, that in no way minimizes the delight that both singers and listeners derive from the performance of this sprightly anthem. The original Latin and German text is given as well as a useful English translation. Explore the possibility of singing the original Latin and German, but always print *all* the texts in the service folder. Duplicating the vocal parts with instruments such as recorders, flutes, woodwinds, etc., either played alone or with the voices, enhances the performance of this work and is very much in keeping with the performance practice of this era. Check out the many other compositions by this outstanding Lutheran composer. Praetorius deserves to be heard in Lutheran worship.

Rejoice in the Lord
John Redford (d. 1547), ed. Edward Klammer
GIA, 1985, G 2810
SATB

Here is another product of the Tudor era that over the years has become one of my all-time favorites. The text is assigned to Advent 3 in Series C and Pentecost 21 in Series A. Philippians 4:4–7 always comes to life in this setting. The final words of the text, "And the peace of God, which passeth all understanding, keep your hearts and minds through Christ Jesus," provide, in my opinion, one of the most sublime and beautiful moments in all of choral literature. The anthem deserves an annual performance because of its quality. Such yearly repetition of worthy anthems helps the choir retain the repertoire in its memory.

Teach Me, O Lord
William Byrd (c. 1540–1623), ed. Edmund H. Fellowes
Oxford, 1999, No. 3953625
Soprano or tenor solo, SSATB organ

Based on Psalm 119:33–38, this English verse anthem alternates passages for solo and choir, all accompanied by an uncomplicated organ part. The solo may be sung by several blending voices in a simple, non-dramatic manner. The traditional Gloria Patri ending is set with typical Anglican splendor. These Psalm verses are assigned to Pentecost 16, Series A.

This is the Record of John

Orlando Gibbons (1583–1625), ed. Edmund H. Fellowes
Oxford, 1924, No. 3520842
Tenor solo, SAATB, organ

This English verse anthem is also a true Gospel motet with alternating parts for tenor solo and choir, which may be accompanied by either organ or instruments. John 1:19–23 is a significant scriptural account of the importance of the forerunner in the celebration of Advent. It is available in several editions in various keys. String parts may be ordered from the publisher. Another Oxford version, edited by Peter Le Huray, gives the solo to an alto. It is a fine composition and it would be very much worth your time to investigate both editions.

Wake, Awake, for Night is Flying

Bartholomäus Gesius (c. 1555-62–1613), ed. Edward Klammer
Concordia, 1963, No.98-1251, print on demand
SATB

This famous chorale of Philip Nikolai, who wrote both text and tune, has become known as "the King of Chorales." The setting by Gesius has maintained the beautiful but rugged rhythmic character of the original chorale. It is especially appropriate for the first Sunday in Advent, which does not seem complete to me without singing this strong hymn that heralds the coming of Christ and which urges us to be ready to receive him. The polyphonic writing will encourage independence of voices in your choir.

Now, here you have *a* list, not necessarily *the* list! What will you do with it? Your music budget in many cases will not be able to immediately bear purchasing quantity copies of every item listed here. Nor would you want to do that. Look upon it as a reference list to which you turn each season after you have acquired the liturgical materials that it is your choir's function to perform in the service.

You will notice that I have listed only one work by J. S. Bach, the master composer of Lutheran music. The reason for this is that Bach chorales are usually found in collections that I heartily recommend. Bach motets, oratorios, and cantatas are extended works that are probably too long for the average service if used in their entirety. However, do not rule out the use of individual choruses, arias, or chorales that relate to the Gospel of the day. In my last full-time position we developed an annual series of Bach cantata services in order to feature these masterpieces in the context in which they were originally intended. I am happy to report that after thirty-five years this series is still alive and well.

But I also want to share with you a few general thoughts that might help you develop skill in selecting music for worship. In my opinion, being a choir director is an on-going process of learning and study. You can have the most beautiful anthems in existence in your library, but if you don't know they are there they are of little use to you. You must be thoroughly familiar with the music in your possession. Perhaps a yearly review of each piece in your library would facilitate this process.

I have also always found it very helpful and enjoyable to sing in a choir myself under an experienced and competent director, who could help me to develop a feeling for good choral writing and performance. Summer workshops and publishers' reading sessions are helpful in becoming acquainted with new choral music. Examine much choral music—old and new—and in time your powers of discernment will become sharper and more focused. Always ask yourself, "How will I use this composition with my choir in a service? Is the textual content worthy of presentation to our congregation? Does it contribute to the proclamation of the Gospel? Will it reinforce the theme of worship of a given service? Is the musical dress worthy of the time it will take to rehearse the anthem in order to perform it well"?

These days music is an expensive item and we cannot afford too many mistakes in our musical shopping excursions. Before you buy, be sure that you like the music and that you can tolerate spending the rehearsal time helping the choir to learn it. Sometimes I only later discovered the superficiality of a piece that, at first, seemed very beguiling.

In my early years as a choir director, I was fortunate to be a part of a group of four or five Lutheran church musicians who periodically met to review choral music. Each of us would bring four or five anthems for review. In these sessions we would gather around the piano, play and sing the music and offer our opinion. Several in the group were more seasoned directors than I, but we all offered an honest appraisal of the music reviewed, and, I must say, we all learned much from each other. I will be forever grateful to my colleagues for this experience, as I was often spared making unwise purchases.

A word about your rehearsal procedures may be of help. Always allow enough time for a choir to learn the music well, no matter what the choir's rate of learning may be. The point is that even if the choir reads quickly and well they must also be given time to *absorb* the music, a process that ultimately will also contribute to a good performance. As an example, begin your more difficult Christmas music in September and spend perhaps five to ten minutes on it in *each* rehearsal so it becomes familiar to the choir. Discuss your rehearsal technique with a colleague if possible. Also, from time to time you might seek advice or a comment from a trusted choir member whose opinion you respect.

If you really enjoy what you are rehearsing, be enthusiastic and point out to the choir particular places in an anthem that really touch you. This enthusiasm imparts itself to a group and serves to develop a bond in the joint effort of turning a printed page into an artistic, devotional, and aural experience.

Always make reference in rehearsal to the text of an anthem and be aware of difficult places in the text that you feel need an explanation. If a text doesn't make sense to you perhaps you need to study it a bit more, or perhaps you need to question the choice you have made. Your pastor is a good resource to help clarify certain biblical phrases. Discuss with your pastor some of the anthem texts you have in preparation and see how they correspond with the planned pulpit message. Reference to the choir's emphasis of the text may even be made later in a sermon, thereby reinforcing the concept that the choir is part of the proclaiming ministry. This helps to develop in the choir recognition of the importance of their participation in the service, not as entertainers, but as proclaimers. This most important function cannot be emphasized enough.

We, who have been fortunate enough to be called as choir directors, have been led into a wonderful ministry in which our choirs are our partners. Therefore, we must be the joint guardians of the goal that should be ours, namely, never to present in worship works that are textually or musically trivial. They must ever and always direct attention to the praise of God. The landmark publications of Georg Rhau, the foremost music publisher and composer of the early Lutheran Reformation, provided choral resources of high quality for the young church, resources that were rooted in sound Lutheran theology and the liturgical heritage of the church. We do well to follow his example.

As church musicians we have a gift from the Holy Spirit to be teachers in the church. According to Ephesians 4:12–13, we are to "equip the saints for the work of ministry, for the building up of the body of Christ, until we all attain to the unity of faith and the knowledge of the Son of God." Your calling requires you through music to equip the saints in your choir and through them your congregation.

May God bless you and help you fulfill your important calling!

Your friend and colleague,

Paul Bouman

P. S.: The liturgical assignments cited above are those of *Lutheran Book of Worship* (St. Louis: Concordia, 1978). Other liturgical designations of texts should be checked carefully in order to coordinate service music with the liturgical assignments of the hymnal or service book adopted locally.

These works may be secured from various music dealers, such as GIA in Chicago, Douglas Williams Music in Chicago, Kephart Music in Decorah, Iowa, or where you would normally purchase choral music for your congregation. From time to time, even "classic" choral pieces go out of print. If such is the case with some of these pieces, it will probably be helpful to consult the publisher or choral holdings of large parishes in your vicinity for a copy that may be duplicated for your choir (after securing approval, of course, from the publisher).

FRANK C. SENN

The Pastor and the Church Musician

The success of the partnership between the pastor and the church musician is crucial to the process of planning and leading the people of God in worship. Like other partnerships, sometimes it works and sometimes it doesn't. This essay argues that the partnership will work best if both pastor and musician are regarded as holding ministerial offices in the church that bind them together on a ministry team. This requires locating the church musician among the ministerial offices of the church. Then we will discuss the relationship between the pastor and the church musician within the theology of worship, identify the pitfalls in this partnership, explore aspects of worship planning which require the knowledge and talents of both pastor and church musician, and finally offer some suggestions for strengthening this partnership by giving attention to the musical formation of the pastor and the theological formation of the church musician.

The Church Musician Among the Ecclesiastical Offices

From the earliest descriptions of Christian liturgy after the New Testament, including but not limited to the *Didache* (late first century), the Letters of Ignatius of Antioch (c. 115), the *Apology* of Justin Martyr (c. 150), and *The Apostolic Tradition* attributed to Hippolytus of Rome (c. 215), we see a differentiation of roles in the liturgical assembly. The *Didache* seems perched at that moment in the history of the church when leadership in the assembly was passing from charismatic to elected ministers. Ignatius of Antioch describes an assembly that includes roles for bishops, presbyters, deacons, and laity. Justin Martyr mentions bishops, deacons, and laity. *The Apostolic Tradition* actually provides ordination prayers for bishops, presbyters, and deacons, procedures for the appointment of widows, readers, and subdeacons, and the recognition of the charismatic ministries of confessors, virgins, and healers. A whole section of the treatise deals with formation of the laity in terms of the catechumenate and the rites of Christian initiation.

In the evolution of Christian liturgy up to this point, references to singing are quite sparse. St. Paul refers to "psalms and hymns and spiritual songs" in Colossians 3:16 and Ephesians 5:19. In the Letter of Pliny the Younger to the Emperor Trajan (c. 112), this Governor of Bithynia and Pontus describes his dealings with Christians and mentions in passing that they assembled "before daybreak" and sang "a hymn (*carmen*) antiphonally to Christ, as to a god."[1] Ignatius of Antioch writes that the church should "form into a choir, so that, in perfect harmony and taking your pitch from God, you may sing in unison and with one voice to the Father through Jesus Christ."[2] There is no mention of a song leader or cantor in any of these documents.

The Tabernacle and Temple in Jerusalem, as described in I Chronicles 25, had a professional choir and orchestra of Levites. Pagan cults in the ancient world also had professional singers and instrumentalists. As Christianity developed in the pagan world, the church at first did without professional musicians. The church fathers were concerned that Christian worship should be differentiated from pagan worship, although it was a constant struggle to do so.[3] But in the fourth century the character of Christian liturgy changed as Christianity became a legal cult in the Roman Empire and moved out of private homes into public buildings called basilicas in order to perform public liturgies. The singing of Psalms covered the processional entrances and exits of the clergy, provided responses between readings, and offered devotional reflection during the gathering of gifts and administration of Holy Communion. The morning and evening prayer offices in the basilicas required the singing of Psalms and canticles. It was also in the prayer offices that the use of non-biblical hymns first emerged.

Writings of the church fathers, such as John Chrysostom, indicate that cantors had been used to lead the singing of Psalms by the congregation. In a homily against talking and gossiping in church during the liturgy Chrysostom uses as an example the fact that ". . . the lector alone speaks, and even the bishop sits and listens in silence. Thus the cantor sings alone, and when all join him in the response it is as though only one voice were sounding."[4] The lack of references to cantors in ecclesiastical documents such as church orders means that these persons did not hold an appointed ecclesiastical office. In fact, the selection of song leaders in the early church may have been an informal process, depending on who had the gift to do the job. That places the role of cantor among the charismatic rather than among the institutional ministries of the church.

By the end of the fourth century, however, choirs were being regularly employed to sing the Psalms, canticles, and hymns in place of the congregation ("another treasure chest that has been robbed of its original beauty," in the opinion of Chrysostom).[5] Choirs of women were common in pagan cults. Choirs of virgins seem to have been first employed by Ephrem in East Syria who used them to sing his hymns.[6] Choirs of boys were also used in pagan cults and by the state on festive civic occasions. By the fourth century the singing of children in church was taken for granted by a number of Eastern church fathers.[7] But not until the fifth century do ecclesiastical documents begin to speak of a *schola cantorum*, i.e. a school of singers attached to a cathedral, who are trained to sing parts of the liturgy not sung by the people.[8]

The reason for the development of the choir is easy to understand. Even though the liturgy was in the language of the people (Syriac, Greek, Latin), the people did not have books in their hands such as modern congregations have. They could easily memorize the standard responses to dialogues and litany-prayers and perhaps even some of the standard canticles. As hymn writers like Ephrem the Syrian or Ambrose of Milan provided hymns for their people, they could learn and sing these also. Daily prayer offices in the cathedrals of the fourth and fifth centuries made use of regularly recurring Psalms and canticles, which made popular participation possible. In fact, popular participation was a characteristic feature of the cathedral office, but that required sameness of structure and repetition of material. With the addition of more Psalms in the eucharistic liturgy and in the prayer offices (especially in the monastic offices), it would have been necessary for a group to gather around a reading stand in order to chant the variable texts. This explains why, in the cathedrals of great cities like Constantinople and Rome, those who did the chanting were first called *schola lectorum* (school of readers). It definitely was a school since its members had to learn to read and sing together. These cathedral schools provided the education of selected boys. In Rome, the *schola* was not called *cantorum* until during or after the pontificate of Gregory the Great (590-604). The Constantinopolitan and Roman *scholae* consisted of men and boys. Since they were also considered readers, this put the members of the *schola* into the ranks of the lower clergy. Thus the original charismatic leadership of the cantor had been transformed into an collective institutional leadership which was regularized by being given a clerical office (even for the boys). This is why, as the alb (and later the surplice) came to be regarded as a vestment, the cathedral choirs were vested (including the boys).

However, not every great church had a *schola*. The growth of monasteries in the fourth century, especially in urban areas, provided a natural source of choirs to provide leadership in liturgical singing. We know that Pope Gregory the Great employed monastic communities attached to the cathedral churches of Rome to provide leadership in the daily prayer offices (e.g. at St. John Lateran). Monks were charismatics, not ecclesiastics. They really were laity who undertook a special vocation of prayer. This is why choirs of monks were not vested in alb or surplice unless they were specifically ordained and were providing a liturgical role (e.g. celebrant, deacon).

When the Carolingian rulers requested Roman liturgical books to be sent to their court so that they could bring some order into the unruly Frankish Church, they were particularly interested in Roman chant and musical organizations. Pippin III (741–768) made an effort to replace the old Gallican chant by importing and introducing Roman chant. Pope Stephen II sent to Pippin an *Antiphonale* and a *Responsale* containing the chants of the Mass and the Office. Bishop Chrodegang of Metz (d. 766), one of Pippin's closest advisers, and Bishop Remedius of Rouen (d. 771), Pippin's half-brother, both set up schools of chant following the Roman model.[9] About 760 Chrodegang brought a singing teacher from Rome to Metz and the *secundus* of the Roman *schola cantorum* was despatched to Rouen. Choirs of men and boys on the Roman model were established in cathedrals throughout Europe, especially in Britain where Augustine of Canterbury, having been sent by Pope Gregory the Great to evangelize the English, founded a Church that was a replica of the Roman model. The British cathedral choirs of men and boys today continue the tradition of the Roman *schola cantorum*.

Unfortunately, we don't know the names of the musicians who provided professional musical leadership for the liturgical offices. Certainly by the early Middle Ages they were all monks or clergy. Among the few names of church musicians that have come to us from the early Middle Ages we may mention the monk Notker Balbulus, who wrote sequence texts in his *Liber Hymnorum* (c. 885); Hucbald (c. 850–930), a monk of St. Amand in the Diocese of Tournai, who was both the author of *De Institutione Harmonca* and a composer of mass settings; and Guido d'Arezzo, a Benedictine who taught at the choir school of the Cathedral of Arezzo between 1025 and 1033 and fostered solmization (*ut, re, mi,* etc.).

From the thirteenth century on an increasing number of musicians are known to us. Many who provided church music were also monks or clerics. Some, like Philippe de Vitry (1291–1361) and Guillaume de Machaut (c. 1300–1377), were ecclesiastics on loan to the courts of kings and wrote secular music as well as liturgical music. By the time of the Renaissance we also find non-ecclesiastics writing liturgical and secular music, men such as Heinrich Isaac (c. 1450-55–1517) and Ludwig Senfl (c. 1486–1542/43). Martin Luther's favorite composer, Josquin Des Prez (c. 1450-55–1521), was an ecclesiastic who had been a member of the Papal Chapel in Rome and ended his career as provost of the Collegiate Church at Condé-sur-Escaut, Flanders. The premier musician of his age, he was comfortable in both secular and sacred musical fields. Ecclesiastical appointment of church musicians continues after the Reformation in Roman Catholic, Anglican, and Lutheran Churches. Giovanni Pierluigi da Palestrina (1525-26–1594), the paradigmatic post-Tridentine composer, held ecclesiastical appointments in Rome throughout his career. Tomás Luis de Victoria (1548–1611) was actually ordained a priest. Comparable roles were served in the Church of England by Thomas Tallis (c. 1505–1585), who held ecclesiastical appointments both before and after the Reformation, and William Byrd (c. 1540–1623), who, though a known Roman Catholic, held an ecclesiastical appointment at Lincoln Cathedral. Both Byrd and Tallis served also in the Chapel Royal and shared a monopoly on the printing of music and production of music paper granted by Queen Elizabeth I. In contrast, the two greatest post-Reformation Lutheran composers, Michael Praetorius (1571–1621) and Heinrich Schütz (1585–1672), held court appointments even though both made important contributions to Lutheran church music. Johann Sebastian Bach (1685–1750) held both court and ecclesiastical appointments. In his position as Thomaskantor in Leipzig (1723–1750), Bach simultaneously held an office in the church, the school, and the city. Christoph Wolff has shown that receiving the office of cantor required passing a rigorous theological examination.[10]

The office of cantor continued after the time of Bach, but there was a diminishing sense that the church musician held an ecclesiastical office, even if he held a church "appointment." In the Age of Enlightenment the best musicians sought employment in the burgeoning venues of the opera houses and concert halls, often leaving musicians of lesser ability to provide music for the church. Indeed, even some of the best church music after the Age of Enlightenment was produced by "secular" composers on commission rather than by church musicians.

In America one can only find the scattered remains of church music institutions. Some larger Episcopal cathedrals and parishes have tried to maintain the tradition of English cathedrals with their organist/choirmasters, assistant organists, organ scholars, choral scholars, and choir schools. The Lutheran Church–Missouri Synod revitalized the role of cantor in the Lutheran tradition, especially in congregations with parochial schools. These Lutheran cantors were and are regarded as "called" teachers of the Church and are listed on the synod's roster of ministers. They had responsibility both for parish worship and music education in the school. Some congregations, especially in the Reformed tradition, developed the position of minister of music, which usually means being the music director of the congregation with supervisory responsibilities for other staff musicians, choirs, and ensembles. In most smaller congregations and parishes in all denominations, the church musician is a part-time employee who may play the organ or direct the choir or lead the praise band or do everything. In some situations the church musician is a volunteer from the congregation. Thus, in most parish settings the church musician is a charismatic leader rather than an ecclesiastical officer.

While the charismatic, as opposed to the institutional, position of the church musician in the church structure does not explain all the reasons for conflict between pastor and musician (personality clashes can never be left out of the equation), conflicts are sometimes the result of the inherent tension between institutional and charismatic ministries. The charismatic appeals more to the authority of his or her gift than to the authority of an office that is responsible to a community. This does not mean that a charismatic leader cannot develop a strong sense of responsibility to a community. But calling the musician to a church office (i.e. cantor), even (especially!) in a part-time position, might help to forge a partnership between the pastor and the church musician by giving both a sense of being colleagues in ministry.

The Partnership of Pastor and Musician Within a Theology of Worship

A partnership between the pastor and the church musician is crucial because both play a role in leading the people of God in the worship of God and proclaiming of the Word of God in the liturgical assembly. Church musicians who are part time, who may even come to church on Sunday morning after performing in a concert hall or a club on Saturday night, must have a sense of a call to an ecclesiastical office extended by a community of faith no less than their full-time church music colleagues. The musician may have a gift of music, but it needs to be honed into a personal sense of a call, communally-extended, to do church music. A call to office with election by the parish governing board and public installation in the congregation will give the church musician more of a sense of responsibility in the tasks of enabling the congregation to praise God in song and proclaim the Word of God through music.

Medieval and Reformation theology understood that there are two directions of communication in worship, which they labeled the *sacrificial* and the *sacramental*. The sacrificial aspect of worship is what the people address to God in prayer, praise, and thanksgiving. The sacramental aspect of worship is what is addressed to the people from God in the Word and the sacraments. These two directions of communication serve to glorify God and edify the people. Church music serves both directions. In some contemporary "praise and worship" services, the pastor turns over to the musician the selection and arrangement of songs. The musician becomes the worship leader, who then makes decisions about what to add or drop or repeat or cut off during the "praise and worship" part of the service, as well as decisions about when the people should stand or sit and even how long the prayers should be. The proclamation of the Word of God in the second part of the service belongs to the pastor.[11] In liturgical worship no purpose served by the pastor in worship is not served also by the church musician, and vice versa. Both have responsibility for praise and proclamation. The musician leads the people in the praise of God through Psalms and canticles just as the pastor leads the people in the praise of God by offering the Great Thanksgiving. The musician proclaims the Word of God to the people through hymns and motets just as the pastor preaches a sermon. Since these leadership roles are exercised in one and the same liturgy, there must be cooperation between the pastor and church musician in planning worship as well as in leading it. Pastor and musician have performance responsibilities throughout the liturgy.[12]

Partnerships between pastors and church musicians in the Lutheran tradition, and more broadly in the Protestant tradition, go back to Martin Luther. In the preface to Georg Rhau's *Symphoniae iucundae* (1538), the great reformer wrote that "next to the Word of God, music deserves the highest praise."[13] Luther's musical education was better than average, and his contribution to liturgical music and hymnody was formidable.[14] He appreciated the work of the best composers of his age. He collaborated with the first evangelical cantor, Johann Walter, in the arrangement of musical scores.

While Luther supported liturgical art music, his primary concern was to restore the people's song to the liturgy. For this reason he supported the efforts of the first and greatest of the Reformation music publishers, Georg Rhau, in the production of hymnals. Congregational song was also the purpose of Jean Calvin (who granted no role to the choir). Inspired by the metrical psalmody he had experienced in the German congregation in Strassburg, when Calvin returned to Geneva in 1542 he collaborated with the court poet Clément Marot and the composer Louis Bourgeois in the production of the French Geneva Psalter (1551, 1562).

We don't know the extent of the collaboration of John Marbeck (c. 1505–c. 1585) with Archbishop Thomas Cranmer or other leaders of the English Reformation, but we may note his work as organist at St. George's Chapel in Windsor Castle, where he provided a complete plainsong setting of *The Book of Common Prayer Noted* (i.e. set to music, 1550). This was music meant for a Protestant cathedral choir. Unfortunately, the revision of the Prayer Book in 1552 set all his work to naught, and he made no attempt to revise it.

Productive partnerships between pastors and church musicians have been possible in instances in which the pastor and church musician respected and supported one another and collaborated in a team effort. The greatest Lutheran pastor-poet of the seventeenth century, Paul Gerhardt (1607–1676), collaborated with the Cantor of the St. Nicholas Church in Berlin, Johann Crüger (1598–1662), and later with Crüger's successor, Georg Ebeling (until 1668).

A collaboration similar to the Gerhardt-Crüger partnership occurred in nineteenth-century Denmark. The lyrics of the priest-hymn writer, historian, and folklorist, Nikolai F. S. Grundtvig (1783–1872), attracted the interest of one of Denmark's leading organists, Andreas P. Berggren (1801–1880). As editor of a Danish chorale book (hymnal) of 1852 (authorized in 1855), Berggren siezed the opportunity to find appropriate settings for Grundtvig's unconventional hymn lyrics by using a new kind of tune styled "religious romance" since it resembled the Danish Romantic lied. A number of Grundtvig's 1500 hymns were included. Berggren's use of triple meters and quicker tempos was considered scandalous by the traditionalists of the time, although this style served Grundtvig's lyrics better than the old chorale tunes.[15]

A similar collaboration occurred in England in 1906 when the Anglo-Catholic priest Percy Dearmer (1867–1936) contracted with Ralph Vaughan Williams (1872–1958) to edit *The English Hymnal* in 1906. Although Vaughan Williams professed to be an atheist (or a "disappointed theist," as his second wife Ursula put it), he provided several hymn tunes distinctly English in character that have endeared themselves to English-speaking Christians in several denominational traditions.

In America one would have to take note of the celebrated partnerships between revival preachers and their musical companions, most famously Dwight L. Moody and Ira Sankey in the late nineteenth century, Billy Sunday and Homer Rodeheaver in the early twentieth century, and Billy Graham and Cliff Barrows and George Beverly Shea after 1950. Rick Warren, writing out of this tradition in *The Purpose-Driven Church*, advises the pastor-developer of a mission church to secure a musician before proceeding with other staffing or erecting a building.

Pitfalls in the Partnership of Pastor and Church Musician

For every successful partnership between pastor and church musician there are unsuccessful partnerships. Ironically, the career of the greatest Lutheran cantor, Johann Sebastian Bach (1685-1750), provides examples of why this partnership has not always worked—even when the church musician held an ecclesiastical office.

Bach did not always get on well with his ecclesiastical superiors, for theological as well as professional reasons. One of Bach's best friends was Georg Christian Eilmar, the orthodox pastor of St. Mary's Church in Mühlhausen (who later served as godfather to Bach's first-born in Weimar) during the time Bach served as organist at St. Blasius Church under the pietist Superintendent Frohe.[16] In the pietist view, public worship should cultivate an individual relationship with God. Pietists evaluated worship and music in terms of how edifying it was to the congregation rather than how it glorified God. The orthodox had a more objective view of worship as a God-centered activity and believed that church music was to be rendered "to the glory of God alone" (*soli Deo gloria*), as Bach wrote on his manuscripts. Caught in the battle between orthodox and pietists, Bach moved on to the court at Weimar.

Bach's disagreements with church and civic authorities in Leipzig are well-known. These disagreements were not only over "practical" issues, such as the disparity between what Bach thought had been promised to him and what was actually delivered. Theological issues lay behind Bach's charges that church music was not being adequately supported by the city council and later by the Enlightenment-espousing rector of the St. Thomas School, Johann August Ernesti. As a lead-up to his conflicts with Ernesti, Bach had composed his well-known memo to the Leipzig City Council in 1730, "A Short but Most Necessary Draft for a Well-Appointed Church Music; With Certain Modest Reflections on the Decline of the Same."[17] Apparently, after seven years in Leipzig, the conditions of Bach's position had not kept pace with expectation, and the result was, in Bach's considered opinion, a deleterious decline in the quality of church music.[18] Ernesti became the rector of the Thomasschule in 1734. He was probably not the most radical proponent of the Enlightenment view that what is valuable is what is useful, but it is also clear that Ernesti placed the study of music far below the core curriculum of the Thomasschule. The relationship between cantor and rector deteriorated when Bach sacked a student prefect for incompetence, a charge which Ernesti thought was overstated. In Ernesti's view the lad "was competent enough" and Bach was displaying musical snobbery.[19] In the rector's view, the opportunity of any student to participate in the church music and derive whatever benefit he could from this experience trumped the cantor's desire for quality performance of church music "to the glory of God" (especially when it was Bach's own music!).

Bach's own experiences suggest two issues that must be dealt with in the relationship of pastor and church musician. First, there must be agreement in the purpose, content, and style of public worship. Bach and Ernesti, for example, disagreed over what music was appropriate at funerals; Bach preferred chorales, Ernesti wanted cantatas. Had Bach lived toward the end of the eighteenth century his disagreements with the rationalist Superintendent Rosenmueller would have resulted in a total impasse. The Age of Enlightenment was a great dividing point in the history of Western worship in which the sacrificial/sacramental balance in worship of previous times was tipped in favor of the sacramental: the purpose of worship was conceived almost exclusively as the edification of the worshiper, with music playing an important role in the manipulation of emotional response.[20] For Bach the role of church music was to glorify God.

Second, there must be agreement about the conditions and resources that will make quality worship music possible. Bach felt that talent must be considered in the selection of choir and orchestra members; town councillors and Ernesti felt that anybody should be able to perform. Here too it is absolutely crucial that the pastor and the church musician have a common understanding of the needs of worship. The musician must have a realistic sense of the financial picture of the parish, and the pastor must understand the performance requirements of the music that is being selected. This includes the issue of how much it costs to hire the instrumentalists who are capable of producing the kind of music desired for worship. True practitioners of "church growth" would not sacrifice quality the way conventional congregations often do. Indeed, one of the lessons to be learned from celebrated megachurches like the Garden Grove Community Church in Anaheim, California (the Crystal Cathedral), and Willow Creek Community Church in Barrington, Illinois, is that quality of presentation is never compromised.

Planning for Worship

The pastor and the church musician must be able to sit down together to plan in detail the music that is appropriate to the congregation's worship. In the context of the worship wars of the last decades of the twentieth century, this means first of all agreeing on the purpose as well as the style of worship. Is the liturgy primarily the congregation's worship of God or is it an evangelism event designed to reach out to the unchurched?[21] These two purposes cannot co-exist equally in one order of service. Partnerships between pastor and musician have foundered over disagreement about the purpose of worship, often with the pastor pressing for a "contemporary service" that the classically-trained church musician has no interest in providing.

This essay focuses on the requirements of liturgical worship, that is, worship that uses the forms of the church's historic liturgy. Such worship may employ music that is "traditional" or "contemporary;" it will probably not use music that is "popular." "Popular music" tends to be generationally-specific. The long-term liability of "popular music" is that what appeals to one generation or sub-culture may not appeal to another generation or sub-culture. Liturgical worship that is "traditional" in the best sense of the word (reflecting the great historic tradition, not just the last fifty years) must appeal to all generations, and the music it uses must therefore transcend differences between the generations. This is an issue on which the pastor and church musician must be in agreement and on which there should be consensus in the congregation.

In my opinion there should be a weekly planning meeting involving the pastor and the church musician. They will look ahead several weeks as well as solidify plans for next Sunday's liturgy. We should note that in parishes that lack a full-time staff musician, this requires the pastor to meet at the convenience of the musician. If several musicians are employed by the congregation (e.g. adult choir director, youth choir director, organist, assistant organist, bell choir director, etc.), it is desirable that they all participate in the planning process. The tendency to rely on e-mail does not work in worship planning; the worship team must be able to look at material that is spread out before them. This material will include hymnals and songbooks (most denominations now have several) as well as choir and organ music.

The first task is to read through the scripture readings in the lectionary, especially the Gospel, the responsorial Psalm, and related texts for the day or season such as the Prayer of the Day and the Proper Preface. The central ideas in the readings and prayers should be discussed. How the pastor might develop these ideas in the sermon should also be shared. Only then does the team turn to the selection of the music that will praise God and proclaim the Word of God.

The first musical decisions concern the selection of hymns, especially the Hymn of the Day. What organ music is available or might be improvised to introduce these hymns? What arrangements of the hymns might be secured or are in the music library to help to convey their true character? Is there a setting of the Psalmody of the Day in the music library that the choir might sing or that the cantor might chant responsively with the congregation? Will the proper Alleluia Verse and Offertory Verse be sung by the choir or a soloist? What anthems are available in the music library or catalogues that relate to the readings? Where might this "special music" be placed in the liturgical order? Sometimes the choir sings a motet after the Gospel is read. At other times the choir sings a motet during the offering or during Communion. Even a cantata by Bach or someone else requires careful placement within the liturgy. In my present congregation we have been fortunate to have Bach cantatas within the Sunday morning liturgy. In some cases placing the cantata around the sermon seemed appropriate (and I have made reference to the cantata text in the sermon). At other times the cantata has been more appropriately sung during Communion. In the case of Bach's cantata, *Christ lag in Todesbanden*, appropriate for Easter Sunday morning, four movements were performed after the Gospel and the remaining four were performed during the administration of Communion.

The flow of the liturgy is a matter of concern in worship planning. Flow is not just a matter of keeping the service within a certain time limit. It is the state in which action follows action according to a logic inherent in the liturgical order. If liturgy has a flow to it, the musical selections seem right in terms of their place within the order and the functions they serve.[22]

Pastor and church musician will look at each piece of music to consider how it might function in the liturgy. They will also look at the overall selection of music for the liturgy to see if there is a variety of expressions or a sameness of character. They will look at the music chosen for the congregation to determine whether some hymns and chants are familiar and others are unfamiliar and will try to achieve a balance. But they will work to expand the congregation's musical repertoire. Through the worship and music committee they will listen for just feedback and will respond in a caring way in their planning. They will try to balance music that is familiar with music that is unfamiliar to a broad spectrum of the congregation. They will try to choose music that has an enduring rather than a throw-away or esoteric quality. There will be an effort to balance traditional and contemporary music. The musician will look for ways of adapting old favorite hymns to twenty-first century sounds by altering the harmonization and using different instruments for accompaniment. This enables congregations to continue to use old favorites in ways that keep them fresh. The planning group will look to see what appropriate global music is available that will support the liturgy and promote the congregation's sense of being part of the global church. They will also consider whether they have the musical resources to perform this music with integrity. Not every organist trained in classical Western music is capable of leading the congregation in singing African call-and-response songs. Perhaps the organ should not be used when such songs are sung. What other instrumental accompaniment is available? Above all, the pastor and church musician will pay attention to the texts of the hymns, songs, and other music selected to achieve a balance between words that focus on the human response and words that focus on God as the object and subject of worship.[23]

The Musical Formation of the Pastor and the Theological Formation of the Musician

The musical formation of the pastor would seem to be an easier matter to address than the theological formation of the church musician because all pastors attend seminaries in which issues of church music can be included somewhere in the curriculum, whereas the education of musicians varies greatly. Unfortunately, that has not always been the case. During my brief stint as a seminary worship professor I included a section on church music in the one required worship course and offered an elective in church music which included guest appearances of practicing musicians and composers in the classroom. Some seminaries are fortunate to have a musician on the faculty and a few even offer degrees in church music. The actual presence of a musician on the faculty makes some interaction with seminarians possible, even if they don't take a course in church music. Much musical formation has occurred through participation in daily chapel services and singing in seminary choirs. Such formal and informal seminary experiences are invaluable to the formation of future pastors and leaders in liturgy.

The theological formation of the musician is a more difficult issue to address because there is no one model of musical education. There are few programs in church music outside of denominational colleges and universities in which courses in theology and worship can be offered and participation in chapel services is a possibility. Nor does every church musician today go through a church music curriculum. So it is necessary for the congregation to make up the difference by providing for the continuing education of the musician. Conferences and institutes are available, but congregations might go a step beyond this and subsidize the enrollment of the musician in an appropriate seminary or university course in worship or theology if he or she has not had such a course. This would at least demonstrate to the called cantor that the congregation is serious about its staff musicians holding a ministerial office in the church.

The possibility of the pastor and the church musician attending together conferences or institutes should be considered. This gives both ministers a common experience that they can reflect on when they return to their home base. Especially when new worship resources are being promoted by the denomination, pastor and musician should attend workshops together and strategize with the worship and music committee on how these resources will be implemented.

Finally, the role of the worship and music committee is crucial in fostering a good working relationship between the pastor and the musician. This committee can provide valuable guidance for the whole liturgical life of the congregation. It is responsible to the congregation council, session, or vestry. The pastor(s) and church musician(s) are *ex-officio* members of this committee along with other persons who have particular responsibilities of oversight in worship, such as the director of the altar guild and the chief usher.

Members of choirs might also be appointed to this committee.[24] The worship and music committee is involved in worship planning only in the general sense of establishing times of worship and approving orders of worship and liturgical material that will be used. This committee solicits feedback from the congregation and educates the congregation on worship practices. As regards music, the worship and music committee plays a role in the selection of musicians when positions are open by collecting applications, conducting auditions and interviews, and making a recommendation to the church council, session, or vestry. The worship and music committee solicits from the musicians information on what is needed to provide "a well-regulated church music to the glory of God," ranging from the care of instruments to the purchase of music. It prepares a budget proposal that is submitted to the council/session/vestry through the finance committee. If, as sometimes happens, the total financial request of the worship and music committee is not granted in the budget process of the congregation, this committee must make decisions on how the monies allocated for worship and music shall be spent and help the musician to work within the congregation's means.

This committee can provide support to the musician by giving advice and consent to ideas and programs. It can negotiate with the personnel committee the salary and benefits of the musician. It can defend the musician from unjust criticism and work with the musician in responding to just criticism. The tenure of the musician, as an office-holder in the congregation, is protected by this committee so that his or her job security is not capriciously determined by the pastor or anyone else in the structure of the congregation. This kind of system has worked reasonably well in many Lutheran congregations and may be commended to other Christian traditions. It recognizes that even the community of the Gospel that should operate by evangelical persuasion is made up of members who are saints and sinners at the same time. The congregation therefore needs structures provided by the law (or at least the bylaws) in order that ministry may flourish to the glory of God and the edification of God's people. The worship and music committee can provide a buffer between the pastor and the musician, if one is needed.

When all is said and done, the relationship between pastor and church musician will flourish best when both hold ecclesiastical offices in the congregation, when both are committed to the same kind of worship practices, and when both strive to maintain excellent liturgical practice and conscientious spiritual care of the members. These two ideals need not be mutually exclusive. The spiritual life of the congregation is not promoted by a haphazard performance of public worship. The pastor must hone the sermon and go over the choreography of the service with other liturgical ministers. The musician must rehearse the music that is to be used and play or lead it with confidence and competence. Removing attention-attracting pratfalls and wrong notes as far as is humanly possible enables the worshipers to focus on the object of worship rather than its forms, which is the encounter between God and humanity in the liturgical assembly.

NOTES

1 *Documents of the Christian Church*, trans. Henry Bettenson (New York: Oxford University Press, 1947), 6–7.

2 "Letter to the Ephesians 4:2," *Early Christian Fathers*, ed. and trans. Cyril C. Richardson. The Library of Christian Classics, I (Philadelphia: Westminster, 1953), 89.

3 See Johannes Quasten, *Music and Worship in Pagan and Christian Antiquity*, trans. Boniface Ramsey, O.P. (Washington, D.C.: National Association of Pastoral Musicians, 1983), 60ff.

4 John Chrysostom, *Homilia 36 in Epist. I ad Corinthos*; PG 61:313.

5 Ibid.

6 Quasten, 75ff.

7 Ibid., 87ff.

8 See Maxime Kovalevsky, "The Role of the Choir in Christian Liturgy," in *Roles in the Liturgical Assembly*. The Twenty-Third Saint Serge Liturgical Conference, trans. Matthew J. O'Connell (New York: Pueblo, 1981), 193–206.

9 See Yitzhal Hen, *The Royal Patronage of Liturgy in Frankish Gaul To the Death of Charles the Bald (877)* (London: Henry Bradshaw Society, 2001), 49. On Chrodegang's zeal see P. Bernard, *Du chant romain au chant grégorien (Vie-XIIIe siècle)* (Paris, 1996), 725ff.

10 Christoph Wolff, *Johann Sebastian Bach: The Leaned Musician* (New York: Norton, 2000), 240ff.

11 See Robb Redman, *The Great Worship Awakening: Singing a New Song in the Postmodern Church* (San Francisco: Jossey-Bass, 2002), 36–37.

12 I use the word "performance" here not in the popular sense of putting on a show, but in the sense of active rather than passive roles for ritual participants. See Catherine Bell, *Ritual: Perspectives and Dimensions* (New York: Oxford University Press, 1997), 72–76.

13 Martin Luther, *Liturgy and Hymns,* ed. Ulrich S. Leupold, Luther's Works, American Edition, vol. 53 (Philadelphia: Fortress, 1965), 323.

14 See Friedrich Blume, et al., *Protestant Church Music: A History* (New York: Norton, 1974), 5ff.

15 See Torben Schousboe, "Protestant Church Music in Scandinavia," in Blume, 622–23.

16 See Günther Stiller, *Johann Sebastian Bach and Liturgical Life in Leipzig*, trans. Herbert J. A. Bouman, et al. (St. Louis: Concordia, 1984), 182.

17 Hans David and Arthur Mendel, eds., *The Bach Reader* (New York: Norton, 1966), 120–24.

18 See Mark Bangert, "Toward a Well-Regulated Church Music: Bachian Prescriptions with Enduring Shelf Life," *dialog* 24 (1985), 107–12.

19 See Jaroslav Pelikan, *Bach Among the Theologians* (Philadelphia: Fortress, 1986), 35ff.

20 See Frank C. Senn, *Christian Liturgy—Catholic and Evangelical* (Minneapolis: Fortress, 1997), ch. 15, "Liturgy in the Age of Reason."

21 See the insightful questions raised by Ronald P. Byars, *The Future of Protestant Worship: Beyond the Worship Wars* (Louisville and London: Westminster John Knox, 2002), 58–59.

22 See Victor Turner, "Ritual, Tribal and Catholic," *Worship* 50:6 (1976), 504–26.

23 See Marva Dawn, *Reaching Out Without Dumbing Down: A Theology of Worship for the Turn-of-the-Century Culture* (Grand Rapids, MI: Wm. B. Eerdmans, 1995).

24 See Frank C. Senn, *The Pastor As Worship Leader: A Manual for Corporate Worship* (Minneapolis: Augsburg, 1977), 100–2.

Part Three
The Life and Works of Carl Schalk

STEVEN WENTE

A Focused Life

The life and work of Carl F. Schalk show a remarkable diversity of achievement within a clearly focused purpose. He has been a successful teacher, author, editor, composer, arranger, choir director, and administrator. The focus of his life has been to proclaim the Gospel of Jesus Christ through the study and revival of the Lutheran liturgical heritage of church music and to inform and invigorate contemporary church music practice. An overview of his life of service to the church reveals the breadth of his achievements in word and music.[1]

Early Life

Carl Flentge Schalk was born September 26, 1929, just days before the "Black Monday" fall of the stock exchange in October 1929. His parents, Erich and Elsie, lived in Des Plaines, Illinois, a western suburb of Chicago, where Erich was a teacher of grades five and six at Immanuel Lutheran School. The school was a part of Immanuel Lutheran Church, a congregation of the Lutheran Church–Missouri Synod. Carl was baptized into the Christian faith at Immanuel on November 10, 1929 (Luther's birthday). His sponsors were his aunt Mame Flentge and Walter Oehler, a friend of the family. As a child in a Lutheran teacher's home, Carl's early family life was very stable (though certainly not affluent). The family was grounded in the piety and activities of the local congregation. Because of the depression-era economy, his father sold insurance in addition to teaching.

When Carl was in elementary school, he sang in the school choir, which often participated in Sunday worship. It was in school that he was first exposed to the strong hymn and chorale tradition represented in *The Lutheran Hymnal*. Carl was also in a school production of *Hansel and Gretel* by Humperdinck. Carl was cast as one of the sandmen. (The head sandman was his cousin, Donald Johns.)

In the fall of 1943, Carl entered Concordia High School, the Lutheran boarding school of the Lutheran Church–Missouri Synod, located on the campus of Concordia Teachers College in nearby River Forest. As a freshman, Carl would return home on weekends; frequently he would sing in the church choir, which was directed by Theodore Markworth. As with so many Lutheran parochial school teachers who had come through the Missouri Synod educational system at that time, Carl's father had had organ instruction in college and took his turn playing the organ for services at Immanuel.

Concordia Days (1943–1952)

Concordia High School was a four-year college preparatory school on the campus of Concordia Teachers College, the alma mater of Carl's father. Its main purpose was the preparation of students for entrance into the college and for later service in the church. When Carl entered high school as a freshman, music was not yet a serious interest for him. That changed during his sophomore year when a new professor came to campus. Victor Hildner, who was an ambitious and enthusiastic conductor, was to inspire many to pursue music as vocation. Carl continued to sing in choir throughout his high school years and also took piano lessons.

Upon graduation from high school, he enrolled in Concordia Teachers College where he continued his music education, which included singing in choir and starting organ lessons. He joined the A Cappella Choir, which Prof. Hildner conducted. Carl credits this choral experience with providing him an excellent musical foundation for his future conducting and composing:

> Part of later being able to write something at all was due to the experience I had in singing excellent choral music through nine years of high school and college. Singing good literature over a long period of time gives one a feel for what is a good, effective, and workable choral style, which one can probably learn in no other way. Certainly singing all of the Bach motets in those nine years had an effect on me.[2]

Prof. Hildner's influence and control over the lives of the choir members was well known on campus. During his senior year in college, Carl was appointed the editor of *Spectator*, the student newspaper. Prof. Hildner was not happy at this move because he thought it would take too much time from Carl's music studies. After serving as editor for one issue, Carl heeded his mentor's advice and resigned. He credits Prof. Hildner with inspiring many of the students who sang in the A Cappella Choir with the vision and confidence to further their music studies at the graduate level.

The late 1940s were a time of musical growth at Concordia as the college music faculty, whose primary focus was the preparation of church musicians, became more aware of the musical heritage of the Lutheran church. Before and during World War II, church music of high quality, such as editions of Bach's works, were sometimes difficult to obtain. After the war, these materials became much more readily available. Connections with West Germany were made more easily, and a number of church musicians from the homeland of Lutheran church music came to teach in this country.

For his first three college years Carl studied organ with Victor Hildner; in his senior year Carl Halter was his teacher. However, between his junior and senior years Carl was asked by the college to teach classes in keyboard skills for a one-year appointment at Concordia. Upon returning to the life of a student the next year, Carl found study with Carl Halter to be a revelation.[3] Prof. Halter had been a teacher and the music director at Grace Lutheran Church and School in River Forest, located on the college campus. Halter, a Concordia graduate himself, was a gifted musician and teacher who had also studied organ in a graduate program at Baldwin-Wallace College with Carl Riemenschneider, the well-known organist and editor of *The Liturgical Year*, a (still) famous edition of Bach's *Orgelbüchlein*.

In his senior year Carl met his future bride Noël Donata Roeder. Actually, they had known each other casually for some time, since both families were active in Lutheran church work in the Chicago area. Carl and Noël both sang in the college A Cappella Choir, and it was during the annual choir concert tour in Carl's senior year that his friend and roommate, Chuck Henke, suggested that they might be interested in each other. Their friendship soon developed into a much stronger relationship.

Carl graduated from Concordia in June 1952 and accepted a position to teach elementary school and direct music (an assignment that the Lutheran Church–Missouri Synod termed a "Divine Call") at Zion Lutheran Church and School in Wausau, Wisconsin. Zion had a large organ and a well-developed music program in its church and school that had been led by Paul G. Bunjes, an outstanding church musician and organist. Quite by coincidence, the Wausau position had become vacant because in 1951, after fifteen years of service as teacher and director of music at Zion, Bunjes accepted a faculty position at Concordia Teachers College, River Forest.

Wausau Years (1952–1958)

In August 1952 Carl began his first regular teaching assignment at Zion Lutheran Church and School. Pastor Luther Roehrs and his father, Paul W. Roehrs, welcomed Carl as one who could continue to develop the high quality of musical and liturgical life of Zion. And they were not disappointed.[4]

Carl was called to teach fifth and sixth grade and direct the school's music program. He, of course, taught all the required subjects in his own classroom, but music was clearly his special interest. Carl worked hard with the children in their singing, and they did well. Carl had a good rapport with the children, one that was no doubt strengthened because of his avocation as an amateur magician, a talent he had developed as an occasional entertainer in high school and college. He didn't often share this talent with the congregation, but it certainly endeared him to his children at school. The beginning teacher's relationship with the pastors was strengthened by the fact that for the first year of his service he lived in the home of Pastor Paul Roehrs.[5]

It was a busy life: Besides full-time teaching of fifth and sixth grades (one year he had fifty-two children in his classroom), Carl also directed the music ensembles of the church. At Zion he directed a large adult choir and a capable children's choir, both of which sang regularly for Sunday services. There was also a chamber choir of approximately eight voices, called the Chapel Choir. This group sang for special services, recorded service music for the local radio station, and once came to River Forest to sing for a weekend festival sponsored by Concordia Teachers College and Grace Lutheran Church. Already at this time Carl was seen as a rising leader in church music.

In addition to the adult and children's choirs, he soon formed a string ensemble of five or six players that functioned in both regular and special services. The quality of the repertoire of the group is illustrated by the fact that it included music of Walford Davies, Corelli, and Walter Piston.[6]

Carl Schalk directing a group of young singers at Zion Lutheran Church, Wausau, Wisconsin.

Zion had an active liturgical life in which music played an important role. In addition to the regular Sunday worship, an evening service of Holy Communion was scheduled once a month. For these evening services Carl began the practice of giving a half-hour organ recital before the service. Sometimes there would be a guest organist. Richard Hillert, already a friend from River Forest days who served at neighboring Trinity Lutheran Church and School, played for one of these recitals. Always wanting to expand the congregation's appreciation of the church's historic repertoire (and his own), Carl programmed the entire *Orgelbüchlein* of J. S. Bach during one year.

Another innovation of Carl at Zion was the inauguration of annual Days of Spiritual Music. Typically, at this time special music was planned for the morning church services followed by an afternoon recital and an evening concert. The idea and the title for the practice came from one of Carl's teachers, Carl Halter, who had instituted something similar at Grace Lutheran Church, River Forest, during his tenure as teacher and church musician.

Various musicians came to Zion for these days. Organ recitalists included Harry Gudmundson and Herbert Gotsch, who was later to be Carl's colleague at River Forest. Carl commissioned new hymns from writers such as Pastor Kenneth Runge from Zion Lutheran Church, Detroit, and musicologist Walter Buszin. Richard Hillert, also destined to be Carl's colleague, contributed compositions for these days. Hillert's *Cantata for the Day of Pentecost* (for SAB, three violins and flute) and his *Prelude and Toccata* (first performed by Herbert Gotsch) were written for these festivals.

The summer of 1953, his first in Wausau, was an especially busy time for the young teacher. He enrolled at the Eastman School of Music in Rochester, New York, and he married his college sweetheart, Noël Roeder. In fact he finished his first six-week term only a week before the wedding. Carl and Noël were married on August 9, 1953, the summer after they had each taught a year in a Lutheran school. Noël had completed her two-year program at Concordia in 1952 and taught for a year in Buffalo, New York, while Carl was in Wausau. Carl and Noël were married at Bethany Lutheran Church, Chicago, where Noël's father, Paul Roeder, was pastor. After the wedding Carl and Noël moved into a small second-floor apartment in Wausau. Activities at Zion occupied much of their attention. The following year they moved again, into a slightly larger apartment that was closer to the church. Throughout the Wausau years, Carl and Noël did not own a car. Carl returned to Rochester and Eastman by train each summer. He stayed in the YMCA, since the Eastman School did not have a dormitory on its campus, and Noël went to Chicago to stay with her parents.

On August 19, 1955, right after another summer session at Eastman, Carl and Noël's first daughter, Jan, was born. Rebecca followed seventeen months later on January 27, 1957. Carl returned to Eastman each summer and graduated in the summer of 1957 with the Master of Music degree in theory. While yet in Wausau in 1958, Carl composed his first hymn tune, ZION, to a text by Martin Franzmann, "Rise again, ye lion-hearted saints of early Christendom." It was first performed at the Day of Spiritual Music that year.

Carl's tenure at Wausau pointed to the future direction of his vocational life in at least two regards: his faithful service as teacher and musician of a church and school while exercising his growing abilities as composer and director, and his increasing awareness of the need of both the parish and the wider church to explore more fully the rich and vibrant Lutheran heritage of music and worship. Soon, he would be called to bring these inclinations to the service of the church at large.

St. Louis Years (1958–1965)

In August 1958 Carl, Noël, and daughters Jan and Rebecca moved to St. Louis, where Carl had accepted a call from the Lutheran Hour to serve as director of music, a position he would hold until 1965. Shortly thereafter, on September 23, 1958, their son Timothy was born.

The Lutheran Hour was the radio broadcasting arm of the Lutheran Layman's League, an independent organization within the Lutheran Church–Missouri Synod. At this time, the Lutheran Hour was broadcast worldwide over a network of 1200 stations. Carl was to organize and direct the Lutheran Hour Choir, a newly formed mixed choir, and to program music for the Sunday broadcasts. He also traveled to represent the Lutheran Layman's League in various locales and to conduct large choirs at the Lutheran Hour rallies that were held throughout the nation. As Carl relates, traveling was difficult, and "not nearly as exciting as it sounds." While in St. Louis he also completed a second master's degree, this time a Master of Arts in Religion from Concordia Seminary, St. Louis.

The Lutheran Hour had a staff of about seven people in those days. As director of music, Carl was charged primarily with providing music for radio broadcasts. But his leadership during these years went much further. First, the music for Lutheran Hour broadcasts now included a combination of music from the Lutheran heritage, e.g. works of Michael Praetorius, Hans Leo Hassler, and Johann Walter, and much newly composed music. The composers whom Carl commissioned to write settings for the Lutheran Hour Choir included Hugo Gehrke, Donald Busarow, Robert Dozien, Ralph Schultz, and Richard Hillert. Carl also contributed a number of settings himself. Some of these compositions were later published in the Chapel Choir series of Concordia Publishing House. During Carl's tenure a Lutheran Hour Music Conference brought some of these composers together to discuss the opportunities presented by religious radio broadcasting.

Carl advocated the building of a small organ for the Lutheran Layman's League Christ of the Nations Chapel by writing a newsletter article, "The Case for the Small Organ." This eventually resulted in the installation in the chapel of a ten-rank Schlicker unified organ, which was hailed as "a significant step in the development of Lutheran Hour recording facilities." In 1959 Carl also spoke on recording and broadcasting church music at the Church

Music Seminar at Valparaiso University, which was held that year at Concordia Senior College, Fort Wayne, Indiana.

In 1963 a unique leadership opportunity arose in the form of a thirty-minute national TV program. In those days, various denominations took turns presenting a scheduled network program. When the Lutheran Church–Missouri Synod's turn came, the responsibility for this New York production fell to the Lutheran Hour. Oswald Hoffmann was the regular speaker of the Lutheran Hour, and Norman Temme was director of public relations for the LC–MS. Carl was appointed to oversee the music. Rather than rely upon standard repertoire, Carl suggested that a chorale Mass be written for the occasion: Lutheran composer Donald Johns was commissioned to write a Mass setting for three solo voices, based on the Lutheran chorales associated with the five parts of the Ordinary. For the performance Carl selected soprano, alto, and baritone soloists from New York. The program was recorded on April 28, 1963, and aired a month or two later. The program included the singing of the Mass and then a discussion with Carl Schalk and the composer Donald Johns. The Rev. John Tietjen, who was also a speechwriter for Oswald Hoffmann, was the narrator. Carl remembers the amazement of the television producers at how well prepared everyone was. Rev. Tietjen in particular had memorized his part. A later outgrowth of this effort was the publication by Augsburg Publishing House of two movements of the Mass.

Carl also took the initiative of editing a newsletter for the Lutheran Hour, called *Lutheran Hour Music News*. In addition to news and program listings for the coming months, he included extracts of recent publications and wrote editorials about music practice. His ecumenical interest was reflected in the sources he quoted in the publication: the National Council of Churches, *Christian Century*, *Lutheran Education*, *The American Organist*, *The Hymn* (The Hymn Society of America), *Concordia Theological Monthly*, *The Cresset*, *Journal of Church Music*, and *Studia Liturgica*.

Lutheran Hour Music News was an important project in Carl's development as an editor and writer. Readers of his later writing will notice his gracious style and thoughtful selection of issues discussed. The "Editorial Comments" of each newsletter reveal remarkable insight and a ready willingness to examine musical issues from various points of view. In these newsletter articles, he promoted thoughtful consideration of new ideas, but always within the framework of the liturgical foundation of the Christian church. Carl did not hesitate to take on sensitive topics and to point out narrowness of viewpoints, whether it was an insistence by some to use only hymns from *The Lutheran Hymnal* or the preference by others for music with "schmaltz" as a way of attracting people. He wrote in favor of an ecumenical selection of hymns for Lutherans. He also pointed out that many of the hymns in the Worship and Praise section of *The Lutheran Hymnal* came from other denominational hymnals.

The 1960s were a time of experimentation in worship using popular styles such as jazz and folk music. Carl's awareness and understanding of this development is shown in an editorial from 1960, which used as its springboard a recent TV program that presented a Methodist jazz-style worship service. In an editorial, Carl spoke about the need to "reach out" and to address concerns of culture. Certain to catch his readers' attention, he wrote, "The self-proclaimed task of the church to speak the Gospel to people in the light of their own times and culture is not particularly aided by the almost cultish rejection by many church musicians of attempts to relate more closely to the music of the church than to the times in which the church finds itself."[7] Later in the column, he gave fundamental advice that continues to be true today, "When we cease to look at music as something to be "used," and rather recognize it as an element of our culture which God has created and which we can "baptize" through our "involvement" in it, we will be on the way toward making our witness of the Gospel truly relevant in a time when, if ever, relevance is sorely needed."[8]

One of Carl's greatest gifts is his ability to turn a phrase. He has the admirable capacity to write about highly charged issues directly without attacking or belittling those who might take exception to his viewpoints. Carl's generation of church musicians found itself very much at the forefront of an issue that still plagues the church today. That is the issue of stylistic appropriateness. In an editorial Carl discussed the use of emotional, "schmaltzy" music in worship. He wrote:

> The question is not whether or not the song of the church will have a warmth to which we can react. It is not—as a writer in the current *Advance* magazine

thinks—that "touching the emotions seems to be regarded as a bad thing." One could hardly imagine a more personal expression of faith than Luther's "A mighty fortress". . . . The point about "schmaltz" is that it is a detour—a detour which prevents us from facing up to the basic Christian facts of life and death. A detour from both the Word and the work of art. A detour which reduces Christian anxiety to a diminished 7th chord and the joy of the Christian life to a waltz in a major key.[9]

In a later issue of the *Lutheran Hours Music News*, Carl took on the topic of worship and evangelism. In a reference to a wildly popular television program of the time, Carl indicated that one approach might be to appeal to the lowest common denominator (à la "Beverly Hillbillies"). Rather, he points out that "What [the media] need is not simply different programs to give each group what they 'want,' but tailor-made vehicles to present to each group what they 'need' in a way more meaningful and relevant than any kind of 'smorgasbord' approach can ever hope to have." Later, he writes, "The implications for the Church's music are great. The Church must continue to offer the substance of its message in music—simple or complex—which stands as a witness to the integrity of its faith as well as a witness to the Church's love for those to whom it speaks."[10]

Carl's support for the chorale—in its original rhythmic form—was demonstrated in a 1964 editorial in which he lifted up the rhythmic form of "A mighty fortress" over the isorhythmic version, stating that the latter has an "increasing pomposity and dirge-like solemnity."[11] This advocacy for the chorale was soon expanded in his monograph, *The Roots of Hymnody in the Lutheran Church—Missouri Synod*.[12] Carl was not hesitant to enlist support for the cause of church music, quoting the president of the Lutheran Church–Missouri Synod, Dr. Oliver Harms, as saying, "I believe we should establish standards of church music, too, since music is such an essential part of worship."[13]

One cannot leave a discussion of Carl's contributions to the church to this point in his career—including his continuing development as a conductor, music editor, and a proponent for a richer and more broadly-based Lutheran music practice—without considering the influence on him of another outstanding Lutheran church musician, Walter E. Buszin. While Carl had known Buszin before, it was in St. Louis where their relationship was strengthened. Buszin was a professor at Concordia Seminary in the field of hymnody and liturgics and was one of Carl's mentors Buszin was a well-known musicologist and in his day was the leading spokesperson in the Missouri Synod on the topics of hymnody and liturgy, much as Carl Schalk is today. Buszin had an interest in aspects of ecumenism having received a graduate degree from Union Seminary in New York, and he had a broad vision for the church and its musical and liturgical heritage. He was also sensitive to Lutherans within the former Synodical Conference, especially those of the conservative Wisconsin Synod and the Evangelical Lutheran Synod, having taught at Bethany College, Mankato, Minnesota. It could be maintained that Carl Schalk, from his service with the Lutheran Hour onward, has had a similar ecumenical interest as well as a concern for all branches of American Lutheranism.

In Carl's service to the church, first as teacher and parish musician and then as music director of the Lutheran Hour, one can see the foundation being laid for his later work as editor, conductor, and college professor. Carl's activities not only prepared him well for his next task, but also brought him to the attention of many within the Lutheran Church–Missouri Synod.

River Forest Years (1965–1993)

In 1964 Concordia Teachers College, River Forest, celebrated its one hundredth anniversary. In the decade of expansion of the student body and the faculty that occurred in the 1960s, the college administration looked to church music as an area in which it might further expand its leadership. Carl Waldschmidt, a musicologist who served for sixteen years as academic dean of the college, and Paul Bunjes, as chair of the music department, sought to produce a journal of church music[14] and to host a conference of church music.[15] In Lutheran Church–Missouri Synod circles, Carl Schalk was the ideal individual to be given charge of leading these ventures. President Martin L. Koehneke and the board of Concordia Teachers College extended a call to Carl Schalk to serve his alma mater as assistant professor of music beginning in the fall of 1965.

In retrospect, one can imagine the great excitement in church music at Concordia in 1965. The college was entering its second century, great change was happening in the wider church especially through Vatican II, and the Lutheran Church–Missouri Synod in convention had just passed the resolution to invite its sister Lutheran bodies to prepare a hymnal.

Immediately upon arriving at Concordia, Carl launched three projects: editorship of a new journal, *Church Music*, a collaborative publication between Concordia Teachers College and Concordia Publishing House; the initiation of the church music conference to be called "Lectures in Church Music;" and, within a few years, the development of the Master of Church Music program.

The first issue of the new journal, *Church Music* 66:1[16] established a pattern of contents that served it well throughout the course of the publication: Each issue had a theme or topic and related articles. These were accompanied by occasional interviews; features (including copies of new music); a focus on a "Composer for the Church;"[17] and several editorial departments, including reviews of books and music scores and and sound recordings, a guest commentary entitled "First Person Singular," and a column entitled "The Current Scene."[18]

Church Music reflected the editor's philosophy in that it was strongly rooted in the Lutheran heritage of church music. It featured as editors and contributors established leaders in Lutheran church music and gradually involved members of the younger generation. It also sought to expand boundaries by including contributions of leading church musicians beyond Lutheran circles (such as Eric Routley, Carlton R. Young, Carlton Russell, William Storey, Elmer Pfeil, and Joseph Gelineau) and people in the wider orbit of music (Paul Henry Lang, Alan Stout).[19] The first issue listed the following goals:

> *Church Music '66* [66.1] will attempt to provide material through which the Christian community, and especially its leaders in worship, may more effectively *grow* in realizing the importance of theology as the basis for the life of worship, *develop* in understanding the significance of an evangelical-liturgical viewpoint for the Christian parish, *enrich* its knowledge and acquaintance with the church's music, *deepen* insights into basic problems confronting the practicing church musician, *evaluate* intelligently current developments in the worship and musical life of the parish, *relate* the musical heritage of the church to itself in meaningful

ways, *acquaint* itself with the historical-musical traditions of the Lutheran churches in America, and *mature* in judgment concerning matters relating to the musical and liturgical life of the Christian congregation.

The editorial stated clearly, "It is to the renewal of the musical life of the church at the parish level that this journal is dedicated."[20]

Carl also established the pattern for Lectures in Church Music. The conferences, begun immediately upon Carl's arrival in River Forest, sought to bring to campus leaders in church music both from within Lutheran circles and from the broader denominational spectrum. Programs from these Lectures form a "Who's Who" of liturgical theologians, choral directors, organists, hymn writers, and others for whom the practice of church music was important.[21] Under Carl's leadership, and with the assistance of members of the music department, Lectures grew from a small seminar to a major conference that at its height could boast an attendance of 250. This was amazing for a conference that did not have the luxury of being held in the summer when, typically, most such conferences occur. In order to attend, many of the Lutheran teacher-organists who came had had to convince their parishes to give them leave from their classrooms and provide them with substitutes. At many churches, this was difficult. At its beginning, Lectures in Church Music drew largely from alumni of the institution; but over the years it has attracted many other Lutherans as well as musicians from other denominations.

Lectures in Church Music always promised a variety of presentations ranging from scholarly papers to practical workshop events. Reading sessions of choral and organ music[22] filled out the presentations. Concerts included various organists and usually a choral program or hymn festival. Carl's leadership of Lectures in Church Music spanned 29 years. In many ways it is a tribute to Carl that the basic format of Lectures, now named the Vi Messerli Memorial Lectures in Church Music, remains much the same as it was at its inception.

A third area that Carl administered was the development of the Master in Church Music degree program. Working together with other members of the music department and the graduate school, Carl planned a unique masters program, one that incorporated broad studies in theology, music theory and history, church music, and applied study. Intended to be practical for the musician serving the parish, the graduates of the Master in Church Music program include many prominent church musicians, some of whom serve as leaders of their respective denominational worship and music staffs. A number of graduates have gone on for doctoral studies. The required recitals and projects, both theses and compositions, reflect a high level of skill and achievement on the part of the students and their mentors. Until his retirement in 1993, Carl served as coordinator of the Master in Church Music program and project advisor for nearly all of the theses.

As part of the masters and the undergraduate programs, Carl was charged with developing a number of courses. These included The Musical Heritage of the Church, The Lutheran Liturgy, Musical Monuments of the Reformation, Historic Rites of the Western Church, Traditions of Christian Hymnody, and Lutheran Hymnody in America. These courses gave the Master in Church Music program a scope and flavor that could not be obtained at a school offering a "church music" degree in performance.

Because of the desire of the administration of Concordia Teachers College that Carl start a church music journal, a church music conference, and assist with beginning a graduate program (much of this with minimal faculty course equivalency credit), it did not recommend that Carl pursue a doctoral degree as had many of his colleagues. There simply wouldn't have been time for that if these initiatives were to be founded and developed. When one looks at Carl's scholarly activity, however, one sees a wealth of important publications and solid academic research in hymnology that he has provided for the church and for the academic community.[23]

During these early years at Concordia, Carl continued to edit and publish, preparing several editions of works of early composers as well as composing many liturgical settings and other choral works. One effort that consumed much time was his membership on the Hymn Music Committee of the Inter-Lutheran Commission on Worship (ILCW) for twelve years in the late 1960s and the 1970s. The work of the ILCW ultimately resulted in the publication of *Lutheran Book of Worship* (1978) which had been prepared jointly by the American Lutheran Church, the Lutheran Church in America, and the Lutheran Church–Missouri Synod.

After the initial stage of getting to know the people from the various Lutheran traditions represented on the ILCW,[24] the committee faced several issues. One of these was the "unison vs.

harmony" issue. There was significant difference of opinion about whether hymns should be printed in the projected hymnal in standard four-part harmony to facilitate singing in parts (as in *The Lutheran Hymnal* and *Service Book and Hymnal*), or as hymn melodies alone for unison singing with organ accompaniment printed separately in another book.

A second issue was whether the form of the various Lutheran chorales was to be rhythmic or isorhythmic. While Carl favored the traditional rhythmic form of the chorales, the committee chose a middle ground. Some chorales appear in *Lutheran Book of Worship* in both forms. A few appear with music in one form for one text and the other form for a different text. For example, EIN FESTE BURG ("A mighty fortress") appears in both forms, but WACHET AUF appears in the rhythmic form with "Wake, awake, for night is flying," but in isorhythmic form with the text "Holy Majesty, before you."

The organization of the new hymnal was yet another issue to be addressed. *The Lutheran Hymnal* had several general sections of hymns (e.g., Worship and Praise, Opening of Service) placed before the church year section began. The argument that was favored by Carl, and which ultimately prevailed, was that, just as the Eucharist is the first order in the hymnal, so the hymns for the church year should appear first in the book, in order of the seasons.

In the mid 1960s, Carl began his long tenure as a member of the Music Editorial Advisory Committee of Concordia Publishing House. Originally, Carl was appointed to replace Walter Buszin who had retired; however, Buszin came out of retirement and served several more years on this committee. The Music Editorial Advisory Committee (MEAC) served the publisher in reviewing proposed publications and in providing guidance for future projects. During this time, under the leadership of Edward Klammer, head of the Music Department, Concordia Publishing House achieved wide acclaim for the high quality and usefulness of its music publications. Over the years, members of the MEAC included Theo. Hoelty–Nickel, Paul Bunjes, Donald Rotermund, Carlos Messerli, Theodore Beck, and David Held. Rodney Schrank, later head of the music department at Concordia, remembers Carl as having excellent insights into proposals and very creative ideas for new projects. Schrank also noted that, at the beginning of each meeting, to set the tone for the serious discussions ahead, Carl would always have three great jokes to tell.[25]

Concordia Publishing House Music Editorial Advisory Committee, mid-1960s: Left to right: Theodore Hoelty-Nickel, Walter E. Buzin, Edward Klammer, Carl Schalk, Paul G. Bunjes.

At Concordia College, Carl continued his leadership of choral groups. During the early 1970s he conducted College Chorus, which sang mostly large choral works. During his tenure with the choir, Carl introduced a number of new pieces to this group. On one program, College Chorus sang the Stravinsky *Symphony of Psalms*, the Hillert *Five Canticles from the Exodus*, and the Schubert *Mass in G*. This was the first time these works had been performed at Concordia. Another program included the Distler *Totentanz* and the Vaughan Williams *Hodie*, sung with the Grace Lutheran School Children's Choir under the direction of Paul Bouman. An example of innovative programming was the "Mostly Handel" program, which consisted of an afternoon concert of a Handel organ concerto, secular Handel arias (upon which *Messiah* arias were later based) and the *Chandos Anthem "O Sing unto the Lord."* In the evening, the chorus sang the *Utrecht Jubilate* and the *Dettingen Te Deum*. In rehearsals, Carl was known as a very firm but energetic and lively director. Students enjoyed the programs and the chance to explore new literature.

During the mid 1970s, Carl completed two major projects of long-range importance for church music: *Handbook of Church Music* and *Key Words in Church Music*. The *Handbook*, edited in collaboration with Carl Halter, was intended to be an updating and expansion of Halter's *The Practice of Sacred Music*, which had been published in 1948. Now in its second edition (2004), *Key Words in Church Music* offers extended definition essays on a wide range of topics in church music history and practice written by thirty-eight authors and edited by Carl.

It was as director of the Concordia Chapel Choir, perhaps, that Carl made his greatest contribution on campus to practical church music for choirs. The Chapel Choir sang once or twice each week for chapel. While the choral repertoire was mostly historic music, Carl would often prepare for the choir a new composition or a new edition of an historic composition. These were favorite occasions for the choir which also enjoyed singing "new" music. Under Carl's direction, the practice of singing the O Antiphons in December and a Passion setting in Holy Week was established. The tradition continues to this day. The *Passion According to St. John* by Richard Hillert was given its first performance by the Chapel Choir at Concordia in 1973.

From 1975 to 1978 Carl also conducted the Lutheran Choir of Chicago, which was made up of singers from various Lutheran congregations and which met on the Concordia campus on Monday evenings. Again, Carl's innovative programming led the choir to sing Randall Thompson's *The Peaceable Kingdom,* Heinrich Schütz's, *German Magnificat*, Felix Mendelssohn's Psalms, and Virgil Thomson's, *Scenes from the Holy Infancy.* Frequently, Carl's programs were structured around Vespers (Evening Prayer) with its opportunities for congregational participation.

Carl Schalk conducting the Concordia Teachers College, River Forest, College Chorus, mid-1970s. Daughters Jan Schalk (flute) and Rebecca Schalk (oboe) are at the right side of the photo.

On two occasions, each coinciding with sabbatical leaves of Thomas Gieschen, the director of the Kapelle, Carl conducted the touring choir of Concordia. He brought his innovative ideas for programming to this choir with such pieces as the Stravinsky *Mass*. It was during the first of these sabbatical years, 1971–72, that the Bach Vesper Cantata series at Grace Lutheran Church, River Forest, was born. Carl was the assistant director of music at Grace, where he and Noël sang in the choir and their children went to school. Paul Bouman, the director of music at Grace from 1953 to 1983, relates that in those early years, Carl would often play organ for the early Sunday service, and Paul would play for the late service.[26] In this way, a regular pattern of leadership of hymns and liturgy was established for the congregation. Singing in the choir regularly, Carl was also a convenient resource for Paul as a conductor. If the choir needed the extra security of a conductor for an accompanied work, Carl was able to conduct while Paul remained at the organ.

When it was known that Carl would be conducting the Kapelle for the 1971–72 academic year, the wheels were set in motion for the initial cantata series at Grace. From the start the plan was developed for a Bach cantata to be sung monthly within the context of a liturgical service, in which there would be a guest preacher and often a guest organist. Because of the demands of presenting eight cantata services during each church year (none in December, when the Grace choirs gave a Christmas concert), the college Kapelle and the Grace choir alternated preparation of the cantata. The Grace choir and a choir from Concordia (either Kapelle or the Chapel Choir) participated in each Vespers; the choir that was not singing the cantata would present a motet. Occasionally, a cantata for solo voice was scheduled, reducing performance demands on the choirs. The first cantata service was held in September 1971, and Kapelle was the Concordia choir to sing. The cantata performed was *Es erhub sich ein Streit* (There arose a great strife, BWV 19). The Kapelle sang the cantata under Carl's direction, and the Grace choir sang the motet. The Rev. Dr. Richard Caemmerer of Concordia Seminary, St. Louis, was the preacher.

This happy arrangement of shared participation allowed the Grace choir to continue its level of service as the main choir for Sunday liturgies while learning several new works. The principle of not slighting Sunday worship for the sake of "bigger performances" still holds true at Grace Church. Concordia Kapelle under Thomas Gieschen's leadership continued to cooperate in cantata services until the late 1970s, when, in a time of crisis in the Lutheran Church–Missouri Synod, Grace Church voted to become an independent Lutheran church, and Concordia broke off all ties with the congregation.

Paul Bouman describes his relationship with Carl at Grace as always harmonious. They each had their special areas of interest to be sure, but their interests were complementary as were their personalities. There was a meeting of minds in selecting cantatas to be sung, in planning pre-service music, and in extending invitations to guest organists. They discussed many aspects of church music and even shared ideas for other projects such as the programs of Lectures in Church Music. In the early years the Sunday evening Lectures concert was sponsored by Grace as a gift to Concordia.[27]

The year 1978 saw the publication of *Lutheran Book of Worship* and, with that, the end of Carl's work with the ILCW. *Church Music* ceased publication in 1980 for financial reasons as well as out of concern for synodical polity. Many musicians "in the field" saw the termination as politically motivated, because *Church Music* 79 featured the publication of the *Lutheran Book of Worship*, which was not accepted by the Lutheran Church–Missouri Synod.

After 1980, Carl turned more to composing and writing. These years saw the publication of many hymn concertatos, which were often based upon texts and tunes that were new to Lutherans from the publication of *Lutheran Book of Worship* and the later publication of *Lutheran Worship* by the Missouri Synod. One only has to think of choral works such as "Lord, It Belongs Not to My Care" (choral anthem), "All You Works of the Lord" (canticle with congregation), "O Day Full of Grace" (hymn concertato), and "Before the Marvel of This Night" (new tune and setting) to see the broad spectrum of choral/congregational compositions that Carl has written. These are only a few of the many that quickly have become standards for church choirs.

Some of Carl's works have achieved even broader status. Shortly after it was published, the Christmas hymn setting of "Before the Marvel of This Night" was featured in the St. Olaf Christmas Concert, where the accompaniment was transcribed for handbells, harp, and string bass. The hymn has been recorded by several English choirs, including the Choir of St. Alban's with

Barry Rose conducting. The "Parish Magnificat" for treble choir and congregation was written for the Covenant Service of the Archdiocese of Chicago and the Metropolitan Chicago Synod of the Evangelical Lutheran Church in America (1989). "Now the Silence" was sung at Westminster Abbey.

If the 1960s and early '70s at River Forest were years of support and encouragement, the change in college administration at River Forest in 1973 brought what could best be described as an attitude of uneasy tolerance. Carl was valuable to the school for his position in the field of church music, but the very nature of his broad appeal across denominational lines was difficult for the new administration to understand. Like many members of the faculty, Carl was questioned and even "scolded" for making presentations at places such as Seminex (the "Seminary in Exile"); fortunately, unlike other faculty members, his position at Concordia was never threatened.

Although Carl Schalk was a noted musician, conductor, and author, it should not be forgotten that in all his many activities Carl was always a teacher. Many of his former students describe him as an unforgettable teacher. He was a careful, well prepared, and interesting lecturer who was known for writing difficult tests! He organized material well and presented it in a way that exposed students to a great amount of information that they were able to retain while enjoying the experience.

Graduate students in particular readily signed up for Schalk courses; they knew they would get a firm grounding in hymnody or church music history and practice One course in particular, "Studies in Christian Worship: Theology and Music," was taught for many years by Carl and Kenneth Heinitz, a member of the theology faculty. This course was affectionately known by students, in a blending of the names of both instructors, as the "Scheinitz" course. Students who took "Musical Monuments of the Reformation" in which they studied the works of Johann Walter, Hassler, Rhau, Praetorius, Schütz, Schein, and Scheidt, saw the inscription of "Schütz, Schein, and Scheidt" on the Holtkamp studio organ on campus as an opportunity to add "Schalk" to the names to be honored in church music. While Carl was an excellent lecturer and teacher, he also had a quick and sometimes biting wit. He had little patience for students who were not prepared or had a lackadaisical attitude. A pointed comment or quip from Professor Schalk could put a student in his or her place. Students knew this

and acted accordingly. One former student remembers a class in which one student, an undergraduate, was late, but could be heard talking loudly in the hall on the way to class. When she entered the room, Professor Schalk stopped his lecture as all eyes followed her to her seat. Needless to say, she wasn't late again.

Long-time colleagues Richard Hillert and Carl Schalk; taken October 2003 at Lectures in Church Music.

Many students have maintained contact with Carl over the years and still look to him for guidance and support. In the early 1980s, after the publication of *Lutheran Book of Worship*, a group of former students honored Carl and Noël and his colleague Richard Hillert and his wife, Gloria, for their contributions to Lutheran church music. In 1990, a group of former students humorously proclaimed September 26 an addition to the church calendar as "Carl Schalk Day." The citation honors (tongue-in-cheek) Carl as "*St. Carl of Melrose, Patron Saint of Church Musicians, Doctor of the Church, Composer Extraordinarius, A Keyword in Church Music.*"

In 1982, Carl was asked to participate in the work leading to the formation of Lutheran Music Program, first as advisor and later as a member of the board of directors. He continues to serve on the board to the present time. Lutheran Music Program is the sponsor of Lutheran Summer Music Academy and Festival, a national month-long program for high school students gifted in music. Its purpose is to encourage young musicians to develop their talents, to remain active in the church, and to provide future leadership in Lutheran church music, all areas dear to Carl's heart. While Carl's particular contribution to this endeavor has been to encourage the program to remain faithful to the Lutheran heritage of music and worship, he has also been influential in promoting the pan-Lutheran possibilities of the organization. In addition, he has encouraged the maintenance of standards of excellence in teaching and performance at Lutheran Summer Music and the need for all students to participate in chamber music and choral ensembles as a way of preparing for more active service in their own congregations.

During his later years of full-time teaching, Carl edited the Church Music Pamphlet series, several series of liturgical choral music and wrote scholarly studies, such as *Luther on Music: Paradigms of Praise* (1988), *Johann Walter: First Cantor of the Lutheran Church* (1992), and *Praising God in Song: An Introduction to Christian Hymnody for Congregational Study* (1993). All were published by Concordia Publishing House, St. Louis, Missouri.

Because of his unique contributions to the university, the church, and church music, the faculty members at Concordia University, River Forest, named Carl F. Schalk Distinguished Professor of Music in September 1993. He retired from full-time service at Concordia on December 1, 1993, receiving the title of Distinguished Professor of Music Emeritus.

The Retirement Years

In retirement, Carl's career has continued very much as it had when he was fully employed. He maintains an active schedule of lectures at seminars and workshops, teaching occasional courses at Concordia, and composing hymn tunes and choral and organ music, the latter often in response to a request from a congregation or an individual. He has contributed to the field of church music through many articles and several significant books for Concordia Publishing house, including *God's Song in a New Land: Lutheran Hymnals in America* (1995), *Source Documents in American Lutheran Hymnody* (1996), and *Music in Early Lutheranism: Shaping the Tradition*, 1524–1672 (2001). In addition, he and Noël continue to travel both domestically and internationally, sometimes in connection with Carl delivering a paper, as he did in Thailand, Hong Kong, and Korea, and at other times for leisure, in trips to England and Scotland, Greenland, and the Fuji Islands.

One of Carl's enduring traits is his ability to stimulate the thinking of others. His suggestions most frequently support the cause of church music and the mission of Concordia, or help to advance another person's career.

One of Carl's recent ideas came at the invitation of Aid Association for Lutherans (now Thrivent Financial for Lutherans) to help create a tribute to the history of Lutheran church music. Thrivent produced the resulting multi-media project, *Celebrating the Musical Heritage of the Lutheran Church*, which was released in 2002. Distributed to every Lutheran congregation, school, college, univeristy, and seminary library in America, this resource surveys Lutheran church music from the sixteenth century to the present day. The study was produced on five audio and one CD-ROM discs. As lead consultant for the project, Carl provided its theme, shape, and outline, and also served as music director.

Carl's loyalty to his alma mater, Concordia, Reiver Forest, can be seen in his creative contributions to the school in many areas over the years: in his desire to stay at Concordia in spite of offers to teach elsewhere, such as the rejection of two invitations to direct the church music program at Westminster Choir College in the mid-1980s, in his continued service to Concordia in his retirement as teacher of occasional courses and as workshop leader, and in his on-going connection with many alumni and friends of Concordia. It can also be seen in the contribution of an endowed graduate church music scholarship to the univeristy by Carl and Noël.

Understandably, Carl has received much recognition and many awards, both within and beyond Lutheran circles, and both before and in retirement. In 1985 Concordia College, Seward, Nebraska, and Concordia College, St. Paul, Minnesota, each recognized his contributions to church music, both academic and practical, by granting him an honorary doctorate. In 1992 he was named a Fellow of the Hymn Society of the United States and Canada. In 1995, along with his colleague Richard Hillert, Carl was granted Honorary Lifetime Membership in the Association of Lutheran Church Musicians. The citation reads:

Carl F. Schalk
Church Musician, Composer, Teacher, Author

His skillful articulation of the Lutheran liturgical and musical heritage and its continuing development has stimulated congregational song and worship with remarkable effectiveness. Church musicians, pastors, and the people of God will forever be indebted to him for music and words of surpassing beauty and clarity.

In 1999 Carl received the prestigious Wittenberg Award from The Luther Institute, Washington, D.C., for his contributions to the Lutheran church. In 2002 he received the Distinguished Composer Award from the American Guild of Organists at its Philadelphia convention. This award has been presented to outstanding composers in the United States writing for the organ and choral music fields, such as Virgil Thomson, Ned Rorem, Daniel Pinkham, Samuel Adler, Dominick Argento, William Albright, Conrad Susa, Emma Lou Diemer, Dan Locklair, William Bolcom, and Alice Parker.

He received the Graven Award from Wartburg College, Waverly, Iowa, in 2004. In part, the award states:

> You have devoted your life to creatively inviting the people of God to marvel at all that God has made. Throughout your life, you have dedicated yourself and your gifts to God in ways that have equipped others to carry on that work. Because of you, the worship life of our church is richer and more rooted in the depth of silence and the joyful celebration of God's grace.
>
> During your lifetime, you have been an inspiration and sign of God's ability to compose new tunes among us, hope out of despair, wonder out of fear, and life out of death. You have lived out your vocation in the spirit of Henry and Helen Graven, for whom this award is named.

Throughout his life, Carl F. Schalk has devoted himself to pointing Lutherans, and indeed all Christians, to the Church's continuing heritage of music and worship. He has done so with eloquence and with grace. He is a supremely gifted, creative, and dedicated servant of God and of the church. But perhaps the truest evaluation of Carl's career is to say that all of his activities—whether composing hymn tunes or choral anthems, editing music or encouraging others to compose, writing books and articles about church music, conducting choirs or giving workshops—derive from his firmly grounded understanding of music in the life of the church, an understanding that is part of the Lutheran heritage of music, which Carl has so faithfully espoused. Carl Schalk, has indeed lived a focused life that has enriched and inspired the church, its pastors, teachers, and musicians, and thereby helped all to proclaim the Gospel in music.

The Carl and Noël Schalk family. First row, left to right: Jan (Schalk) Westrick, Noël Schalk, Samuel Nagel, Ingrid (Pierson) Schalk, Carl Schalk, Rebecca (Schalk) Nagel. Second row: Brian Westrick, Greg Westrick, Peter Westrick, Timothy Schalk, grandson Aaron Schalk, Ed Nagel.

NOTES

1   Other studies of the life and work of Carl F. Schalk include "Contemporary Lutheran Hymnody: An Interview with Jaroslav Vajda and Carl Schalk," *CrossAccent* 1, no. 2 (July 1993): 19–24; Martha Rohlfing, "Servant of the Word: Composer Carl Schalk," *Christianity and the Arts* 4, no. 3 (August–October 1997): 14–18; Richard Hillert. "Composers for the Church: Carl F. Schalk," *Cross Accent* 10, no. 1 (Spring 2002): 12; David W. Music, "The Hymn Tunes of Carl Schalk," *The American Organist* 36, no. 4 (April 2002): 66-70; and Janet M. Neumann, "A Study of the Life and Work of Carl Flentge Schalk, Lutheran Church Musician," (DMA diss., New Orleans Baptist Theological Seminary, New Orleans, Louisiana, May 2005).

2   Richard Hillert, "Composers for the Church: Carl F. Schalk," *Cross Accent* 10, no. 1 (Spring 2002): 12.

3   Carl Schalk, interview by author, July 20, 2004.

4   Luther Roehrs, interview by author, April 19, 2005.

5   Ibid.

6   Carl Schalk, interview.

7   *Lutheran Hour Music News*, March 1960.

8   Ibid.

9   Ibid, April 1961.

10 Ibid, February 1963.

11 Ibid, August 1964.

12 This monograph was advanced by Paul Bunjes before the 1965 convention of the Lutheran Church–Missouri Synod to hold before the convention the heritage of that church body. The LCMS was considering an overture to stop work on its own hymnal and to invite the other Lutheran bodies—the American Lutheran Church and the Lutheran Church in America—to join it in a common hymnal. Bunjes's preference was to bring the work of the LC–MS, which had been ongoing for a number of years, to fruition in a hymnal for Missouri.

13 *Lutheran Hour Music News*, December 1963.

14 The CTC faculty already produced *Lutheran Education*, the longest continuously running journal of education in the United States.

15 A centenary college forum had presented the noted composer Howard Hanson in 1964. The following year, the highly respected musicolgist Hans T. David was the first major speaker at what was to become Lectures in Church Music.

16 Each issue had a number for the year and the issue, thus 67.1, 67.2. The first issue was produced in the fall of 1966; thus it was numbered 66.1, and there was no 66.2.

17 Composers featured included Richard Wienhorst (68.1), Ludwig Lenel (69.1), Daniel Moe (70.1), Jan Bender (71.1), Gerhard Krapf (74.1), Paul Bunjes (74.2), Paul Manz (79), and Leland Sateren (80).

18 *Church Music* 66.1, "The Hymn in Christian Worship," presented articles by Reuben Pirner, Fred Precht, Ralph Gehrke, Paul Henry Lang, Rhea Felknor, Oliver C. Rupprecht, Richard Hillert, and an interview with Eric Routley. Two "features" were "Three Advent and Christmas Chorales in New Translations and Musical Settings" (translations by F. Samuel Janzow and settings by Richard Hillert, Paul Bunjes, and Jan Bender) and "Some Early American Hymnals," which reprinted the title and other pages of significant American hymnals. The first "First Person Singular" column was by Edward Klammer, "The Lutherans' 'Common Book': A Proposal." "The Current Scene" highlighted Richard Wienhorst's "Canticle of the Three Children," written for the dedication of the new campus of Christian Theological Seminary in Indianapolis.

19 The Editorial Board of *Church Music* at its inception included Walter E. Buszin, Jan Bender, M. Alfred Bichsel, Hans Boeringer, Edgar S. Brown, Eugene Brand, Mandus Egge, A.R. Kretzmann, Ulrich Leupold, Daniel Moe, Fred L. Precht, Paul Rosel, and Carl Waldschmidt. The Editorial Staff was Carl Schalk, editor, Richard Hillert, assistant editor, Paul G. Bunjes, Carl Halter, Charles Ore, Theodore Hoelty-Nickel, Edward Klammer, and Martin L. Koehneke, president of Concordia Teachers College, *ex officio*. Contributing editors included Charles Anders, Theodore Beck, Robert Bergt, Thomas Canning, Leonard Ellinwood, Rhea Felknor, Paul Foelber, Regina Fryxell, Philip Gehring, Hugo Gehrke, Ralph Gehrke, Thomas Gieschen, Herbert Gotsch, Donald Johns, David Johnson, Charles Krutz, Ludwig Lenel, Paul Manz, Joseph Mc Call, Louis Nuechterlein, Ruth Olson, Reuben Pirner, Johannes Riedel, Evangeline Rimbach, Oliver C. Rupprecht, Erik Routley, Leland B. Sateren, Berthold von Schenk, Ralph Schultz, Alan Stout, George Weller, and Richard Wienhorst.

20 *Church Music* 66.1: 37.

21 Major presenters at Lectures in Church Music during Carl Schalk's years of

leadership included Jaroslav Pelikan, Lincoln Spiess, Arno Schoenstedt, Leonard Ellinwood, Walter Bouman, Mandus Egge, Paul Foelber, Daniel Poellot, Paul Bunjes, Erik Routley, Mons Teig, Philip Pfatteicher, Aidan Kavanagh, Harold Samuel, Frank Senn, Robert Hovda, Austin Lovelace, Don Saliers, Gracia Grindal, Richard Benedum, Richard Resch, and Robert Jenson.

22 Originally, only two publishers were represented: Concordia Publishing House and Augsburg Publishing House. Over the years that number grew to a total of six publisher sessions in the early 1990s.

23 In addition to his numerous publications, Carl has also presented papers at many institutions and events, including the following: The 14th Annual Moravian Music Festival, Waukesha, Wisconsin, 1981; Lutheran Theological Seminary at Gettysburg, Pennsylvania, 1982; Concordia College, St. Paul, Minnesota, 1983; the Staley Foundation Lectures, Concordia College, Seward, Nebraska, 1984; Valparaiso University, Valparaiso, Indiana, 1985; Regional Conference of the Association of Lutheran Church Musicians, Muhlenberg College, Allentown, Pennsylvania, 1988; 9th Annual Festival of the Resurrection, The Evangelical Lutheran Church of St. Luke, Chicago, Illinois, 1989; Regional Conference of the Association of Lutheran Church Musicians, Concordia University, River Forest, Illinois, 1990; Good Shepherd Institute, Concordia Theological Seminary, Ft. Wayne, Indiana, 2003; and Institute on Preaching, Worship, and Church Music, sponsored by the Commission on Worship, The Lutheran Church–Missouri Synod, Carthage College, Kenosha, Wisconsin, 2005.

24 Leland Sateren was the only member of the ILCW hymn committee who had also served on the committee for the *Service Book and Hymnal*.

25 Rodney Schrank, interview by author, April 22, 2005.

26 Paul Bouman, interview by author, April 8, 2005.

27 Ibid.

The Works of Carl Schalk

This catalog is arranged according to the following outline by category and chronology. Sections I, II, and III include printed books, articles, and music; IV, and V reveal the widespread distribution of the composer's hymn tunes and the sound recordings of his compositions. Entries are based upon information supplied by Carl Schalk to the editor.

I. Books and Articles

A. BOOKS

1963

Planning the Wedding Service. Minneapolis: Sacred Design Associates, 1963.

1965

The Roots of Hymnody in The Lutheran Church–Missouri Synod. St. Louis: Concordia, 1965.

1975

Hymnals and Chorale Books of the Klinck Memorial Library. Carl Schalk, comp. River Forest, Illinois: Concordia Teachers College, 1975.

1978

Key Words in Church Music. Carl Schalk, ed. St. Louis: Concordia, 1978.

A Handbook of Church Music. Carl Schalk and Carl Halter, eds. St. Louis: Concordia, 1978.

Source Documents in American Lutheran Hymnody. edited, annotated, and translated, Carl Schalk. [River Forest, Illinois:] Concordia Teachers College, 1978.

1980

Music for the Wedding Service. Booklet for the parish musician. St. Louis: Concordia, 1980.

1983

The Hymn of the Day and Its Use in Lutheran Worship. Church Music Pamphlet Series. St. Louis: Concordia, 1983.

Music in Lutheran Worship. Church Music Pamphlet Series. St. Louis: Concordia, 1983.

The Pastor and the Church Musician: Thoughts on Aspects of a Common Ministry. Church Music Pamphlet Series. St. Louis: Concordia, 1983.

1988

Luther on Music: Paradigms of Praise. St. Louis: Concordia, 1988.

1989

The Carl Schalk Hymnary. Forty-Seven New Hymntunes and Carols. Chicago: GIA, 1989.

1991

The Carl Schalk Hymnary Supplement. Sixteen New Hymntunes and Carols. Chicago: GIA, 1991.

1992

Johann Walter: First Cantor of the Lutheran Church. St. Louis: Concordia, 1992.

1993

Praising God in Song: An Introduction to Christian Hymnody for Congregational Study. St. Louis: Concordia, 1993.

1995

God's Song in a New Land: Lutheran Hymnals in America. St. Louis: Concordia, 1995.

Guide to Basic Resources for the Lutheran Church Musician. A Project of the Educational Concerns Committee, Association of Lutheran Church Musicians. Carl Schalk, ed. St. Louis: MorningStar, 1995.

1996

Source Documents in American Lutheran Hymnody. St. Louis: Concordia, 1996.

Thine the Praise: The Hymntunes and Carols of Carl Schalk. Including Sixteen New Hymntunes with various texts. Chicago: GIA, 1996.

1998

First Person Singular: Reflections on Worship, Liturgy, and Children. St. Louis: MorningStar, 1998.

2001

Music in Early Lutheranism: Shaping the Tradition (1524–1672). St. Louis: Concordia Academic Press, 2001.

2003

Our Voices Raise. Twenty New Hymn Tunes. Chicago: GIA, 2003.

2004

Key Words in Church Music. 2nd ed. rev. and enlarged, Carl Schalk, ed. St. Louis: Concordia, 2004.

B. ARTICLES

1956

"A Second Look at the Heritage," *Lutheran Education*, October 1956 (Vol. 92, No.2), 66–72.

1959

"Music and the Word," *Lutheran Education*, March 1959 (Vol. 94, No.7), 350–60.

1961

"New Music for the Church," *Walther League Messenger*, March 1961, 12–17.

1961–63

A series of articles for *This Day* magazine:

"The Church's New Song," July 1961 (Vol. 12, No. 11), 14–15.

"New Life in the Church," October 1961 (Vol. 13, No. 2), 17.

"That New Look in Churches," June 1962 (Vol. 13, No. 10), 20–21.

"Christian Art in the Iowa Country," January 1963 (Vol. 14, No. 5), 26–27.

"The Quiet Healers," March 1963 (Vol. 14, No. 7), 30–31.

"Songs Before Unknown," April 1963 (Vol. 14, No. 8), 16–17, 42–43.

1962

"Religion in America and the Churches' Use of the Mass Media," *Concordia Theological Monthly*, June 1962 (Vol. 33, No. 6), 337–49.

1963

"The Case for the Small Organ," *Lutheran Education*, February 1963 (Vol. 98, No. 6), 260–61.

1964

"Is Your Sunday School Music Sound?" *Interaction*, July 1964.

1964–70

Various articles published in *Spirit* magazine:

"Your Worship . . . Heritage or Hootenany?" November 1964.

"Folk Songs for You," December 1964.

"Teen-Agers Take a New Look at Music," February 1970.

"Where Summer Is Music," May 1970.

"Fire at Concordia Teachers College: A Professor and Student Report," with Marva Gersmehl. October 1970.

1965

"Reexamine the Choir Program," *Advance*, December 1965 (Vol. 12, No. 10), 17–20.

"Musical Style and Interpretation: Some Observations," *Lutheran Education*, March 1965 (Vol. 100, No. 7), 300–309.

"The Dilemma of the Contemporary Composer of Church Music" *Response*, St. Michael and All Angels 1965 (Vol. 7, No. 2), 69–78.

1967

"Music in Lutheran Worship," *Crisis in Church Music*. Proceedings of a meeting on church music conducted by The Liturgical Conference and the Church Music Association of America. Washington, D.C.: The Liturgical Conference, 1967, 40–51.

1968

"The Forgiveness of the Christ Child," *Young Church*, January 1968 (Vol. I, No. 4), 4–5.

1970

"The Shape of Church Music in the '70s," *The Christian Century*, December 2, 1970 (Vol. LXXXVII, No. 48), 1445–49.

1973

"Church Music in Transition: The Change in Change," *The Christian Century*, December 19, 1973 (Vol. XC, No. 46), 1251–54.

"Psalm Singing," *Church Music Memo*, Pentecost Issue, 1973, 1–5.

"Lutheran Hymnody in America," *Motif*. River Forest, Illinois: Concordia Teachers College, 1973, 17–18.

1975

"Old Song, New Book," *The Lutheran Witness*, September 14, 1975 (Vol. 94, No. 15), 10–11.

1977

"New Hymnals: Shaping the Future of Congregational Singing," *The Christian Ministry*, March 1977 (Vol. VIII, No.2), 4–7.

1981

"German Hymnody," in *Hymnal Companion to the Lutheran Book of Worship*, Marilyn Kay Stulken, ed.. Philadelphia: Fortress Press, 1981, 19–34.

"Worship and Teaching the Faith," with Kenneth Heinitz, *Lutheran Education*, May–June 1981, 260–67.

"Two's Company, Three's a Marriage," *The Lutheran Witness*, June 1981 (Vol. 100, No. 6), 10–11.

"Lutheran Church Musicians in the 1980s." Address delivered at the Annual Worship Consultation, Yahara Center, Madison, Wisconsin, September 27, 1981. Subsequently published in *Church Music Memo*, Easter Cycle, 1982, Issue No. 30.

"Thoughts on Smashing Idols: Church Music in the '80s," *The Christian Century*, September 30, 1981 (Vol. XCVIII, No. 30). See also "Readers' Response," December 2, 1981.

1982

"Getting More for Less: Church Music in the Smaller Parish," *The Christian Ministry*, July 1982 (Vol. 13, No. 4), 20–23.

1983

"A Lament for Resounding Praise," *The Christian Century*, March 23–30, 1983 (Vol. 100, No. 9), 269–71.

"Martin Luther's Hymns Today," *The Hymn*, July 1983 (Vol. 34, No.3), 130–33.

"Why Christians Sing: Paradigms and Proposals," *Liturgy: A Journal of the Liturgical Conference*, 1983 (Vol. 3, No. 3), 7–15.

1984

"Approaches to Writing Hymn Tunes," *The Hymn*, April 1984 (Vol. 35, No. 2).

"What Did Luther Say About Music?" *Pastoral Music*, June–July 1984 (Vol. 8, No. 5), 13–14.

1985

"J. S. Bach's Music: The Context of Creativity," *Lutheran Education*, January–February 1985 (Vol. 120, No .3), 141–47.

1986

Five articles for the *Evangelisches Kirchenlexikon: Internationale theologische Enzyklopaedie*. Goettingen: Vandenhoeck & Ruprecht, 1986ff. (English ed. William B. Eerdmans Publishing Company). "Gesangbuch 2," "Gradual," "Graduallied," " Gospelsong," "Motette."

"Renewing Parish Worship," *The Christian Century*, June 5–12, 1985 (Vol. 102, No. 20), 585–87.

1988

"A Song for Silent Praise," *The Christian Century*, March 23–30, 1988 (Vol. 105, No. 10), 300–301.

1988–

A series of "First Person Singular" articles for *Lutheran Education* beginning in 1988, later collected and expanded for *First Person Singular* (see Books).

1989

"The Hymn in the Liturgy: A Lutheran Perspective," *Currents in Theology and Mission*, June 1989 (Vol. 16, No. 3), 210–20.

1990

"German Church Song," in *The Hymnal 1982 Companion*. Raymond F. Glover, ed. New York: The Church Pension Fund, 1990, vol. 1, 288–309.

1989–90

Two articles for *Grace Notes* (Newsletter of the Association for Lutheran Church Musicians):

"Labels, Liturgy, and Dinosaurs: Comments on Some (Non-) Liturgical Terminology." November 1989 (Vol. V, No. 4).

"Worship, Church Music, and the Lack-of-Information Age." February 1990 (Vol. VI, No. 1).

1990

"Luther on Music: Paradigms of Praise. An Interview with Carl Schalk." *Lutheran Worship Notes.* A Publication of the Commission on Worship and Concordia Publishing House. Winter 1990.

"Church Music in the '90s: Problems and Prognoses." *The Christian Century.* March 21–28, 1990 (Vol. 107, No. 10), 306–8.

1991

"The Challenge for Lutheran Worship in the '90s," A Paper of the Association of Lutheran Church Musicians. No. 5, March 1991.

1993

"Music and the Liturgy: The Lutheran Tradition" in *Lutheran Worship: History and Practice.* Fred L. Precht, ed. St. Louis: Concordia, 1993, 243–62.

1995

"Some Thoughts on the Writing of Hymn Tunes," *CrossAccent*, November, 1995.

1997

"A Brief History of Hymnals in the LC–MS," *Lutheran Witness Reporter*, 1997.

1998

"A Tribute to Paul Bunjes (1914–98)" in *Worship: A Lutheran Perspective.* A publication of the LC–MS Commission on Worship and Concordia Publishing House. Issue No. 38.

2000

"The Church and the Composer," *CrossAccent*, Journal of the Association of Lutheran Church Musicians. Spring 2000 (Vol. 8, No. 1), 3–8.

22 brief articles contributed to *Worship Music: A Concise Dictionary*, Edward Foley, ed. Collegeville, Minnesota: The Liturgical Press, 2000.

2002

"Voices of the Early Reformers: Their Message for Today," *CrossAccent*, Summer 2002 (Vol. 10, No. 2), 3–10.

"Hymnody and the Proclamation of the Gospel," in *Not Unto Us: A Celebration of the Ministry of Kurt J. Eggert.* Milwaukee: Northwestern, 2001, 129–39.

2003

"Some Thoughts on the Hymnody of *Lutheran Book of Worship*: Context, Issues, and Legacy," *Currents in Theology and Mission*, October 2003 (Vol. 30 No. 5), 366–73.

2004

"The Roots of American Lutheran Hymnody," in *Hymns in the Life of the Church.* Daniel Zager, ed. Journal for the Fourth Annual Conference, November 2003. Ft. Wayne, Indiana: Concordia Theological Seminary Press, 2004, 101–15.

"Richard Hillert, a Personal Memoir," in *This is the Feast, A Festschrift for Richard Hillert at 80.* James Freese, ed. St. Louis: MorningStar, 2004, 1–11.

C. EDITORIAL ESSAYS AND ARTICLES IN *CHURCH MUSIC*
1. Editorial Essays

"The Living Hymnody of American Lutheranism," *CM* 66.1, 40–42.

"Church Music and the Sacred-Secular Syndrome," *CM* 67.2, 40–41.

"New Music for the People's Song," *CM* 68.1, 30–31.

"The Opportunities for Music in the Small Parish," *CM* 68.2, 38–39.

"The Congregational Singing of the Psalms," *CM* 69.1, 42–43.

"Martin Luther Is Alive and Well and Writing Acid Rock Hymns in the Wartburg," *CM* 69.2, 31–32.

"Using the Resources that are There," *CM* 71.1, 29.

"The New Music—Where Do We Go From Here?" *CM* 72.1, 35.

"Worship in Wonderland," *CM* 73.1, 54–55.

"Beginning the Conversation," *CM* 78.2, 1.

2. Articles

"The Shape of Church Music in the 70s," *CM* 70.2, 1–11.

"Solo Literature for the Liturgical Service," *CM* 70.2, 5–11.

"Composers for the Church: Richard Hillert," *CM* 72.1, 21–33.

"In Memoriam: Walter Edwin Buszin (1899–1973)," *CM* 73.2, 65.

"The Search for a Useable Tradition of Church Music," *CM* 75.1, 1–10.

"Lutheran Hymnody in America: Problems and Possibilities," *CM* 76.1, 16–19.

"Music in Lutheran Worship: A Primer," *CM* 77.1, 1–9.

"Georg Rhau: First Lutheran Printer of the Reformation," *CM* 78.2, 30–33.

"The Seduction of Church Music," *CM* 79, 2–10.

"The Pastor and the Church Musician: Thoughts on Aspects of a Common Ministry," *CM* 80, 23–28.

D. FOREWORDS

Jaroslav J. Vajda. *Now the Joyful Celebration*. St. Louis: MorningStar, 1987.

Robin A. Leaver. *The Theological Character of Music in Worship*. Church Music Pamphlet Series. St. Louis: Concordia, 1989.

Jaroslav J. Vajda. *Sing Peace, Sing Gift of Peace: The Comprehensive Hymnary of Jaroslav J. Vajda*. St. Louis: Concordia, 2003.

Herbert Brokering. *Earth and All Stars: Hymns and Songs for Young and Old*. Minneapolis: Augsburg Fortress, 2003.

E. BOOK REVIEWS

Lutheran Education

Johannes Riedel, ed. *Cantors at the Crossroads: Essays on Church Music in Honor of Walter E. Buszin*. St. Louis: Concordia, 1967. In *Lutheran Education*, October 1967.

The Journal of Religion

Quentin Faulkner. *Wiser Than Despair: The Evolution of Ideas in the Relationship of Music and the Christian Church*. Westport, Connecticut: Greenwood Press, 1996. In *The Journal of Religion*, April 1998.

The Christian Century

Friedrich Blume. *Protestant Church Music: A History*. New York: Norton, 1974. In *The Christian Century*, September 17, 1975.

Conrad L. Donakowski. *A Muse for the Masses: Ritual and Music in an Age of Democratic Revolution, 1770–1870*. Chicago: University of Chicago Press, 1977. In *The Christian Century*, May 17, 1978.

Donald P. Hustad. *Jubilate: Church Music in the Evangelical Tradition*. Carol Stream, Illinois: Hope, 1981. In *The Christian Century*, April 7, 1982.

"Record Reviews: Nudgings Along the Way," in *The Christian Century*, March 31, 1982.

Church History

Bernarr Rainbow. *The Choral Revival in the Anglican Church, 1839–1872*. London: Oxford, 1970. In *Church History*, December 1971 (Vol. 40, No. 4).

Notes

David W. Music. *Instruments in Church: A Collection of Source Documents* (Studies in Liturgical Musicology, 7). Lanham, Md.: Scarecrow, 1997. In *Notes*, December 1999.

Rochelle A. Stackhouse. *The Language of the Psalms in Worship: American Revisions of Watts' Psalter* (Drew Studies in Liturgy, 4). Lanham, Maryland: Scarecrow, 1997. In *Notes*, June 1999.

CrossAccent

Philip H. Pfatteicher. *The School of the Church: Worship and Christian Formation*. Valley Forge, Pennsylvania: Trinity Press International, 1995. In *CrossAccent*, 1998, January 1998, 56–57.

Basil Smallman. *Schuetz*. New York: Oxford, 2000. In *CrossAccent*, Fall 2002, 38–39.

Timothy Dudley-Smith. *A House of Praise: Collected Hymns 1961–2001*. Oxford, England and Carol Stream, Illinois: Oxford University Press and Hope Publishing Company, 2003. In *CrossAccent* 2004 (Vol. 12, No. 2), 38–39.

The Hymn

Robin A. Leaver, ed., et al. *Ways of Singing the Psalms*. London: Collins Liturgical Publications, 1984. In *The Hymn*, July 1985 (Vol. 36, No. 3).

"New Hymns for the Lectionary—To Glorify the Maker's Name" (a review article). In *The Hymn*, January 1987 (Vol. 38, No. 1), 40–41.

"Sounding in Glad Adoration: Critical Impressions of *The Hymnal 1982*" (a review article). In *The Hymn*, April 1987 (Vol. 38, No. 2).

David Ashley White. *Sing, My Soul: The Hymns of David Ashley White*. Kingston, New York: Selah, 1996. In *The Hymn*, January 1998 (Vol. 49, No. 1).

II. Choral, Solo, and Instrumental Music

A. CHORAL OCTAVOS

1957

Four Choruses from the Lamentations of Jeremiah. SATB. St. Louis: Concordia, 1961. Reissued 2000.

1963

A Processional Carol for Christmas. Unison voices and organ. St. Louis: Concordia, 1963.

A Canonic Litany for Children. SS and organ. St. Louis: Concordia, 1963.

1964

Christ the Lord Is Risen Again. Two-part (men/women) and organ. (Excerpted from *The Crown Choir Book*. St. Louis: Concordia, 1964.)

Two-Part Canons on Classic Hymns and Chorales. Set II. Two equal voices. St. Louis: Concordia, 1964.

> All Praise to God, Who Reigns Above
> How Lovely Shines the Morning Star
> From Depths of Woe I Cry to Thee
> When I Survey the Wondrous Cross
> Lord Jesus Christ, Be Present Now
> Jesus Christ, Our Blessed Savior
> O Sacred Head, Now Wounded
> The King of Love My Shepherd Is
> Come, Follow Me, the Savior Spake

1965

Two-Part Canons on Classic Hymns and Chorales. Set I. Two equal voices. St. Louis: Concordia, 1965.

> All Glory be to God on High
> Arise, Sons of the Kingdom
> To Shepherds as They Watched by Night
> Now Thank We All Our God
> Lamb of God, Pure and Holy
> Draw Us to Thee
> Come, Holy Ghost, Creator Blest
> A Mighty Fortress Is Our God

Two-Part Canons on Classic Hymns and Chorales. Set III. Two equal voices. St. Louis: Concordia, 1965.

> Praise to the Lord, the Almighty
> Almighty God, Thy Word Is Cast
> Lord, Keep Us Steadfast in Thy Word
> Wake, Awake, for Night Is Flying
> Now Sing We, Now Rejoice
> When I Survey the Wondrous Cross (II)
> We Now Implore God the Holy Ghost
> O Gladsome Light, a Grace

1968–71

Settings for the Concordia Music Education Series (1968–71). Various voicings (unison, SA, SSA, men/women), piano accompaniments, vocal and instrumental descants

> BOOK 1 (1972)
> "Snow is Falling on the Ground"
>
> BOOK 2 (1972)
> "Clouds"
>
> BOOK 5 (1968)
> "Father, Let Me Dedicate," "Old Texas," "Cielito Lindo," "Jesus, I Will Ponder Now," "There's Music in the Air," "The Shepherd"

BOOK 6 (1968)
"With Flame of Might," "O Thou of God the Father," "O Sacred Head, Now Wounded"

BOOK 7 (1970)
"From Depths of Woe," "God Who Madest Earth and Heaven," "The Ash Grove"

BOOK 8 (1971)
"Jesus Christ, Our Blessed Savior," "Come, Holy Ghost, God and Lord," "Thee Will I love," "The Curtains of Night"

1969

My Shepherd Will Supply My Need. Two parts (men/women) and organ, with descanting instrument. (Excerpted from *The Second Crown Choir Book.* St. Louis: Concordia, 1969.)

1972

A Child Is Born in Bethlehem. Setting of an old Latin hymn for unison voices, keyboard, and descanting instrument. Published in *Christmas: An American Annual of Christmas Literature and Art.* Minnespolis: Augsburg, 1972. Published separately by Augsburg in 1974.

1973

O Kingly Love. Setting for SATB choir, brass, organ, and timpani of the tune "Kingly Love" by Richard Hillert. St. Louis: Concordia, 1973.

1974

Thy Strong Word Did Cleave the Darkness. Hymn concertato on the tune "Ebeneezer" for congregation, choir (SATB), two trumpets, and organ. St. Louis: Concordia, 1974.

1975

There Through Endless Ranks of Angels. SATB and organ. Text by J. J. Vajda. Minneapolis: Augsburg, 1975.

1976

Four Slovak Carols. SATB. English translations by Jaroslav Vajda. St. Louis: Concordia, 1976.

The Pentecost Celebration. SATB, congregation, brass (2 trpts., 2 trbns.), and organ. St. Louis: Concordia, 1976.

1977

A Child Is Born in Bethlehem. Arr. of a traditional Danish tune. Unison voices and keyboard. Published in *Christmas: An American Annual of Christmas Literature and Art.* Minneapolis: Augsburg, 1977.

Come Ye Faithful Raise the Strain. Hymn concertato on "Ave virgo virginum" ("Gaudeamus pariter") for congregation, choir (SATB), two trumpets, and organ. Chicago: GIA, 1977. Written for the Chicago Archdiocesan Choral Festival, May 22, 1977, and first performed at Holy Name Cathedral.

See Amid the Winter's Snow. Arr. of the carol by John Goss for SATB and organ. Minneapolis: Augsburg, 1977.

A Short Hymn Mass (Missa Brevis) *on Traditional Melodies.* For congregation, choir (SATB), and organ. St. Louis: Concordia, 1977.

Gabriel's Message Does Away. A Carol for Easter for SATB and brass (2 trpts., 2 trbns.). St. Louis: Concordia, 1977.

1978

Jesus, Jesus, Rest Your Head. SATB. St. Louis: Concordia, 1978.

Alleluia To Jesus. SATB. St. Louis: Concordia, 1978.

Verses and Offertories/Pentecost 12–20. For unison and two-part choir (men/women) and organ. Minneapolis: Augsburg, 1978.

Lord, It Belongs Not To My Care. SATB and organ. Minneapolis: Augsburg, 1978.

Rejoice Jerusalem. SATB with SA or children's choir, and organ. Minneapolis: Augsburg, 1978. (Arrangement of carol originally published as "A Child Is Born in Bethlehem" in *Christmas: An American Annual of Christmas Literature and Art,* 1977).

The Church's One Foundation. Hymn concertato for congregation, choir (SATB), and organ. St. Louis: Concordia, 1978.

1979

O Jesus Christ, Thy Manger Is. SATB and organ. St. Louis: Concordia, 1979.

The Head That Once Was Crowned With Thorns. Hymn concertato on "St. Magnus" for congregation, choir (SATB), and organ. Chicago: GIA, 1979.

1980

Three Slovak Carols. SATB. St. Louis: Concordia, 1980.

Lift High the Cross. Hymn concertato for congregation, choir (SATB), brass (2 trpts, 2 trbns), and organ. Composed for the installation of Rev. James Wind, Grace Lutheran Church, River Forest, Illinois. St. Louis: Concordia, 1980.

O Day Full of Grace. Hymn concertato for congregation, choir (SATB), brass (2 trpts., 2 trbns.), and organ. Minneapolis: Augsburg, 1980.

Verses and Offertories/Easter Day through Easter 7. SATB and organ. Choir part, acc. volume. St. Louis: Concordia, 1980.

Alleluia, Sing to Jesus. Hymn concertato on "Hyfrydol" for congregation, choir (SATB), organ, and 2 trpts. ad. lib. Chicago: GIA, 1980.

Here, O My Lord, I See Thee Face to Face. Hymn concertato on "Farley Castle" for congregation, choir (SATB), organ, and desc. instr. ad. lib. St. Louis: Concordia, 1980.

1981

All You Works of the Lord (Benedicite, omnia opera). For single or multiple unison choirs, congregation, organ, brass (2 trpts., 2 trbns.), and timpani. Commissioned for the 100th anniversary of Zion Lutheran School, Wausau, Wisconsin. Chicago: GIA, 1981.

Ride On, Ride On in Majesty. A hymn concertato on the tune "Winchester New" for congregation, choir (SATB), brass (2 trpts, 2 trbns.), and organ. St. Louis: Concordia, 1981.

1982

Look from Your Sphere of Endless Day / We Come, by Thankful Hearts Made Bold. SATB and organ. St. Louis: Concordia, 1982.

Jesus, I Live to Thee. SATB and organ. Commissioned by the Senior Choir of St. John's United Church of Christ, Chambersberg, Pennsylvania. Minneapolis: Augsburg, 1982.

Before the Marvel of This Night. SATB choir and organ. Instrumental parts (strings) ad. lib. Text by Jaroslav Vajda. Minneapolis: Augsburg, 1982.

Creator Spirit, Heavenly Dove. A hymn concertato on "Komm, Gott Schöpfer" for congregation, choir (SATB), brass quartet (2 trpts., 2 trbns.), timpani, and organ. St. Louis: Concordia, 1982.

Christ Is the King. Hymn concertato on "Gelobt sei Gott" for congregation, choir (SATB), brass (2 trpts, 2 trbns), timpani, and organ. Written for the 10th annual Choral Festival of the Archdiocese of Chicago at Holy Name Cathedral, Spring, 1982. Chicago: GIA, 1983.

Lord Christ, When First You Came to Earth. A Hymn Concertato on "Mit Freuden zart" for Congregation, Choir (SATB), strings, and oboe. Written for the choir of Christ Seminary Seminex, Mark Bangert, director.

1983

Victimae Paschali Celebration. "Christians to the Paschal Victim" and "Christ Is Arisen" for choir and organ (congregation optional). Philadelphia: Fortress, 1983.

Thine the Amen, Thine the Praise. A Post-Communion Hymn for congregation, choir (SATB), and organ. Text by Herbert Brokering. Minneapolis: Augsburg, 1983.

Who Knows When Death May Overtake Me. Written in memory of Viola Gotsch Roeder (1902–1980) for 2 equal unison treble choirs, 2 four-part choirs (SATB), and organ (2 trpts., 2 trbns. ad. lib.). Minneapolis: Augsburg, 1983.

Festival Propers (Psalm 96, Verse, Offertory). For choir, organ, brass, and congregation. Written for the joint convention of the Lutheran Church in America, the American Lutheran Church, and the Association of Evangelical Lutheran Churches. First performed June 4, 1983, Peoria, Illinois.

The Works of Carl Schalk ■ 297

O Lord God, You Have Called Your Servants. SATB and organ. St. Louis: Concordia, 1983.

O Lord, Support Us All the Day Long. SAB and organ. St. Louis: Concordia, 1983.

The Lamb. An Easter Processional for choir (SATB), brass (2 trpts, 2 trbns) timpani, congregation (opt.), and organ. Text by Herbert Brokering. Score, choir part, instr. pts. St. Louis: Concordia, 1983.

1984

Lord God, the Holy Ghost. A hymn anthem on the tune "Des Plaines" for SATB and organ. Commissioned by the choir of Immanuel Lutheran Church, Des Plaines, Illinois, Paul Haberstock, director, for the 110th anniversary celebration of the congregation (August 13, 1981). Minneapolis: Augsburg, 1984.

God, Who Made the Earth and Heaven / Go, My Children, with my Blessing. SATB, opt. congregation, and organ. Opt. text by J. J. Vajda. St. Louis: Concordia, 1984.

Lord, as the Grain. A motet for the Eucharist for SATB and organ. Minneapolis: Augsburg, 1984.

Not Unto Us, O Lord. Written in 1984 for the retirement of Edward Klammer for two equal voices, oboe, and organ. Included in the *Third Crown Choir Book*. St. Louis: Concordia, 1989.

Jesus Christ, the Apple Tree. A Processional Carol for SATB and hand bells. St. Louis: Concordia, 1984.

Eleven Psalm Antiphons. Written for GIA.

1985

The Day You Gave Us, Lord, Is Ended. A hymn anthem for SATB and organ (cong. opt.). Dedicated to Jan and Gregg Westrick. Minneapolis: Augsburg, 1985.

Where Charity and Love Prevail. For two-part treble voices, oboe, and organ. St. Louis: Concordia, 1985.

I Will Sing My Maker's Praises. A concertato for congregation, choir (SATB), brass, timpani, and organ. For the choir of Zion Lutheran Church, Dallas, Texas, Donald Rotermund, director.

Remember, O God. Collect for mixed voices (SATB) and organ. Written for Henry Gerike.

1986

I Will Sing to the Lord. Verses from the Psalm for Pentecost for unison children's voices, handbells, and organ. Included in *Alleluia! I Will Sing*. Minneapolis: Augsburg, 1986.

On Christmas Morning Children Sing. For unison voices, flute (oboe), handbells, and organ. Text by Henry Lettermann. For Aaron Michael. St. Louis: Concordia, 1986.

Now. Setting of the tune "Now" for SATB. Text by J. J. Vajda. Carol Stream, Illinois: Hope, 1986.

O God, Our Help in Ages Past. A hymn concertato on the tune "St. Anne" for congregation, choir (SATB), brass (2 trpts, 2 trbns), timpani, and organ. Commissioned by the choirs of Holy Cross Lutheran Church, Ft. Wayne, Indiana, John Mueller, director. Score, choir pts., instr. pts. Minneapolis: Augsburg, 1986.

O Jesus, Joy of Loving Hearts. SATB and organ. Minneapolis: Augsburg, 1986.

1987

Rejoice, O Pilgrim Throng. A hymn concertato on "Marion" for congregation, choir (SATB), brass (2 trpts, 2 trbns), and organ. Commissioned by St. Paul Lutheran Church, Trenton, Michigan, William Heide, director. Minneapolis: Augsburg, 1987.

Where Shepherds Lately Knelt. Christmas carol for SATB and organ. Text by J. J. Vajda. Minneapolis: Augsburg, 1987.

Propers for the Vigil of Pentecost (Psalm 33 and Offertory). For unison and 4-part choir and organ. Written for the 1st Convention of the Metropolitan Chicago Synod of the Evangelical Lutheran Church in America.

Gather Your Children, Dear Savior, in Peace. SATB and organ. Text by J. J. Vajda. St. Louis: MorningStar, 1987.

How Lovely Is Thy Dwelling Place. Motet for SATB. Commissioned for the 100th anniversary of Emmanuel Lutheran Church, Baltimore, Maryland. St. Louis: MorningStar, 1987.

1988

Those Who Are Wise. Motet for SATB. For the choirs of Grace Lutheran Church, River Forest, Illinois. St. Louis: MorningStar, 1988.

Return to the Lord, Your God. Setting of the Verse for Lent for SATB. St. Louis: MorningStar, 1988.

This Touch of Love. A Communion hymn for congregation, choir, and organ. Text by J. J. Vajda. St. Louis: MorningStar, 1988.

See This Wonder in the Making. A Baptismal song for unison voices (or solo voice), flute (ad. lib.), and organ. Text by J. J. Vajda. St. Louis: MorningStar, 1988.

Jesus, Jesus, Light from Light. Two equal voices, flute (or oboe), and 8 handbells, organ. Text by Herbert Brokering. For Brian Paul. Minneapolis: Augsburg, 1988.

Propers for Pentecost 4 (Psalm 100, Verse, Offertory) and *In Thee Is Gladness.* Unison, two- and four-part choir. Written for Lutheran Summer Music.

Glory of God, Around, Around. Unison voices with oboe or other C instr., handbells, and organ. Text by Herbert Brokering. For Brian Paul. Minneapolis: Augsburg, 1988.

The Child Lay in the Cloth and Hay. SATB, organ, and strings. Text by Herbert Brokering. For Brian Paul. Minneapolis: Augsburg, 1988.

Three Carols. ("The Child Lay in the Cloth and Hay," "Mary Had a Little Lamb," and "Round Around Around and Round.") Unison and two-part children's voices, desc. flute, and organ. Text by Herbert Brokering. Minneapolis: Augsburg, 1988.

Two Common Seasonal Responses. "We Praise You, O Lord" and "Lord, Send Out Your Spirit." In *Service Music for the Mass*: Vols. 1, 2, and 5. SATB with congregational refrain and organ. Schiller Park, Illinois: J. S. Paluch, 1987–88.

Hail, O Favored One. SATB, op. sop. solo, and organ. Written in 1988 for the choir of Grace Lutheran Church, River Forest, Illinois. St. Louis: Concordia, 1990.

Be Known to Us, Lord Jesus, in the Breaking of the Bread. An Entrance Processional for the Easter Season. For SATB choir, brass (2 tpts, 2 tbns), timpani, organ, children's choir (ad. lib.). For the choirs of Trinity Lutheran Church, Sheboygan, Wisconsin, Mabel Schmidt, director. St. Louis: Concordia, 1995.

1989

Lord of Feasting and of Hunger. Hymn anthem on the tune "Cronmiller" for SATB and organ. St. Louis: Concordia, 1989.

Christ Is Made the Sure Foundation. A hymn concertato for congregation, choir (SATB), brass (2 trpts., 2 trbns.), and organ. Commissioned for the 100th anniversary of Emmanuel Lutheran Church, Baltimore, Maryland, Richard Durham, director. St. Louis: MorningStar, 1989.

I Have Set the Lord Always Before Me. Motet for choir (SATB). For the choir of Grace Lutheran Church, River Forest, Illinois. St. Louis: MorningStar, 1989.

God of the Sparrow, God of the Whale. Setting of the hymn ROEDER for choir (SATB), organ, and descanting instrument ad. lib. St. Louis: MorningStar, 1989.

Light the Candle. An Advent Candlelighting Carol for unison voices and organ. St. Louis: MorningStar, 1989.

A Parish Magnificat. For congregation, cantor, choir, and organ. Commissioned for the Covenant Service of the Archdiocese of Chicago and the Metropolitan Chicago Synod of the ELCA. First performed on May 13, 1989, James Michael Thompson, director. St. Louis: Concordia, 1990.

All Things Are Yours, My God. A hymn concertato on the tune DALLAS by Carl Schalk, set to an original text by Jaroslav

J. Vajda, for SATB choir and organ. Commissioned by the Worship Committee, Texas District, The Lutheran Church–Missouri Synod, for the Pastor-Educator Conference, Fort Worth, Texas, October 1989. St. Louis: MorningStar, 1990.

The Best of Gifts, The Gift of Peace. A hymn concertato on the tune SALEM for congregation, SATB choir, brass, timpani, and organ. For Salem Lutheran Church, Tomball, Texas.

Children of the Heavenly Father. For SAB, flute, and piano. For the choir of St. Paul Lutheran Church, Danbury, Connecticut, Rev. Donald Larson, pastor.

Wake, Shepherds, Awake. An original setting for SATB choir, flute, hand bells, and organ of the Rhine carol "*Ihr Hirten, erwacht*" in a new translation by Jaroslav J. Vajda. For Peter Charles. St. Louis: Concordia, 1990.

Let Our Gladness Know No End. TTBB and handbells. For Richard Resch and the Concordia Seminary Kantorei. St. Louis: Concordia, 1992.

Triumphant From the Grave. TTBB and brass. Text by Werner Franzmann. For Richard Resch and the Concordia Seminary Kantorei, Ft. Wayne, Indiana.

Noël, Noël. For SATB choir, organ, hand bells. St. Louis: MorningStar, 1992.

Blessed Are the Dead Who Die in the Lord. SATB. A motet for All Saints Day. In memory of Louise Nolde Ladwig. St. Louis: Concordia, 1995.

Come, Sing, Ye Choirs Exultant. SATB, organ. For the Lutheran Choir of San Diego, Frank Williams, director. Minneapolis: Augsburg Fortress, 1991.

Sweet Was the Song the Virgin Sang. SATB choir, organ (strings ad. lib.). St. Louis: MorningStar, 1993.

Propers for The Holy Trinity (Verse and Offertory) and *Go Therefore and Make Disciples of All Nations.* For the Youth Choir, Trinity English Lutheran Church, Ft. Wayne, Indiana. Two-part choir, organ.

1990

O God of God, O Light of Light. A hymn concertato on the tune "O Grosser Gott" for SATB choir, congregation, two trumpets, two trombones, timpani, and organ. Commissioned by the Lutheran Chorale of Milwaukee, Wisconsin, Kurt Eggert, director. St. Louis: Concordia, 1990.

Psalm 110. For the Ascension. SATB choir antiphon and chanted verses.

He Who Dwells in the Shadow of the Most High. SATB. Commissioned for the 25th anniversary of Holy Cross Lutheran Church, Jenison, Michigan. St. Louis: Concordia, 1991.

O Lord, Thou Hast Been Our Dwelling Place. SATB. For the 125th anniversary of St. Paul's Lutheran Church, Oconomowoc, Wisconsin, Glenn Mahnke, minister of music. Minneapolis: Augsburg Fortress, 1991.

1991

Sent Forth by God's Blessing. A hymn concertato on "The Ash Grove" for congregation, choirs (SATB, treble), brass, and organ. Commissioned by the choirs of St. Mark Lutheran Church, Houston, Texas, Metford E. Mountford, director.

Go Therefore and Make Disciples of All Nations. A setting for two-part choir and organ. Commissioned for the Youth Choir of Trinity English Lutheran Church, Ft. Wayne, Indiana, Robert Hobby, director. St. Louis: MorningStar 1990.

I Come with Joy to Meet My Lord. An anthem for Holy Communion for SATB, organ. Text by Brian Wren. Carol Stream, Illinois: Agape, 1993.

Jesus Take Us To the Mountain. SATB, congregation (opt.), and organ. Commissioned by St. Luke Lutheran Church, Silver Spring, Maryland, on the occasion of their 50th anniversary. St. Louis: Concordia, 1994.

Three Descants (FLENTGE, ISTE CONFESSOR, ALLEIN GOTT IN DER HÖH SEI EHR). Chicago: GIA.

Fill My Cup, Lord. SATB, organ. St. Louis: Concordia, 1992.

1992

Born to Be Our Savior (Let Us Sing with Heart and Voice). SATB, organ. Text by Jaroslav J. Vajda. St. Louis: MorningStar, 1993.

Strengthen for Service, Lord. SSA, organ. Written for the 25th Biennial Convention of the International Women's Missionary League, June 1993, Edmonton, Alberta. St. Louis: Concordia, 1993.

1993

Catch the Vision! Share the Glory. SATB and organ. St. Louis: MorningStar, 1995.

Hymn to God, My God. SATB, flute, and organ. Commissioned by University United Methodist Church, Austin, Texas, Suzanne Schulz-Widmar. First performed on the First Sunday of Lent, February 20, 1994. St. Louis: Concordia, 1995.

Lord, When Your Glory I Shall See. TTBB. For the Wisconsin Lutheran Seminary Male Chorus, James P. Tiefel, director. Honoring the ministry of Rev. Kurt Eggert. First performed May 27, 1993. St. Louis: Concordia, 1995.

Where the Swallow Makes Her Nest. For congregation, choir (SATB), brass, and organ. Text by Jaroslav J. Vajda. Text, tune, setting written for the 150th anniversary of the Evangelical Lutheran Church of St. Lorenz, Frankenmuth, Michigan, in 1995. St. Louis: Concordia, 1995.

Show Me Your Ways, O Lord. SATB. For the choir of Zion Lutheran Church, Dallas, Texas, Donald Rotermund, director, honoring the musical ministries of Herbert and Louis Nuechterlein. St. Louis: Concordia, 1995.

1994

Now I Will Walk at Your Side (Ps. 116) and *Let Us Go Rejoicing* (Ps. 22). Two Psalm settings for unison voices with refrains. Included in *Sing Out: A Children's Psalter.* Schiller Park, Illinois: World Library Publications, 1994.

Verses for the Sundays of End Time with Congregational Refrains. Unison choir with accompaniment. Milwaukee: Northwestern, 1995.

Our Soul Waits for the Lord. SATB. Commissioned by Guardian Lutheran Church, Dearborn, Michigan, on the occasion of the retirement of Clifford Halter, June 1994. St. Louis: Concordia, 1994?

Let Our Gladness Know No End. SATB and hand bells. St. Louis: Concordia, 1994.

How Good, God Said, and Blessed the Two and *How Sweet the Name of Jesus Sounds.* SATB, organ, flute, and congregation (opt.). Commissioned by Bill and Nancy Raabe for David L. and Paula J. Raabe. Minneapolis: Augsburg Fortress, 1966.

Evening and Morning. SATB, brass (3 tpts, 2 tbns), organ, congregation (opt.). Written for the 1994 Fort Wayne Lutheran Choral Festival. St. Louis: Concordia, 1996.

I Was Glad. SATB, flute, clarinet, and organ. Commissioned for the 50th anniversary of Peace Lutheran Church, St. Louis, Missouri, Sherry Bierwagen, director. Pittsburgh: Selah, 1998.

1995

I Saw a New Heaven and a New Earth. SATB, alto and tenor soli (opt.). Commissioned for the choir of the Dauphin Way United Methodist Church, Mobile, Alabama, John Ricketts, director, to remember the life of Margaret Campbell Patton. Written at the Episcopal Seminary of the Southwest, Austin, Texas, in the spring of 1994. Minneapolis: Augsburg Fortress, 1997.

In Thee Is Gladness. Two-part mixed choir, organ, congregation (opt.). St. Louis: Concordia, 1995.

Psalm 100. Unison choir and/or soloist (cantor), descant, congregation, organ. St. Louis: Concordia, 1995.

His Voice Is In the Thunder. Concertato on the tune FLENTGE for SATB, congregation (ad. lib.), and organ. Written for the eucharistic celebration of the NPM convention, Cincinnati, Ohio, in the summer of 1995. Chicago: GIA, 1998.

Joyous Light of Glory. SATB. Written for Carlos Messerli on the occasion of his retirement as executive director of Lutheran Music Program in the summer of 1995. St. Louis: Concordia, 1997.

My Soul Gives Glory to the Lord. SATB, children's choir (ad lib.), flute or handbells, and organ. Written for the 50th anniversary of Holy Cross Lutheran Church, Ft. Wayne, Indiana, John Mueller, director. St. Louis: MorningStar, 1966.

1996

Paschal Lamb, Who Suffered for Us. SATB, unaccompanied, brief divisi. Text by J. Michael Thompson. St. Louis: Concordia, 1997.

The God of Love My Shepherd Is. Unison and SATB choir, 2 violins, and organ. For Ellen June Bowlin on the 25th anniversary of her service as a church musician. St. Louis: MorningStar, 1998.

1997

Have Mercy On Me, O God. SATB. Written for the Lutheran Choir of Chicago, Don Oberg, director. Minneapolis: Augsburg Fortress, 1998.

Settings of Eight Congregational Refrains for the Easter Season (Year C). Unison voices with accompaniment. Published as bulletin inserts. Minneapolis: Augsburg Fortress, 1997.

Who Is the One We Love the Most? SATB, organ. Commissioned by the Presbyterian Association of Musicians for the 1998 Montreat Conference on Worship and Music. St. Louis: Concordia, 1997.

Come, Oh, Come, Our Voices Raise. SATB, organ. Commissioned by Fellowship Lutheran Church, Tulsa, Oklahoma, for the dedication of their new sanctuary, May 1977. St. Louis: Concordia, 1998.

As the Dark Awaits the Dawn. SATB, organ. Anthem commissioned by White Memorial Presbyterian Church, Raleigh,

North Carolina, in memory of Herbert K. and Carolyn G. England. Minneapolis: Augsburg Fortress, 1999.

1998

From Distant Lands the Wise Men Come. SATB, organ, handbells. For Samuel Nagel. St. Louis: Concordia, 1999.

Out of the Depths. SAB choir, organ. Text: Psalm 130. Written in memory of Dr. Leslie Zeddies and commissioned by Ruth Zeddies. First performed on May 15, 1998, at Trinity English Lutheran Church, Ft. Wayne, Indiana. St. Louis: MorningStar, 1999.

1999

All the Ends of the Earth. SATB, organ. Commissioned for the 50th anniversary of Gloria Dei Lutheran Church, Downers Grove, Illinois. Psalm 22:27. St. Louis: Concordia, 1999.

Day of Arising. SATB, organ. Text by Susan Palo Cherwien. Written at the request of William and Nancy Raabe. Minneapolis: Augsburg Fortress, 1999.

Around the World the Shout Resounds. SATB, brass 2 tpts, 2 tbns), and organ. Original text by Jaroslav J. Vajda. Commissioned by the choir of Our Savior's Lutheran Church, Sioux Falls, South Dakota, celebrating the music ministry of Donald O. Levson on the occasion of his retirement. First performed on May 16, 1999, by the church choir. St. Louis: MorningStar, 2000.

Songs from Isaiah. Four choruses for 1 and 2 SATB choirs. Commissioned by the Oak Park Concert Chorale, Victor Hildner, director, and first performed by this group on April 9, 2000, at Grace Episcopal Church, Oak Park, Illinois. St. Louis: Concordia, 2000.

Christ Be Our Seed. SATB, organ, and oboe. Text by Herbert Brokering; based on the tune WHEAT RIDGE; written for Wheat Ridge Ministries. St. Louis: Concordia, 2000.

When Time Was Full. TTBB, organ. Text by Stephen Starke. Written for the male chorus of Concordia Theological Seminary, Ft. Wayne, Indiana, Richard

Resch, director. First performed by this group on its Easter 2000 tour.

2000

Easter. For Bar. Solo, choir (SATB), brass (2 tpts, 2 tbns), organ. Text by Gerard Manley Hopkins. Commissioned by Douglas and Ann Anderson honoring the ministry of F. Dean Lueking.

Jesus Lover of My Soul and *Watchman, Tell Us of the Night.* SATB, brass (2 tpts, 2 tbns), timp., organ, and congregation (opt.). Commissioned by the Institute for the Study of Evangelicals at Wheaton College in connection with the Hymns in American Protestantism Project through a grant from the Lilly Foundation. Pittsburgh: Selah, 2000.

Six Motets from Isaiah. For four choirs, (2 SATB choirs, male chorus, treble choir), organ, and congregation (opt.) First performed on Sunday, April 1, 2001, by the choirs of Martin Luther College, New Ulm, Minnesota, Roger Hermanson, Joyce Schubkegel, John Nolte, and Kermit Moldenhauer, directors.

2001

Cradle Hymn. SATB, flute, and organ. Text by Isaac Watts. Commissioned by the choir of St. John Lutheran Church, La Grange, Illinois in honor of Virginia Marohn on the occasion of her retirement. Minneapolis: Augsburg Fortress, 2001.

How Lovely Is Thy Dwelling Place. SATB. Text from Psalm 84:1–3. Commissioned for their centennial celebration by Emmanuel Lutheran Church, Aurora, Illinois.

Baptized in Living Water. Concertato for SATB, brass, timp., congregation. Commissioned for the 25th anniversary of the dedication of the Faith and Life Center, Luther College, Decorah, Iowa. First performed on October 14, 2001 at Luther College. Chicago: GIA, 2004.

Lord, Now You Let Your Servant Go in Peace. 2-part male chorus, organ, opt. bells. For the Concordia Seminary Chorus, Henry V. Gerike, dir., on the 100th anniversary of the chorus'

founding. First performed on January 13, 2002, at the Epiphany Celebration at Concordia Seminary, St. Louis, Missouri. St. Louis: Concordia, 2003.

A Carol for Christmas (A Little Child There Is Born). SATB, organ, and clarinet. Commissioned by David and Connie Zyer. St. Louis: Concordia, 2002.

2002

Oh, How Blest Are You Whose Toils Are Ended. SATB, organ. Dedicated to the memory of Eugene F. Panhorst (1933–2001). St. Louis: Concordia, 2003.

The Spring Wind. SATB, flute, wind chimes. For Jan. St. Louis: Concordia, 2002.

The Good Shepherd. SATB, organ, and oboe. Commissioned by Russell Schulz for the Choir of the Episcopal Church of the Good Shepherd, Austin, Texas. Pittsburgh: Selah, 2002.

Stir Up Your Power, O Lord, and Come. Collect for 1 Advent for SAB and organ. St. Louis: MorningStar, 2003.

Lord, We Will Remember Thee. SATB, organ, and congregation. For First Lutheran Church of West Seattle, Washington. St. Louis: Concordia, 2003.

A Christmas Slumber Song. Unison or 2-part choir, organ, and flute. For Samuel Nagel. Minneapolis: Augsburg Fortress, 2003.

Jesus Christ, Our Blessed Savior. A motet for SATB for Holy Communion. Commissioned for the 125th anniversary of St. John Lutheran Church, Merrill, Wisconsin.

Te Deum (We Praise Thee, O God). For SATB choir, brass, organ, and congregation (opt.). Commissioned by St. John Lutheran Church, Wheaton, Illinois, observing the 40 years of ministry of Rev. Dennis Schlecht. First performed June 23, 2002.

Draw Near and Take the Body of the Lord. A Communion Motet for 4-Part Choir. For the 100th Anniversary of Grace Lutheran Church, River Forest, Illinois. First performed May 25, 2003.

O How Amiable Are Thy Dwellings. SAB and organ. For the dedication of Bethlehem Lutheran Church, Sturbridge, Massachusetts. First performed November 3, 2002.

Before the Marvel of This Night. Arr. for 2-part mixed choir. For the *Augsburg Easy Choirbook,* Volume One. Minneapolis: Augsburg Fortress, 2003.

Be Still and Know That I Am God. A Motet for SATB. For Tom Giordano.

2003

For the Lord God Is Sun and Shield. Motet for SATB. For Roger and Delayne Thake on their 50th wedding anniversary.

I Will Sing to the Lord. A Psalm Motet for SATB. For Rhonda Zacharias.

Three Refrains, Antiphons, and Acclamations for Baptism, Marriage, and Funerals. For the Renewing Worship Project of the ELCA.

Christ Sits at God's Right Hand. Concertato for SATB, brass, organ, and congregation. Hymn tune and concertato setting commissioned by St. Lorenz Lutheran Church, Frankenmuth, Michigan, for the Ascension service, 2003.

Fairest Lord Jesus. Unison and two-part children's choir, organ, hand bells. Dallas: Choristers Guild, 2003.

A Child Is Born In Bethlehem. SATB, organ, and strings. Based on an original carol commissioned by Kurt and Kathryn Petersen. St. Louis: Concordia, 2005.

Jesus, Redeemer of the World. An Evening Hymn for Choir (SATB), Congregation, and Organ. Commissioned by St. Francis Episcopal Church, San Francisco, California on the occasion of the 75th anniversary of the church building. First performed February 8, 2004.

All Creatures of Our God and King. For choir (SATB), organ, and strings. For the choir of St. Francis Episcopal Church, San Francisco, California, Robert Kerman, director, on the occasion of the 75th anniversary of the church building. First performed February 8, 2004.

2004

Hear Me, O My Precious Love. SATB, organ. Commissioned in memory of Herbert G. Jarosch, Aurelia and Joseph Musia, and H. Jack Stoffregen for the choir of Holy Spirit Lutheran Church, Elk Grove Village, Illinois, Richard Rose, director. First performed March 21, 2004.

My Wartburg. For SATB and piano. Text by Herbert Brokering. First performed at the Spring Commencement 2004.

They Are Before the Throne of God. SATB, organ. Commissioned by Gerald Kuker in memory of the life and devoted ministry of Rev. Lester H. Kuker (Jan. 24, 1914–Jan. 11, 2004).

Before the Marvel of This Night. Arranged for TTBB and organ (optional strings). Commissioned by the Appleton Boychoir Mastersingers, Austin Boncher, director, and the choir of Faith Lutheran Church, Appleton, Wisconsin, Robert Unger, director.

Begin the Song of Glory Now. SATB, brass, timpani, and organ. Commissioned by Pastor Lowell and Sally Almen in honor of Paul I. Hanson on the occasion of his 40th anniversary as organist and choirmaster at Our Saviour's Lutheran Church, Arlington Heights, Illinois. Text by Jaroslav J. Vajda.

Thy Strong Word Did Cleave the Darkness. For TTBB, brass, timpani, organ, and congregation. This setting was written for the Concordia Seminary Chorus, St. Louis, Missouri, Henry Gerike, director. Text is by Jaroslav J. Vajda.

Psalm 100 (O Be Joyful in the Lord, All You Lands). For choir (SATB and TTBB), brass, organ, and timpani ad. lib. Commissioned by William and Joanne Musselman on the occasion of the centennial of Trinity Lutheran Church, Kalamazoo, Michigan (1904–2004).

Day of Arising. For two-part mixed choir and organ. Written at the request of Carol Carver.

O Christ the Same, Through All Our Story's Pages. A hymn anthem for choir

(SATB) and organ based on the tune RED HILL ROAD, commissioned in honor of 35 years of music ministry of Ann Mangelsdorf at St. Peter Lutheran Church, Mishawaka, Indiana.

B. CHORAL COLLECTIONS

1963

Festival Chorale Settings for the Small Parish. The Easter Season. Organ and two trumpets. St. Louis: Concordia, 1963.

1964

The Crown Choir Book. Easy Anthems for the Small Parish. Two parts (men/women) and organ. St. Louis: Concordia, 1964.

1966

Chorales for Lent. Unison or solo voices with instruments, instruments only, or accompaniment to congregational singing. Minneapolis: Augsburg, 1966.

1968

The Star Carol Book. Unison carols for all seasons. St. Louis: Concordia, 1968.

1969

A Second Crown Choir Book. Easy Anthems for the Small Parish. Two parts (men/women) and organ, with occasional instruments. St. Louis: Concordia, 1969.

1971

Make We Joy Now in This Fest. The Christmas Story in Old and New Carols. SATB choir, flute and oboe (or other descanting instruments). St. Louis: Concordia, 1971.

Make We Joy Now in This Fest. The Christmas Story in Old and New Carols. SAB choir, flute and oboe (or other descanting instruments). St. Louis: Concordia, 1971.

1972

Chorales for Advent. Unison and SAB choirs; organ, and two descanting instruments. Minneapolis: Augsburg, 1972.

1973

Chorales for Christmas and Epiphany. Unison and SAB choirs, organ, and two descanting instruments. Minneapolis: Augsburg, 1973.

1975

Psalms for the Church Year. For congregation and choir. Choir edition, Congregational edition. SATB and congregation. With Paul Bunjes and F. Samuel Janzow. Minneapolis: Augsburg, 1975.

1978–82

Hymns of Martin Luther. Simple settings of Luther's hymns in new translations by F. Samuel Janzow for varied voicings, descanting instruments, and organ, in six vols. With Paul Bunjes and Richard Hillert; includes score, choir part, and instr. parts. St. Louis: Concordia, 1978–82

Vol. I (Advent–Christmas)
Vol. II (Lent–Easter–Pentecost)
Vol. III (Hymns for Liturgical Worship)
Vol. IV (Post-Christmas, Epiphany)
Vol. V (Teaching the Word)
Vol. VI (Sundays after Pentecost)

1984

Festival Hymn Settings for the Small Parish. The Easter Season. Settings of 14 Easter hymns for congregation, opt. unison choir, one or two descanting instruments, and organ. St. Louis: Concordia, 1984.

1985

The Great O Antiphons of Advent. A revised edition of the 1958 Concordia ed. of the settings of Healey Willan adapted to the new translations in *Lutheran Book of Worship* and *Lutheran Worship,* together with Gregorian melodies. St. Louis: Concordia, 1985.

1986

Oremus: Prayers for the Church. Set I and II. Settings of ten collects for unison, two-part (men/women), and SATB voices and organ. Instr. pts. ad. lib. Written for the 1984–85 series of Bach Vesper Cantata services, Grace Lutheran Church, River Forest, Illinois. St. Louis: Concordia, 1986.

Set I
O Holy Christ, O Lord of Light
Teach Us, Good Lord
Lighten Our Darkness
O Holy Jesus
O Lord God, You Have Called Your Servants

Set II

Thou That Has Given So Much to Me
God Be in My Head
Watch Thou, Dear Lord
God of Majesty
O Lord, Support Us All the Day Long

1988

A Third Crown Choir Book. Easy Anthems for the Small Parish. Ten settings for unison, two-part (men/women), and SAB choir, occasional descanting instruments and handbells, and organ. St. Louis: Concordia, 1988.

1996

The Concordia Book of American Carols. Carl Schalk, ed. St. Louis: Concordia, 1996.

1999

Hymnal Supplement 98: Vocal Descant Edition. Carl Schalk, ed. St. Louis: Concordia, 1999.

C. EDITED CHORAL SERIES

1960–75

The Chapel Choir Series. St. Louis: Concordia, 1960-1975.

Settings by Carl Schalk

O Love, How Deep, How Broad, How High and *Lord Jesus Christ, My Savior Blest.* SATB and organ. 1960.

God of Mercy, God of Grace. SATB and organ. 1960.

The King of Love My Shepherd Is. SATB. 1960.

Awake, Thou Spirit Bold and Daring, God Is Our Sun and Shield, and *How Blest Are They.* SATB. 1961.

Ye Servants of God, Your Master Proclaim. SATB and organ. 1961.

God the Father, Son, and Spirit. SATB and organ. 1961.

When Came in Flesh the Incarnate Word. SATB, organ, and two violins. 1962.

In Adam We Have All Been One. SATB, organ, and oboes. 1963.

Let All That Are to Mirth Inclined. SATB. 1964.

Gabriel's Message. SATB, T solo. 1964.

Jesus Shall Reign Where'er the Sun. SATB and organ. 1965.

When Morning Gilds the Skies. SATB and organ. 1965.

A Mighty Fortress Is Our God. SATB and organ. 1966.

In Thee Is Gladness. SATB and organ. 1975.

Settings by other composers (Carl Schalk, ed.)

Who Are These That Earnest Knock, by Walter Pelz. SATB and organ. 1962.

Holy Ghost with Light Divine, by Richard Hillert. SATB and organ. 1962.

Bless We the Name, by Robert Dosien. SATTBB and organ. 1962.

As Lately We Watched, by Richard Hillert. SATB, S solo. 1964.

Four Hymns for Choir: "We Are the Lord's" by Ludwig Lenel, "Ye Lands, to the Lord Make a Jubilant Noise" by Daniel Moe, "Lord of Our Life, and God of Our Salvation" by Hugo Gehrke, and "Rejoice, My Soul, Declare and Sing" by Richard Hillert. SATB. 1964.

Christmas Song, by Thomas Gieschen. SATB. 1966.

1982–86

Hymn Concertato Series. For the Hymn Society of America. Carol Stream, Illinois: Hope, 1982–86.

God Hath Spoken By His Prophets (EBENEEZER) by Robert Powell. 2 mixed voices, congregation, organ, 1982.

Hope of the World (DONNE SECOURS) by Carl Schalk. SATB, congregation, 2 trpts., 2 trbns., timp., and organ, 1982.

A Hymn for Confirmation (HAWLEY) by Alice Parker. SAB, congregation, and organ, 1982.

First Fruits (FOREST GREEN and KINGSFOLD) by Austin C. Lovelace. SATB, congregation, organ, flute, and trpt. ad lib., 1985.

Creating God, Your Fingers Trace (KEDRON) by Walter 1. Pelz. SATB, congregation, flute, and organ, 1985.

God Whose Giving Knows No Ending (BEACH SPRING) by Richard Hillert. SATB, congregation, organ, oboe, and strings ad lib., 1986.

1984–90

Concordia Hymn of the Day Concertato Series. St. Louis: Concordia, 1984–90. For choirs with limited resources.

On Jordan's Bank the Baptist's Cry by Donald Busarow (Advent 2), 1984.

Let All Together Praise Our God by Richard W. Gieseke (Christmas 1), 1984.

With High Delight Let Us Unite by Barry L. Bobb (Easter 3), 1984.

The King of Love My Shepherd Is by Gerhard Krapf (Easter 4), 1984.

The Day Is Surely Drawing Near by Theodore Beck (Pentecost 27), 1984.

Oh, Wondrous Type! Oh, Vision Fair by S. Drummond Wolff (Transfiguration), 1985.

O Lord, We Praise You by Allan Mahnke (Maunday Thursday), 1985.

Up Through Endless Ranks of Angels by Henry V. Gerike (Ascension), 1985.

Of the Father's Love Begotten by Thomas Gieschen (Christmas Day), 1986.

O Morning Star, How Fair and Bright by Donald Busarow (Epiphany), 1988.

God the Father, Be Our Stay by John Eggert (Lent 1), 1988.

Dear Christians, One and All Rejoice by James Engel (Easter 5 & 6), 1988.

Son of God, Eternal Savior by Thomas Pearce (Pentecost 15 & Epiphany 4), 1989.

The Only Son from Heaven by Donald Rotermund (Epiphany 2), 1989.

Sing Praise to God, The Highest Good by Walter Pelz (Epiphany 8), 1989.

At the Lamb's High Feast We Sing by David Cherwein (Easter 5), 1989.

To God the Holy Spirit, Let Us Pray by Philip Gehring (Pentecost 2), 1989.

When in the Hour of Deepest Need by Jan Bender (Pentecost 13), 1990.

Hail to the Lord's Anointed by Mark Bender (Epiphany 5), 1990.

1994–95

The Proclaim Series. St. Louis: Concordia, 1994–95.

Hans Leo Hassler, *O Sacred Head Now Wounded*, SATBB (1994).

Heinrich Isaac, *Now Rest beneath Night's Shadow,*. SATB (1994).

Leonhard Schroeter, *All Glory be To God On High*, SATB (1994).

Benedictus Ducis, *My Faith Is Sure*, SATB (1994).

Michael Praetorius, *Let All Together Praise Our God* (1994).

Johannes Eccard, *When to the Temple Mary Went*, SATBB (1994).

Michael Praetorius, *A Child Is Born In Bethlehem* (1994).

Melchior Franck, *Come, O Blessed of My Father*, SATB (1994).

Martin Luther, *I Shall Not Die But Live*, SATB (1995), ed. William Braun.

D. EDITED OLD MASTERS

1963

Felix Mendelssohn, *Chorale Harmonizations by Felix Mendelssohn.* From the Oratorios and Cantatas. SATB. St. Louis: Concordia, 1963.

1968

Hans Leo Hassler, *Laudate Dominum, omnes gentes.* SSAB & ATTB choirs. St. Louis: Concordia, 1968.

1969

Hans Leo Hassler, *Dear Christians, One and All, Rejoice.* SATB. St. Louis: Concordia, 1969.

Michael Praetorius, *Sing with Joy, Glad Voices Raise.* SS & SSATB choirs. St. Louis: Concordia, 1969.

1970

Georg Forster, *To You This Night Is Born a Child*. SATBB. St. Louis: Concordia, 1970.

Balthasar Resinarius, *Come, Holy Ghost, Creator Blest*. SATB. St. Louis: Concordia, 1970.

Michael Praetorius, *Christ, Our Lord, Who Died to Save Us*. Four SATB choirs, instruments ad lib. Minneapolis: Augsburg, 1970.

Michael Praetorius, *All Glory Be to God on High*. Two four-part (SATB) choirs. Minneapolis: Augsburg, 1970.

1971

Johann Walter, *Now Sing We, Now Rejoice*. SATB. St. Louis: Concordia, 1971.

Michael Praetorius, *Four Chorale Harmonizations*. SATB. St. Louis: Concordia, 1971.

1973

Michael Praetorius, *O Lord, We Praise Thee*. Settings for the Communion Service. SATB, SAB solo voices, instruments ad lib. St. Louis: Concordia, 1973.

1974

Felix Mendelssohn, *Grant Peace, We Pray*. SATB and organ. St. Louis: Concordia, 1974.

1976

Michael Praetorius, *Easy SATB Settings* from *Musae Sioniae*. SATB. Carol Stream, Illinois: Hope, 1976.

1982

Johann Walter, *O Lord, My God, If I Have Thee*. SATB. St. Louis: Concordia, 1982.

Michael Praetorius, *Oh, Be Joyful in the Lord God*. For 2 equal voices (SS/TT), 4 trbns. (or 2 trbns. and 2 B voices), and continuo (From the *Polyhymnia Exercitatrix*). St. Louis: Concordia House, 1982.

1984–86

Christopher Tye, *Easter Motets*. An edition of Christopher Tye's fourteen motets from "The Actes of the Apostles" (1553); set to new paraphrases of the lessons from the Book of Acts appointed for the Easter season by Jaroslav J. Vajda. SATB. Minneapolis: Augsburg, 1984–86. Series A (1986), Series B (1984), Series C (1985).

1988

Heinrich Schuetz, *Eight Psalms*. Music from the "Becker Psalter" in new paraphrases by Jaroslav J. Vajda. Texts and music prepared for the 15th Annual Bach Cantata Series of Grace Lutheran Church, River Forest, Illinois. Minneapolis: Augsburg, 1988.

Michael Praetorius, *The Lord Ascended Up on High*. Alternate text: "Do Not Despair, O Little Flock." For the choirs of Grace Lutheran Church, Northbrook, Illinois, Elizabeth Gotsch, director. St. Louis: Concordia, 1988.

E. VOCAL SOLOS

1982

Where Will Mercy Be Tomorrow. For solo voice and piano. Text by Herbert Brokering.

1990

The Lord's My Shepherd. For solo voice (S/T), guitar, and flute, based on the tune PRIMROSE. For the 40th wedding anniversary of Raymond and Lucia Pierson.

1993

Lord, What I Once Had Done With Youthful Might. For solo voice and piano, text by George McDonald. For Richard Hillert on his 70th birthday. First performed by Susan Krout-Lyons, March 14, 1993.

1999

Reflections of the Centurion. For solo voice (T/S) trumpet, and organ (piano). In memory of Tim Wnuk (May 17, 1982–February 2, 1998). Original text by Tim Wnuk. First performed June 4, 1999, Concordia Kirkwood Lutheran Church, Kirkwood, Missouri.

F. ORGAN AND INSTRUMENTAL MUSIC

1963

Ricercare on an Old English Melody. Three violins. St. Louis: Concordia, 1963.

1982–86

Preludes and Intonations for Organ. Written for the following tunes in the *Concordia Hymn Prelude Series.* 42 vols. Herbert Gotsch and Richard Hillert, eds. St. Louis: Concordia, 1982–1986.

CAROL (vol. 2)
CITY OF GOD (vol. 21)
DIR, DIR, JEHOVA (vol. 23)
GOTTLOB, ES GEHT NUNMEHR ZU ENDE (vol. 7)
HAMBURG (vol. 7)
HANOVER (vol. 26)
KING'S LYNN (vol. 15)
KINGDOM (vol. 17)
LAUREL (vol. 30)
LEUPOLD (vol. 30)
MORESTEAD (vol. 32)
NOEL NOUVELET (vol. 11)
O DURCHBRECHER* (vol. 34)
O GROSSER GOTT* (vol. 6)
O GROSSER GOTT* (vol. 34)
O PERFECT LOVE (vol. 35)
RESIGNATION (vol. 36)
SIEH, HIER BIN ICH (vol. 38)
ST. CHRISTOPHER (vol. 9)
ST. LOUIS (vol. 5)
UNE JEUNE PUCELLE (vol. 5)
WINDHAM* (vol. 42)

*Tune appears in more than one setting or key.

2002

Easy Hymn Preludes for Organ (Vol. 1 in the *Musica Sacra* Series). St. Louis: Concordia, 2002.

III. Congregational Song

A. HYMNS

1958

Rise Again, Ye Lion-Hearted Saints of Early Christendom. This hymn tune, the first written by Schalk, was composed for the Fifth Annual Day of Spiritual Music, Zion Lutheran Church, Wausau, Wisconsin, to a translation by Martin Franzmann of a German text of unknown authorship that first appeared in 1712. This cento is composed of stanzas 1, 2, 4, and 5 of the original. The tune name is ZION.

1966

Sing, My Tongue, the Glorious Battle. This setting the ancient text of VENANTIUS FORTUNATUS, was written for *Spirit* magazine and appeared for the first time in its March 1967 issue. The choice of FORTUNATUS NEW as the tune name is obvious.

1967

Come, Holy Ghost, Creator Blest; Hail the Day That Sees Him Rise; We Thank Thee, Jesus, Dearest Friend. "Come, Holy Ghost. Creator Blest" is the first of three hymns for unison voices with guitar accompaniment, written for use by the Chapel Choir of Concordia College, River Forest, Illinois. The accompaniment should be strummed simply, one strum for each dotted half note. The hymn tune is SEVENFOLD GIFTS.

"Hail the Day That Sees Him Rise," GLORIOUS TRIUMPH, is the second of three hymn tunes for unison voices with guitar accompaniment, written for use by the Chapel Choir of Concordia College, River Forest, Illinois. The accompaniment should be strummed simply but vigorously, one strum for each dotted half note.

"We Thank Thee, Jesus, Dearest Friend," ASCENSION, is the third of three hymn tunes for unison voices with guitar accompaniment, written for use by the Chapel Choir of Concordia College, River Forest, Illinois. The accompaniment should be strummed simply and quietly, one strum for each quarter note.

Lord God, Reform Our Heart. The text for "Lord God, Reform Our Hearts" was written by Henry L. Letterman. The tune REFORM was written for this text. Both appeared for the first time in the October 1967 issue of *Lutheran Education.*

1968

We Lift Our Hearts, O Father. This hymn tune, WE LIFT OUR HEARTS, was written for *Worship Supplement* (1969), where it appeared with this text by Edward Welch (1860–1932) in the section "The Church: Marriage."

Now the Silence. The irregular tune Now, written for this unique text by Jaroslav J. Vajda, was composed for and first appeared in *Worship Supplement* (1969). It begins quietly, builds to the middle of the tune, and ends quietly once again. It should be sung easily with one beat for each dotted quarter-note. It was written as an Entrance Hymn for Holy Communion.

Look, Now He Stands. Written to an Easter text by George Utech, PARSONS first appeared in *Contemporary Worship I: Hymns* (1969).

1971

Give Thanks to God, the Father. NEW PRAISE was written at the request of the International Commission on English in the Liturgy, and first appeared in *Resource Collection of Hymns and Service Music for the Liturgy* (1981).

Spirit of God Unleashed On Earth. Written for this text by John Arthur, DONATA first appeared in *Contemporary Worship 4: Hymns for Baptism and Holy Communion* (1972).

1973

Hymn in Honor of the Holy and Undivided Trinity. TRINITY was written for the text by F. Pratt Green entitled "Hymn in Honor of the Holy and Undivided Trinity." The refrain may be sung by the congregation, the choir singing the verses, or the entire hymn may be sung by the congregation.

1974

There Through Endless Ranks of Angels. This hymn tune was written at the request of Augsburg Publishing House for a series of new hymns published in bulletin inserts to acquaint congregations with a number of new texts which would appear in *Lutheran Book of Worship* (1978). The text for the Ascension is by Jaroslav J. Vajda. The tune was called FIRST TUNE.

1975

Lord God. the Holy Ghost. The tune DES PLAINES was written to this text by James Montgomery at the request of the Hymn Tune Committee of the Inter-Lutheran Commission on Worship and first appeared in *Lutheran Book of Worship* (1978).

1976

Amid the World's Bleak Wilderness. VINEYARD, the tune for this eucharistic hymn, was written for this text penned by Jaroslav J. Vajda.

1979

I Greet Thee, Who My Sure Redeemer Art. The tune WAUSAU was written at the request of Russell Schulz-Widmar and first appeared in the collection *Songs of Thanks and Praise: A Hymnal Supplement* (1980), where it appeared with this text attributed to John Calvin.

Eternal Spirit of the Living Christ. The second of two tunes written at the request of Russell Schulz-Widmar, FLENTGE first appeared in the collection *Songs of Thanks And Praise: A Hymnal Supplement* (1980), where it was joined with this text of Frank von Christierson.

1981

Thine the Amen, Thine the Praise. This tune, originally called THEN and subsequently renamed THINE, was written in the summer of 1981 at Holden Village, Chelan, Washington, and first sung there to this unique text by Herbert Brokering. It was written as a post-communion canticle for the Eucharist.

Take the Bread, Children, Take the Bread. The tune BREAD was written and first sung at Holden Village in the summer of 1981 to this text by Herbert Brokering. It is intended to be sung during the distribution of Holy Communion.

1982

I Lift My Eyes to Worship. The tune SHEPHERD was written to a text by F. Samuel Janzow; both text and tune were commissioned by Shepherd of the Hills Lutheran Church, Rancho Cucamonga, California.

1983

How Good It Is, In Praise and Prayer. ST. ANDREWS RICHMOND was commissioned by St. Andrew's Methodist Church, Richmond, Virginia, where it was sung to this text of Fred Pratt Green which was also commissioned by the congregation.

God of the Sparrow God of the Whale. The tune ROEDER was written for this text by Jaroslav J. Vajda and was first sung at the 1987 convention of the Hymn Society of America in Fort Worth, Texas. It first appeared in *Hymnal Supplement* (1987) published by Hope Publishing Company.

1984

Love Is His Word, Love Is His Way. The tune EUCHARISTIC HYMN was written for this text by L. Connaughton. The verses may be sung by cantor or choir, the refrain sung by the congregation.

1986

Catch the Vision! Share the Glory! VISION, set to this text by Jaroslav J. Vajda, was commissioned by the Division for Life and Mission in the Congregation of the American Lutheran Church.

God Is One, All Places Here. The tune DAVENPORT was written to this text by Herbert Brokering; both text and tune were commissioned by Zion Lutheran Church, Davenport, Iowa.

1987

This Touch of Love. The tune TOUCH OF LOVE was written for this Communion text of Jaroslav J. Vajda.

We Meet You, O Christ. The tune STANLEY BEACH was written at the request of the Tune Sub-Committee of the Hymnal Revision Committee of the General Conference of the United Methodist Church. It first appeared in *The United Methodist Hymnal* (1989). The text is by Fred Kaan.

Christ Goes Before. The tune RIVERSIDE was commissioned by Ascension Lutheran Church, Riverside, Illinois, and sung to this text of Jaroslav J. Vajda. The refrain may be sung by the congregation, the verses by the choir, or the entire hymn may be sung by the congregation.

1988

Holy Spirit on the Earth. This tune, HOLDEN, was written for a text by Herbert Brokering for Holden Village, a Lutheran retreat center in the state of Washington, reflecting their theme for that year: "There is something afoot in the universe."

Astonished by Your Empty Tomb. Both the text written by Jaroslav J. Vajda and the tune KEMPER were written for the 50th anniversary of the Southeastern District of the Lutheran Church–Missouri Synod at the request of Rev. Frederick Kemper.

1989

The Best of Gifts, the Gift of Peace. This hymn tune, SALEM NEW, together with its text by Jaroslav J, Vajda, was commissioned by Salem Lutheran Church, Tomball, Texas.

Name of All Majesty. This hymn tune was written at the request of Russell Schulz-Widmar to a text by Timothy Dudley-Smith. The tune name is MAJESTY.

There Was a Maid in Nazareth. Set to a text by Herbert O'Driscoll, this tune— NAZARETH—was written at the request of Russell Schulz-Widmar.

All Things Are Yours, My God. Both text and tune were commissioned by the Worship Committee, Texas District, of the Lutheran Church–Missouri Synod. The hymn was first performed at the Pastor-Educator Conference, Fort

Worth, Texas, in October of 1989. The tune name is DALLAS.

Today Again, the Gift of Life. This hymn tune, TURCO, together with its text by Jaroslav J. Vajda, was commissioned by the First Presbyterian Church of Dearborn, Michigan, and dedicated to "Alexander J. Turco in appreciation and celebration of his twenty-five years as director of music, September, 1989."

1990

Walls Crack, the Trumpet Sounds. Set to a text by Jaroslav J. Vajda, both tune and text were commissioned for the fiftieth anniversary of Trinity Lutheran Church, Mission, Kansas. The tune name is MISSION.

A Woman and a Coin—the Coin Is Lost. Both tune—NYGREN—and text by Jaroslav Vajda were commissioned by the First Presbyterian Church, Champaign, Illinois, in honor of the ministry and service of the Rev. Dr. Malcolm Nygren.

1991

Jesus Take Us to the Mountain. The tune SILVER SPRING was written to a text by Jaroslav J. Vajda. Both were commissioned by St. Luke Lutheran Church, Silver Spring, Maryland, on the occasion of the congregation's fiftieth anniversary.

Be Happy, Saints. The tune ARLINGTON HEIGHTS was commissioned as the Centennial Hymn for the Hundredth Anniversary (1892–1992) of the Lutheran Home for the Aged in Arlington Heights, Illinois. The text, written by Jaroslav J. Vajda, was commissioned for this occasion, and both appeared in the anniversary collection, *Be Happy Saints: A Collection of Hymns for the Second Half of Life.*

Creator Spirit, Heav'n and Earth; O Lord, Increase Our Faith; With Head on High the World Goes By. These three hymns tunes—NORTHAMPTON, ABINGDON, and RED HILL—were commissioned for inclusion in the collection *100 Hymns of Hope* (1992). The texts of these hymns are by J. R. Peacey (1896–1971).

I Come with Joy to Meet My Lord. The tune BALLACHULISH was written in 1991 as a demonstration example at a hymn writers' workshop led by the composer and Brian Wren, who wrote the text for this hymn. Ballachulish is the name of a small town in Scotland where Schalk stayed on several occasions.

1992

What Would the World Be Like? This hymn tune, DES MOINES, was commissioned for the Region III Conference of the Association of Lutheran Church Musicians, Des Moines, Iowa, in 1992. The text, also written for this occasion, is by Jaroslav J. Vajda.

Blessed, Chosen Generation. The tune HAMPTON, together with the text by Jaroslav J. Vajda, was commissioned by the International Lutheran Laymen's League, St. Louis, Missouri, for its 75th anniversary celebration. It was first sung in the chapel of Concordia Seminary, St. Louis, Missouri.

1993

One by One the Spirit Calls Us. Commissioned for the 40th anniversary of Faith Lutheran Church, Lincoln, Nebraska, the tune LINCOLN sets a text also written for that occasion by Jaroslav J. Vajda.

Shine Like Stars. The tune STARS was written for the Great Commission Convocation, Minneapolis, Minnesota, which was held October 7–10, 1993. The text was written for this occasion by Jaroslav J. Vajda.

Where the Swallow Makes Her Nest. The tune FRANKENMUTH was commissioned by St. Lorenz Lutheran Church, Frankenmuth, Michigan, on the occasion of its 150th anniversary, which was celebrated in 1995. The text by Jaroslav J. Vajda was also commissioned for this occasion.

Add One More Song to That Unending One. The tune PARK RIDGE was commissioned, together with the text by Jaroslav J. Vajda, for the 150th anniversary celebration of the Park Ridge Community Church, Park Ridge, Illinois.

1994

What Does the Lord Require. The tune EVANSTON was written in May 1994 at the request of Ruth Duck, set to a text by Albert F. Bayly.

As the Sun with Longer Journey. This tune, NAGEL, was written in 1994 for the hymnal supplement, *With One Voice*, where it is set to a text by John Patrick Earls.

How Good, God Said. The tune BENISON was commissioned by William and Nancy Raabe for David L. and Paula J. Raabe, and set to a text by Gracia Grindal.

1995

Preach the Word! The tune FT. WAYNE was commissioned to commemorate the 150th anniversary of the founding of Concordia Theological Seminary, Ft. Wayne, Indiana. The text is by Stephen P. Starke.

Rejoice My Soul, Declare and Sing. The tune BROOKWOOD, together with a concertato based on this tune, was written to commemorate the life and work of John A. Mueller, Lutheran teacher and active lay leader in the Lutheran Church. Mr. Mueller was also the author of this text. Both tune and concertato were commissioned by the choirs of Holy Cross Lutheran Church, Ft. Wayne, Indiana, and first performed by them in 1996.

A Life Begins, A Child Is Born. GRACE CHURCH NEW was written for the l00th anniversary of Grace Lutheran School, River Forest, Illinois. The text was written by Jaroslav Vajda. The hymn was first performed in May, 1996.

1997

As the Dark Awaits the Dawn. The tune LUCENT was written at the request of Augsburg Fortress Publishers for this text by Susan Palo Cherwien.

Simon, Simon, Do You Love Me? The retirement of Rev, Theodore Laesch as president of the Northern Illinois District of The Lutheran Church–Missouri Synod was the occasion for the writing of the tune LAESCH at the request of the family of Pastor Laesch.

By a Lake We Come to Know You. Both text, by Jaroslav J. Vajda, and tune—ARCADIA—were written for the 75th anniversary of Camp Arcadia, Arcadia, Michigan, and commissioned by David and Pat Leege.

Come, Oh Come, Our Voices Raise. This tune, together with a choral composition based on the tune, was commissioned by Fellowship Lutheran Church, Tulsa, Oklahoma, for the dedication of their new sanctuary in May of 1997. The tune name is TULSA.

Children Are a Gift of God; Abba, Father, Hear Me Pray. These two texts by Steve Allmon were written on the occasion of the retirement of Doris Rotermund as a Lutheran teacher. The original intent was that the five stanzas of the tune ROTERMUND ("Children Are a Gift of God") are sung in four parts by a mixed choir alternating with the tune DOEHRMAN ("Abba, Father, Hear Me Pray") sung by children in unison accompanied by organ.

1998

Christ Be Our Seed. The tune WHEAT RIDGE was commissioned in 1998 by Wheat Ridge Ministries for a text by Herbert Brokering on health and healing.

God Beyond All Worlds and Time. Commissioned for the 50th anniversary of Gloria Dei Lutheran Church, Downers Grove, Illinois, the tune GLORIA DEI is set to a text by Jaroslav J Vajda that was also commissioned for this occasion.

1999

Around the World the Shout Resounds. The tune SIOUX FALLS was commissioned by Our Savior's Lutheran Church, Sioux Falls, South Dakota, on the occasion of the retirement in 1999 of their director of music, Don Levsen. The text, by Jaroslav J. Vajda, was also written for this occasion.

Day of Arising. The tune RAABE was commissioned in 1999 by William and Nancy Raabe for a text by Susan Palo Cherwien.

The Greatest Joy of All. Written for the 125th anniversary of Lutheran Child and

Family Services of Illinois in 1999, the tune ADDISON is set to a text by Jaroslav J. Vajda, also written for this occasion.

As Newborn Stars Were Stirred. The tune NEWBORN STARS was commissioned in 1999 by Hope Publishing Company for a text by Carl P. Daw, Jr.

2001

Baptized in Living Water. The tune DECORAH was commissioned on the occasion of the twenty-fifth anniversary of the Center for Faith and Life of Luther College, Decorah, Iowa, in 2001. The text is by Alan J. Hommerding.

2002

Good Shepherd. The tune LAGUNA GLORIA was written at the request of Russell Schulz in 2002 for a collection of new hymns for the Episcopal Church of the Good Shepherd, Austin, Texas.

Lord, We Will Remember Thee. Written to a communion text by Martin Franzmann, this tune—SEATTLE—was written at the request of First Lutheran Church of West Seattle, Washington, for the dedication of their new organ.

Since an Empty Heart Collects. This tune, DANIEL STEPHEN, with text by Thomas H. Troeger, was commissioned by Rev. Martha Klein-Larsen in memory of her son Daniel Stephen, who was killed in a tragic accident at the age of eighteen years.

2003

Christ Sits at God's Right Hand. This hymn tune, BETHANY MISSION, was commissioned by St. Lorenz Lutheran Church, Frankenmuth, Michigan, for their Ascension service, May 29, 2003. The text was written for this occasion by Rev. Stephen Starke.

Jesus, Redeemer of the World. This tune—ST. FRANCIS—set to the text of a Latin evening hymn from the 10th century, was commissioned for the occasion of the 75th anniversary of the church building of St. Francis Episcopal Church, San Francisco, California. It was first performed on February 8, 2004.

O Christ the Same Through All Our Story's Pages. Timothy Dudley-Smith's text is set to the new tune RED HILL ROAD.

The Lord Who Seeks, Creator God. The tune CENTENNIAL HYMN was commissioned for the 100th anniversary of the Texas District of The Lutheran Church–Missouri Synod. Various stanzas are in English, German, Wendish, and Spanish, written by different authors.

2004

Christ Jesus Was For Us Made Poor. Set to a new text by Stephen Starke, this new tune, SEBASTOPOL, was commissioned for the anniversary of Mt. Olive Lutheran Church, Sebastopol, California.

Thankless for Favors from on High. Set to an 18th-century text by William Cowper, this tune—KIERKEGAARD—was commissioned for the 25th anniversary of the investiture of Ronald Marshall as pastor of First Lutheran Church of West Seattle, Washington.

Begin the Song of Glory Now. Commissioned in honor of Pastor Lowell G. Almen on the occasion of the 50th anniversary of Our Savior's Lutheran Church, Arlington Heights, Illinois, the tune—ALMEN—is set to a text of Jaroslav J. Vajda.

B. CAROLS

1963

Let Sighing Cease and Woe. This processional carol for Christmas, CHRISTMAS PROCESSIONAL, was the first of a series of carols written for *Spirit* magazine and first appeared in the December 1963 issue of that publication.

1965

We Christians May Rejoice Today. The tune RIESS was written for *Spirit* magazine and first appeared in the December 1965 issue of that publication. The text is by Caspar Fuger, 1592, in a translation by Catherine Winkworth, 1863.

To You, O Comforter Divine. This Pentecost carol, COMFORTER DIVINE, was written for *Spirit* magazine and first appeared in the May 1965 issue of that publication. The text is by Frances Ridley Havergal, 1982.

1966

With Flame of Might. This carol for St. Michael and All Angels, FLAME OF MIGHT, was written for *Spirit* magazine and first appeared in the September 1966 issue of the publication. The text is by Henry L. Letterman.

A Strangely Quiet Bethlehem. This Christmas carol, with original text by Henry L. Letterman, was written for *Lutheran Education* magazine and first appeared in the December issue of that publication. The tune name is RADKE.

O Sons and Daughters ot the King. This Easter carol, SONS AND DAUGHTERS, is set to a text attributed to Jean Tisserand (d. 1494) in a translation by John Mason Neale (1818–1886).

Hail the Day That Sees Him Rise. This Ascension carol, KING OF GLORY, is set to the traditional text by Charles Wesley.

1967

Jesus! Name of Wondrous Love. This carol, JESUS' NAME, was written as a processional carol for the Circumcision and Naming of Jesus. The text is by William W. How, 1854. The refrain may be sung in parts (SAB) by a group in a separate part of the church.

1972

A Child Is Born in Bethlehem. This carol for Christmas, CUM NOVO CANTICO, was commissioned for *Christmas, The Annual of Christmas Literature and Art,* Augsburg Publishing House. It first appeared in the 1972 issue. It is set to an ancient text of unknown authorship.

1977

The Name of Jesus Sweetly Sounds. This Christmas carol, SIMEON, was written to an original text by Henry L. Letterman and first appeared in the December 1977 issue of *Lutheran Education.*

1978

Someone Special. This carol was commissioned by the Board for Parish Education of the Lutheran Church–Missouri Synod in connection with the "Year of the Child." The original text is by Jaroslav J. Vajda. The tune name is EISENBERG.

1979

Before the Marvel of This Night. This Christmas carol, MARVEL, was written for an issue of *Christmas, The Annual of Christmas Literature and Art*, Augsburg Publishing House. The original text is by Jaroslav J. Vajda.

1980

Best You Sleep Now, Little Jesus. Originally entitled "Lullaby for Baby Jesus," this Christmas carol is set to an original text by Henry L. Letterman and first appeared in the December issue of *Lutheran Education.* The tune name is LULLABY.

1981

Brightest and Best of the Stars of the Morning. The tune DAWN is set to the traditional text by Reginald Heber, 1811. The exotic sounds of the accompaniment attempt to reflect the coming of the Magi to the child Jesus.

Glory of God Around Around. Written at Holden Village, Chelan, Washington, in the summer of 1981, this is the first of a series of six carols for children written to texts of Herbert Brokering to celebrate the Nativity. It should be sung with an easy swing, one beat per measure. The tune name is GLORY OF GOD.

Mary Had a Little Lamb. The second in a set of six carols for children to celebrate the Nativity, this carol is a gentle lullaby that lends itself to accompaniment by guitar or similar instrument. The tune name is LITTLE LAMB.

The Child Lay in the Cloth and Hay. The third in a set of six carols to celebrate the Nativity, MESSIAH is a lullaby that should be sung quietly and simply.

Oh the Wailing and Lamenting of the Woman by the Tree. This carol, celebrating the Holy Innocents, is the fourth in a series of carols celebrating the Nativity. The tune name is RACHEL.

Round Around Around and Round.
NEWBORN CHILD, the fifth in a series of six carols celebrating the Nativity should be sung in a sprightly manner.

Jesus, Jesus, Light from Light. This Epiphany carol, the sixth in a series of carols celebrating the Nativity, is set for two groups of children's voices singing the alternate stanzas. LIGHT should be sung easily with two beats per measure.

1983

On Christmas Morning Children Sing. Written for the December issue of *Lutheran Education* magazine with an original text by Henry L. Letterman, this is a playful carol which should be sung with buoyancy. The tune name is AARON MICHAEL.

1986

Where Shepherds Lately Knelt. This carol, MANGER SONG, with original text by Jaroslav J. Vajda, was written for the 1987 issue of *Christmas, The Annual of Christmas Literature and Art*, Augsburg Publishing House.

1988

Light the Candle. This Advent candle lighting carol was written to a text by Jaroslav J. Vajda. The tune is ADVENT CAROL.

A Shadow upon Cheops Sat. This Epiphany carol was written for the Chapel Choir of Concordia University and first sung by them in 1988. The text is by Fred Durbin, a member of the choir at that time. The tune name is CHEOPS.

1990

The Whole Bright World Rejoices Now. This German text from the seventeenth century was set to a new tune, GARLAND, at the request of the Choristers Guild.

Son of God, Which Christmas Is It? Both text—written by Jaroslav J. Vajda—and the tune MONTGOMERY were written at the request of Our Redeemer Lutheran Church, Montgomery, Alabama, in tribute to Karl Albrecht.

2000

Cradle Hymn. This carol was commissioned by the choir of St. John Lutheran Church, LaGrange, Illinois, "as a tribute to Virginia Marohn on her retirement after forty-three years of service as Lutheran teacher and church musician." The tune LAGRANGE is set to a text by Isaac Watts.

2003

A Child Is Born In Bethlehem. This carol—together with a choral arrangement for strings and mixed choir—was commissioned by Curt and Kathryn Petersen in connection with the hundredth anniversary of Grace Lutheran Church, River Forest, Illinois, in 2003. The text is a translation of a traditional sixteenth-century German text. The tune name is PETERSEN.

IV. Hymn Tunes in Hymnals and Supplements

A. HYMNALS

United States

Book of Worship for United States Forces (1974)—Harmonizations: IN BABILONE.

Ecumenical Praise (1977) — Original Tunes with Harmonization: NOW.

Worship II (1975, Roman Catholic)— Original Tunes with Harmonizations: NOW; FORTUNATUS NEW. Harmonizations: ISTE CONFESSOR

Lutheran Book of Worship (1978, ELCA)—Original Tunes with Harmonizations: FORTUNATUS NEW; PARSONS; DES PLAINES; NOW; PARSONS. Harmonizations: DIVINUM MYSTERIUM; DEO GRACIAS (2); FREUT EUCH, IHR LIEBEN CHRISTEN; CHRISTE, DU LAMM GOTTES; PANGE LINGUA; CHRIST IST ERSTANDEN; VICTIMAE PASCHALI LAUDES; MIT FREUDEN ZART; ALLEIN GOTT IN DER HÖH; KYRIE, GOTT VATER IN EWIGKEIT; CHRISTE SANCTORUM (2); ST. PATRICK'S BREASTPLATE; MITTEN IN DE DOOD; FARLEY CASTLE; GOTT SEI GELOBET UND GEBENEDEIET; JAM LUCIS; NUN FREUT EUCH; GOTT DER VATER WOHN UNS BEI; CONDITOR

ALME SIDERUM; ES WOLLE GOTT UNS GNAEDIG SEIN; WIR GLAUBEN ALL; ACK, BLIV HOS OSS; MIT FREUDEN ZART; VERLEIH UNS FRIEDEN; SONG 34; IN BABILONE; JESAIA, DEM PROPHETEN; LOBE DEN HERREN, O MEINE SEELE.

Lutheran Worship (1982, LCMS)— Original Tunes with Harmonizations: FORTUNATUS NEW. Harmonizations: CONDITOR ALME SIDERUM; MIT FREUDEN ZART; IN BABILONE; ST.PATRICK'S BREASTPLATE; CHRISTE SANCTORUM (2); SONG 34; ALLEIN GOTT IN DER HÖH; VERLEIH UNS FRIEDEN; GOTT SEI GELOBET UND GEBENEDEIET; FARLEY CASTLE; DEO GRACIAS; NUN FREUT EUCH; LOBE DEN HERREN, O MEINE SEELE; JAM LUCIS; ACK, BLIV HOS OSS.

ICEL Resource Collection of Hymns and Service Music for the Liturgy (1981, Roman Catholic)—Original Tunes with Harmonization: NEW PRAISE (2).

The Hymnal 1982 (1982, Episcopal Church USA)—Original Tunes with Harmonization: NOW; FLENTGE.

The Summit Choirbook (1983, Roman Catholic)—Original Tunes with Harmonizations: FORTUNATUS NEW; YE SONS AND DAUGHTERS; COMFORTER DIVINE.

Worship: A Hymnal and Service Book for Roman Catholics, 3rd ed. (1986)— Original Tunes with Harmonizations: FLENTGE; NOW. Harmonizations: ISTE CONFESSOR (2)

Psalter Hymnal (1987, Christian Reformed Church)—Original Tunes: FLENTGE. Harmonizations: DEO GRACIAS

Hymnal for the Hours (1989, Roman Catholic)—Original Tunes: FORTUNATUS NEW.

The United Methodist Hymnal (1989)— Original Tunes: ROEDER; STANLEY BEACH; NOW.

The Presbyterian Hymnal (1990)— Original Tunes with Harmonizations: ROEDER

The Collegeville Hymnal (1990, Roman Catholic)—Harmonizations: ISTE CONFESSOR.

The Worshipping Church: A Hymnal (1990)—Original Tunes: FORTUNATUS NEW

Worship Songs: Ancient and Modern (1992)—Original Tunes: NOW (2).

All God's People Sing (1992, LC–MS)— Original Tunes: ROEDER; EISENBERG.

Hymnal: A Worship Book. Prepared by Churches in the Believers Tradition (1992)—Original Tunes: NOW.

A New Hymnal for Colleges and Schools (1992)—Original Tunes: MAJESTY; ROEDER; NOW; THINE; FORTUNATUS NEW.

Christian Worship: A Lutheran Hymnal (1993, WELS)—Original Tunes with Harmonization: MANGER SONG; FORTUNATUS NEW; NOW (2). Harmonizations: DEO GRACIAS; MIT FREUDEN ZART; IN BABILONE; ALLEIN GOTT IN DER HÖH SEI EHR; FARLEY CASTLE (2); CHRISTE SANCTORUM; VERLEIH UNS FRIEDEN GNÄDIGLICH; JAM LUCIS

Singing the Living Tradition (1993, Unitarian Universalist)—Original Tunes: FLENTGE

Moravian Book of Worship (1995)— Original Tunes: ROEDER (3); DONATA; NOW; FORTUNATUS NEW.

The New Century Hymnal (1995, United Church of Christ)—Original Tunes: ROEDER; SILVER SPRING; FORTUNATUS NEW.

Chalice Hymnal (1995, Disciples of Christ)—Original Tunes: ROEDER; NYGREN; STANLEY BEACH (2); NOW.

Ritual Song: A Hymnal and Service Book for Roman Catholics (1996, Roman Catholic)—Original Tunes with Harmonization: MARVEL; MANGER SONG; BREAD. Harmonizations: ISTE CONFESSOR.

Gather: Comprehensive (1998, Roman Catholic)—Original Tunes with Harmonizations: NOW.

Hymns of Truth and Light (1998)— Original Tunes with Harmonizations: NYGREN; ROEDER.

Worship and Rejoice (2001)—Original Tunes: ROEDER; STANLEY BEACH (2); NOW

Canada

The Book of Praise (1996, The Presbyterian Church in Canada)— Original Tunes: MANGER SONG; ROEDER; STARS; NOW.

Voices United (1996, The United Church of Canada)—Original Tunes: MARVEL; ROEDER; NOW.

Spanish

Libro de Liturgia y Cantico (1998)— Original Tunes with Harmonizations: ROEDER.

Slovak

Evanjelický Spevnick (1992)—Original Tunes with Harmonizations: NOW.

Southeast Asia

Hymns of Praise (Revised Edition) (1994)— Original Tunes with Harmonizations: NOW; DONATA.

B. SUPPLEMENTS

United States

Worship Supplement (1969)—Original Tunes with Harmonizations: FORTUNATUS NEW; NOW; WE LIFT OUR HEARTS. Harmonizations: PSALM 146; MIT FREUDEN ZART (2); VICTIMAE PASCHALI; LAUDES/CHRIST IST ERSTANDEN; KING'S WESTON; ST. PATRICK'S BREASTPLATE; DEO GRACIAS; IN BABILONE (2); FARRANT; FARLEY CASTLE; SONG 34; ISTE CONFESSOR (2); PAX (2); CHRISTE SANCTORUM (2); JAM LUCIS (2).

Contemporary Worship 1: Hymns (1969)—Original Tunes with Harmonizations: PARSONS; NOW.

Contemporary Worship 4:Hymns for Baptism and Holy Communion (1974)— Original Tunes with Harmonizations: NOW; DONATA.

Songs of Thanks and Praise: A Hymnal Supplement (1980)—Original Tunes: WAUSAU; NOW; FLENTGE; FORTUNATUS NEW.

Lift Up Your Hearts (1988)—Original Tunes: NOW; THINE.

Hymnal Supplement 1991 (1991)—Original Tunes with Harmonizations: MARVEL;

TOUCH OF LOVE; THINE (THEN); RIVERSIDE; VISION; ROEDER. Harmonizations: ISTE CONFESSOR (2).

Hymns of Hope (1992)—Original Tunes: NORTHAMPTON; ABINGDON; RED HILL.

See This Wonder (1994)—Original Tunes: VISION; RIVERSIDE; ROEDER; ADVENT CAROL; NOW; STARS; EISENBERG; MONTGOMERY; TOUCH OF LOVE; MANGER SONG.

Sing for Peace (1994)—Original Tunes: ROEDER.

With One Voice (1995)—Original Tunes with Harmonizations: MARVEL; NAGEL; THINE.

Supplement 99 (1999)—Original Tunes: NEWBORN STARS.

Wonder, Love, and Praise: A Supplement to The Hymnal 1982 (1997)—Original Tunes with Harmonizations: FLENTGE.

Hymnal Supplement 98 (1998)—Original Tunes with Harmonizations: MANGER SONG; NOW; THINE (2). Harmonizations: FARLEY CASTLE.

Worship Supplement 2000 (2000)— Original Tunes with Harmonizations: SIOUX FALLS; NOW; MANGER SONG. Harmonizations: DEO GRACIAS.

Great Britain

New Songs of Praise 3 (1987)—Original Tunes with Harmonizations: NOW.

Canada

Songs for a Gospel People: Supplement to The Hymn Book of the Anglican Church of Canada and the United Church of Canada (1987)—Original Tunes: NOW.

V. Sound Recordings

1957

Hymns by the Parish School Choir of Zion Lutheran Church, Wausau, Wisconsin, Carl Schalk, director (45 rpm).

> All Hail the Power of Jesus' Name
> Holy God, We Praise Thy Name
> Abide, O Dearest Jesus
> Upon the Cross Extended
> Come Thou, Almighty King
> All Ye Who on This Earth Do Dwell

1959–1965

A Mighty Fortress: Music of the Lutheran Church. The Lutheran Hour Choir with Orchestra, Carl Schalk, director. Recorded in Holy Cross Lutheran Church, St. Louis, Missouri. Produced by Paul Mickelson, Word Records W 4017BLP.

A Mighty Fortress Is Our God–J. S. Bach

All Glory Be To God On High–Leonhart Schroeder

Once He Came In Blessing–Richard Wienhorst

Beautiful Savior–arr. Carl Schalk

Praise We the Lord in Highest Heaven–Melchior Vulpius

I Heard the Voice of Jesus Say–Thomas Tallis

Our God, Our Help in Ages Past–arr. Victor Hildner

Praise God from Whom All Blessings Flow–J. S. Bach

Christ Is Arisen–Latin Hymn–arr. Carl Hirsch

From God Shall Naught Divide Me–Johann Jeep

Comfort, Comfort Ye My People–Paul Bunjes

Alas, My God, My Sins are Great–Friedrich Riegel

Children of the Heavenly Father–Swedish Folk Song

O God, Our Lord, Thy Holy Word–Thomas Canning

Praise to the Lord. The Lutheran Hour Choir with Members of the St. Louis Symphony Ensemble, Carl Schalk director; Thomas Zehnder, organist. Recorded in the Chapel of Washington University, St. Louis, Missouri. Produced by Kurt Kaiser, Word Records W 4019BLP.

The Old Hundredth Psalm Tune–Ralph Vaughan Williams

The King of Love My Shepherd Is–arr. Carl Schalk

Meditation on "Hyfrydol"–Thomas Canning

God Is Our Sun and Shield–arr. Carl Schalk

Jesus, Lover of My Soul–arr. Carl Schalk

Praise the Almighty, My Soul, Adore Him–Paul Bunjes

Prelude on "Come Thou, Redeemer of the Earth"–Healey Willan

O Rejoice, Ye Christians, Loudly–Andreas Hammerschmidt

Awake, Thou Spirit Bold and Daring–arr. Carl Schalk

Rejoice, My Soul, Declare and Sing–Richard Hillert

How Blest Are They Who Hear God's Word–arr. Carl Schalk

Alleluia, Sing To Jesus–Thomas Canning

Christmas Carols. The Lutheran Hour Choir, Carl Schalk, director. With members of the St. Louis Symphony Orchestra. Donald Petering, organist, Bud Bisbee, soloist. Recorded in Resurrection Lutheran Church, Sappington, Missouri (LP).

A Child Is Born In Bethlehem–J. S. Bach

Three Medleys of Familiar Carols, with original music for brass–Richard Hillert

Thee With Tender Care I'll Cherish–J. S. Bach

Gabriel's Message–arr. Carl Schalk

Babe of Beauty–John Boda

Coventry Carol (brass)–Richard Hillert

Before the Paling of the Stars–John Boda

Jesus, Jesus, Rest Your Head–arr. Carl Schalk

As Lately We Watched–Richard Hillert

Praise God, the Lord, Ye Sons of Men–Paul Bunjes

The Works of Carl Schalk ■ 319

Songs from the Psalms. The Lutheran Hour Choir, Carl Schalk, director, with members of the St. Louis Symphony Orchestra. Soloists: Kenneth Jorgensen, Katherine Hoyer; organist, Donald Petering; produced by Kurt Kaiser. Recorded in Resurrection Lutheran Church, Sappington, Missouri. Word Records WSTB9023BLP.

A Mighty Fortress Is Our God–arr. Carl Schalk

When Morning Gilds the Skies–arr. Carl Schalk

Meditation on the 23rd Psalm for Harp and Strings–Jerome Neff

How Lovely Shines the Morning Star–arr. Carl Schalk

Jesus Shall Reign Where'er the Sun–arr. Carl Schalk

Our God Our Help in Ages Past for Strings–Thomas Canning

How Lovely Is Thy Dwelling–Heinrich Schütz

I Will Lift Up Mine Eyes Unto the Hills–Jan P. Sweelinck

Praise God, Ye Lands, Throughout Earth's Frame–Heinrich Schütz

To My Humble Supplication–Gustav Holst

1991

Sing Ye Choirs Exultant: The James Chorale Sings Music of Carl Schalk. The James Chorale, James Rogner, director. Recorded at Grace Lutheran Church, River Forest, Illinois, October 1990 (CD).

Come, Sing Ye Choirs Exultant

Parish Magnificat

Wake, Shepherds, Awake

Where Shepherds Lately Knelt

Noël

Four Choruses from the Lamentations of Jeremiah

Come, Ye Faithful, Raise the Strain

How Lovely Is Thy Dwelling Place

O Day Full of Grace

Alleluia to Jesus

This Touch of Love

Lift High the Cross

O Lord, Thou Hast Been Our Dwelling Place

Blessed Are the Dead

God Who Made the Earth and Heaven

All You Works of the Lord

2000

Christ Be Our Seed: The Choral Tradition of Carl F. Schalk. The American Repertory Singers with the Washington Symphonic Brass; Leo Nestor, Artistic Director and Conductor. Recorded at St. Luke Church, McClean, Virginia, March 27–28, 2000 (CD).

Creator Spirit, Heavenly Dove

Who Is the One We Love the Most?

Where Shepherds Lately Knelt

Be Known to Us, Lord, Jesus, in the Breaking of the Bread

Out of the Depths

Paschal Lamb, Who Suffered For Us

Four Choruses from the Lamentations of Jeremiah

Christ Be Our Seed

Four Songs of Isaiah

Evening and Morning

Joyous Light of Glory

I Saw a New Heaven and a New Earth

Thine the Amen, Thine the Praise